March 2022   NF
Brooks, Alvin   977.84
Binding Us Together

DATE DUE			

Praise for *Binding Us Together*

"This book gives us a close-up of pivotal events with insights into the man who turned those events toward justice."

—Reverend Dr. Vern Barnet, founder of the Kansas City Interfaith Council

"Al Brooks is a national treasure. This important book tells you why. In his long and amazingly generous life of public service, he has faced family crises as well as unjust racial and economic systems. Those systems were designed to keep Black men like Brooks in his place. But he publicly named those evils and worked to replace them with moral systems offering opportunity instead of social immobility. Read this book and weep. Then read it again and cheer."

—Bill Tammeus, former Kansas City Star *columnist and author of*
Love, Loss and Endurance: A 9/11 Story of Resilience and Hope in an Age of Anxiety.

"The streets of a city are daunting to most young children. Not to the six-year-old Alvin Brooks. With his shoeshine box under his arm, he shined shoes on the corners and in shops in the busiest, most notorious areas in Kansas City. That fearlessness nestled into the psyche of that little boy who would grow to serve the community, such as head of the AdHoc Group Against Crime and as mayor pro tem, but most importantly as the man that the community recognized as the bridge from them to city power."

—Carmaletta M. Williams, PhD, executive director of Black Archives of Mid-America in Kansas City

"My mom and I read Al's book. He's a really great guy who has been through a lot and he always perseveres and he made Kansas City a better place for everyone."

—Lorenzo Guezuraga, age nine

"Al Brooks's strength has benefitted Kansas City for decades. His quiet determination, his soft smile, and his generosity of time and effort have given the community countless moments of justice and real progress. I'm so proud to call him my friend. His story is important."

—Claire McCaskill, former US senator for Missouri

"Al Brooks is one of the most dedicated public servants I've ever met. I am impressed by the knowledge and dedication he has for social justice for all. I hope many will get to read his evaluation of a very important time."

—*Richard "Dick" Berkley, former mayor of Kansas City, Missouri*

"What a terrific person with a fascinating life story to tell! Al's story is rich, eye-opening, and inspirational . . . an amazing example of a life full of challenges, insights, and success. He opens our eyes to the harsh reality of racism and the never-ending need to confront the ills of our society, along with the tenacity to seek common ground with others different from ourselves. Great book, great person!"

—*Kay Barnes, former mayor of Kansas City, Missouri*

"Too often, those who actually make history are distant figures who, although important, are impersonal. Alvin Brooks is an historic figure personal to those of us honored to know him. Through his dedication and service to community, he has blessed so many with his unique blend of knowledge, grace, and activism. He has made his history our treasure and his friendship our honor."

—*Sly James, former mayor of Kansas City, Missouri*

"Alvin Brooks is a legend in our community, having worked for decades to build a better life for all in Kansas City. One cannot ask for a better mentor, legislator, teacher, or friend. I am honored to have heard his stories over the years, and I am delighted he memorializes them here for generations to learn the story of our country, our city, and our people."

—*Quinton Lucas, mayor of Kansas City, Missouri*

BINDING US TOGETHER

BINDING US TOGETHER

A CIVIL RIGHTS ACTIVIST REFLECTS ON A LIFETIME OF COMMUNITY AND PUBLIC SERVICE

ALVIN L. BROOKS

Foreword by John Kurtz

Andrews McMeel
PUBLISHING®

DEDICATION

I dedicate this book to three beautiful, loving women. First, my wife, Carol Rich, who at fourteen, when I was seventeen, became the love of my life, my soul mate, my lifeline, my very being, from our marriage August 23, 1950, until her transition July 21, 2013. Carol was the mother of our six children. She was the woman who made me who I am. Only the good side, of course!

Second, my adoptive mother, Estelle Brooks. Estelle adopted me when she was thirty-three and raised me until her transition March 20, 1950, when I was seventeen. My mother, Estelle Brooks, gave me love.

Third, Thomascine Gilder, who was fourteen years old and unmarried when she gave birth to me. In those days, an unwed teen mother-to-be would be an embarrassment and sent away to live with other relatives. But in North Little Rock, Arkansas, Uncle Willie Whitson did not like having a pregnant teen in the house. So, Aunt Mozzella, Thomascine's older sister, approached the neighbors—Cluster Brooks, then forty, and Estelle Brooks, then thirty-three—about permitting my mother to stay with them until I was born. The Brookses had no children and were happy to accept my mother into their home. My mother, Thomascine Gilder, gave me life.

Finally, I want to include our children in this dedication as well: our late son, Ronall, and five beautiful daughters, Estelle, Carrie, Rosalind, Diana, and Tameisha.

CONTENTS

DECENDENTS OF ALVIN AND CAROL BROOKS

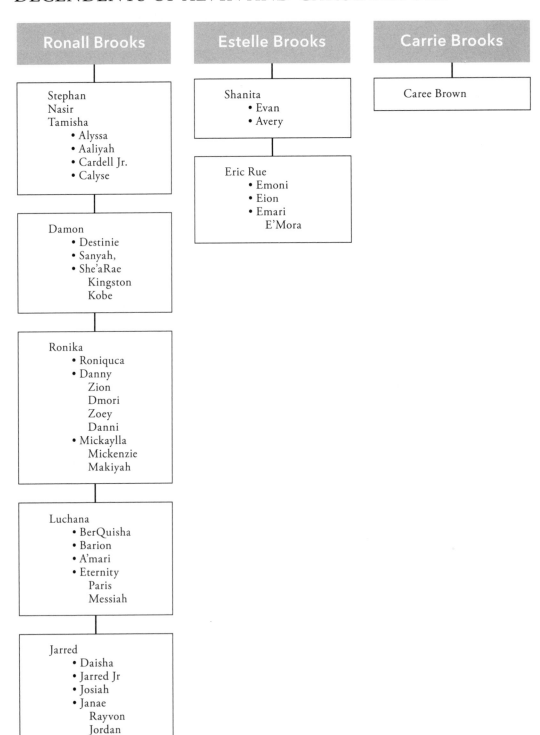

Ronall Brooks

Stephan
Nasir
Tamisha
- Alyssa
- Aaliyah
- Cardell Jr.
- Calyse

Damon
- Destinie
- Sanyah,
- She'aRae
  Kingston
  Kobe

Ronika
- Roniquca
- Danny
  Zion
  Dmori
  Zoey
  Danni
- Mickaylla
  Mickenzie
  Makiyah

Luchana
- BerQuisha
- Barion
- A'mari
- Eternity
  Paris
  Messiah

Jarred
- Daisha
- Jarred Jr
- Josiah
- Janae
  Rayvon
  Jordan

Estelle Brooks

Shanita
- Evan
- Avery

Eric Rue
- Emoni
- Eion
- Emari
  E'Mora

Carrie Brooks

Caree Brown

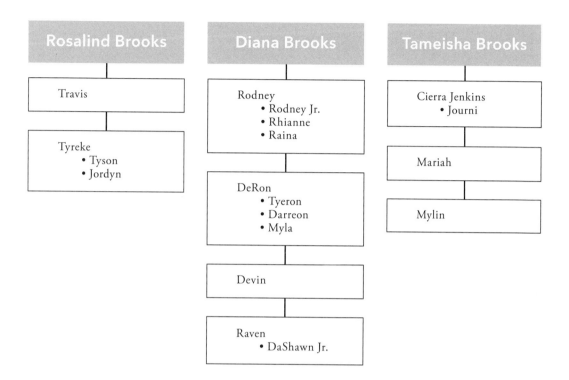

Rosalind Brooks

Travis

Tyreke
- Tyson
- Jordyn

Diana Brooks

Rodney
- Rodney Jr.
- Rhianne
- Raina

DeRon
- Tyeron
- Darreon
- Myla

Devin

Raven
- DaShawn Jr.

Tameisha Brooks

Cierra Jenkins
- Journi

Mariah

Mylin

ACKNOWLEDGMENTS

The Reverend Dr. Vern Barnet, John Kurtz, Sallie Guezuraga, John Dill, Bill Tammeus, John and Bonnie Martin, Gayle Krigel, Carrie Brooks-Brown, Patricia Kurtz, Allison McDonald, Raven Lloyd Stubbs, Dr. Carmaletta Williams, Angela Curry, Tamika Pouncil, Deputy Chief of Police Karl Oakman, Sergeant Joe Bediako, Marlon Buie, Christopher Bumpus, Minnette Bumpus, Patrick Neas, Bill Pryor, Bradley Poos, Jeff Simon, Wade Kerrigan, and Buck Wimberly.

I want to thank all those mentioned above, but there are two people who I must single out. During an event, I mentioned I was writing my memoir. Afterward, a person asked if I had an editor. My response was, "No!" He said, "I would love to work with you pro bono. Your life seems so interesting, and it would be so worthwhile sharing it with others." Almost three years ago, Vern Barnet joined the journey by editing hundreds of pages. Our favorite place to meet and discuss my writing was the Westport Branch of the Kansas City Public Library. The second-floor meeting room overlooked Vern's home. I would watch Vern cross the street with the flash drive with my manuscript around his neck, and I always admonished him to look both ways! Thank you, my dear friend Vern.

The other person I must single out is Carrie Brooks Brown, daughter #2. Carrie joined the journey and came to stay with me from her home in Phoenix. I wanted a local publisher that not only wanted to publish the book but believed in my dream of creating a movement that increases awareness of diversity and human rights through everyday conversations. Carrie and I met with Andrews McMeel Universal CEO Andy Sareyan, president and publisher Kirsty Melville, and senior editor and director of partnerships Jean Lucas. After an hour of exchanging ideas, we discovered the team at Andrews McMeel Publishing was right for the job. Carrie and Jean got to work, and have spent countless hours completing the book. Andy has reached out to collaborate with Carrie on the next phase of our journey, which is creating the actual movement. I can't thank Andrews McMeel enough and I look forward to seeing the positive actions that the next phase of our journey will create. Carrie, on my behalf, and on behalf of the seventy-one other descendants of your mom and me, you've made us proud! We love you dearly! May God continue to bless you with your extraordinary talents.

FOREWORD

How do I begin to write a foreword to the autobiography of Alvin Brooks? He is, after all, the most virtuous person I have ever known. Eventually, I found my reference points by going to Alvin's Roman Catholic faith and to the classic virtues identified and extolled in that faith down through the millennia. I think that is the best way I can express my regard for him and prepare the reader for what they can learn from his extraordinary life.

In the Catholic catechism, the seven Christian virtues (sometimes called "heavenly virtues") refer to the union of two sets of virtues. The first four are the cardinal virtues, from ancient Greek philosophy: prudence—justice—fortitude—temperance.

The last three are the theological virtues, from the letters of Saint Paul of Tarsus, particularly as found in I Corinthians 13: faith—hope—charity (or love).

The life of Alvin Brooks exemplifies all seven virtues and does so in ways only the most saintly have ever been able to do.

PRUDENCE

The wisdom of Alvin Brooks is something upon which so many of us have relied now for so many decades. His prudent advice to all of us about how to live our lives, how to solve problems, how to serve others, and how to advance mankind has been treasured by the mighty and the lowly—and equally so! We all have relied upon him for prudence and wisdom.

When he became the highest-ranking person of color in the history of the City of Kansas City, Missouri (as director of the Department of Human Relations and thereafter the assistant city manager), everyone knew that he had gotten there by a lifetime of wise choices and careful planning. Alvin Brooks has always been an inspiration to people—of all colors—to believe in themselves, to realize their dreams, and to live meaningful and worthwhile lives.

JUSTICE

Alvin Brooks has always had a heart and soul for justice. He has basically always been around the justice system. In one way or another—from his early work as a police officer to his creating the AdHoc Group Against Crime and to his just showing up in courtrooms on all sorts of cases—for decades. The judges have always taken note. Recently, his presence was so strong that a judge actually commented that Alvin Brooks's affiliation with one side of a civil case—as the "next friend" for some children in the case—would certainly make the result come out in their favor. I have never known anyone whose pure goodness was so strong and so obvious that it alone could determine the outcome of a case.

I warmly recall having breakfast with him one morning at the Denny's restaurant located at 15th and Broadway in Kansas City. A telephone call came across his cell phone. I have been with people who receive such calls to check on their stocks, to make social arrangements, to deal with the high and mighty. This call was from a mother whose son was wanted by police and who wanted to turn himself in but was afraid to do so. Alvin arranged to meet that young man at eight o'clock that evening and assist him with the self-surrender. I remember thinking at the time how Alvin's life has always been dedicated to "the least of these."

FORTITUDE

Alvin Brooks's fortitude—his courage, his bravery, his strength—has never been in doubt. In 1991, he left the safe confines on the upper floors of city hall in Kansas City so that he could devote his full-time energy to the AdHoc Group Against Crime, a broad-based, grassroots community organization that he had founded in November 1977. The group was created in response to unsolved murders of Black women in the urban core. From 1991 forward, Alvin's offices have always been in that same urban core.

I have introduced him more than once by noting that he is the only person known to have a range of people needing him that runs from someone in the White House to someone in an Operation 100 house. Alvin Brooks can be in the Oval Office with the president of the United States on one day and then, on the next day, be the person called to an Operation 100 (police code for escalated situation) by a deranged person isolated in a house and hollering out that Alvin Brooks is the only person to whom he will speak.

He has gone to drug houses along with other courageous people, going to the front door and knocking on it and talking to the persons inside. He has been dedicated to making our streets and neighborhoods safer for everyone.

His courage knows no bounds. He has stunned all the rest of us by what he has been willing to do.

TEMPERANCE

March 27, 2007, was one of the saddest days of my life. That night, my wife and I were with Alvin and Carol Brooks at what was hoped to be a victory celebration in the Kansas City mayoral race. Unfortunately, the final vote count was 42,799 votes for his opponent and 41,949 votes for Mr. Brooks.

Alvin and Carol had zero bitterness after that election. They harbored no ill will for those 42,799 people. I have been with Alvin when people have come up to him and apologized for failing to vote for him. He was unfailingly gracious to every such person. He has always lived a forgiving life. On election night and thereafter, he basically accepted it as God's will that he was meant for something else in the years starting in 2007.

FAITH

Alvin is a dedicated Roman Catholic. However, he has always been inclusive of all persons of faith and even inclusive of persons who have no faith. He is a "big tent" person of faith whereby there is room for everyone. Not only is there room, but he has always welcomed everyone.

We in Kansas City know that he, more than anyone else, has been there for grieving families who have lost loved ones as a result of murders. His strong and obvious faith enables him to bring comfort to the families otherwise torn apart by violence.

All his work exemplifies his steadfast belief in his Maker, that being the same Maker of all persons whom he sees as his sisters and brothers—and that includes EVERYONE!!!

HOPE

It seems that Alvin Brooks must believe there are no such things as hopeless situations, only people who have grown hopeless about them. He maintains eternal hope for the betterment of Kansas City, for the betterment of mankind. A prime example is the death of a three-year-old girl eventually known to be Erica Michelle Marie Green. Her murdered and decapitated body was discovered on April 28, 2001. The identification did not take place until four years later, May 5, 2005. During that period, the child was known as "Precious Doe."

Alvin Brooks helped to make sure this child "mattered," that this act of violence on an innocent child would be raised up, made known to the public, and converted into a transformational time when people of good will would be called upon to support the effort to learn why and how she had been killed and by whom. That effort was successful. It was a watershed moment in Kansas City's social history.

CHARITY (OR LOVE)

1 Corinthians 13 indicates that these three things abide: faith, hope, and love. But the greatest of these is love.

I close with a paraphrase of parts from an old Christian hymn. I obviously draw parallels here between Alvin Brooks and his Savior. I know that Alvin Brooks has been in close touch with Him for all his life.

Alvin loves us, this I know
For his actions tell us so.
Little ones to him belong.
They are weak, but he is strong.
Alvin loves us still today,
Walking with us on our way,
Wanting as a friend to give
Light and love to all who live.

This hymn was first published in 1860 as a poem within a novel where the words were spoken to comfort a dying child. Alvin Brooks has always been a comforting force of love and charity for everyone who has known him.

His virtuous and remarkable life has been an incredible blessing and inspiration to us all.

—John Kurtz, attorney and trusted friend

Chapter 1

MY ORIGINS AND YOUTH

My Teenage Mother and My Early Childhood Illness, 1932

I was born in the Brookses' home, Route 8, Box 58, North Little Rock, Arkansas, on May 3, 1932, at about 4:30 a.m., according to my birth certificate. I was attended by a midwife—Mrs. Fannie Adams—who signed my birth certificate. My birth certificate has "Alvin Lee Herring or Gilder." Later the Brookses adopted me.

There is no way of knowing now what the relationship was like between my mother Thomascine and my mother Estelle. I recently found a postcard from Thomascine to Estelle dated August 28, 1941. Thomascine signed it, "Your Cousin, Thomascine Austin." I also recall from attending, with Carol, a 2004 Gilder Family Reunion, when my then ninety-two-year-old cousin, Virgil Bynum (my oldest living relative at the time), told me that Thomascine was adopted by the Brookses. As I write these memoirs, I seem to be the oldest living Gilder.

Sometime after my birth mother left me with the Brookses, I developed a condition where I could not keep food down for full digestion. Until recently I didn't know what the situation was. I was literally dying of malnutrition. After being fed milk or baby food, my adoptive mother, Estelle, told me I would regurgitate it. My mother knew something was wrong. I was sickly. Because of the race issues in the health system in Arkansas, Estelle decided to take me to St. Louis, Missouri, where her sister Matilda Miller lived. I was about seven months old and, of course, not walking yet. My mother, with me in her arms, caught a Greyhound bus and headed north to St. Louis.

According to my mother, shortly after arriving at her sister's home, together they took me to what I believe was the Homer G. Phillips Health Center, long before it became the Homer G. Phillips Hospital for Negroes, a free clinic for Black residents of St. Louis. My mother gave her sister's St. Louis address, and I became eligible for service there.

I underwent a battery of exams and tests. Then my mother and aunt were given the findings. The doctors stated they didn't know the exact cause of my ailment, but their prognosis was that I was suffering from a state of malnutrition. They didn't know how long I could live—probably not more than six years old, if that long. That lack of food over time would cause me to become very ill. Unless something came into play to reverse the trend, I would eventually die from malnutrition. My mother and Aunt Matilda left the center in tears. My mother said my aunt, who was religious, had taken her Bible with her, and soon as she got back home, she began to read it and pray for me. Sometime later, we returned home to Arkansas.

My mother told me she and my father, Cluster Brooks, had no idea what they could do to help me. They had no place they could take me for further diagnosis or treatment. My mother said she stopped giving me milk and baby food but started feeding me from the dinner table. She said what she and my father ate, I ate. She would take a little food from her plate and ball it up and feed me that way. She said I began to keep this food down, and most times it would stay down.

The Herb Doctor Came for Dinner; Dad Bought a Goat That Saved Me

Sometime later, one of my parents' friends stopped by our house and was asked to share dinner with us. He accepted the invitation. He was viewed throughout the area as the "herb doctor." An herb doctor was one who searched the woods for various plants, roots, and leaves. They would gather these different ingredients and would either find names for them or give them names that over time became standardized or common throughout the community. My father was also called an herb doctor.

During dinner, my health came up. My mother explained to their visitor what the Homer G. Phillips doctors had said.

Our dinner guest suggested to my father, "Brooks, I think you ought to find a goat and put the boy on goat's milk." The herb doctor said he had heard of children, as well as adults, having the same problems I was going through. Adults were given goat's milk because they were suffering from ulcers, what people used to call an ulcerated stomach. He told my parents that he had heard that goat's milk, unlike cow's milk, coated the stomach and eased the pain in adults who were suffering from this malady. With babies, he thought it was the same: their stomachs would be coated, and their food would stay down and digest.

The best my mother could remember was that my dad learned that a white man raised goats in Lake Village, Arkansas, maybe 100 miles away.

My mother told me my dad left home early one morning with $10 in his pocket and a tank of gas in his old car. Just before noon he came back with a white goat in the back seat. Daddy told her he paid $1.25 for the goat that had just come fresh (this term, "fresh," refers to a female goat able nurse her kid). Her breed was Saanen, white in color. The goat had pink eyes, nose, and inside the ears: all pink. Dad was told she gave four quarts of milk a day, two quarts in the morning and two in the evening. We began to call the goat Nanee. Why Nanee? Neither of my parents knew.

Momma said three or four days after she gave me the goat's milk, the milk stayed down and all other foods did, too. Some way, she wanted to get the message back to the doctor at the Homer G. Phillips Health Center that goat's milk was helping me. Maybe it would help others if they knew. She said she told Aunt Matilda and asked her if she would call the center and let them know what goat's milk had done for me. She said Aunt Matilda told her she wasn't about to tell those folks anything. She was still mad that they told them that I wasn't going to live beyond the age of six.

My Daddy Killed a White Man

It must have been the late spring of 1933 when my parents and I ended up in Kansas City, Missouri. I must have just started walking. We stayed with Aunt Mittie, my dad's sister, and her husband then, M. T. McDonald, in the Leeds-Dunbar area. We lived with them until my dad found a job and built our first home.

One day my parents and I went to visit my aunt and her new husband, John. I was about fourteen or fifteen years old. I left the adults talking and walked around with some of the kids in the neighborhood for a while. When I returned, I sat on the front porch, but the adults didn't know I was back. They were talking about numerous things. Then my mother asked Aunt Mittie, "Mittie, did Cluster ever tell you why we really left Arkansas?"

Aunt Mittie said, "No! Cluster had told me so many different things, but go ahead. Cluster, you be quiet and let Stella tell the truth. You know I can't believe you, especially when you're drinking that stuff. Come on, Stella, tell it. What happened?"

My mother said to my dad, "Do you want to tell Mittie why we left Arkansas, or do you want me to tell her the truth?" They all laughed.

My dad said, "It don't make me no difference. But you can go on. I'll cut in when you leave something out."

My aunt said, "No, you've been in Kansas City for over ten years and we've talked often, even on the phone, and you've never said why you-all left Arkansas. Go on, Stella, and you be quiet, Cluster. You had your chance."

My mother began. "Mittie, Cluster killed a white man over whiskey that he made in one of those things they called a still, making moonshine. The whole thing was illegal. But the sheriff was the one who set Cluster up in business and protected him when all other folks were being arrested."

Aunt Mittie said, "The sheriff set Cluster up in a business that was wrong, that he could have gone to jail if caught? Cluster, you should know when the mess hits the fan, that white man goin' to turn on you. You should know better than that. Go on Stella, tell the truth.

Cluster, you're my brother; you let a white man set you up to go to jail for him? Go on, Stella."

My dad said, "I didn't go to jail, did I? We've been here since 1933 and I ain't in jail yet. I got us out of Arkansas and only spent one night in jail. So, go on, Stella, tell it."

My mother said, "Well, Cluster said he got turned loose because of my spitting on the judge with some kind of root. He called it John the Conqueror root. You know, he went out there in the woods and brought back different kinds of funny-lookin' stuff. Folk around bought that stuff, too."

Aunt Mittie said, "You did what? Who spit on the judge? You spit on the judge, Stella? You're just as crazy as Cluster. You deserve each other. One of you got to have some sense for that boy out there. Then I wouldn't have had a fine nephew, 'cause you two crazies would be in jail or you, Cluster, be dead."

My mother said, "Mittie, let me finish about my spitting on the judge. I really did, like Cluster told me to do. When I went down to see him in jail that Monday with little Alvin, he told me to go back home and get a piece of that root and come back and put a piece of the root in my mouth and see the judge and get close enough where I can get some spit on him, cough or sneeze, and make sure I got some on the judge. I did get that nasty-tasting stuff and caught the judge as he was going out of the courtroom for lunch with the sheriff. The sheriff tried to keep me from the judge. But I got to speak to him anyway. I told the judge, 'Please, your honor, sir, I really need to have word with you, sir, about my husband, Cluster. That man he killed came in our yard shooting at Cluster.'

"The judge was very rude, and I could tell he didn't like colored folks. But I think he thought I was white because he gave me permission to speak with him. He questioned whether the baby was mine. We sat at a table in the courtroom. Mittie, I was scared to death. I was sweating all over, and that stuff that I had in my hand left my hand brown. And now it was in my mouth. I thought I was going to puke any minute. But I got my question in. Was Cluster going to be allowed to come home without any charges? I said, 'The man was in our backyard shooting at Cluster, judge, your honor.' Then I faked a sneeze. Spit went everywhere! Over the judge, me, and little Alvin. I think the judge thought I dipped snuff.

"The judge jumped up and tried to brush my spit off of his arms and white shirt. He said, 'You go home, girl. I haven't decided what I'm going to do with Cluster. He killed a well-respected white man, and for a nigger to kill any white man, he should be tried for murder. You ought to know that. You and your colored baby get out of here. I'll make the decision when I get back from lunch.'

"I thanked the judge and hurried out of that courthouse," my mother said. "I had to pee so bad but knew I couldn't till I got back home. And little Alvin was soaking wet and needed to be changed. When I got home, I rushed into our toilet. I sat little Alvin on the back steps. When I picked him up and got in the house, Cluster was walking around in the house. Scared me to death! I asked him what he was doing home. I thought, *my God, he didn't escape, did he?* I asked him again, 'What you doing here?'"

My mother said, "Come on, Cluster, you tell the rest. Go ahead, Cluster, you tell what happened." My dad laughed, and so did my mother, Aunt Mittie, and Mr. John, who never said a word.

"Well, my friend the sheriff brought me from the jail cell to the back door to the courtroom. He opened the door. Court was in session with a lot of white folks. The judge came out and closed the door behind him. He asked me, 'Is that woman who came down here earlier today your wife and that boy you'alls?' I told him, 'Yes, your honor, sir, she's my wife and the boy's ours.' The judge said, 'Your colored nigger ass is in trouble. You killed a well-thought-of white man. And don't tell me about no self-defense.'

"The judge then told me, 'You listen here and listen damn good. You killed a white man here in Arkansas, Pulaski County. Your nigger ass should be put in the 'lectric chair. But I'm gonna let your nigger ass go. But you had better get out of this county, in fact the whole state of Arkansas, by Saturday. You understand English, don't you, nigger?' I said, 'Yes, your honor, sir. I understand.' He told the sheriff to 'get this nigger's stuff and get him on his way. And you check back at his house Saturday. If they're not gone, bring his Black ass back and his so-called colored wife, and put both their asses in jail and charge him with murder, her for passing to be colored. You got that?' The sheriff said, 'Yes, your honor, I'll check as you ordered.'"

My aunt Mittie, Mr. John, and my mother really began to laugh now. Aunt Mittie said, "Cluster, my brother, you killed a white man and is living to tell it. You know I wouldn't believe it if you told it, but I know Stella ain't gonna lie. Man, you is crazy and lucky as hell. You ought to be on your knees till they are raw." All four of them had a long, hard laugh.

My mother came to the door to call me. They were ready to go home. She was surprised when she saw me sitting on the porch. She said, "I thought you were out there with those kids. How long have you been sitting out here?"

I didn't want them to know that I heard everything, so I said, "I just got here."

Mother went back inside. I was sure she whispered to everyone that she believed I heard them. But the subject never came up again.

The sheriff had returned dad's rifle to him before my folks left Arkansas. I still have it and the knowledge of how I came to Kansas City.

To Kansas City!—Late 1932 or Early 1933

The night we were preparing to leave, my daddy went to gas up. The service station was also the Greyhound bus stop. Daddy said he woke the owner up to get gas, check his oil, air, and everything, and to pay the owner for previous bills. Just as he began to drive away and head back home, his good friend Tom Ousley was talking to the station owner. My daddy said he asked Mr. Ousley where he was he going. Mr. Ousley said he was going to St. Louis to visit his brother. My dad then said, "Tom, why don't you come to Kansas City with me, the wife, and the boy and help me drive? Then you can go to St. Louis from Kansas City. From Kansas City to St. Louis is about the same distance as from North Little Rock to St. Louis. And my old car doesn't have a first gear. Some of those Arkansas mountains I may have to back up the hill. The old car won't pull those mountains in second gear. You may have to walk outside behind me to make sure we don't get hit by some car that can't see us." Mr. Ousley told my dad he would go and help him drive to Kansas City. The car was already packed. Only Nanee, my mother, and I were left.

Shortly after midnight, we were on our way. My dad had already written his sister Mittie in Kansas City to tell her he was coming. He hadn't received any response, but he was sure she had gotten his letter and that our staying with them until we found a place was okay. He didn't know anyone in Kansas City but his sister. He had never even met his sister's husband, M. T.

The four of us and Nanee arrived, safe and sound, at Aunt Mittie's. No one said where Mr. Ousley stayed. My aunt and uncle had a small two-bedroom house at 3405 Quincy. Uncle M. T. rarely stayed at home. Neither he nor Aunt Mittie told my parents what kind of work he did.

Nanee was like a novelty to our new neighbors. My parents said they acted as though they had never seen a goat before. Nanee was tied to a tree in my aunt's backyard. Nanee had a feast. My aunt had tin cans all around the tree. Nanee ate all the paper labels off the cans. She got loose one day, my mother said, and one of Aunt Mittie's neighbors called her outside and said that Nanee was up in her backyard eating on some of their clothes hanging on their clothesline. My aunt offered to pay for anything that Nanee had eaten. Her neighbor wouldn't accept any money.

My daddy was out half of the day looking for a job. The other half he was looking for someplace for us to live. Daddy found a job working for the WPA, the Works Progress Administration, which was the most important program under President Franklin D. Roosevelt's New Deal. It was a work-relief program that employed some 8.5 million people, whose average monthly salary was $41.57. Soon my dad announced he had bought a couple of lots to build us a house.

Daddy Built Our First Kansas City Home

My daddy began to build our first house in Kansas City at 3421 Quincy by working evenings and weekends. When it was completed, there was no electricity, only kerosene lamps, also known as coal oil lamps. There was no running water or inside toilet. In fact, several houses got their water from the same source, a city water supply in the middle of the block. In the winter, those families on Quincy had to take turns letting the water run because it would freeze in the frigid temperature. I often would be told to go out and thaw the faucet by piling newspaper and starting a fire around the pipe. The short-lived fire often still left the faucet frozen.

The only way we could wash our faces in warm water or take a bath was by warming the water on the stove. I was the only one who took a bath, and that was in a No. 2 galvanized tin bathtub—which I still have today. It was also used to wash clothes and clean chitterlings. My mom and dad just used a small wash pan. The soap we used for bathing was Proctor & Gamble. To wash clothes, we used the No. 2 bathtub with the lye soap my mother made in the backyard. My parents used baking soda as a deodorant and to brush our teeth. When I became old enough, I also used baking soda as a deodorant.

So, what if we had to go to the toilet during the night? Or when the weather was bad and we couldn't get outdoors? We used a "slop jar," a porcelain two-gallon bucket with a beautiful print on it and a matching lid, or a galvanized bucket filled with ashes from the stoves. If we had to use one or the other of these pots during the night, which one or more of us always did, it was emptied the next morning, depending on the weather, by me. In the winter when there were times I couldn't get outdoors, we had to endure the stench, especially after the house heated up. Both pots had covers, which helped somewhat. Only somewhat. Also, the pee and slop jar would freeze and couldn't be emptied until it thawed out. Oh, the aroma!

Our house basically had just two rooms. One was a small kitchen with a large coal cookstove, a few wooden shelves around the wall, and a closet with two printed flour sacks sewn together for a door. The other room was long from south to north. I slept on an old sofa at the south end of the room, a few feet from the potbelly wood and coal stove. In the middle of the long room was my parents' bed. There was a big trunk at the foot of their bed where they kept linen, some clothes, and important papers. Chairs were placed around the rest of the room.

I Start School at Six and Avoid Circumcision, 1938

I didn't start school until I was six years old because I was very skinny and sickly. I had every conceivable childhood disease except smallpox. And even after I started school at age six, I was out of school almost more than I was in. My friends my age were going to school every day, but I stayed home sick a lot.

I remember one occasion when the school nurse, Mrs. Coleman, checked on me at home. As soon as she walked into our house, I threw up everywhere. Mrs. Coleman could see that I had whooping cough. Without ever taking a seat, she looked at my mom and said, "I have seen enough." She turned around and left.

Sometimes when I felt better, my mother would let me go outside. One day, I was outside throwing my tennis ball against the front of the house and the ball rolled under the front porch. My father had stacked several bricks at the corners and in the middle of the porch, which was very low to the ground. I was able to slide under the porch and get my ball, but then I couldn't squeeze back out. I began to holler for my mother. She came out on the porch and stood right on top of me. I hollered and cried. My mother realized that she was standing on top of me and stepped off the porch. Some men who were working down the street came and lifted the porch up, and I got up and ran to my mother. My mother and the men had a good laugh over what had happened to me.

My mother took me to Dunbar Elementary School, and we met the principal (also a teacher), Mrs. Daisy Trice. Mrs. Trice welcomed me to school, and my mother left me with my lunch in a brown bag. Mrs. Trice took me to my classroom and introduced me to my teacher. My kindergarten teacher was Mrs. Emma Stokes. Whatever kindergarteners did their first day of school at the time, I must have done it. Then there was recess, and all of us went outside. We played and the bell rang, and I went home. When I got home, my mother asked me, "Baby, is school out?"

I said, "Yes, ma'am."

"Did you like school today?" she asked.

Again, I answered, "Yes, ma'am."

Later that day, Jacob Armstrong, who lived down the street from us near the corner of 35th Street and Quincy, came up to my house and told me I was in "big trouble," that I had left school too soon, that I left at recess and school was not out. My mother overheard Jacob. She said she would take me back to school the next day and everything would be all right. Jacob was about two years older than me. His sister, Evelyn, and I were the same age and both in kindergarten. Jacob must have been in the second or third grade.

The next day, my mother took me back to school and all was fine.

Sometime during these early years, the nurse at school told my mother that I should be circumcised. About the same time, Jacob Armstrong got circumcised. So, Mother discussed it with Mrs. Armstrong, and she told my mother of the pain Jacob was going through. He even had to stay at home for a couple of days. She said she told Mrs. Armstrong that she was not going to let me go through what Jacob was going through, that "circumcision is too painful for my baby." My mother told me about this when I was in high school.

My Main Chores at an Early Age, 1939

We now had four goats: Nanee, Billy, Babe, and Bob. We had a large red rooster, also named Bob. My chore was to take care of the goats. I would water them, feed them, and take them out of their pen and put them out to graze. One day when I was taking Billy out, he ran in circles and my legs got tangled up in his chain. I tripped, and the chain also wrapped around a small bush that was the home of a yellow jacket nest. The yellow jackets came at Billy—and me. We both got stung.

My mother heard me hollering and crying and came to our rescue. She ran to me, unwound the chain around my legs, and ran with me into the house. Billy ran to the end of his chain. Mother also got stung a couple of times, but I was stung numerous times on my head, face, and arms. I was crying to high heavens. My mother got some of my daddy's chewing tobacco, placed it in her mouth until it was good and wet, and placed it on each of my stings. That was supposed to reduce the swelling. And it did.

Someone Stole Five Baby Pigs from Our Sow, 1939

The Brooks family had a miniature farm. We had several hogs, and our sow had five pigs. After they were weaned, all five of them disappeared one night. Someone stole them. After finding that the pigs were missing, my dad told my mother that he heard the pigs squealing the night before but didn't think much of it. Our neighbor next door to the south of us was Mrs. Ida. I never knew Mrs. Ida's last name. To all the kids, she was Mrs. Ida. I later learned that Mrs. Ida liked younger men. At the time our pigs got stolen, there was a young man staying with Mrs. Ida. I think my daddy suspected he stole our sow's five pigs.

The next evening my dad told my mother, "Stella, I'm going down to Richardson's tavern to find out who stole the pigs."

She said, "Cluster, don't go down there gettin' any trouble over no pigs." My daddy didn't say anything.

The actual name of the tavern was Liberty Tavern, but it was owned by Mrs. Myrtle Richardson. I loved to go with my dad down to Mrs. Richardson's. He let me sit at the end of the bar. Mrs. Richardson would give me a big bottle of Nehi red strawberry soda pop.

This evening was a little different. My daddy turned to me. "Come get your coat on." My mother told my daddy, "You don't need to take that baby with you. He's got school tomorrow, and you've been drinkin' anyway." My daddy said, "Not that much. I won't be down there long. We'll be right back. Come on, boy, let's go." I looked at my mother. She wasn't happy. She was mumbling something to herself as we walked out the door.

My dad always carried his pistol. He had already drunk part of a half pint of some kind of whiskey in the truck on the way to the tavern. After downing a couple of beers at the bar,

Daddy all of a sudden pulled out his pistol from his overalls pocket, slammed it on the bar, and hollered out, "Some son of a bitch stole five pigs from my old sow, and if those five pigs aren't back by tomorrow morning, I'm going to kill the son of a bitch."

Some of the folks were mumbling things like "Brooks will do what he says" and "Don't fool with Brooks."

Shortly after Dad made his announcement, he said, "Come on, son, let's go."

When we got home, my mother scolded my dad for keeping me out so late. She told him, "Tomorrow is a school day. This baby should have been in bed. You said you were coming right back. What happened?"

My dad said, "I just had two beers and talked to Mrs. Richardson for a minute while the boy was drinking a soda pop she gave him." Dad did not tell Mother of the ultimatum he had thrown out to the men at Mrs. Richardson's.

Yes, you guessed right. The next morning all five of the old sow's pigs were back in their pen. My mom and dad had the biggest laugh as we ate breakfast together that morning before I went to school.

Our First Winter in Our New Home, the Flu, and the Rabbit, 1939

I don't remember the year, but I know it seemed as though it snowed for days without stopping. I must have been seven or eight years old. My mother, father, and I were all down with the flu (we called it influenza then). The coal for the heating stove was all gone, but we had lots of wood piled up outside by the back door, plus a small pile by the stove. Coal burned slow and held heat much longer than wood. The wood burned fast. The heat went out when the wood burned down. Then Dad or I would put more wood in the stove. We kept a gallon can of water on top of the stove because the air became so dry without it.

Then there was a substance from the coal called "slack." It was more like ground-up coal. I was taught to first put the wood in the stove, then, after it got a good start, add the coal. The slack was not placed on the coal until night. My dad called it "bedding it down" or "banking" it. In other words, the slack would hold the fire through the night. And if you banked it well, you wouldn't have to get up during the night and place anything else on the fire until the next morning

The house only heated close around the stove. It could hardly be felt at my parents' bed, which was several feet away. We had nothing to eat but potatoes, rice, onions, oatmeal, flour, and cornmeal. All except the potatoes and onions were infiltrated with little bugs. And they were alive. My mother used a sifter to separate the bugs just before she cooked.

Thank God for Mrs. Ina Williams and her father, Mr. Willie Williams, our neighbors up the street at 3400 Quincy. Mrs. Ina hadn't seen my dad in a couple of days, or the tracks from his truck indicating he had gotten out. With her dad's tall rubber boots on, she managed to come down the hill to our house in knee-deep snow. There were no snowplows for us. Even if there were, they couldn't do us any good on our street because there were rocks between 34th and 35th Streets on Quincy.

Mrs. Williams came inside our house and my parents told her our situation. We had no telephone, but the Williamses did. My dad asked her if she would call the coal company where Mr. Martin "Shugg" Brown worked on 18th Street and "order us a half ton of coal." Mrs. Williams knew Mr. Brown and where he worked and promised to make the call. She also said she and her father were going hunting that day and if they killed any rabbits, she would bring us one.

Later that day the "coal man," as he was called, brought our coal. He had a hard time getting to our house because of the deep snow, but his truck made it with chains on the tires. The coal was dumped by the back door. Because my dad was so weak, the coal man brought in a lot of the coal and put it in the coal box Dad had made and put behind the stove. Still later that day, Mrs. Williams came back and gave us a large rabbit, one of three she had killed during their hunting. Mrs. Williams had already dressed it, so all my dad had to do was cut and cook it. Now we had heat and food! We must have eaten that rabbit cooked a dozen different ways with potatoes, rice, and gravy. Mother sifted out the little bugs.

Several days after the coal man had delivered the coal and Mrs. Williams had left us the rabbit, another big snow fell. I can remember when my dad opened the back door to go out and get some more coal, nothing could be seen except snow. It had really drifted this time at that corner of the house, and Dad could not get out to get any coal. He had to improvise.

We slept in the clothes we wore during the day, so Daddy put on more clothes and galoshes (rubbers over his shoe, if you wonder what galoshes are). He took a chair out the front door and used it to edge along in the snow and carried a shovel with him. My mother and I could see him as he passed the window at the front of the house. Then we saw him pass the window on the north side. He used the chair to support himself and shoveled to clear some of the snow away.

Finally, we heard Daddy in the back of the house. It took him some time, but after a while, he said, "Alvin, open the back door." And I did. And there stood Daddy, covered in snow, along with the chair and shovel. He had been out long enough to shovel some of the snow off the pile of coal and the small pile of slack. Mother told Daddy to come in to rest and warm awhile, but he refused. I handed him the coal bucket and he started putting coal in it. Little by little, the coal and slack boxes were full. I must have made twenty-five trips from the back door to behind the stove.

Our House Burned so We Lived in a Barn, 1939

It must have been March of '39 or '40, following the hard winter that year. It was still cool enough that my mother wrapped a blanket around me as I sat on the running board of Dad's truck, watching our first house go up in flames.

My father said the fire started in the chimney where the heating stovepipe had gotten cherry red, from the top of the stove to where it went into the chimney. It was believed to have stayed hot so long that the ceiling caught fire. That's the information the fire chief passed on to my parents after they got to us. I think 35th Street East was still under construction for paving, and the fire trucks could not get to our house. They had to turn around and take Elmwood to Linwood Boulevard. If they had gotten there in time, they would have had to use the water from the fire truck because there wasn't a fireplug anywhere near our house.

By the time they arrived, the house was just a pile of smoldering wood. We lost everything. My dad said if it hadn't been for my dog, Midnight, we would have died in the fire. Daddy said Midnight started barking and pawing at the bed and woke him up. My mother was so happy we had survived. But we didn't really have anyplace to go. Aunt Mittie no longer lived a couple blocks away because she had moved to Kansas City, Kansas, and all our neighbors had homes too small to have three guests. No Red Cross came to our aid.

Mrs. Williams and her father, Willie, helped us again. She told my parents that we could live temporarily in a barn across the street from her house until we could do better. I don't remember what the barn was used for, but it was filled with a lot of junk.

My dad had no choice but to accept the invitation. He and some other men rearranged it so it would fit a bed and a stove. Mrs. Williams, her dad, and her boyfriend would help my dad make it livable.

The weather was still cool. We had one bed and two mattresses and sets of springs and bed covering. Someone gave us a heating stove like the one lost in the fire. The stovepipe had to be run out of an opening over the side door. There was no cookstove. My mother cooked on the top of the heating stove. The Williamses and other neighbors brought us breakfast, lunch, and dinner. Once it rained for a couple of days.

My dad joked about the arrangements years later. He said he didn't think the Williams family owned the barn, which stood on a vacant lot across the road from their house. No one ever said who owned it or what it was used for. It sat at the end of 34th Street. It was white stucco. The roof was bad in more places than good. The front and back doors were always open. Only one door was in place. My dad replaced the other door.

We kids played in and around the barn. There were owls, bats, and squirrels nesting in the upper part of the barn. The Williamses would run us off, not because it was theirs but because they didn't want us to get hurt.

My dad bought plywood to fix the leaky roof. And Mrs. Williams and her boyfriend, as promised, helped Dad make the barn suitable for us to live in, at least until Dad could find us another place. The plywood had to be arched to direct the rain away from the bed someone had given us and to shelter us from the bird and bat droppings. The three of us slept together again, and I remember a couple of days when it rained and we had to sit on the edge of the bed to keep from getting wet.

Our livestock were still down the hill where our house had once stood, except the four goats. They grazed around the barn and in the open pasture behind the barn.

The teachers at my school, Dunbar, took a collection and gave the money to me to give to my parents. A couple of classes at school brought clothes, shoes, and even some food to help. People in the neighborhood brought clothes for my parents. My parents didn't like that but had no choice because we lost everything.

Daddy Found Us a Home to Rent on Colorado Avenue, 1940

I don't remember how long we stayed in the barn, but I remember when Dad came home one evening and announced that we had a house to move into. My mother and I were overjoyed. The house was at 3419 Colorado, about three blocks from the barn. I went with my parents to see our new home. I had a small bedroom to myself. This was the best house we'd lived in, even better than Aunt Mittie's. We had a water faucet and a sink inside the small kitchen.

We even had a dining room that was open to the front room. For once we had some furniture. Although used, it was better than we'd ever had. At this location I was closer to my school than before. And we were able to bring all our livestock with us. Although we were renting the house, my parents treated it like it was ours by doing needed repairs. My dad and mother were still looking for a place that they could call theirs.

Two Tornadoes and Dull Needles, 1941

My parents were at work on Monday, October 6, 1941. I was home alone. It got so dark in the middle of the day. There was no breeze; all the trees were still. Suddenly, it sounded like a train coming down our street. My mother called me (we finally had a phone) and told me to go next door to the Joneses' house. I knocked on their door, and Clytee, the oldest girl, let me in.

I told her my mother had called from her job and said that she heard on the radio that there was a tornado in the area. The train sound got louder. I started to go back home for something and opened the Joneses' door, and I saw lumber, chickens, tree limbs, and trash blowing over our houses. I was aware of World War II and shouted to Clytee and others in the house, "The Germans are coming! The Germans are coming!" I shut the door, and Clytee told us we should go downstairs to the basement. We had all gone through tornado drills at school, but Clytee was the one who guided us.

We could hear things hitting the house, and the lights went out. We were all scared, including Clytee. Then it got still again. Clytee took us back upstairs and we went outside. Our block didn't look the same. Lumber from the new houses they were building for white folks up and around 39th and Hardesty had blown our way. Chickens were walking in folks' yards who had no chickens before the storm. Trees were uprooted. There was no electricity. The phone would not work. Luckily, my mother made it home and later my dad.

A short time after the tornado, all the kids at Dunbar had to take a series of shots. I don't remember exactly where this took place, but I think it was at our school site that they administered the shots to us—until the needle got dull. Today, after each shot, there's a new needle. Not so then. They used the needles until they got dull.

Then they tried to bribe us by taking us on buses to what I believe was like a "petting farm." I wasn't impressed—we had almost as many different animals as they had—but I couldn't enjoy any of what I saw, or the hot dogs, potato chips, and pop that they served us. After the dull needle exercise, my arm had swelled up and was hurting so bad that I lost my appetite. Many, like me, were walking holding our arms up from the elbows because it hurt worse when you allowed your arms to hang down. The kids who had little reaction to the shots would walk up to us and yell loud. That would cause us pain. They would just run and laugh and tell others, and the others would do the same. We were defenseless. But thank God, in a couple of days, we were able to function again.

The tornado had blown over the outdoor toilets on our school grounds, and the roof on the school was partly blown off. We could not return to school until the roof was repaired.

My dad was renting the house where we lived on Colorado. He and my mother talked often about owning our own home. Dad bought two lots just three or four blocks down on Drury, the 3600 block, just south of our school. My dad had completed the concrete floor and the frame. He had all the materials, lumber, nails, and all, but then the tornado came. Everything was blown away except the flooring. All the lumber my dad had bought and had piled up in the yard was gone, and the frame had also been blown away.

We Integrated a Poor White Neighborhood, 1942

My dad found another home for us at 3240 Quincy. We were buying the house from an attorney named Joseph H. Glass. All our neighbors were poor whites. None were poorer than our next-door neighbors, the Finleys—Mr. and Mrs. Finley and their two kids,

Tommy and Lela. Lela and I were the same age, and Tommy was two years older. Then there were the Joneses who lived on Brighton, one block over from us. After being called "nigger" numerous times by both families' kids and occasionally fighting, we finally became friends. Friends to the point that when they were seen with me, their friends would call them "nigger lovers." My neighbors ended up fighting their friends over me because they didn't want to be called "nigger lovers."

This new home had no running water inside either. We had a cistern, and my dad fixed it so we could use it as an ice box. The cistern stayed cool enough to keep things from spoiling. Plus, we drank water from the cistern. Unlike with a well, water in a cistern came from rainwater off the roof of the house and was filtered to make it drinkable. My mother also used it to wash clothes and for bathing.

My daddy explored with the city the possibility of having water run to our house. The city sent out a representative from the water department, and he told my father that the best and least expensive way to get water to our house was to give so many feet in the front of our property to the city to place a fire hydrant in front of our house and have a water line run from the fire hydrant to our kitchen. They placed the water meter right at the fire hydrant. And they also paved the rest of Quincy, a dead end. We could now drive up to the front of our house on pavement. We used to have to park 100 feet or more down the street where the pavement ended. Before the street was paved, when it rained, the entire area was nothing but mud.

I Was a Successful Shoeshine Boy Until Gum Got Me Fired, 1942

My dad helped me make a shoeshine box, which I still have, along with the black shoe brush. He took me to the Katz Drug Store and bought me polish, brushes, and shine rags.

My mother now worked different Saturdays—once or twice a month for a white family on South Benton, the other Saturdays for white families who lived where we called "out south." She caught the streetcar at 31st and Linwood, then transferred at 31st and Main Street and caught the Main streetcar south to the Waldo and Brookside areas.

I would ride the streetcar on Saturday with my mother and get off with her at 31st and Main and, when the weather was good, would stay on the corner shining shoes. Shines were five cents, but most of my customers gave me an extra nickel, sometimes even a quarter. I made $2.00 to $3.00 for five or six hours, almost as much as my mother made working for the white folks all day.

My shine spot was on the southeast corner of 31st and Main, right in front of the Junior League Thrift Shop. Around the corner was Cargile Shoe Repair at 3 East 31st Street. After two or three Saturdays, the owner of the shoe repair shop came out and asked me if I had a license to shine shoes on the street. I told him, "No, sir!" I didn't know what he was talking about. He then told me that I should get off the corner before the police came to arrest me. I caught the next streetcar and went home.

That evening, I went to meet my mother at the streetcar stop when she got off from work. She asked me why I hadn't waited for her. I told her what the man at the shoe shop had told me and that I was scared that he was going to call the police and they would arrest me. My mother told me the police weren't going to arrest a ten-year-old.

So, the following Saturday, I was back on the corner with my box. I kept looking for the man from the shoe shop and the police. I made it through that Saturday. I was developing quite a clientele. Men would come back Saturday after Saturday, and they all gave me a tip. Occasionally, I had one or two men waiting in line to get their shoes shined. The women at the thrift shop told me I could come in and use their restroom if I needed to. They thought what I was doing to help my family was good. Sometimes they would give me a sandwich and a bottle of pop and sometimes homemade cookies.

The owner of the shoe shop saw the women at the thrift shop tell me I could come in and use their restroom. I think he saw them as kinda supporting my shoeshine business.

He came out one Saturday and asked if I wanted to work for him in his shoe shop. He invited me in to see his shine stand. I had seen his shine stand because my mother had left shoes there to be repaired and I was with her. I went in to look. I told him I would ask my mother, which I did when she got off the streetcar.

Mother said she'd talk about it with my father. My dad said he thought I would lose my clients if I moved inside and there was no way to tell them I had moved inside. He said, "The shoe repair man knows you're taking his customers, but you would be out of the heat and the cold weather." Mother said she would go in with me to talk to him next Saturday.

The following Saturday, my mother took me to meet with the owner of the shoe shop, Mr. Ray Cargile. I still had my shine box across my shoulder. He told my mother he thought I did a good job at shining shoes on the corner, but I could make more money and do a better job on his shine stand. His shines were ten cents. I would get five cents from each shine, but I would have to clean up and sweep up the shop at the close of the day. My mother told him maybe my father would let me work a couple of hours on Friday evenings and half days on Saturdays, maybe noon to 6:00 p.m. Mr. Cargile said I would have to be consistent so my customers would know my days and hours. My mother told him she and my father would discuss it and she would be back and let him know. We thanked him and went home.

That evening when my dad came in from work, we discussed the job offer. After some talking, my parents said okay. My mother stopped by and told Mr. Cargile that it was okay that I start work the following Saturday. They agreed upon the hours, noon to six, and four to six on Friday evening.

After a couple of Saturdays, my parents said it was okay if I worked from four to six on Fridays and four to six on Saturdays.

My customer base became rather good. My former customers on the corner found me in the shop. I got the chance to offer a shine to those who came in for shoe repairs. Some even began to drop their shoes off for me to shine and pick them up in the evening.

While working at the shoe repair shop, one of my customers asked me if I wanted to make extra money buying and selling chewing gum. I believed he either worked at the Wrigley gum factory or somewhere that he got cartons of gum, twenty-four packages per carton, I think. I forget how much I paid him per carton, but I remember I made fifty cents per carton. So, I became a businessman.

My business was flourishing, and my parents were proud of me. I sold gum to all my regular customers and others who came to me for shoe repair. Some Saturdays I brought home as much as my mother earned working eight hours for the white folks out south.

But my business came to an abrupt halt.

Mr. Cargile told me one Saturday afternoon that he didn't need me anymore. When I asked why, he said, "You know that man you're selling that gum for is stealing it. You are selling stolen property. I'm not going to have my business closed because some damn kid is selling stolen gum. So get going."

I begged him not to send me home. I was mature enough to tell Mr. Cargile that the man who sold me the gum was a regular customer before I started to work there. I told him that I didn't know the gum was stolen and that my parents didn't know either. He said again, "Get out. You're a thief, too. The police are going to arrest both of you."

My plea made no difference. I was fired. I left crying, both because I had been told to go home and couldn't work there anymore and because the police were coming after me for selling stolen chewing gum.

That evening, I told my mother. I asked her if I could go back on the corner and shine shoes. She told me maybe I should not, that Mr. Cargile might call the police on me and bring up the gum incident.

That ended my shoeshining career.

"Run, Nigger, Run!"

Our neighborhood was all white and poor, and I mean poor. We were poor, but the white folks were what my parents and other Black folks called "po." I ran with three or four white youth, all around my age. They were the Jones boys, Billy, Bobby, and Eddie Jr.

And Max—I can't remember his last name. Max was Italian. I knew this because other boys, sometimes playfully, sometimes when they were angry with him, called him "dago," an ethnic slur. It was like calling me "nigger." And Tommy Finley ran with us sometimes. He was about three years older than us. He was always telling us what to do and putting us up to do stuff that would always get us into trouble.

One day we were just walking, talking, and looking for pop bottles to sell for money to buy ice cream. We walked through the wooded area west from my house and ended up on Elmwood, then walked over to Linwood Boulevard and up Linwood toward Indiana. Just as we approached Jackson, two policemen drove up and told all five of us to get into the back seat of the police car.

We asked what for, and one of the cops said they had a report that some boys were throwing rocks at the dogs in a woman's backyard where her baby was in a playpen. She told the police that she had hollered at the boys and told them to quit throwing into her yard, and they cursed her. We tried to explain to the cops that it wasn't us. We did walk past her house on our way through the wooded area, but there was no baby in the yard in a playpen.

The cops told us to get in the police car to take us back to the woman's house to see if it was us. They took us to the house where the Gores lived at 3240 Brighton.

We were told to get out and stand next to the police car. The Gores' daughter came to the door. One of the officers, the younger of the two, asked if we were the boys who threw the rocks and cursed her. She said no. She said, "I saw these boys walking just outside the yard before I put my baby into the playpen" and that she knew me and my mother well and that I often went to the store for her.

The older officer, who had done all the talking when we first got picked up, told us to get back in the car. One of my friends asked the officer if we could go "just over there" and pointed to my house, which was less than a half block away. It was easy to see.

The older cop was big bellied, and we could smell liquor on his breath, both inside and outside the police car. The older cop ordered us into the police car and had the younger cop drive us away. As soon as we got out of sight of the Gores' daughter, who was still standing in her front yard, the older fat cop began to call me nigger and told my white friends, "You white boys have no business hanging around with this nigger. If I catch you with him again, I'm going to put all your little white asses in jail, you little white trash. You hear me?"

My friends responded, "Yes." Tommy, who was the oldest among us, probably around thirteen, asked the older cop why they couldn't be with me.

The cop said, "Because I said so. I don't like niggers, and I don't want to see you with him again. You hear me?"

By this time, we were near the foot of the Brighton Street hill. The older cop told the younger cop to stop the car. He got out and told us to get out of the car. I saw him draw his gun. He turned to me and said, "Okay, nigger, see that hill? Start running. If you can make it over that hill before I shoot you, you're a free nigger." I began backing up toward the foot of the hill. I was screaming and crying, begging him not to shoot me. I was backing up faster and faster but never turned my back to him. He had the gun raised and was pointing it at me. I heard him cock the gun. He was hollering, "Run, nigger, run! You better git running before I shoot you right here."

All my little friends were hollering and screaming, "Don't shoot Alvin, don't shoot Alvin!" As they were hollering and screaming, little Billy jumped up and grabbed the cop's arm. The gun fired. I turned and ran as fast as I could up the hill. My friends followed. The cop who threatened to shoot me got into the police car, and he and the younger cop sped off.

By that time, my friends had almost reached me at the top of the hill. We just laughed, all of us, and told Billy how crazy he was. We began re-creating what had occurred and were still laughing. My friends even imitated the cop calling me nigger, saying, "Run, nigger, run!" I told them that was not funny and don't call me a nigger again. They apologized.

We agreed that we wouldn't tell my mother what had happened. We looked for a piece of glass to go through the ritual of cutting our fingers so they would bleed, then let the blood touch "finger to finger"—that meant we were "blood brothers" and would not talk about it.

I walked the short distance to my backyard and my friends followed me. My mother came out after hearing us and asked me where I had gone because she had been calling me. I told her we had walked up on Linwood Boulevard, just walking.

Billy spoke up and said, "I jumped up on that cop's arm that was going to shoot Alvin."

My mother said, "What cop? Where? Why was he going to shoot Alvin?"

And Billy went on (although we were whispering to him, trying to tell him to be quiet), and we began to fill in the blanks.

My mother went in the house, saying, "I'm going to call the police station and report this." My mother hollered back out to us, saying, "Don't any of you leave here."

We reminded Billy that we had sworn not to tell and he violated our brotherhood. I was Billy's biggest critic, but I finally said, "I'm glad you talked, 'cause that cop could have killed me, and you all would have been scared to tell." They said they wouldn't have been so scared, but I knew they would have.

We continued to talk about our experience. And how big the older cop's belly was, and how he had been drinking, and how he smelled.

A half hour or so passed and a white cop drove up to the front of our house. Tommy said he was a sergeant because he had three yellow stripes on his jacket.

My mother began to tell the sergeant what we had told her. Then she asked us to tell the sergeant what had happened. The sergeant never took out a pencil or pad. Tommy Finley, remember, was the oldest of the five and was eager to respond first. He told how all five of us started out from my house and decided to walk up to the Velvet Freeze ice cream store and get ice cream cones. I could not go inside Velvet Freeze; my white friends had to buy my cone or ice cream bar for me.

But that day, before we got to Velvet Freeze, we were picked up by the cops. Tommy gave the number that appeared on the side of the police car and described what the two officers looked like and that the older officer with the big stomach "smelled like he was drunk."

The sergeant stood there and never asked a question. My mother did most of the talking and introduced us one after another. Each of us stated almost verbatim what the other said. Billy was the one who said, "That cop was going to kill Alvin unless I had jumped on his arm." Others chimed in about what took place after that. All of us used the word "nigger" to describe what happened. We also laughed when the story got to the cop's gun going off, how everyone ran after hearing the shot. And how I was running faster than they were—even though I was running backward.

The sergeant told my mother he would check it out and get back with her. My mother never heard anything further from the sergeant or anyone else from the police department.

Before Brown v. Board of Education

My white friends and I, despite our close friendships, lived in two different worlds. We were living "separate and unequal" lives in so many ways. Even as children, we saw the different ways I was treated. We lived three blocks, no more, from Milton Moore Elementary School. But because of discrimination, separate and unequal, my friends and I could not attend the same school. We were victims of a system we could not at our ages understand. We never knew the term "racist" or "bigot." But we did know about indifference.

It was the summer of 1942 or 1943. There was a drive-in restaurant (like today's Sonic) just east of the intersection of Linwood Boulevard and 31st Street, next to the Missouri State Highway offices. The owner hired only boys as carhops. He sold only hot dogs on buns and frozen mugs of root beer. The boys delivered the orders from a window outside the business to trays that hung on the doors of parked cars. If they were not being served in their cars, my white friends could walk up to the "to go" window and place an order. I could not be served either way.

I did land a job at the drive-in when I was ten or eleven years old. I was with my white friends, and we were walking down the street toward the drive-in. One of our friends worked there and cooked the hot dogs. He would intentionally burn hot dogs, and since the owner would not let his carhops (all of them white males) serve any burned hot dogs, our friend would slip us the burned ones out the back door, maybe three or four an hour. We didn't have any buns or mustard, but the hot dogs still tasted pretty good.

On one occasion, we got to the drive-in before it opened. Our friend was already at work. We just kinda stood around across the street from the drive-in, just messing around. The owner came out of the back door and pointed at us. All of us answered, almost like a quartet, "Who? Me?"

The owner said, "You, Snowball!" He was talking and pointing to me. I wondered what I had done for him to call just me and why he called me Snowball.

I didn't feel good about being called Snowball, but I walked over to him. He said, "Snowball, you want a job?"

"Doing what?" I asked.

He said, "Cleaning up the parking lot every morning before we open for business. But," he said, "you can't bring them little peckerwoods with you. You have to sweep and pick up the paper every morning before we open at eleven."

I told him, "Yes, I want the job. How much do you pay me?"

He said, "Twenty-five cents a day, six days a week, just until I close for the winter."

I told him I would have to ask my parents. "Can I come back and tell you tomorrow or this afternoon?"

He said, "Yes, but I'll have to know right away before I give it to someone else. But you can't bring those others with you. They can't even hang around you while you're working. You understand? Am I making myself clear?"

I said, "Yes, sir."

"Okay, Snowball, you got the job if your parents approve."

Both of my parents were at work. I went back across the street and told my friends that I had a job making twenty-five cents a day working every morning except Mondays. I hadn't forgotten the Snowball thing, but I didn't bring it up. But my friends did. They started calling me Snowball. Someone even called me Colored Snowball. I knew I didn't like to be referred to that way, either by the drive-in owner or by my white friends. I told him so.

Later that evening, my friends and I met my mother at the streetcar stop right across the street from the drive-in. I told my mother about my job offer, and she said it was okay. One of my friends told my mother the owner called me Snowball. They all laughed, but my mother didn't think it was funny. She told them that my name was Alvin, not Snowball. She said she was going to go over and talk to the owner, but I begged her not to because I wanted to work. We walked past the drive-in, but she didn't stop. I knew if my mother said something, I wouldn't get the job. She told me if he called me "Snowball" again to walk off the job and come home. She would deal with it when she came home. I worked for about a month before school started. The owner never called me "Snowball" again.

"Grandson, You Keep Drinking That Coffee, You're Going to Turn the Color of Alvin"

My mother was one of the many women across this country who worked for white families. They were called "domestics." My mother worked for $5.00 a day and car fare, which was twenty cents. Ten cents each way. You got your transfer and got it punched when you changed streetcars. My mother worked five and a half days a week, Monday through Friday, 8:00 a.m. to 4:00 p.m. and 8:00 a.m. to noon on Saturday. Sometimes she stayed all night—several days a week. Because of my dad's drinking, I was often home alone. Sometimes, several of my Black friends would stay all night with me.

My mother worked for a white woman in an all-white, working-class community. This woman was a grandmother whose son was in the service. This was during World War II. Her daughter-in-law worked at the defense plant. The grandmother babysat her three grandkids. Two were twins my age. The third grandchild was a baby. Mother went to this job only on Saturdays, for a half day. I went with her when I didn't shine shoes. I helped. I swept the porch, the sidewalk, and the driveway. My mother taught me how to wash the window in the front of the house so there were no streaks. I cut the grass in the front yard. If I hadn't done the outside work, my mother would have had to do it.

On Saturday mornings when my mother first got to work, she and the kids' grandmother would sit in the kitchen and drink coffee and just have small talk. The twins and I would have milk and rolls. Often after the twin boy finished his milk, he would go to his grandmother's coffee cup, take a spoon, and dip coffee from her cup into his glass. Occasionally, he would go to my mother's cup and do the same thing.

One morning before my mother and I started our chores, after the twin boy finished his milk, he went to my mother's cup and then his grandmother's and dipped spoons of coffee from their cups to his glass. His grandmother said, "Grandson, you keep drinking that much coffee, you're going to turn the color of Alvin."

When she said that, my mother looked very strange. She immediately stood up and said to me, "Come on, baby, let's go to work."

What was said, and my mother's reaction, troubled me, even though I was just nine or ten.

Later, when we were waiting for the streetcar at 36th and Prospect, I asked my mother, "What did it mean when she said that if her grandson kept drinking that coffee, he was going to turn my color?"

My mother only responded, "You'll understand one day, baby."

I saw tears in her eyes and asked, "Mama, why are you crying?" She didn't answer. The streetcar came and we went home.

When we got home, my mother pulled off her coat and took off her shoes. She picked up her Bible and sat in her old lime-green rocking chair with the wooden back and called me to kneel and place the left side of my head in her lap. She still had her apron on. On it, I could smell what she had prepared for lunch for all of us before we had left that home.

This was not the first time my mother had done this. Every time something happened where I was the victim of a racial situation, my mother would do this ritual. She patted me on my right cheek while I lay with my head in her lap. She read several verses from the New Testament. Then she'd sing a few verses of "Precious Lord, Take My Hand" and would pray this prayer: "Lord, please help my baby become the kind of man you want him to be." I'd kneel there for a while, with my head in her lap, waiting for more patting of my cheek. Then she would get up with no further explanation about what happened.

My mom did the same thing with the incident of the cops drawing the gun on me and threatening, "Run, nigger, run."

She did it many times when I told her about something that happened, even though I often did not fully understand how racist it was.

The Light Bill, That Segregated Coke, and How I Became a Member of the Exclusive Kansas City Club

My mother and I often went downtown together. We would first go to the Jones Store, one of the three big downtown department stores, along with Kline's and Emery, Bird & Thayer. Then we'd walk through what I remember was the restaurant section of Jones. A woman from our neighborhood worked at the restaurant as a bus girl. She spoke to my mother and me. I never thought about all these people, their race or their color. I smelled the food and saw them eating, and all I knew was that I was hungry.

Before we got downtown, my mother would say that we were going to stop and get something to eat. To me, that meant Kresge's. The streetcar would let us off right in front of Jones. Mother would do some shopping, then we'd go across the street to Kresge's. My mother ordered the usual, the only thing on the menu—Cokes and hot dogs. We ate, went into Jones for more shopping, and then caught the 31st Street streetcar in front of the cigar store on the northwest corner and headed home.

When I was nine or ten, after going downtown so many times with my mother, I was old enough to ride the streetcar by myself and to go pay our monthly light bill at the downtown Kansas City Power and Light building at 1330 Baltimore. It was the tallest building in Kansas City. On the very top, different colored lights would come on at night and you could see it from miles away.

I loved to go downtown by myself to pay the light bill. We lived at 3240 Quincy, so to get to Kansas City Power and Light, I had to walk down the Brighton hill to the streetcar stop where Linwood Boulevard crosses 31st Street. I would stay on the streetcar until I got to

14th and Main. Then I'd walk up the hill to this very tall granite stone building and enter the revolving doors. Inside, just to the right, were women—all white—sitting behind what I call a caged-in counter. I would walk up to one of them and hand over our light bill and the money. The woman behind the counter would count my money and place the bill in a machine that perforated the bill to show it was paid.

Most of the time my mother would give me the change for the exact amount of the bill and an extra quarter. As I remember, ten cents was for the streetcar fare (going and coming), and fifteen cents was for me to go to Kresge's Dime Store at 12th and Main and order a ten-cent hot dog and a nickel Coke. I couldn't sit down because there was no place to sit, but there was a counter, bar-type arrangement where I had to stand up to be served and eat my hot dog and drink my Coke.

I didn't know why I never saw anyone of my color sitting on the upper level, where the fountain and the stools were. I didn't know anything about racism, segregation, or discrimination. But to a nine- or ten-year-old kid, those racist hot dogs and Cokes were the best! And I looked forward to the next time I got to pay the light bill.

I don't remember what time of year it was. I know it wasn't winter; but, oh, what a day.

In my haste to get to that "segregated" hot dog and Coke, one day on the streetcar I passed by the 14th and Main stop and pulled the cord for the next stop, which was 13th Street. I didn't waste any time and ran up the hill to Baltimore to pay the light bill. When I got inside the revolving door, everything had changed. There were no white women sitting behind the caged-in counter. No machines that made those funny noises when the woman would place our light bill in it to mark it paid.

Instead, there were two tall white men in uniforms. They wore tall hats. I was lost. I had never been in this building before. I was not in the Kansas City Power and Light building at 1330 Baltimore, but a block up the street that I later learned was the exclusive all-white, all-male Kansas City Club at 1228 Baltimore. The two white men didn't waste any time approaching me and starting their racist game-playing.

They began jostling me around from one to the other as they laughed. Then one grabbed me and began to rub my head. He also told his partner to rub my head for good luck. They called me nigger, little nigger, Little Black Sambo, Buckwheat, burrhead, and many other names. I began to cry. I was so scared. I tried to run out the door, but they held me. They weren't finished with their play.

They kept jostling me and rubbing my head with their knuckles for good luck. They finally took me outside. I tried to run, but they held me. Both men picked me up and slung me back and forth like a bag of something, like they were going to throw me out into the street. My God, they were having fun at my expense. I was screaming and crying more now. I just knew they were going to throw me into the street.

While they were slinging me back and forth, my light bill money fell out of my pocket. About that time a white woman was driving up the street and saw what they were doing to me. She stopped and walked across the street and admonished them, "Why are you all doing this to this child?" They didn't answer her, but they let me go and then went back inside the building, laughing.

The woman helped me find my money for the light bill and walked me across the street to her car. She got a handkerchief from her purse, wiped my nose and eyes, and gave me the handkerchief. She asked my name and my age. I told her and she told me her name. Then she asked me what I was doing in that building. I told her I had to pay the light bill. She said that building was down the street on the next block.

I told her that I wanted to go to Kresge's to eat. She said, "You're hungry? Well, get yourself something to eat and then come back down there and pay for your lights. Do you know how to get home? Where do you live?"

I told her my address. She asked if I wanted her to take me home. I told her, "No, ma'am. I have streetcar fare." She told me to get in her car and she would take me around the corner to Kresge's.

I could see the two white men had come back outside and were still laughing, and they waved at me. We drove to 12th and Main. I pointed out Kresge's and told her, "There it is!"

She stopped to let me out. But before I got out, she told me to hold on. She searched in her purse, found several coins, and handed me a solid quarter. I thanked her as I was taught to say to anyone who gave me something. I crossed the street and entered Kresge's.

That hot dog and Coke became my primary interest now. The light bill would have to wait. My God, now I could buy three hot dogs and two Cokes! And I did! When I finished, I walked up the hill to the northwest corner of 12th and Main and waited for the 31st Street streetcar.

When I returned home, I did what I always did. I placed the receipt under the scarf in the back part on the dresser where there were numerous receipts. Only this time, I brought the entire bill back and the money. Mother asked me later, "Did you pay the bill, baby, and get your hot dog and Coke?"

I replied, "Yes, ma'am."

Several days later we got a cutoff notice from Kansas City Power and Light. My mother told me about the cutoff notice and asked me to go get the receipt showing the bill was paid. I went where I had placed the whole bill and the money. I tore off the larger part that should have been stamped "paid." I took that portion of the bill and gave it to my mother. She looked at it, ran her hand over it, and held it to the light.

She said, "Baby, they didn't mark this paid!"

I said, "Yes, mama, they did. Let me show you." I tried to convince her that the bill had been paid, but after further questioning, I broke down and told her what had happened. She said she understood.

In the early '70s, when I was still director of Kansas City's Human Relations Department, a friend, a local real estate agent, called me. He was responsible for providing the next month's program for the luncheon of the organization of real estate agents of which he was a member. He wanted me to be their luncheon speaker. He said I could choose my topic, but he wanted the group to be challenged out of their comfort zone. He said normally the speakers were given about a half hour: twenty minutes for remarks and ten minutes for Q&A. The group met from 12:00 to 1:30, but he said the group gets a little restless after 1:30. He told me I would get a good free lunch because the club's chef was excellent.

I asked what club it was. He said the Kansas City Club, 13th and Baltimore. I told my friend "no way" and why—about what had happened to me as a boy and that I had promised God and a few other responsible persons that I would never set foot in that building.

After hearing my story, he responded, "Al, I didn't know about that. That's all the more reason you ought to speak to this group. Most of them are members, as am I, of the Kansas City Club, as were many of our fathers and other male relatives—although to the best of my knowledge, I'm the first generation in my family to hold a membership. We all need to hear your story just as it happened. Please, Al, you need to speak to us." After playing tennis with our conversation, I gave in and told him I would speak.

About six weeks later, my friend picked me up at city hall. After parking, we walked to the doors of the Kansas City Club. I had driven by a hundred times and cursed every time! Sometimes, when someone was with me, I would mention the childhood incident.

Before I entered, I stood and looked at that door, the closest I had come since that awful day some thirty years ago. Talk about post-traumatic stress! I had it right there for a moment. Tears came to my eyes. I pulled out my handkerchief and wiped them away.

My friend placed his arm on my shoulder and said, "Al, I'm so sorry, man. I am so damn sorry."

I said, "That's okay. I'm all right now."

There were no doormen this time. But several men spoke to my friend as we waited for the elevator. He tried to introduce me, but all of them responded, "Oh yes, I've seen you on television. Thank you for joining us today. We look forward to hearing from you." About thirty men and a couple of women were already there, sipping drinks. My friend began introducing me around. Someone offered to buy me a drink. I declined. I felt my stomach churning. Not scared as I was downstairs thirty years ago. Not crying, screaming for my life. But I was getting angry as I looked around and saw all those white men, some old enough to have been members in the early '40s. I wondered if one of them had been sitting downstairs when those racist bastard doormen were jostling me, using their knuckles on my head, calling me burrhead, nigger, Little Black Sambo.

The room filled up with about eighty people, including about a half dozen women. One man called them to order and asked everyone to stand for the Pledge of Allegiance. Afterward he welcomed everyone and announced, "Lunch is served." I sat at the table with my friend and the man who seemed to be the convener, at least for the occasion.

I didn't eat. The waiter asked if I wanted to take the meal with me. I said no. After lunch, the convener made a few remarks, asked for a few reports, and said they should dispense with some things to get a chance "to hear our speaker for the hour."

My friend rose and said that he wanted to apologize to me but would wait until after I spoke. I wish I could have seen all those faces. I saw the ten or twelve in my view, and they looked like they were thinking, "What the hell is he talking about?" My friend then introduced me from my biographical brief.

My friend shook my hand, gave me a hug, and whispered, "Okay, Al, let us have it." I saw that he had tears in his eyes.

There was a lectern with a mike. I thanked my friend for the introduction and stepped away from the lectern. I began to pace right in front of them, to focus their attention on me. I looked down for a minute or so and stood without moving. I gave them every chance to see I was a Black man. Then I shouted out the poem by African American poet Langston Hughes, "Dream of Freedom."

When I ended reciting the poem, I said, "African American poet Langston Hughes, 1964." I believe the most important point of this poem is that to save the dream for one, it has to be saved for everyone. Then I told about when my friend first asked me to speak some six weeks earlier, and then I told the story of being abused as a child at the Kansas City Club. At times I felt angry. I couldn't help it. But I kept my anger to myself.

I continued to pace but met the eyes of almost everybody in the room, about eighty members and guests. All the women were crying. One got up and walked out but came back during the Q&A. At the end, my friend then explained why he was apologizing to me, and he said everyone in the room should also. They responded with a standing ovation. Each woman came up and apologized with handkerchiefs or the table napkins in hand. About a dozen men came up, one or two of the old-timers. Most of them left without saying anything.

One of the women, the one who got up and walked outside the room, came up to me and asked, "Alvin, would you mind if I gave you a hug?" I thought quickly. She held out her arms and I responded, and we hugged. She whispered, "I'm so sorry." I thanked her.

Arriving about three weeks later in the mail at home was a membership card to the Kansas City Club marked "Alvin Brooks, #U212." The reverse side had a place for my signature and information about club rules.

I called my friend and asked him why he paid for a membership for me in the Kansas City Club. "What membership?" he asked. He swore he didn't buy me a membership. The next day he came to city hall to have lunch with me and to see the membership card. He laughed. He took his out of his billfold. The only difference between our cards was the name and number. He made me believe him. We suspected it was one of the women, although women couldn't belong. My friend even said he thought he knew who it was but asked me to never say anything to her. He believed it was the middle-aged woman who got up and walked out and was the first to come forward, holding back tears and asking if she could hug me.

About a month later, my friend sent me a copy of the organization's newsletter. Although a few of my remarks were mentioned, they missed the point of my remarks, but it did report that I had given a moving speech to the membership and received a standing ovation.

That person continued to pay my membership for years. I never used the club. But I still have the card today. It's a little mutilated for showing it so many times, worn but legible. I still carry it. The Kansas City Club, founded 1882, closed May 23, 2015.

Stand by the Door or Take Your Coke Outside

My daddy worked as a track laborer for the Missouri Pacific Railroad. He also hauled trash in his truck from several different businesses to earn additional money. One business was a drugstore near 31st and Indiana. I often went with him on his trash route. Sometimes my white friends went with us. We all loved to ride in the back of the old truck.

At the drugstore, my daddy taught me how to clean up behind the soda fountain. I emptied the metal receptacle under the soda counter where the broken Coke glasses, used straws, straw wrappers, Lily paper cone-shaped cups, and napkins were thrown. I also learned how to rinse the receptacle out with water with a small amount of Clorox after emptying and drying it. I also emptied the wastebasket behind the pharmacy. The owner was a pharmacist.

While I was inside, my dad was outside breaking down all the cardboard boxes and placing them in the truck. My dad and the owner would always engage in small talk while we were at the business. The owner's son was a senior at Central High School.

My white friends told me about how much fun it was when they went to the drugstore and bought a Coke, how much fun it was to take straws from the glass straw holder and pull the metal top of the straw holder so that all the straws could come up so you could take one to drink your Coke with.

My friends told me they'd always take more than one while the owner or his son was drawing Coke from the fountain. Then they'd wet the end of the wrapper over the straw, just enough so they could slide the other side of the wrapper down to put their lips on the tip of the straw, and BLOW. That wrapper would take off around the fountain once or twice, and that would give the kids much joy to watch that wrapper go up and down and around and land somewhere around the fountain. That was more fun than drinking the Coke.

I got my chance to experience this straw wrapper phenomenon. One day we each had our nickels for a Coke. We all entered the drugstore and spoke to the owner's son, and each of us ordered our Coke and sat down at the fountain. There were several straw holders on the fountain counter. My friends immediately pulled up on the metal top. I followed. We had already placed our nickels on the counter. The blowing of the wrappers began. We'd see who could blow theirs the farthest and whose made the most twists and turns in the air before it landed somewhere. God, that was fun.

The son had delivered our Cokes in glasses. We put one or two straws in our Coke glasses but still each got two or three straw wrappers airborne. My first day of this fun-filled activity with my white friends was spoiled when the owner came from behind the pharmacy side and walked over to us kids as we were sucking up our drinks. He reached and took my Coke from me and threw the straws and my glass into that metal receptacle that I emptied when I was cleaning up with my father. He reached and got a Lily cone-shaped paper cup, poured the remainder of my Coke in it, threw the glass in that metal receptacle under the counter, handed the paper cup to me, and said, "You take this and stand over there by the door."

I was almost in tears. I called the owner by his name and asked, "What did I do? What did I do?"

My friends asked, "What did Alvin do?"

The owner said, "You shut up, or you can stand up there with him. Or, better yet, finish your Cokes and all of you get out of here."

I was scared now. I must have done something wrong; and if the owner told my dad, I was in big trouble. I could feel the whipping already.

I called the owner again by his name and asked, "What did I do? I'm sorry. I'm sorry." I was crying now.

The owner responded, "All of you go now! Get out of here. Now!"

I was the only one who still had some Coke. My friends drank their Cokes quick and followed me outdoors. I gave the rest of my Coke to one of my friends. I lost my "Coke appetite." I was scared that whatever I had done, the owner was going to tell my dad, and I knew what my daddy would do to me. As we walked back home, we were trying to figure out what I had done wrong. We retraced all our activities before the owner took my Coke and poured it into that paper cup. We never came up with a rational answer.

We did make another one of our "brother-to-brother" commitments. We couldn't figure out what I had done to get into trouble that caused the drugstore owner to make me stand by the door, but we knew we didn't want my dad to hear about it and hoped that the owner wouldn't tell him the next time we went there to pick up the trash. So, to keep the whole event secret among us, we found that piece of glass, pricked our fingers until they drew blood, and touched our fingers together. We were now blood brothers. Silence among us!

We decided to head back toward my house. We played all the way. When we got to 32nd and Brighton (that infamous Brighton hill), just a block from my house, we noticed it was about the time when my dad would be coming home. So, we decided to wait on him. He'd be driving his old truck. We would hitch a ride with him to our house on Quincy.

While we waited, we played around the bottom of the Brighton hill. We would be able to tell when he was coming, either when we saw the truck or when he was close enough for us to hear the truck's loud muffler.

And then there he was! We piled on. Billy always jumped in the front seat with my dad. And he did that day.

While my dad was waiting for us to get on the back of the truck safely, Billy disclosed to my dad what had occurred earlier at the drugstore. He didn't honor our "brother-to-brother swearing in blood not to tell."

Almost as soon as Billy got in and shut the truck door, my dad put the truck in reverse. Rather than go up the hill as he did most of the time, he drove exceedingly fast up to Quincy in front of our house. When Dad arrived in front of our house, he stopped the truck abruptly. Daddy jumped out, left the truck rocking, and came up the yard to the house. Billy was following behind him. Just as Daddy was coming out, Billy was standing on the porch. We could hear my mother yelling, "Cluster, don't take that gun out of here. Please don't take that gun!"

Dad came down the stairs, Billy right behind him. We could see the gun hanging out of my dad's pocket. He told us, "Get back on the truck."

My mother was standing on the porch, still yelling, "Cluster, come back with that gun! Please don't leave here with that gun. Don't take those kids with you."

Daddy never responded. He backed up and turned around and reversed his direction. Billy again sat in the front seat. We were just hollerin' and hollerin' as my dad drove west, up Linwood Boulevard. We really didn't know where my daddy was taking us. We didn't know until later that Billy, sitting in the front seat, told my daddy what had occurred to us earlier at the drugstore.

My dad drove to the drugstore, right up to the door, so close that the door could hardly be opened. But there was enough room for my dad to open the door and step inside. He told us, "Come on down here." We climbed down and stepped inside beside my dad.

He called the owner by his last name. Before this, every time I was with my daddy, when we were at the drugstore, the owner was always addressed as "Mister" and my dad by his first name, although my dad was considerably older.

This time, "Mister" did not precede his name. My dad pulled out his gun and held it down to his side. The owner came out from behind the counter. He was alone in the store. My daddy began to curse him, calling him all kinds of names. He asked him repeatedly, "Do you hear me?"

Each time, the owner responded, "Yes, sir, Mr. Brooks, I hear you."

And finally, my daddy said, "You see these boys? If you ever treat them like you did today, I'll come here and take care of you. You understand, you no-good son of a bitch?"

"Yes, sir, I understand," the owner responded. Dad told us, "You all get back on the truck." We drove off back toward my house.

We were talking about what my daddy said. My friends were saying how bad my daddy was. "Mr. Brooks is tuff!"

Daddy went up the Brighton hill this time, drove down the unimproved 33rd Street, and turned off the engine. He told us, "Get off the truck and go play somewhere."

My mother was standing in the back door. He pushed past her. Moments later, he came back. He had changed his pants and shirt and got back in the truck and drove off. My mother called me in the house and told my friends to go home. She asked me what happened. I told her the whole incident and how we had not planned to tell anyone, but Billy told Daddy what had happened earlier at the drugstore. Then I told her what Daddy had told the owner when we returned to the drugstore. My mother began to cry. She sat down in her favorite chair and began to rock. I sat on the floor beside her and continued to ask her why she was crying. She never responded.

She finally asked me if I was hungry. I said, "No, ma'am." I was scared now. No appetite. Then a police car with two white police officers arrived. They walked up to our porch, and just as one of them was starting to knock, my mother opened the door.

He asked, "Is Cluster Brooks here?" He pronounced my daddy's first name incorrectly.

My mother told him, "No!" He asked if she knew where he was.

She said, "No."

He told her, "When he comes back, tell him we're looking for him." My mother didn't respond. We didn't see my dad for several days. He talked to my mother by phone every day. I was not allowed to be in the room where our phone was when my mother talked to my father.

Finally, after about a week, my father came back home. He had been going to work every day. I never heard where he had been staying. I never heard what finally occurred except my daddy never got arrested and we no longer had the drugstore as our customer.

My mother said to me. "When that little Billy Jones comes here again, you tell him I need to talk to him and his parents." I don't remember whether or not she ever talked to Billy's parents, but she did talk to him. He told my mother and us kids that he was sorry and would never "tell anything again"!

My First Horse, Betty, Was Bought for $1.75

My father had another drinking partner, Mr. Ernest Butler. Mr. Butler worked at the stockyards, and one day Mr. Butler came walking past our house with a baby female yellowish-colored pony. The pony had a bad bruise on one of its back legs. Mr. Butler stopped to see if my father was at home, but it was too early in the day. My mother came outside, and Mr. Butler told her that he was helping farmers unload their cattle and other animals sold and traded at the stockyards. He sat awhile and then walked to his house just across the field.

Several days later, I was visiting with my friend Maurice Green and we walked a couple houses down to the Butlers'. The pony was tied in their backyard. Her back leg was healing. The Butler kids were feeding their pony oatmeal. They named her Betty, I think after their mother. Maurice and I were told that Betty was palomino-colored. Betty never was big and strong enough to ride. As time passed, Betty grew to the size of a Shetland pony. The smaller kids around the neighborhood were able to ride her when she was being led by the rope. After more than a year, Betty's growth had stunted because of her injury as a baby and her diet of oatmeal.

One evening Mr. Butler was returning from work and was walking past our house. I spoke to him. He began talking to me about Betty. He asked if I had any money. I said yes. He asked if I wanted to buy Betty. I yelled, "Yes! How much?" He asked me how much money I had. I ran in the house. Mother asked me what I was running about, and I said, "I'm going to buy Betty from Mr. Butler."

Before she could say anything, I ran back outside and told Mr. Butler I had $1.75. He put out his hand and took the $1.75 and said he was going to get Betty and bring her back. My mother came to the door and saw Mr. Butler walking away. She asked me, "What do you mean, you're buying Betty?"

I told her Mr. Butler took my $1.75 and went to get Betty. My mother called out Mr. Butler's name several times. I believe Mr. Butler heard her, but he did not go directly toward his house. He was headed down toward 31st and Van Brunt to the liquor store.

My mother said, "Butler's got your money and gone to the liquor store." She scolded me for giving Mr. Butler my money for his kids' horse. She asked me, "How would you like it if your daddy tried to sell something of yours? You're not going to buy those kids' horse."

I cried because I gave Mr. Butler the money I had saved from selling goat milk and eggs, and here I was, no money and no horse.

My mother tried to reach Mrs. Butler to tell her what Mr. Butler had done. Mrs. Butler apparently had not gotten home from work. It was just about time for my dad to get home. Mr. Butler arrived with my horse Betty. My mother told Mr. Butler that he should be ashamed of himself for trying to sell his kids' horse. She told him she wanted the $1.75 back and that he didn't have any business selling me anything without the consent of either her or my father. Mr. Butler told my mother he had spent the money for something to drink, but he had to go to work the next day and would bring me my $1.75. But I didn't want the $1.75. All I wanted was my horse.

Several days passed. No one said anything more about my money. Then one day when I came home from school, Betty was tied to a pole in our yard! Neither of my parents had gotten home yet. I didn't know what to say or do. I don't remember what time of year it was, but it must have been summer because it was hot. I moved Betty from the sun to the trees on the south side of our house. I also gave her some water and got some hay out of our barn. I felt so good. I had my horse. I kept patting her and went and got one of our big horse's brushes. I then began to do my chores, check the water for the pigeons, the rabbits, the chickens. Then I led the big horse down to the water hole and put water in the hog's pen. I brought the horse back and took the cow down to the water hole and the goats to a better place to graze.

Lessons from Pat's Pig Restaurant

It was fall, I was thirteen years old, and it was time for me to go back to school. Shortly after school started, I was able to get a part-time job at a restaurant called Pat's Pig just six blocks from my house. I worked Friday and Saturday, 6:00 to 9:00 p.m.

Just before the 1946–47 school year started, my mother's nephew, Jeffrey Miller, Aunt Matilda's son, moved to Kansas City from St. Louis. My parents had bought the house next door to where the Finleys lived. Arrangements had been made to rent it to Cousin Jeffrey, who had gone through a divorce but remarried. He had two sons: Raymond, who was fifteen, and Herbert, who was twelve. His wife, Stella, also had two boys, Junior, twelve, and Aaron, ten.

I was an eighth-grader at R. T. Coles Vocational High School. Raymond was a sophomore and was taking a trade in electricity. The other three boys attended Dunbar Elementary School. Raymond was now looking for a job.

I heard that there was an opening for a dishwasher at Pat's Pig. I told Raymond about it and he was hired. We both worked part-time, different days and different hours.

Mr. Johnny Goldston was an elderly Black man who was a World War I veteran. He worked at Pat's Pig full-time and had been there for some years before I began. More about Raymond and Mr. Goldston later.

People always said Pat's Pig was owned by a true Klansman, minus the robe. One evening when Raymond and Mr. Goldston had off, the owner of Pat's Pig was standing right outside the kitchen door and was telling his friend about his recent trip to his home in Rogers, Arkansas. I could see and hear the conversation from the door and the window. They had their backs to me. He told the man that at the entrance to Rogers there was a big boulder with a live bear tied to it. The boulder had a sign in large letters: "Nigger, Don't Let the Sun Catch You in Rogers After Dark." They laughed. And then he said, "You see that big oak tree over there?"

The friend said, "Yeah!"

The owner said, "That's the size tree you hang a nigger on." Again, they laughed. When they stepped back into the kitchen door, I was washing dishes just a few feet away from the door. They both looked at me and at each other—and laughed. I didn't know what to do. I really wanted to ease off my apron, slip out the back door, and go home. And never come back to Pat's Pig. I was scared. But I never said anything to my parents about what I heard. I was afraid they would make me quit the job.

Later that evening when I got home, I shared with Raymond what I had heard the owner say and how his friend had looked at me. Raymond said, "Let's continue to work there until we can find something different. But tell Mr. Goldston what happened."

Mr. Goldston suffered from what they used to call "shell shock," tremors from the war. He shook constantly, and his voice sounded the same way. He was also a dishwasher at Pat's Pig. I liked Mr. Goldston. He taught me a lot, from his experiences being Black in America during World War I, and in Europe, to how Black soldiers were treated when they returned home. Sometimes he said, "Alvin, there were times when we were treated better in countries in Europe than we were treated here at home." Mr. Goldston had no children. His wife died while he was on the battlefields in Europe. He was a victim of the gas the Germans used. He told me how the white officers, and sometimes even their sergeants, treated the "Negro soldiers." And how they survived the discrimination and prejudice overseas from their fellow white soldiers who, along with Black soldiers, were dying defending America.

The elderly woman manager at Pat's Pig liked me. She also lived just a few blocks from the restaurant. She and Mr. Goldston always argued with each other. She tried to fire him, telling him, "Time out, Johnny, go home, you're fired. You can't talk to me like that."

Mr. Goldston would just mumble and kept on working. The manager would take his time card out of the holder, write something on it, and put it under the counter where the cash register was. Mr. Goldston stayed until the end of the night. I got off an hour earlier and left him there. Mr. Goldston didn't take any mess from white folks, not even the owner.

Raymond told me he thought the owner's wife and Mr. Goldston had something going on between them. Mr. Goldston didn't drive because of his physical condition. The owner's wife would take him home and many times pick him up and bring him to work. The manager would fire Mr. Goldston, and the owner's wife would pick him up the next day and scratch out what the manager had written on his time card. Mr. Goldston got full pay regardless of the days he got off and took off.

When Mr. Goldston came back to work, I told him what the owner had said to the other white man when I had overheard them. Mr. Goldston carried a switchblade knife with a red pearl handle. He said he used it for protection. He said whenever he walked in the area where he lived, "I walk with my blade in my hand. I have not spent all that time over there on foreign soil and come home to get killed on the damn streets by some little 'bugs.'" Mr. Goldston said, "I wish I been here and heard what that prejudiced bastard said. I would mess up both of those bastards. I would have pulled off this damn apron, changed my clothes, called me a cab, and gone home—or I might have called the old bastard and went to him with my blade."

Mr. Goldston had talked to my mother numerous times. She asked him to look out for me and Raymond and call her if we got out of line.

Although Mr. Goldston had the physical conditions I mentioned, he was a proud, handsome Black man. He had the most beautiful mustache. He wore good clothes and knew how to coordinate colors. He came to work like he was an executive. He left a change of clothes at work and changed back when he got off.

I wanted a mustache like Mr. Goldston. One evening I asked him how he grew such a good-looking mustache. He told me that he grew up on a farm. He killed chickens almost every day. Mr. Goldston said, "I cut the ass off every chicken I had to kill at home. I rubbed that chicken ass, the greasiest part of the chicken, over my top lip. That's what you have to do if you want a mustache like mine."

Fried chicken at Pat's Pig was one of its favorite dishes. So, we always had a walk-in freezer full of chickens. Mr. Goldston took me into the freezer and pulled one of the chickens off the rack. He pulled out his knife and cut what he called an "ass" off the chicken. He had second thoughts and cut "asses" off three or four more chickens. We walked out of the freezer. Mr. Goldston handed me one of the chicken behinds. He wrapped the others in foil for me. He then showed me how to use the chicken "ass" on my lip.

When I got home, I hid them in our icebox. I used that fatty part, what Mr. Goldston call the chicken's ass, for weeks. No mustache was growing. But my upper lip was getting lighter. One day my mother looked at me and said, "Baby, what's wrong with your top lip? Why is it getting so much lighter than any place else on your face?"

I told her that I was trying to grow a mustache like Mr. Goldston. My mother said, "You are not old enough to have a mustache. John Goldston is a grown man. What's John Goldston got you doing?"

I told her about the back part of the chicken and how Mr. Goldston had showed me how to rub it on my top lip. She said, "John Goldston knows darn well no chicken's behind is going to make you grow no mustache. Even if it did, it'll be a long time before you need a mustache. You wait till I talk to John Goldston, making my baby turn white around his mouth."

She called Mr. Goldston at Pat's Pig. He was working. Someone took the number and said they would give the message to Johnny Goldston. About ten minutes later he called my mother back. She balled him out. He didn't get a word in. Then she kinda laughed. And told him he better not pull any more tricks like that.

Although Goldston had tricked me, I still liked and admired him and maybe learned something from his prank.

Mr. Goldston was a lot of fun, too. When he went to the toilet, he couldn't hardly zip up his pants. Often, he would come out and his pants would be unzipped. I would say, "Mr. Goldston, your pants are unzipped."

He'd say, "Boy, when you get my age, it doesn't make no difference. If it can't get up, it can't get out." We both would laugh.

A few weekends later, a Friday, which was payday, I stayed to help Raymond close. I timed out earlier but just stayed and helped him so we could walk home together. We got paid every Friday. The manager figured our time and wrote the gross pay and the deductions on the back of a small brown envelope. The net income was also shown on the front of the envelope. We were paid in cash. Raymond always opened his envelope and counted his money. I'd always leave my pay in the envelope until I got home.

As we were walking toward our houses, a police car was coming toward us. Just as it passed us, I looked over my shoulder and saw it was turning around. I don't know what came over me, but I took my pay envelope out of my pocket and tucked it in my shoe. The police car with two white officers drove up beside us.

"Hey, where you two colored boys going?"

Almost like a duet, we responded, "Home!"

They got out. They began to search us. I had a Boy Scout knife in one pocket. The officer who searched me took it and laid it on the hood of the police car along with my billfold. The officer searching Raymond placed Raymond's billfold on the hood of the police car with the empty pay envelope. The one officer took my knife and said it was against the law.

Then we were told to put the stuff back in our pockets and go straight home. They drove off.

Raymond began to search all his pockets. He said, "My money's gone. That cop took all of my pay." We got down on our knees and looked all around the area. We searched in the street in front of where the police car had been and searched the grass next to the curb. Raymond start crying.

I said, "Let's go home and get a flashlight."

Raymond said, "It ain't going to do no good. That cop took my money out of my pocket. It was in the same pocket with my pay envelope."

I saw a beer bottle and got it and placed it where we had been standing and where we had been searching. I repeated, "Let's go home and come back with a flashlight and be sure." We ran home.

Our houses were next door to each other. I went in the house and woke my mother up and told her what had happened. Our flashlight had no batteries in it. My mother told me to go and get the lantern. Raymond had awakened his brother, Herbert. They had a flashlight. We went back to where I had placed the beer bottle. We looked everywhere. The streetcar driver saw us on our knees and stopped and asked what we were looking for. We told him that a police officer had taken Raymond's money. He told us to call the police station and ask for the sergeant and report it to him. We thanked him and went back to my house. My mother was still up. We told her what the streetcar driver had told us. She called the police dispatcher and told him what had happened. The dispatcher took our phone number and told her he would send a sergeant out.

The sergeant called my mother. My mother relayed to him what we had told her. The sergeant told my mother he would call the officers in, but he knew none of his officers would steal anything. He asked my mother how much money it was. Raymond handed my mother his pay envelope. My mother told the sergeant the amount.

In about forty-five minutes, the sergeant came to our house and brought the amount my mother had told him. The sergeant said, "We chipped in and gave your nephew the money he lost down there because we didn't want you all to think our officers were thieves." My mother thanked him. He told us boys, "Be good boys. Respect the police."

When he left, Raymond said the money the sergeant gave him was the same money the officer took. The money was in the same denominations. And one of the bills had part of the pay envelope stuck to it. (When he had opened the envelope to count his money, the flap was stuck to one of the bills.) The officer did steal all of Raymond's money.

Raymond said both of those cops knew him and where he worked because they came in regularly and talked to the owner. Sometimes the owner would go out and sit in the police car with them. Sometimes they would come in the back door and the cook would fix them a sandwich and fries. "The young cocky one is the one who searched me. He never would speak when he came in the back door. The other cop at least would nod."

My mother said, "Maybe you all should quit that place. Those police may place something on you to arrest you. And you won't be able to do anything about it. It's your word against theirs, and theirs will count."

Raymond said, "Aunt Stella, I need to work. I'm saving money to buy me a car. I'll just have to be careful."

I told my mother that I wanted to work, too. I never told her about what the owner had said about hanging one of us.

Mother wouldn't let me work but a couple of weeks after the police officer took Raymond's money. Raymond worked there and finally bought himself a car. The next summer, Raymond said the owner wanted me to come back to work. My mother said okay. I went down and talked to him.

He wanted me to sit on a platform he had had made with Arkansas watermelons all around it. He wanted me to eat some melon off and on. I would sit there under the big umbrella, and when someone wanted to buy one, I would have the customer take the watermelon to the side door and pay for it.

I didn't have to ask my mother about this job. I wasn't gonna sit under an umbrella on our own street and eat watermelon.

I told the owner I would have to ask my mother. I was afraid to tell him to his face I would not do it. I hadn't forgotten what he had said just a few months earlier about the big oak tree. I told my mother what he wanted me to do but I didn't want to do that.

She said, "Then you don't have to. You don't let no white man put you out there like a trained monkey. You don't need to work anyway."

Delivery Boy for Lyon's Drugstore

In the spring of 1947, Clarence Grayson, another one of my best friends, was working as a porter and delivery boy at Lyon's Drugstore on the corner of 55th and Troost. The job consisted of general custodial work including sweeping, emptying trash, light mopping, sorting pop bottles, and making deliveries on a bicycle. Clarence had been working there several weeks. Business was so good that Mr. Lyons asked Clarence if he knew a "colored boy" who was as good as he was who could work evenings. Clarence was working afternoons. I was fifteen, and I went to meet Mr. Lyons one evening after school as Clarence (I think about a year older than me) was about ready to get off.

Clarence told me to ask for Mr. Lyons, who was not only the owner but also the pharmacist. He called Clarence from the basement, and the three of us talked about being on time; good work habits; being a self-starter, which meant always being busy; doing things that needed to be done; being polite to customers (who were all working-class whites in that area of the city); and taking care of the bike. I got hired and worked evenings from 5:00 until closing time at 9:00. Seems as though Clarence and I split the week, but I worked evenings.

I can so vividly remember riding that Troost streetcar at night. Most of the time no one was on it except me and the motorman. It was the same thing when I transferred at 31st and Troost to the 31st streetcar. The white kids in the area were not too friendly toward us in "their" neighborhood. But I bragged about boxing at Gateway, which was popular then and which turned out some of the greatest fighters. I wasn't one of them, but the white boys didn't know it. In fact, my boxing days had ended several years earlier.

Clarence and I both did well with tips plus an hourly wage. Between Lyon's Drugstore and setting pins at the Pla-Mor Ballroom bowling alley, I saved enough money to buy my first car. I resigned from Lyon's in good stead and left Clarence there working.

My First Car at Fifteen

In the late fall of 1947, when I was fifteen, I paid $125 in cash for a 1934 Ford Tudor using the money I saved from setting bowling pins at the Pla-Mor bowling alley and working at Lyon's Drugstore. My dad went with me and signed the title application for it. My dad taught me how to drive in the big pasture where the Veterans Hospital was erected in 1950. I must have had a driver's permit because my dad wouldn't let me drive unless he was in there with me. Raymond could drive. Once in a while Daddy would let him drive my car.

When I turned sixteen on May 3, 1948, I was able to drive my car. I got only two traffic tickets before I joined the police department in 1954. I don't recall too many young brothers from Leeds driving legally at my age.

I didn't like the gray paint on my car, so I got a paint kit from a Western Auto store that let you paint the whole car with powder puffs and painted it black. It looked pretty good, too, except the wind was blowing and one of the fenders and doors had small particles of dirt that dried in the paint. It was a fast-drying paint. But you really couldn't tell. People thought I had gone to a professional paint shop.

Regular passengers in my car were Maurice, my cousin Raymond, and later my cousins Herbert and Junior—when they left Dunbar to go to R. T. Coles. I always had a car full of people.

Another Encounter with a Racist Cop

We had two large horses and my little horse, Betty. We could only ride one of the larger horses. The other was not broken, not rideable. Daddy took him on a trade thinking he would have him broken. Beauty, which was the horse used to plow, was the better horse to ride. She was gentle and would let anyone ride her. She would even ride three deep. One day, I was with cousin Raymond and my friends Maurice Green, Richard Fuller, Ernie Gillespie, and Richard Smith, who had his own horse. Our horses were grazing. I was on Beauty, leaning back. We were all just talking teenage boy kinda talk. We were at the end of the pasture at 35th and Elmwood. A police car with two white cops drove up. They drove across the brush, weeds, and grass. The one driving got out and approached us.

"Where'd you niggers steal these horses?" he said.

Richard spoke up and said, "This is my horse."

I said, "This one and the one over there belong to my daddy."

One of the cops said, "You two. Get down off those goddamn horses. Now!" The other cop, who was older, got out of the car and just stood by the open door. The cop who was doing all the talking asked everyone for identification. Everyone had a Social Security card. He asked our ages. The only one who was eighteen was Raymond. He asked Raymond for his draft card.

Raymond said, "I don't have a draft card; I haven't registered yet. I just turned eighteen."

The cop grabbed Raymond by his shirt, right up to his neck, and began twisting it. He was left-handed. He had gloves on and a nightstick in his left hand, drawn back. As he twisted Raymond's shirt, it began to choke Raymond. Tears began to come out of his eyes. He was gasping for breath. The cop told Raymond, "You see this nightstick?"

Raymond murmured yes and nodded his head.

The cop said again, "Nigger, you see this stick?"

Again, Raymond nodded yes.

I was afraid Raymond was going to push him off or hit him. Raymond was short and muscular, strong as an ox, as the old folks used to say. The cop went on to say, "The next time I see you, you'd better have that draft card, or I'll beat your Black nigger ass until you can't stand up. You hear me, nigger?"

Raymond nodded yes.

The cop let him go. Raymond was coughing and gasping for breath and spitting up. The cop told us, "Get out of here, all of you. Take those damn horses and get out of here before I shoot all of you." He got back in the car. The older officer was the first to get in. They drove off. We decided not to say anything to our parents. Shortly thereafter my cousin moved his family to the Rosedale community of Kansas City, Kansas.

There is more to tell about this left-handed officer after I became an officer myself.

I Met a Thirteen-Year-Old Girl Who Became My Wife for Sixty-Three Years

I don't remember why I got rid of the 1934 Ford, but I traded it in for a black 1942 Ford Tudor. I was sixteen and in my junior year of high school. That second car is what got me into trouble. I make it sound like I committed a crime, don't I? Well, it was when my friend Maurice Green introduced me to a cute little eighth-grader named Carol Rich, who I thought at first was his girlfriend. Carol and I met between the main building at R. T. Coles and the annex in what I referred to as "the alley." Carol always got upset with me when I describe our meeting "in the alley."

Another one of my best friends was Paul Holt. He was also in the band and played the baritone horn. His dad was a pharmacist for Parkview Drugstore. We became close when I began to see Carol and he became interested in Carol's younger sister, Naomi. I began to take Maurice by Carol and Naomi's house because their older sister, Ruby Alberta Rich, was the same age as Maurice. We came to find out that Maurice, Ruby Alberta, Carol, and Naomi all had the same father, Albert Rich. Enough said about that.

It wasn't too long before it became a habit that Maurice walked over to my house on school days. Then, I drove to Paul's house, about four blocks from Carol's. I then picked up Carol and Naomi. And away we went, making our first stop at Lincoln, where Naomi and Carol got out. My last stop was R. T. Coles. At the end of the high school day, I reversed my travel. Maurice and Paul piled into my car and to Lincoln we went. Carol started riding in the front seat with me at the request of Maurice. Naomi sat in the middle between Paul and Maurice. Soon we began to attend movies together.

In those days, of course, you didn't go to a girl's home without meeting everyone in the household. So, I met Mrs. Carrie McCoy, Carol and Naomi's grandmother, and Mrs. Ruby Rich, their mother. Mrs. Rich was a beautician and did not stay at their house too often. I found out that my dad and Carol and Naomi's grandfather, Mr. Will McCoy, were close friends. Their grandmother, Mrs. McCoy, also knew my father. My mother knew Mr. McCoy, but to my knowledge, Mrs. McCoy and my mother never met.

Obviously, Paul and I felt we were dating Naomi and Carol, but Mrs. McCoy didn't. And she let it be known. But after a while, Mrs. McCoy respected Paul and me. I believe Mrs. McCoy and possibly Carol's mother sensed we were boyfriend and girlfriend. The five of us (including Maurice) went everywhere together. I was told by Mrs. McCoy that if she was not at home, I should not come inside the house. And she told Carol she should not invite me into their house if she wasn't there. I respected what Carol's grandmother said and can't recall ever disobeying—except once or twice.

On one occasion, Carol and some girl got into a fight at school over another boy. I was furious. We had an argument that must have lasted a week. Carol got the best of the girl. I found out all of this later from Mr. Robert Randolph, my summer school math teacher at Lincoln. I took summer school classes at Lincoln when I was not able to get a job. Mr. Randolph had just come to Kansas City. I think his first classroom experience in Kansas City was the summer of 1949, my senior year. He asked me several times to give him a ride home in my 1942 Ford. Sometimes I even picked up Mr. Randolph at his home on Flora, behind Paseo Baptist Church.

One day when I was giving Mr. Randolph a ride home and Carol was in the car, he asked, "Aren't you the cute little girl who fought with another girl over some boy and got blood over everything, including me? You whipped that girl over that boy, didn't you?"

Carol said, "Yes, sir!"

I saw red. My girl fought some girl over another boy. And to have her answer Mr. Randolph's question with "yes" really angered me. I didn't say anything until we let Mr. Randolph out at his house. Carol gave a good explanation about the fight. It appears the boy had eyes for Carol and thought Carol was interested in him. She said she wasn't, but before she could explain, the fight with the other girl was on. School officials were not as quick to suspend you back then as they are today. Both Carol and the other girl got eighth hours, meaning they had to stay one hour after school. I finally got over it.

Paul's father had given him a car. During the winter of 1949–50, Paul could not get his car started. He called Naomi and said, "Naomi, when Alvin comes to pick up Carol, tell him my car won't start and have him bring you and Carol over to pick me up." It was snowy and cold. After picking up Paul, I was driving west on 26th Street from Benton to Brooklyn. A car was coming head-on toward me. I swerved but still got caught by the oncoming car because there was a car parked in front of me. I should have waited until the oncoming car passed, then proceeded around the parked car. The police were called, and I got my first traffic ticket for "failure to yield." I made everyone late that morning. When I went to court, I got fined.

I don't think I had ever introduced Carol to my mother or father at this time.

Losing My Mother

It must have been around Thanksgiving in 1949 when my mother became very ill and was admitted into General Hospital #2, the "colored hospital," at the insistence of Dr. George H. Taft. Dr. Taft, a graduate of all-Black Meharry Medical College, had not been in Kansas City long. I remember when my mother first began to have health problems, someone recommended Dr. Taft because he made house calls. It was in the wintertime and the snow around the area where we lived was knee-deep. Dr. Taft parked his car on the Brighton hill almost a block from our house, and he walked to our house to see my mother. He was like a country doctor.

The wood-coal cook-and-heating stove was warming the house, and Dr. Taft examined my mother. He told my dad and me that my mother needed to go into the hospital. I don't know if he gave her any medication or a shot or what, but we had no way to get my mother from our house to someone's car or to an ambulance because of the heavy, deep snow. No snowplow came up the Brighton hill or Quincy, which was not paved, or in front of my house. So, my mother had to wait until the weather broke before my dad could take her to the hospital.

Several days later, my dad got Mother checked into General Hospital #2. Christmas was just around the corner. My mother checked herself out of the hospital to go back to work as a domestic for several white families. She checked herself out of the hospital so she could go back to work and buy me a suit and class ring for my graduation coming up the following April. My mother was still out of the hospital at Christmas and working for "the white folks." My mother's money plus mine, which I made setting bowling pins, allowed me to get a suit (my first suit) and my class ring.

Being out of the hospital did not fare well with her. In fact, she got sicker. After Christmas, there was snow still on the ground and my mother was back in the hospital. My dad and I went to see her daily. She was having severe kidney pains. On Sunday afternoon, March 19, I went to visit my mother and my dad was already there. She seemed as though she didn't know me. I kept saying, "It's me, Mama. See my class ring?" She tried to acknowledge that she saw it and knew what I was saying. She kept trying to raise up to see my dad, who was pacing the floor at the foot of her bed. She kept mumbling something seemingly directed at him.

The nurse came in and brought some broth with a straw and told her, "Brooksie, come on, let's drink some of this." She put the straw in Mama's mouth, and she sucked on it. A little broth was sucked up, but she immediately regurgitated it. Mother would not take her eyes off Daddy. As he paced the floor—still at the foot of her bed—she continued to mumble, trying to say something to him. We both had to leave; visiting hours were over. In those days, they would come over the loudspeaker and tell you what time it was and that visiting hours were over. I hated to leave my mother, but my dad said, "Let's go." I kissed my mother's forehead and told her I loved her and I would be back later, the next visiting hour.

That evening on my next visit, for the first time, I took Carol with me to meet my mother. She wanted to go. Mother seemed to be a little better. My dad was not there yet. I walked up to the bed and told my mother, "This is my girlfriend, Carol Rich."

My mother mumbled something, and Carol spoke.

She told her, "I hope you get well, Mrs. Brooks." Mother was going in and out, nodding. I told her that Carol and I were going to the movies and that I would see her the next day after school. We left and went to the Carver Theatre at 26th and Prospect. After the movie, I took Carol home, just around the corner, and went home myself.

I slept on the sofa that opened into a bed. Soon the phone rang. I answered it. A woman's voice at the other end asked, "Is this the Brooks residence?"

I said yes.

She called herself "nurse somebody" and said, "I want to inform you that Mrs. Brooks expired this morning at 12:30."

I told her thank you. My dad, who slept in the only bedroom, asked me who it was on the phone. I told him it was the nurse at the hospital and that she said Mother had passed a short time ago. I began to cry. We both just lay there in our bed not saying anything for a while. I got up and sat on the side of my bed thinking, *How I am going to make it without my mother?* I wished I had died first. What was I going to do without my mother?

My daddy got up and turned on the light. "Well, boy, she's gone," he said in a very weak voice just short of crying. I began to cry silently. I kept asking myself, *What am I going to do without my mother?* We sat up until daybreak.

I was really freaking out. I didn't go to school that Monday morning. I called Carol, Paul, and Maurice. I called Watkins Brothers Funeral Home on Lydia near 18th Street. They needed to speak with my father. They said they would pick up my mother midmorning.

My mother passed away at General Hospital #2. She was seen by Dr. E. Frank Ellis from March 4, 1950, to her death on March 20, 1950. She was born March 1, 1899, in Kirkwood, Missouri. She was fifty-one years old at the time of her death. According to the death certificate, the disease or condition directly leading to death was uremia, with antecedent causes chronic nephritis with other significant conditions, carcinoma gastric malignancy (X-ray).

My mother's funeral was held on Wednesday, March 22, 1950, at Watkins Brothers Funeral Home. The Reverend F. D. Robinson, pastor of the Pilgrim's Rest Baptist

Church, officiated. Her cousin Clova Mae from Little Rock, Arkansas, attended the funeral but did not go to the cemetery. While here, she stayed with her sister-in-law, Mrs. Martha Newton, in Kansas City, Kansas.

My mother was buried at Lincoln Cemetery, the "colored cemetery," Grave 8, Row 10, Block 5 (2635).

A Romance: I Think Mrs. Carrie McCoy Has Begun to Accept That Carol and I Were Going Together

Mrs. McCoy, Carol's grandmother, took a liking to me early on. She would occasionally ask me about my dad and talk to me about being a Christian and living a Christian life. Mrs. McCoy, to my knowledge, never met my mother. But she had met and knew my dad well because my dad and Mr. McCoy were close friends. I remember on one occasion Mrs. McCoy told me she liked me because I was "so well mannered" and "seemed to be a nice young man." Mrs. McCoy, Naomi, and Carol all belonged to a Church of God in Christ at 23rd and Olive.

I started seeing Carol shortly before her thirteenth birthday. When I went to her home, it was always with Maurice and under the guise of being with him to visit with his sisters because I had the car, the transportation.

As did Carol's mother (Mrs. Ruby Rich), Carol's grandmother finally accepted that I was "going" with Carol. Later on Mrs. McCoy begin to attend Barker Temple Church of God in Christ. Sometimes Carol and I would show up and not tell her beforehand. She was proud to see us. We always got introduced as visitors and had to stand and remain standing until we had been given an "accorded welcome." Carol and I didn't really like to get there when the service first started. It was nothing for their service to start about eleven o'clock and go nonstop to one thirty, two, or longer. Some Sundays, although Mrs. McCoy and her congregation talked, taught, and preached against it, we sometimes left church and went down the street to the Lincoln Theater. Mrs. McCoy knew the occasions when there was a program where food was being served at the end, and she would tell Carol to tell me. On those occasions, we made sure we slipped in late so we wouldn't have to stay through the long service.

Speaking of Sunday eating, Mrs. McCoy's routine was after church on Sundays, she would come home, change her "church clothes," put on her apron, and begin her Sunday dinner. Sometimes, she would cook it all before she went to church. Most of the time, fried chicken was on the menu—and candied yams, some kind of greens, and corn bread. I enjoyed sitting with family members eating Mrs. McCoy's Sunday dinners—before and after Carol's pregnancy.

A Romance: Carol Got Pregnant, or I Got Carol Pregnant, 1950

Carol was not "fast." In fact, Carol and I were both virgins when we started going together. It's true that that status didn't last too long. After a while, it became clear that soon others would have to know that we were no longer virgins.

Shortly after my graduation, Carol called me and said she needed to talk to me and that it was important. It was a weekend, and when I picked her up at home, we went to the Carver Theatre at 26th and Prospect. We sat in the back of the theater, like we always had, where we could hug and kiss. Carol asked me to feel her stomach and her breast. She asked me, "Don't it feel like my stomach and breasts are swelling?" I felt her breast and her stomach again. I told her, "I can't tell about your stomach, but your breast is." Before I could say anything else, she said, "I've missed my period for the second month. I think I'm pregnant."

I said, "Let's go so we can talk." We drove around and ended up at Spring Valley Park—just two or three blocks from Carol's house. We often went there. We first sat in the car. Then we got out and walked around the lake. I was scared. Really scared. Carol asked if I would be mad at her if she were pregnant. I told her no.

She said, "Well, what are we going to do?"

I said, "I don't know, but I hope you're not because you have two more years in school. You need to graduate. And I want to go to college this fall. But if you are, we'll have to figure out what we're going to do."

Carol said, "Maybe we should tell my grandma rather than my mother."

Carol's grandmother was a true Christian. Carol had a feeling that her grandmother would understand and not fuss or criticize us but would advise us what to do.

I said, "But suppose'n you're not pregnant and we tell her. She might not want us to see each other anymore. Maybe we should wait another month."

Carol said, "I forgot to tell you that I'm going through morning sickness. I spit and spit."

"Maybe we should tell your grandmother, if you're getting sick already," I told her.

It was getting late, and we always respected and adhered to Mrs. McCoy's rule that Carol be in by eleven o'clock. So, I took her home, walked her to the door, kissed and hugged her, and told her that I loved her and left. I didn't go straight home. I drove by Paul's house near 27th and Benton Boulevard but didn't stop. I drove home, but since my dad wasn't home, I decided to drive over to Maurice's house, thinking since it was warm, some of the family would be outside. I was right.

As soon as I drove up, Maurice and a couple of his brothers came out to my car. Maurice and I had been together earlier, but, of course, I didn't know at that time that Carol might be pregnant. I asked Maurice if he could go riding. He said yes and told one of his brothers to tell his mother that he was going with me but would be right back. I just started driving with no particular place in mind. I began telling Maurice what Carol had told me. Somewhere, somehow, I don't remember when or why, Maurice began calling me "Huss." He gave me his own "personal" nickname. He said, "Huss, what are you going to do? Weren't you using rubbers?" He laughed.

It wasn't funny to me and I told him, "Man, this ain't nothing funny."

He said, "I'm sorry, Huss. I was just trying to make you feel better."

I don't know if I ever answered Maurice's question about the rubber.

He asked me again what I was going to do. "Are you going to tell your dad?"

I told him I would eventually, but I had to know if Carol was pregnant first. I told him not to tell anyone, that if it were true, everyone would know sooner or later anyway. He promised not to say a word to anyone. I told him Carol and I had decided to wait and tell her grandmother and later I would tell my father. It was a little after midnight and I had to be at work the next day. Maurice did, too.

A Romance: Conversation with Mrs. McCoy

Carol and I planned to approach her grandmother when she was home alone. For the life of me, I cannot remember ever seeing Carol's younger sister, Naomi, during this time. Naomi wasn't there the day we chose, only Mrs. McCoy and her young grandson, a toddler, Badger McDonald. Badger's mother was Alverna, who was married to his daddy, Eugene McDonald, who joined the US Air Force. Alverna was the youngest daughter of Mr. and Mrs. McCoy. Alverna left Kansas City and lived in Denver, Colorado, but her son, Badger, stayed with Mrs. McCoy. He was asleep the day we got up enough nerve to tell Mrs. McCoy that Carol was pregnant.

Carol said I had to start the discussion with her grandmother. Carol met me at the door and whispered, "Grandma is here. Let's tell her before anyone comes." I entered the house just behind Carol. How was I going to tell her that I had gotten her granddaughter pregnant? Mrs. McCoy was sitting in her favorite chair. Badger was asleep across her lap. I spoke to Mrs. McCoy.

"Mrs. McCoy, can Carol and I talk to you about something very important to us and get your advice?" Carol and I were sitting on the sofa, but not too close together. When Mrs. McCoy wasn't looking, Carol slid her hand over to mine, signaling me to talk to her grandmother about what we had rehearsed.

Mrs. McCoy said, "Yes, what is it?"

I replied in a weak voice, "Mrs. McCoy, Carol thinks she is pregnant. We don't know what to do if she is. Carol wanted us to talk to you first and ask you what you thought we should do."

Mrs. McCoy's first response was to Carol. "Why haven't you said anything to me before now?" Carol started crying. "You see me every day—why didn't you say something?" Tears were rolling down Carol's cheeks. She was squeezing my hand.

I broke in and said, "She didn't say anything, Mrs. McCoy, because we weren't sure, and she was scared. We both were. She didn't know what you or Mrs. Rich would say, but we thought we should come to you first."

Mrs. McCoy said, "I asked Carol the question. I didn't ask you."

I said, "I'm sorry, Mrs. McCoy."

Based on the tone of her voice, I thought to myself, *Oh, I've messed up.*

Mrs. McCoy asked Carol, "How far gone are you?" Carol was shaking and squeezing my hand and crying steady now, not loud, so she couldn't answer her grandmother. So, I had to take another chance at telling Mrs. McCoy. I told Mrs. McCoy that she thought she had missed at least two of her periods in April and May or May and June.

Before Carol or I could say anything else, Mrs. McCoy said, "I knew Carol was pregnant all this time. I could tell it in her eyes. And she was filling out. Her breasts and her stomach. And the mornings before you picked her up for school, I saw that she was spitting a lot, and her appetite was not as good as it had been. And when she went to the bathroom, she began to lock the door, even though we were the only ones here most of the time." She looked at Carol. "I also checked the box of Kotex and you haven't used any for some time. So, I knew something was wrong, that you were pregnant. And I knew if you were pregnant, Alvin had gotten you pregnant."

I didn't know whether to cry or holler, "Hallelujah! Praise the Lord!" Mrs. McCoy didn't seem to be angry. She didn't criticize us. I felt much better now. Carol still hadn't said anything since we sat down but continued to cry.

Mrs. McCoy asked Carol, "What are you crying about? It's too late now. You should have done that before you did what you did to get pregnant." That's all she said that was somewhat critical of us. "Well, you better tell your mother."

Carol said, "Grandma, can't you tell her?"

Mrs. McCoy said, "No! I ain't pregnant. You'all tell her. Your mama will be over here today or tomorrow sometime. You will be here with Badger. I have to go to work."

Carol said, "I just want the two of us to talk to her. Can't you talk to her, Grandma?"

Mrs. McCoy said, "Yes, I can, but I ain't. I told you, that's you'all's doings. If the two of you are grown enough to make a baby, then be grown enough to tell your mama. Both of you. Just like you did with me."

Carol asked, "What is Mama going to say, Grandma?"

Mrs. McCoy said, "Ruby ain't going to say nut'n criticizing you. She had Alberta when she was seventeen and married Albert Rich, you'all's daddy, when he was twenty-two.

You won't be the first young girl in high school that got pregnant, although I wish you hadn't. The thing is what the two of you are going to do about it. That's what the two of you ought to be concerned about."

She asked me, "Have you said anything to your daddy, Mr. Brooks?"

I said, "No, ma'am."

"Well, you should," she said. I thanked her. Carol and I went and sat on the porch. I told both Mrs. McCoy and Carol I was going to tell my father that evening.

I went home. Later that evening my dad came home, but the time was not right. He had been drinking. I felt uncomfortable telling my dad when he was drinking. I just didn't know exactly how I was going to approach him. I wanted to make sure he was sober. Carol called me and asked if I had told my dad. I told her not yet and why.

She said, "Please hurry up. I'm scared what he might say." The next day, Carol said her grandmother asked if I had talked to my father. She told her she wasn't sure.

I hadn't been to Carol's for a couple of days. She was getting scared that I had changed my mind, but I never would. I cared too much about her. And although I wish I hadn't gotten her pregnant, I did, and I knew I had to go through with talking to my dad. I wanted to make sure Carol understood that, that I loved her and would not desert her regardless of what my father said or what her mother said. A couple of days later, the opportunity presented itself. I asked my dad if he remembered Carol. He said, "Oh, yeah, Will McCoy's granddaughter. What, you got her pregnant?" That really caught me off guard, but it certainly made it easy!

I said, "Yes, sir. I think I've gotten her pregnant."

He looked at me and came right back, "Is it yours?"

I said, "Yes, sir."

He said, "How do you know?"

I said, "I just know, Daddy."

He said, "What do you mean you just know?"

I said, "Because I just know it."

He came right back with, "What do you mean you just know it?"

I responded, "I know it because I'm the only one that's been mess'n 'round with her."

He asked, "Are you sure?"

"Yes, sir, I'm sure."

"Well, what about school? You can't take care of a family working at Scott's. You're going to have to get a real job." (I started working at Scott's grocery store as soon as I graduated.) I told him I was going to get another job and would still get into college. He asked if Carol's mother knew. I said, "I don't think so, but Mrs. McCoy, her grandmother does. We told her the other day."

"Boy, I hate for you to be a father and not finish school," my dad said. "You know that's all me and your mother talked about. White folks can and will take anything you got in your hands, but if you've got it in your head, they can't take that." Then he asked, "When you met with Will's wife, what did she say? Did she say anything about you and Carol getting married?" I said no, although Carol and I hadn't discussed it. It was Carol's suggestion that we discuss it first with her grandmother. I wanted to put it all out there since I had my dad's attention and he wasn't condemning us except to say he wanted me to go to college.

I told him that I wanted to get married and Carol did also. He said, "If you're sure that's what you want to do, you'all can stay out here. I'll find someplace to stay. But I don't know what you'all gonna do when winter comes. This ain't no place for someone who's pregnant." I was really surprised and relieved. And happy. I thought he would condemn us, especially me, because he and my mother talked about my education as long as I could remember. I thanked him. He said, "Will's people are good people," referring to Carol's grandpa. He and my dad were close. They all had lived in the Leeds community where Carol was born.

I don't recall when Carol's mother found out. I do remember she accepted me every time I saw her. I can remember her saying one time, "So you and Carol are going to have a baby? Now ain't that something? Which means I'm going to be a grandmama." Her boyfriend, Ollie Robinson, was with her at the time. Ollie had a funny kind of laugh. He seemed to laugh from the bottom of his stomach and kind of grunted and shook. He seemed as though it strained him to laugh. Carol's mother formally introduced Ollie and me.

Well, the word was out. "Alvin got Carol pregnant." I had to do what my dad said: get a better job than working for Scott's.

A Romance: Carol Was Beginning to Look More Like a Mother-to-Be

Carol was beginning to show. I bought her three sets of maternity clothes. She looked so cute. I often told her that she had the "cutest little butt, especially in the skirt of that little blue two-piece suit." Before she got pregnant, she wore it almost every Sunday. When I told her that, she would smile and ask me, "Do you still love me, and is my butt still cute?"

I told her, "Yes, I love you, and that cute little butt, too."

I would turn around and ask her the same that she had asked me: "Do you still love me?"

She also replied, "Yes, and I want to be your wife, and we can have more children."

When we got older, Carol mentioned that when she was a child, people would ask the children what they wanted to be when they grew up. They gave all kinds of answers. Carol's was always consistent: "I want to get married and have lots of children."

I used to tease her about what she said. "Is that why you got pregnant? Was it intentional, so you could start living out what you had been telling adults all the time, that you want to get married and have lots of children?" Of course, she denied that. And I didn't believe it, anyway.

It became a habit when we were driving alone that I would reach over and rub her stomach. She would put her hand on top of mine and rub her stomach with both our hands. Then there came a time when Carol could feel the baby kicking and she would ask me to feel it. Sometimes I could feel the kicking. Then it became much more obvious. You could see her stomach moving when there was kicking.

Hunting for a Real Job, from Age Thirteen to Eighteen at Katz Drug Store

Now that I was to be a father and was going to get married, I had to take the conversation I had with my dad seriously. I had to get a "real job." I began to make applications all over the place—at drugstores and grocery stores as "store porters," at Crown, Parkview, and Katz. I went to the Fegan Employment Agency at 18th and Brooklyn, owned by Mrs. Ardella Fegan. Mrs. Fegan's was one of a few Black employment agencies providing candidates for both short-term employment as domestics and special events and full-time employment with companies in the area. I told Mrs. Fegan I was getting married. She asked me to whom. I told her, "To Carol Rich." Mrs. Fegan knew Mrs. McCoy and Carol's mother. Mrs. Fegan asked if we were getting married because Carol was pregnant. I told her yes.

Mrs. Fegan had several jobs she could place me on, but they were just one day here, two days there, and on and on. Nothing permanent. None were "real jobs."

I got a call about the third or fourth day from Katz's personnel office at 12th and Walnut, which was also Katz's corporate office. The woman who called me said she had noticed that I had worked at their store in Waldo during the summer five years previously and I was seen as a good worker by the manager. She said there was some discrepancy regarding my age. She said, "On the application you made in July of 1945, you said you were sixteen, born May 3, 1929, which would mean you just turned twenty-one. But the application you made just last week, you wrote that you were born May 3, 1932, which means you just turned eighteen." She went on to say, "Your Social Security numbers are the same, though."

I thought fast and replied, "Ma'am, I want to be honest with you. I needed to work really bad as I do now, so I put my age up. I was only thirteen. Now I'm eighteen years old. I graduated from high school in April, and I want to go to college this fall and major in business, and I need a job really bad."

That was true: I had planned to attend college and take up business. But getting a job was important now because I was going to get married in two months and was going to have a wife and a baby.

There was a pause on her end. She came back on the phone and said, "Can you report to our Katz store at 63rd and Brookside tomorrow afternoon at two?"

I quickly said, "Yes, ma'am, I'll be there." She told me the name of the store manager who would be expecting me.

She said, "You don't be late."

I told her I wouldn't and said thank you. It was my first full-time job. My first "real job."

Now I had to tell Mr. Scott I had another job. I think I just happened to be at home on my lunch period when I got the call from Katz. I drove back, to around the corner from the store. I told Mr. Scott that I had just been offered a job at the Katz Drug Store as a porter. I didn't know what he was going to say.

"Alvin, you're going places, boy," he said. "I've watched you around here. You're not like these others. I'm proud of you and I know Brooks is, too. Good luck, boy."

I told him if he wanted me to come in the morning, I would because I didn't have to be at Katz on 63rd and Brookside until two. Mr. Scott said, "No. Thank you, though. Take your time and get ready for your new job. Now you know those white folks don't want us out there anyway, so always keep that in mind. And don't give up on school." I thanked him. Since Mr. Scott paid me every day, at the end of my workday, about four o'clock, he paid me. He said, laughing, "This is in full!" I thanked him for the advice and for giving me a job. I told him that I would stop by to see him and Mrs. Scott. I forced myself to add that because Mrs. Scott was not friendly to anyone.

Well, I knew when I took the job at Katz that I had to do better. An education was my goal and my only chance. I remembered what my parents had tried to drill into my very being: "White folks can and will take from you if it's in your hands, but if it's in your head, they can't take that . . . They really don't know all that you know. And don't ever let them know just how much you know." I went over to Carol's and told her I had a job as a store porter at Katz's and was to report to work the next day. She was happy. I also told my father. He said, "I'm sure glad for you. Getting married and having a child, you need to be able to take care of them. But don't forget your education. You promised."

I again promised him I would get into school. I told him that I didn't want to be a store porter all my life. That I also wanted Carol to get back in school and get her high school diploma and go to college.

He said, "Just make sure you get yours."

"I will, Dad; I promise."

My First Day at Work at Katz Drug Store

I arrived at work the next day at 1:30. I went to the corner of the soda fountain where I saw two Black women. One was cooking; the other, the younger one, was clearing dishes off the fountain counter. I asked the younger woman, "Hi, could you tell me where I could find the store manager?"

She said, "Go back to the pharmacy and they will page him." I thanked her. She told me his name was Mr. Doug Griffin.

She asked me, "Are you looking for a job?"

I told her, "Yes, but I think I'm hired. I hope so anyway." She laughed.

As I walked away, I looked back over my shoulder. She had said something to the older woman, and they were both looking my direction and laughing. I wondered what was funny but didn't go back to ask. I approached the white man in the white jacket at the pharmacy counter. He had his name and his title, "pharmacist," in red letters over his jacket pocket. I introduced myself and asked if he would page the manager for me. The manager walked up behind me before the pharmacist was able to page him. I extended my hand to shake his and at the same time said, "Hi, sir, my name is Alvin Brooks, and I was told by a lady in the personnel department to report here to you today at two to start work."

He hesitated before he reached for my hand, but I continued to hold mine out to him. Taking my hand, he finally said, "I'm Doug, the store manager." He let my hand go. I could tell Doug probably had never shaken a Black man's hand.

I said, "Pleased to meet you, sir." He said that one of the women at the fountain, Marie, had told him I was looking for him.

He said, "I got a call from the personnel office this morning. They told me who you were and that you had worked at our 75th and Wornall store before."

I said, "Yes, sir, I did."

He asked, "Why did you leave?" I told him to return to school. He turned and introduced me to the pharmacist. I reached out to shake his hand. He gave me a very weak handshake and mumbled his name, "Dr." something.

The manager told me to follow him to his office. He handed me an application and told me to sit in the chair out by the pharmacist station, fill it out, and bring it back to him when I completed it. When I completed the application, I returned to his office and handed it to him. He looked over it and said, "You just graduated from high school this spring?"

I said, "Yes, sir." He asked me what school. It was on my application, but I told him R. T. Coles Vocational High School, but I also attended Lincoln. He asked me what vocation I chose. I told him band and orchestra. He asked me what instrument I played. I told him tenor saxophone and trombone.

He was kind of smiling and asked if I wanted to be a professional musician like "Satchmo." I told him yes, but that I planned to go to college in the fall and take up business.

He said, "Why not follow your music in college?"

I hesitated for a couple of seconds. I didn't dare tell him I was going to get married in a few weeks.

Then I said, "I've had some bad experiences with professional musicians. Too many were drug users. I don't want to be around people who use drugs."

He responded, "That's damn good thinking, Alvin. If you keep that attitude, you can make it."

I said, "Thank you," and he told me I would be working the 2:00 to 10:00 p.m. shift and off Sundays with the day porter, Mr. Sanders. He asked me to follow him to meet Mr. Sanders, who would show me around and tell me what my responsibilities were. I was also to meet the assistant manager when he came in later in the evening.

Mr. Sanders, a gray-haired, middle-aged Black man with glasses, was in the little shed outside, sorting pop bottles into their respective cases. He wore a pair of white coveralls with "Katz" on the back. This shed was where all the different sodas and the empty bottles were stored.

The manager introduced us. "Raymond, this is Alvin Brooks. I'm hiring him starting today. He'll be working the evening shift. I brought him to you so you could show him around and teach him the ropes." He and Mr. Sanders laughed.

I said, "Hello, Mr. Sanders, my name is—"

He interrupted and said, "I'm Raymond Sanders."

I came back extending my hand again and said, "I'm happy to meet you, Mr. Sanders. My name is Alvin Brooks." Mr. Sanders gave me a firm handshake and looked me dead in the eyes, and I did the same to him.

The manager said, "I'll leave you two now."

My Orientation at Katz Drug Store

Mr. Sanders was a very soft-spoken man. My orientation began right there in the pop shed. Mr. Sanders asked, "Have you timed in?"

I said, "No, sir."

"Did Doug make you a time card?"

I said, "No, sir."

He said, "Come on. Let's get you on the clock so you can get paid on payday." That sounded good to me. We went to Doug's office. He knew why we were there. He was filing out my time card with my name and my Social Security number. He handed it to me. I thanked him. I went back downstairs where the time clock was and timed in.

Mr. Sanders reached in a closet where several pairs of Katz coveralls were. "You'll probably wear a size 38. Here, step in there," he said, pointing to the mop room, "and try these on." I stepped out of my clothes and slipped on the pair of coveralls. They fit pretty good. Mr. Sanders told me, "Take your money and billfold out of your pocket and anything of value. A lot of people come in and out of here. Let's go back upstairs and out to the shed."

He told me about sorting the various soda pop bottles in their respective cases. The full soda cases were stacked along one wall and the empties were along the opposite wall. Mr. Sanders told me it was my responsibility to keep the space for the pop in the store always filled. He also told me what to do if the respective pop distributors happened to come on my shift. The distributors knew where the key was kept. But it was my role to count with them how many empties they took and how many full ones they left. I was to initial the invoice and give it to the assistant manager or place it on his desk in the office. If the office was locked, I was to slip the invoice under the door.

Then we went downstairs. He showed me our eating quarters, telling me, "Son, you know we can't eat at the fountain upstairs where the white folks eat. You can buy anything off the menu, but you can't eat it up there. And they don't want you sitting at the end of the fountain waiting for your food. After you tell one of the cooks upstairs what you want, one of them, Rose Marie Johnson or her daughter Hazel, will take your order, and when it's ready, they will look for you on the floor and tell you your food is ready or they'll holler down the steps at you. One of them will give you the check and the food, and you're to go over to the nearest cash register and pay for it."

He paused a minute and said, "I see you're frowning a little. Son, many of these Jews aren't any more ready for us to be equal than other white folks. You understand, don't you?"

I said, "No, sir, not really."

He went on to say, "Jews have been treated differently in this country like we have, but they're white and have become more accepted because they're white. But they are good people to work for. They'll treat you good as long as you do your work. They are fair that way. But they discriminate like other white folks. You can see this right here at this store. Keep living, you'll see what I mean. But get your education, as my wife and I tell our children, so you can be ready when the change comes. And God will see to it. Change will come. But I pray every day for your generation, which is my kids' generation, that you will be able to enjoy those changes. I can't do anything about it but pray."

He showed me both upstairs and downstairs, what I was to do every night, and what I might be asked to do by other employees who he said were all white. But most of them were nice, except the pharmacist and a white woman who worked days in cosmetics. "I'm convinced," Mr. Sanders said, "they don't like us. But son, I treat them to death with kindness. If you get caught working with either of them, you'll know what I'm talking about. You do the same thing. Because you're young, they might say or do something to test you. Treat 'em with kindness. Let them make a fool of themselves. Follow what I've told you and shown you, and you'll keep your job until you're ready to leave."

The Katz family members all seemed to reside in the area of the 63rd Street store. I had an opportunity to meet several when taking various things to their cars. Sometimes I made deliveries to the homes of those who lived within walking distance. One of the Katzes' grown sons had a physical disability and had a chauffeur who was Black, Phillip Ramsey, who was in his early thirties. Phillip lived around 13th and Euclid and graduated from Lincoln High School.

I never really knew anyone who was gay, except a classmate of mine who grew up in the Leeds community. We went to the same grade school and high school. He left Kansas City shortly after graduating from high school. If there were others, I didn't know that they were gay.

Phillip was very muscular and tall. When he came into the store, I often heard some of the younger white women employees' comment about how tall, dark, and handsome he was. Then they would laugh. They, of course, didn't know that I overheard them.

I told Phillip one time what I had heard. He just laughed and said, "Shit, I'm looking for the same damn thing they're looking for, except it's Black." I then began to suspect he was gay. But it was soon fully revealed. He invited me to go out with him and some of his "girlfriends who were all men." I declined but told him I respected him for what he was but that was not for me.

When I joined the police department, I would often see Phillip around the clubs at 12th and Vine and 18th Street, especially when I worked the "dogwatch" shift, midnight to 8:00 a.m. Occasionally, I would be parked in front of one of the clubs or restaurants and he, with one or more of his friends, would see me. He called it "flirting with me." It was all in fun. Phillip had told them where I stood, but I respected them.

The job at Katz wasn't too bad, considering. Considering I needed a full-time job and it paid a lot more than Mr. Scott. Plus, they carried some meats, canned goods, bread, and some produce, all on sale with a coupon in both the *Kansas City Star* and *Kansas City Times* newspapers. I was able to buy at the sale prices without the coupon—and get items early before they sold out. And the members of the Katz family who I met knew me by name and were friendly.

A Romance: The Wedding Rings—The Engagement One, 1950

We were now in early July, and somehow, we came up with August 23 as our wedding date. In the meantime, I wanted to get Carol a set of rings. She wanted an engagement ring.

I still had my saxophone. I called Carol's mother and told her I wanted to sell my saxophone to buy Carol some rings. She laughed. I asked her if she would go with me to pawn it. She agreed to go with me. I picked her up where her boyfriend, Ollie Robinson, lived. We went to George's Loan on 18th Street just east of Vine Street. I pawned my sax for fifty dollars. I don't believe I ever thought about getting it out of hock.

We left the pawn shop and went directly to find Carol's rings. We ended up at a Katz Drug Store at 12th and McGee. This drugstore sold some of everything. I remember they had rings, watches, and bracelets—all on a wire hanging around the wall. I told the clerk that I wanted to see some wedding rings. He pulled down one of the strings, and Mrs. Rich and I looked at set after set of rings. Finally, I saw one that looked like it was gold, or at least gold-colored. I thought Carol would like it.

Mrs. Rich said, "That's pretty. That is a nice one." While she looked at them, I told the man assisting us that I was getting married and was getting the rings for my wife-to-be. We both laughed.

The clerk looked at the tag on the rings and said, "This one is $11." I bought the set of rings and Carol's mother and I went to the house. Carol was there, babysitting Badger. Mrs. McCoy was at work. She, like my mother, was a domestic, working in white folks' homes "out south."

I took the ring box out of the small brown paper sack. I opened the beautiful little velvet-covered ring box. When we were at the drugstore, Mrs. Rich had explained the difference between the two rings. The larger one with the stone setting was the engagement ring—the one the man gave to the woman before they got married. That meant they were engaged. I was grinning from ear to ear. I felt so good and happy.

When we went in the house, Carol was sitting on the sofa. She looked shocked that her mother and I were together.

She said Badger was asleep. "Where you all been?"

Her mother said, "Aren't you gonna speak first?"

"Hi, Mama, where you-all been?"

Her mother didn't immediately respond but finally said, "Hi, baby, how are you feeling? You're filling out, girl." We all laughed.

Carol again asked, "So, where you-all been?"

Her mother said, kinda laughing, "Alvin picked me up to come and see my daughter. Is that all right?" Carol sensed something was just not right, but she didn't ask the question again.

I asked Carol how she was doing.

She said, "All right, just spitting a lot." She had a roll of toilet tissue beside her on the sofa and a pile of used ones on the floor beside the sofa.

Mrs. Rich said, "Well, you-all, I need to go. Alvin, come on, take me back where you picked me up, unless you're gonna do what you said you were gonna do."

Carol asked, "Do what?"

I said, "Yes, ma'am, I'm coming, but I need to do what I told you first."

I had taken the ring box out of the brown paper bag before I got out of my car. I was sitting next to Carol on the sofa. Her mother stood up and was walking toward the door. I just kinda slid to the floor on one knee and looked up at Carol. She looked at me as if to say, "What are you doing?"

Before she could say what she was thinking, I had already pulled the rings out of my pocket and held them by my side. I opened the ring box and took out the one that I'd been told was the "engagement" one. As I separated them, I looked up at Carol. She put her hand over her mouth and looked wide-eyed, and I said, "Carol, will you marry me?" She started crying. Her mother walked over and sat next to her, laughing.

She said, "Honey, you better say yes before Alvin changes his mind." She continued to laugh. Carol was really boo-hooing now. Her mother laughing didn't help either.

I sat up beside her. She leaned over on my shoulder, crying away, real tears.

Her mother said unsympathetically, "Come on, Carol, say yes so Alvin can take me back." Her mother began laughing again. "You're getting ready to get married and have a baby. It's gonna be all right. This is the right way. Alvin is assuming his responsibility." Carol continued to cry hysterically. She must have cried for a good two to three minutes. I really didn't know what to say, especially since her mother was sitting there. I reached down and grabbed the roll of toilet paper. I unrolled a wad and put it in one of her hands to wipe her eyes and blow her nose. She finally calmed down, blowing her nose. (You know how people who cry have a little whimper as they calm down.)

She finally stopped crying and whimpering and began to laugh with us.

"Whew," I said, "I thought for a minute you were crying because your answer was no."

Her mother said, "It better not be." I got down on both knees this time and again asked, "Carol, will you marry me?" She said yes and started crying and laughing at the same time. I put the engagement ring on her finger. Lo and behold, it fit. I was glad it did, because all I knew to do was to wrap some tape around the ring until it fit snug. We all laughed.

Her mother said, "You'd better kiss her!" I did. But not like I normally did. We hugged. Her mother hugged her. Her mother stood up and said, "Well, kids, I've done what I left home to do. Come on, Alvin, take me home. You can come back. Is there anything you want Alvin to bring back?"

Carol said, "Yes, a dill pickle and some jaw breakers from Ben's."

Her mother said, "A dill pickle and jaw breakers?" We all laughed.

I said, "I knew what she was going to say to bring her back because I've been bringing dill pickles back for several days now."

I drove her mother where she wanted to go. I told her, "Thank you for going with me."

She said, "Thank you, baby, for asking me to go. Don't forget what Carol told you to get for her and you-all's baby." We laughed. I stopped by Ben's Market. Got the dill pickle and jaw breakers and delivered them to Carol. After a while, I told Carol that I was going home to tell my father what I had done.

A Romance: It's Wedding Time—Time to Say "I Do," August 23, 1950, at 8:00 p.m.

I still cannot recall what was so significant about Wednesday, August 23, at 8:00 p.m., the date and time of our wedding. I had been transferred to work Mr. Sanders's day shift, 7:00 a.m. to 3:00 p.m., while Mr. Sanders was on vacation. I hadn't told anyone at Katz that I was getting married. I was forbidden from seeing Carol at all that day. The older folks said it was bad luck if you saw the bride during the day of the wedding. I don't even remember talking to her.

I went home and dressed. My dad was not at home. I had to find him. I really wanted him at the wedding. I thought he might be down at Richardson's tavern on Raytown Road. I found him sitting at the corner of the bar, a bottle of Budweiser in front of him, and talking to Mrs. Richardson. But he was dressed for the wedding. When I got closer and spoke to him and Mrs. Richardson, I saw a half pint of his favorite drink, gin, in his back pocket. I didn't know how much he had drunk out of it, but I knew my dad and his drinking habits, and his conversation told me how much he had been drinking. I was asking myself if he should come to the wedding if he was "spaced out" on his gin. He hadn't drunk too much from the gin bottle, but a lot could happen between now and eight.

My dad had told Mrs. Richardson about the wedding. She said, "Congratulations, Alvin! So, you're getting married tonight?"

I said, "Yes, ma'am."

Mrs. Richardson reached into the soda pop cooler and handed me a bottle of strawberry pop. "That's what your daddy always bought you when you were younger when he brought you in here with him. Put me down for giving you your first wedding gift." We all laughed.

Several other men were in the tavern, sitting at a table and listening. One of them said, "So, you're getting married tonight, Little Brooks?"

I said, "Yes, sir."

He said, "Okay, everybody, let's toast Little Brooks on his getting married." Everybody stood up, holding their beer bottles up. The same man said, "Here's to Little Brooks, who's getting married. May he be happy and have a house full of chillin."

Everyone laughed and took a drink out of their beer bottles. All of them came over to the bar and shook my hand. Each said, "Good luck, Little Brooks." I thanked them and headed for the door. I turned around and thanked Mrs. Richardson.

My dad said, "I'm coming on behind you. See you in a little while. That's at Will's house, ain't it? Over on Park?"

I said, "Yes, sir. 2632 Park." I was wondering whether I should have given him the exact address.

I left my dad standing outside beside his old truck talking to Mrs. Richardson. Since I couldn't go to Carol's house until eight, I decided to go to one of our favorite places to rendezvous, Spring Valley Park at 27th Street right off Woodland. I got out and walked around the park and threw a few rocks into the spring-fed lake. The park was crowded. There was a baseball game across the street from the shelter house and the lake. Plus, there was a large group of people in the shelter house. I guess people thought I was crazy walking around the park alone at 7:30 p.m., wearing a two-piece blue suit, white shirt, a red polka dot tie—and black shoes, of course. I got a few stares.

Then it was 7:55 p.m., according to my watch. I jumped in my car and headed to 2632 Park to get married. When I arrived at the house, the street was lined with cars up and down the block on both sides. I had to park several houses down the block and walk up to the house. When I opened the screen door and entered, my dad said, "Boy, we thought you had changed your mind." Everyone laughed. I was scared. I was sweating. I could feel the sweat crinkling down my back. The palms of my hands were sweating. Some of it might have been due to the heat outside and inside the house. It was August, and there was no air-conditioning, but there was an electric fan.

Everybody was there. Pastor Luther W. Smith of Mercy Church of God in Christ, 2839 Bell Street, Kansas City, Missouri, officiated. With us were Nan Cunningham (Carol's best friend and bridesmaid), Paul (my best man), Maurice, and Mr. and Mrs. Carter, the next-door neighbors. The house was full of neighbors and some of Carol's friends. Carol, her mother, Naomi (I think), and several other women were upstairs. Pastor Smith hollered out, "Is the bride ready?" Someone hollered back, "In a few more minutes." Someone led off humming out the Bridal March. Others joined in: "Dom, dom da dom. Dom, dom da dom," and so on. Everyone's eyes were on the stairs. Here she comes. You could see the white shoes with short heels and long, beautiful white dress before you could see Carol. Then you saw more dress dragging on the steps. Carol was holding it up in the front so she wouldn't step on it. Then she appeared with a white veil over her face, all smiles, and everyone began applauding.

The women were whispering how pretty Carol looked. Her mother and other women were following her, holding each side of the back of the dress. Carol walked over and stood facing me. Nan was slightly behind her and Paul was slightly behind me. He had the ring. Pastor Smith began the wedding. Now I was really getting scared. I was sweating so, all down my back. I could feel sweat running down each side from my underarms. From between my legs. My hands were sweating. My forehead. Some of it was due to the heat. But most of it was because I was just downright scared of what was about to take place. I wondered what Carol was thinking and going through. I imagined her mind was going through the same thing mine was going through.

I could see Carol shaking. She glanced at me and tried to smile. Why couldn't we have gone to the courthouse and been through with this? Or we could have stood in front of the fireplace and Pastor Smith could have just said, "I now pronounce you husband and wife. You may kiss the bride." But Pastor Smith had to go through the formal stuff.

We all adjusted to our assigned places. Pastor Smith began with prayer. Then he read from a little black book and went through the ritual. Now, here we go.

"Alvin Brooks, do you take this woman, Carol Rich, to be your lawful wedded wife, to have and to hold, this day forward, for better, for worse, for richer, for poorer, in sickness and in health, to love and to cherish from this day forward, till death do you part, according to God's law?"

I responded, "I do."

He then turned to Carol. "Carol, do you take Alvin to be your lawful wedded husband, to have and to hold, this day forward, for better, for worse, for richer, for poorer, in sickness and in health, to love and to cherish from this day forward, till death do you part, according to God's law?"

Carol responded, "I do."

Pastor Smith said, "Is there a ring?" Paul reached into his pocket. It seemed like he couldn't find it. I knew I had given it to him. Did he lose it? Everybody got quiet. It seemed liked it took a lifetime for him to find the ring. He dug it out and handed it to me. Pastor Smith said, "Put it on her finger." I followed his instructions and placed the ring on Carol's finger next to the ring with the high stone. Pastor Smith then said, "If there is anyone present who feels that this couple should not become involved in holy matrimony, speak up now or forever hold your peace."

There was silence. I couldn't forget that my daddy had been drinking quite a bit before the wedding. He was feeling pretty good. He was "in his sin," as the old folks used to say when someone had consumed more than his share of alcohol. I was hoping and praying that he hadn't changed his mind despite me admitting that the baby was mine and that I wanted to marry Carol. I wanted to tell Pastor Smith to hurry up before my dad responded to his call. The pause seemed like an hour. Pastor Smith said, "Hearing none, by the powers vested in me as an ordained licensed minister of the Gospel, I pronounce you man and wife. I present to you, ladies and gentlemen, Mr. and Mrs. Alvin Brooks. You may salute your bride." (That meant kiss.)

I raised the veil and kissed Carol very gently and cautiously. Carol was my wife now, but I still knew how to act in the presence of all those adults. So, I gave Carol a "smack" on the lips.

Her mother yelled out, "Oh, you can do better than that."

Others chimed in. "Yeah, you can do it like you did before you said 'I do.'"

Someone else said, "Do it like you do when we aren't around." Everybody laughed. I was embarrassed and still scared to do any more than we had done, but I did give Carol another kiss a little longer than the first. There was a big burst of applause and folks saying a lot of different things, mostly congratulations. Someone even said, "You are a beautiful young couple."

My dad and Carol's mother received congratulations from a host of people. Everybody hugged Carol and told her how cute she looked. After thanking everyone, Carol, Nan, Paul, Maurice, and I left for the photographer at 18th and Vine Street. Carol and I got in my car. Paul, Nan, and Maurice were in Paul's car. Going down Brooklyn from Carol's house, I pulled over. Paul was ahead of me. I kissed Carol as I had in the past and rubbed her stomach. We told each other how much we loved each other—"for a lifetime!"

When I drove up to the house and went up the stairs, I told Carol that I was going to carry her over the threshold. I picked her up, stepped inside, and we were home. We laughed and prepared for bed. We got down on our knees and held hands, and I began to pray, thanking God for our marriage and asking that our child be born healthy, to bless our marriage and all our children, and I gave thanks for those who had helped us. The rest of our first night sleeping together is history.

I Enroll in College, 1950

I enrolled in Lincoln Business College night classes in September 1950. The college was in the Lincoln Building at 18th and Vine on the second floor. It was an eighteen-month program. It was really a school for veterans; only a few of us were non-vets. Uncle Sam paid for the vets, but we non-vets had to pay our own way.

There were some good teachers. Many taught either at the high school or Lincoln Junior College. There were accountants, businesspeople, a lawyer, and others teaching all the courses that led to a diploma in business administration.

I was supposed to get a diploma in January 1952, but the Feds came in, I believe, the end of December 1951. They placed padlocks on the doors and there were some indictments. Some of the teachers—and possibly some administrators—were allowing some of the veterans to pay them for counting them present and allowing them to take tests with notes provided by faculty members. The vets would pay the teachers or administrators so much money from the monthly check they got from the government.

The few of us who were non-vets lost our money and got no credit for attending. In fact, for two years, I placed Lincoln Business College on my applications to become a police officer, and no record of my attending could be found. All I had to show were the books I bought, classwork I'd done, and receipts showing I had paid my tuition in full.

When I reached Carol's, family members were eating dinner. Rarely did I go to Carol's family home when it wasn't like the lobby of a hotel or a cafeteria, where everyone was eating everywhere—Mrs. McCoy and her daughter, Allene; Allene's daughter, Alverna, and Alverna's husband, Eugene McDonald; John "Buddy" Fletcher; and Mr. McCoy at times also. And there might have been others as well. It was a "family home." Carol and I walked out on the porch. I wanted to hear what had happened to her earlier today at our house.

"Well, baby, I was sitting on the toilet reading one of my magazines. I had kinda eased in there past some men working on a light pole out there. When suddenly, that door to the toilet that your dad made of burlap feed sacks and has hanging up there flew up and I was all exposed. All three of those men looked my way. I know they saw me sitting on the toilet. I grabbed the curtain and pulled it back, but it was too late. They had seen me. So, I had to sit there peeping through the curtain until they got deep in their work again, pull up my clothes, and ease out and back into the house. Then I peeped out of the window to see if they had been looking. I don't think they were. But, baby, I can't really use that bucket in the house, or whatever you call it. And I really have problems using the one outdoors. You'll have to bring me over here to Grandma's on your way to work and then pick me up in the evenings so I can cook. Then you can take a bath over here, and then we can go home."

I apologized, "Baby, I understand, and it's going to be getting cool soon, and you can't stay out there with no heat. You can't take a bath or use the toilet. I'll have to find us someplace else to live and soon. It'll be winter soon. If there's room here at your house, you think your grandma would let us rent a room?"

Carol said, "I don't know; you want me to say something to Grandma? She may not charge us. Maybe we can stay over here."

I said, "You think she'd let us? It's crowded here now."

"Yes, but everyone may not be staying for long. I'm going to ask Grandma tomorrow anyway. Let's go in and tell everyone we're leaving."

Mrs. McCoy said, "Where have you all been? We thought you had gone. Come on in here and eat. Everyone else has eaten. There's plenty left. Or you can fix yourselves a plate and take it with you. Save what you've cooked, Carol, and you can eat that tomorrow." So, we sat down and ate. I went upstairs and took a bath, and we went home.

We stayed at 3240 Quincy until mid-September, when the weather began to change. The only time we spent at home was at night. Carol even stopped cooking, except breakfast. I would take her every morning to her grandma's and then come back in the evening, eat, stay there until almost dark, and then go home. I told my father that I couldn't keep Carol there much longer, and I certainly didn't want us to be there when our baby was born. He asked where we were going to go. I told him that Carol was going to ask her grandmother.

When I came to pick Carol up the day after our discussion, Mrs. McCoy was not at home, but Carol said she had talked to her grandmother about us moving in there and that I had said I would pay rent to her. Mrs. McCoy told Carol that "no one else pays any rent or anything else, so you kids won't have to pay either." Carol's grandmother said that there was the kitchenette upstairs. If we could get some bedroom furniture, we could move in there.

That weekend, Carol and I went to Montgomery Ward and paid down on a five-piece blond-colored bedroom set and a kitchen table with four chairs. I went home and told my father where we were in connection to our moving. Daddy was happy for us and said, "Well, that's good 'cause I don't want my grandson to be around all these animals and stuff until he's old enough."

I asked, "Daddy, how do you know whether our baby is going to be a boy or girl?"

He said, "I'm hoping for a boy. Tell Carol what I said." We laughed.

Montgomery Ward delivered our furniture to 2632 Park. Carol's family home became our family home. Four of our six children were born while we lived there: Ronall, Estelle, Carrie, and Rosalind. Carol's grandmother moved to Denver with her youngest daughter shortly after Ronall was born.

From Waldo, to Brookside, to Downtown, to North KC with Katz

Shortly after I got married, Doug, the Katz store manager, told me to see him after I changed into my work clothes. I didn't like the way he said it. I was thinking, *If I'm going to be fired, he wouldn't have had me change clothes.* After changing, I went to his office.

He said, "Alvin, I hate to lose you, but personnel called this morning and said they needed someone to run the elevators at night at Katz's headquarters at 12th and Walnut. They told me to have you report there at 5:30 tomorrow evening. Maybe I bragged on you too much to personnel. I was told they needed someone dependable at headquarters. So good luck. Everyone around here's going to miss you."

I thanked him and shook his hand. All day I was telling folks that I was leaving and where I was going. Everyone hated to see me leave. I never did tell anyone that I had just married and had a baby on the way. The next day, I reported to 12th and Walnut to the personnel office. I met the woman with whom I had been talking when I first got hired. She greeted me and I thanked her and shook her hand. She had a white man show me what I would be doing until about 12:30 a.m. I would be running the one elevator for those staff persons who worked late—and would carry janitorial workers from one floor to the other and their trash down to the basement.

After about a month, I got reassigned again. When I came in one evening, there was a note on my time card: "Alvin, report to personnel after you time in." I met the same woman. After speaking, she said, "Alvin, you shouldn't do such good work. They need a dependable janitor at one of our newer stores in North Kansas City, and I'm sending you. Congratulations!"

I was happy where I was, but I didn't tell her that. In fact, I liked the elevator assignment. After all the office staff cleared out, I sometimes read magazines and my schoolwork. I think some of the brothers on the night cleanup crew were jealous. They were older. In fact, I called all of them "Mister." Occasionally, one of them would tell me, "Boy, you don't do shit. You just sit on your Black ass, read, and take us up and down." I don't think their attitude had anything to do with my transfer, though.

More Racist Cops: North Kansas City

When I first arrived at the North Kansas City Katz store, my car was running okay. After about the first week, I had car trouble. My starter went out. I didn't have the funds to take it to a regular mechanic shop, so I had to wait until my cousin Raymond could come to my house and help me take the starter off and then go to a shop that rebuilt starters.

In the meantime, for almost two weeks until my next payday, I had to ride the 31st Street streetcar from 31st and Linwood to 10th and Main and there catch the North Kansas City bus to Katz at Armour Road and Swift. The last night bus from North Kansas City to 10th and Main left North Kansas City at 10:15. Although the store closed at nine, I had to stay and run the dust mop and the damp mop and empty the waste baskets before I could time out. Which meant I didn't finish those until about 10:20 or 10:30. Therefore, I missed the last bus and had to walk from the store at Armour Road and Swift to 10th and Main.

The same police officers came in and out of the store several times between 4:00 and 9:00 p.m. I spoke to them each time I saw them in the store. But almost every night as I walked from the store to 10th and Main, they would stop me—sometimes just as I was partway across what is now called the Heart of America Bridge. Two police officers riding together would take me through the same routine each time.

"Come here, boy. What's your name? Where you coming from? Where you going? What are you doing over here in North Kansas City? Let's see some identification. What you got in your pockets?" I got searched. After all that, "You can go."

When they rolled upon me after I had gotten onto the bridge, they couldn't turn around because of the concrete barricade between the southbound and northbound lanes and had to drive to the Kansas City end and turn around. Once or twice I asked, "Sir, can you give me a ride across the bridge?" They would only say, "The only way you can ride in this car is to go to jail."

Raymond had signed up to go into the army and was busy getting his business straight to leave. I finally caught up with him early one Saturday morning before I went to work. We took the starter off and took it to the shop. We left it and were told to come back in about three hours. We got the starter back and back on my car in time for me to drive to work. Thank God!

But even after that, the same cops would stop me once or twice a week. Same routine, except they'd go through my car from the trunk to under the hood. The city of North Kansas City had a reputation of being anti-Black for a long time.

Fegan's Employment Agency

I got a call one morning from Mrs. Ardella Fegan, owner of the Fegan Employment Agency. Mrs. Fegan asked me, "Alvin, are you working?"

I said, "Yes, ma'am, at Katz Drug Store in North Kansas City."

She said, "I know there's only one thing you can be doing at Katz, and that's sweeping and mopping. Come by and see me. I might have something for you better than that, and it might pay you more money. And you'd work forty hours a week and straight days."

I went to see Mrs. Fegan one morning before I got ready to work at Katz. She said, "You got married on me, didn't you? You married one of the Rich girls, Carol?"

I said, "Yes, ma'am, we got married in August." Mrs. Fegan asked how Carol was and when the baby was due.

I said, "The doctor said sometime in January."

"Well, you need something better. And in Kansas City, everybody knows the reputation of North Kansas City. Those folks don't like Negroes. Most of us don't even like to drive through there. That's Little Dixie over there."

Mrs. Fegan said the company was A. J. Griner. The job was truck driver, delivering chemicals and equipment to labs in companies in the Kansas City area with a little office cleaning in between deliveries. The hours were 8:30 a.m. to 5:00 p.m. Mrs. Fegan asked, "How does that sound?"

I told her okay. One of her final comments was, "The company is family-owned. Mr. and Mrs. Griner. Mrs. Griner really runs the company. She is the one who called me, and we've talked a couple of times. She is very curt and short in her conversation. So, keep that in mind when you interview with her, okay?"

I said, "Yes, ma'am. I understand." She asked me if I was going down there now. I told her no because I had to go to work at two at Katz, but I would go the next morning. Mrs. Fegan gave me a referral letter.

The A. J. Griner Company

I started work at the A. J. Griner Company in September 1950. It wasn't long before I found out that none of the employees liked Mrs. Griner—except the person who ranked second in authority, Mr. Griner.

The only other Black employee, Mr. Glen (I called him by his first name), had been there several years. He told me why no one liked Mrs. Griner. Mrs. Griner always had to have the last word on everything. If Mr. Griner told you to do something and Mrs. Griner told you something else, you did what Mrs. Griner told you to do.

As for Mr. Griner, all he did was walk around all day with that cigar in his mouth, looking important. He would meet and greet customers. But when it came to making decisions, Mrs. Griner had the last word.

My first week, I worked inside cleaning, which seemed as though it hadn't been done in years. I also made three or four deliveries, but they were emergency in nature. The second week, I was out making deliveries. I had never heard of most of the streets and places. Mr. Glen knew the streets well. He showed me how to put a system to my deliveries, how to line up the items according to the direction from the store. The third week I was getting better. There was no GPS in those days. I got a map and a pocket-size street guide. As I was lining up my deliveries, I used both maps. By the fourth week, I could find almost any address in the metropolitan area.

I tried to stay out of Mrs. Griner's way, but finally, I had to do some things around the office and in the shop where the chemicals were kept and the paperwork was done. I learned how to deal with Mrs. Griner. Today it would be said that I "played her." I learned how to flatter her, although she rarely smiled or said a kind word to anyone or about anyone. Another term would be "brown-nosing." The Black community would also call it "Tom-in'."

The Griners were well into their sixties, maybe early seventies. Mrs. Griner showed her age; she looked old. I would play her with lines like: "Mrs. Griner, you sure know this business; you know what every one of us is doing; I'm learning so much from you in just a short period of time; I'm enjoying working here and watching how you do things; you know everybody's job; I bet you could make the deliveries if you had to."

Mrs. Griner would respond with, "When you been in this business as long as I have, you'd better know everyone's job. The business is not theirs, but mine. I'd better know."

I'd then say something like, "You know, Mrs. Griner, I'm going to enroll in night school and take business. What are your thoughts about that?"

"My God," folks around the company began to say, "Alvin is the teacher's pet."

The workday started at 8:30 a.m., and everyone came in the back door. Mr. Griner was all over, meddling into whatever. But I always made my way to the front office to speak to Mrs. Griner first. "Mrs. Griner, how are you this morning?" Then I would say good morning to the others. Sometimes I would say to Mrs. Griner late in the afternoon, "Mrs. Griner, you work awful hard and long hours. Do you ever think about you and Mr. Griner just going on a cruise or train ride just to get away and have time to yourselves? We can hold things together until you all get back." Staff then began to say, "Alvin's got the old lady bullshitted. You talk about 'brown-nosing'! Where'd you learn that, boy?" I'd just laugh and give some off-the-wall answer.

Our Son Wants to Be Born and Carol's Mother Wants to Go to the Movies, 1951

Carol went into labor early Sunday evening on January 11, 1951. We had everything ready. Carol's robe, toiletries, house shoes, and a few other items her grandmother told us she would need. Mrs. McCoy was so helpful to both of us. She counseled us all during Carol's pregnancy. We didn't know whether our baby was a boy or a girl. Remember, this was 1951, and sonograms had not yet been invented. Since Carol's labor pains were coming close together, Mrs. McCoy told us it was time for Carol to go to the hospital—General Hospital #2, the "colored hospital."

Carol called her mother. I picked her up, and she accompanied us to the hospital. Carol checked in, and her mother and I followed the nurse who was pushing her in a wheelchair to her room. Her mother and I stayed with her until visiting hours were over. Remember, at that time when visiting hours were over, an announcement would come over the public address system to tell you "visiting hours are over." If you weren't out of the patient's room, the nurses would come around and say, "Sorry, visiting hours are over."

As I recall, there were three other expectant mothers in the room with Carol. Carol's mother kissed her and told her, "It's going to be all right. Go ahead and have that boy—so go ahead and have him!" We all laughed.

Carol's pain was becoming more intense. The nurse came around again. "Okay, folks, you must leave. We'll take care of Carol. She's in good hands."

I rubbed her stomach, kissed her, and told her, "I love you, little mother. See you again real soon." We left.

Carol's mother said, "Let's to the movie. Maybe Carol will deliver while we're there. We can call back to the hospital when we get out of the movie." Her mother suggested the movie at the Lincoln Theater since the last movie there hadn't started yet. After the movie, I used the pay phone in the lobby and got the nurses' station. The duty nurse to whom we had been talking earlier answered the phone. I asked her if Carol had delivered.

She said, "No, but it probably won't be long. If it's while I'm on duty, I'll call you or your mother-in-law. I get off in a couple hours but will leave the information with my relief to call you." I thanked her and told Carol's mother what the nurse said. I took Carol's mother to her boyfriend's residence.

It's a Boy at Five Pounds, Four Ounces, 1951

It was early Friday morning, January 12, when I received a call from a nurse that Carol had delivered a baby boy. She said, "Is this Alvin?"

I said, "Yes, ma'am."

"Okay, Alvin, you are the proud father of a five-pound, four-ounce baby boy. Congratulations! Carol and the baby are fine. She's calling for you."

I said, "Thank you so much. Tell her I'll be there shortly."

"Okay, congratulations again. Your boy is handsome. Carol's nursing him now."

I told her, "Please tell Carol thanks for my son." We both laughed. I called Mrs. Griner and told her that I had an emergency come up and I asked her if I could come in about ten o'clock—would that be okay? She said yes.

I called Carol's grandmother and her mother and my father. I picked up her mother, and we both went to the hospital after I got off work. Carol was glad to see us, but she looked so tired and weak. Both her mother and I kissed her. She said she was in a lot of pain.

Her mother said, "You look tired, honey. You just had a big ol' baby boy. You should be tired." Carol said she had nursed him for the first time and that he was greedy. Afterward, she said they took him back into the nursery. She told us the visiting hours so that we could see him.

"Are you satisfied that I gave you a son?" she asked. I kissed her.

"Yes!" I said. "You did good. Just what I ordered." We all laughed. I asked her, "When did they say you could go home?"

"If no complications occur, I can go home Friday or Saturday," she said.

They made the announcement that the babies now could be seen in the nursery. Carol's mother and I almost ran to the nursery. The nurses began to push the babies up to the nursery glass so parents' other relatives and friends could see their respective newborns. We looked. And there he was.

The ID card at the end of the crib said "Baby Brooks." He was so red. But you could see the dark skin around his ears and fingertips. Carol's mother said, "Yeah, he's yours. He gonna be your complexion. Look at that head of hair! Don't worry; it'll change real soon." We laughed. Others who overheard what she said laughed, too. My son was fast asleep.

When we went back to Carol's room, she asked, "Did you'all see him? Isn't he beautiful?"

Her mother said, "Yeah! And he looks just like Alvin. He is going to have his complexion. And that hair is gonna kink up, too!" We all laughed.

Carol kept inquiring, "Are you happy for your son? I think we ought to name him Ronall. Whad'ya think?"

Her mother said, "Sounds good to me. How about you, Alvin—Poppa?"

I said, "Ronall sounds good to me. Let's think about a middle name later." I was thinking more about "Alvin Junior," but I never said anything to the contrary. *I'll yield,* I thought.

I took Carol and our son home the following Saturday. Dad came over to see his grandson. Everyone who came by said, "That boy looks just like you! What did you'all name him? He's sure yours." You know how that made me feel . . . "cheezing" (smiling) ear to ear.

By that time, we had given Ronall his middle name: Lavern, the same as Carol's. "Your son is the spitting image of you"—everybody was telling me that.

Then the real learning how to care for a baby took place. Mrs. McCoy was our teacher. Thank God for her. I often told her that, too. We had a supply of baby bottles, Enfamil, diapers, and blue and yellow baby clothes. Carol's breasts were filling up more than Ronall could keep up with. Mrs. McCoy said it was better if Carol breastfed Ronall rather than put him immediately on the bottle.

Employment from A. J. Griner to Ford Motor Company

Another call from Mrs. Fegan led me from my work at A. J. Griner to the Ford Motor Company. Around June 1952, she called to inform me that she had received some information that the Ford Motor Company, new to the area, was hiring in Claycomo, Missouri. "They're making airplane wings there," she said. "You may want to check it out." I told my friends Maurice, Paul, George Lucas, and "Peck" (his nickname—I don't remember his real name), and I drove all five of us to the Claycomo plant because I was the only one who had a car. Well, we all got hired.

Now the interesting thing is that the only jobs we Blacks could get hired for were cleaning up the plant. They were still building the facility and setting up to build B-47 bomber wings. All the office workers were white and, of course, the custodians were Black. These were mostly night shift jobs. I had planned to start Lincoln Junior College in September. My foreman knew this. I had asked him for a transfer to the evening shift, but he denied my request. He didn't give any reason, although most of the men didn't want to work evenings despite a night shift pay differential.

As the plant was nearing completion to accommodate building the bomber wings, many employees from the Ford plant in northeast Kansas City were transferred to Claycomo. They went through the necessary training and were assigned to the assembly line. That's when a few Blacks were placed into new positions. None were in management or non-union positions. All non-management employees were members of Union Local 249, AFL/CIO.

As far as we knew, the union did not fight for equal rights and employment opportunities for Black union members, although we paid the same union dues as white members. All foremen and superintendents were white. When we were hired, most of the white workers were farmers from the small towns north of the Missouri River in Clay and Platte counties. Many of them took off or were allowed to change shifts to harvest their crops in the fall and plant in the spring.

The foremen, especially ours, did all kinds of things to catch Black workers committing the least infraction to be written up for termination. I'll never forget one of our coworkers who was working two jobs, at Ford during the day and running his own janitorial service at night. Someone talked too much, and our foreman heard that he owned his own company. The foreman transferred him to the evening shift. None of us felt favorable toward our foreman. He earned the reputation of being hard on Blacks but treating the whites under his supervision differently. It was obvious.

The union representative, Mr. Mosby, who was a kind and humble Black gentleman in his sixties, had been with Ford for years and had been transferred from the plant in northeast Kansas City. He wrote up our various grievances, but they never seemed to go anywhere. You see, he was somewhat new to this group of white folks. I understand he had some semblance of authority as a committeeman at the old plant where he came from, but here there were racist whites. Of all our grievances, the company representative never found the supervisor wrong or in error. Never.

Curtis, one of my Black coworkers who had two jobs (Ford and his janitorial service) would regularly have a run-in with our foreman, but he was sharp enough to stay just one step ahead. It became a game. He would say, "Watch this," and then he'd do something crazy that made us all laugh—Blacks and whites and even the foreman. Many of us figured the foreman thought Curtis was crazy. The foreman always watched Curtis and the rest of us like we were on a plantation pickin' cotton and he was the overseer. But Curtis was just "borderline" enough and knew the rules and nothing the foreman did ever got acted on by the superintendent the foreman reported to.

Curtis would never file an official grievance. He'd tell Mr. Mosby, "Mr. Moz, I got this. I don't want to get you in any trouble. You're up in age and need to get your time in." Mr. Mosby would always try to debate with Curtis but found out repeatedly it was no use. Curtis did what he did pragmatically and always came out on top. "Mr. Moz, I don't want you to get fired over me because I'll be here as long as I want to. So just sit back and go with me for the ride." We all would laugh. So did Mr. Mosby.

Curtis was funny. He could compete with Redd Foxx, the stand-up comic. All of Curtis's capers were humorous, but one stood out over all others. The foreman saw Curtis go into the men's restroom. Although we were working, we had our eyes on Curtis and the foreman, who was peeping around the corner from one of the offices. Curtis was in the restroom for what seemed like a long time. The foreman kind of tiptoed to the restroom door. Three or four of us who were watching hollered, "Curtis!" The foreman went back to his office in a hurry, but Curtis didn't come out of the restroom. We huddled and decided one of us was going to see what Curtis was doing when the foreman came walking back fast with a security guard. Then it dawned on us that when someone said or did something that was an infraction of the rules, there must be a witness. Someone said, "Oh, shit. Curtis is in there asleep on the pot!"

The foreman and the security guard eased the door open and let it close behind them very softly. All of a sudden, we heard Curtis loudly cursing at both the foreman and the security guard, and they were backing out of the restroom. When Curtis got outside the door, cursing and pointing his finger at them, he said, "Goddammit, don't you fuckers ever interrupt me when I'm saying my prayers, you hear? I'm going to report your asses to Henry Ford." Both men walked on down the hall occasionally looking back at Curtis, who was still cursing and hollering at them. Curtis hollered again, "Now I've got a real grievance to file against both of you. Send one of the white committeemen around here and not Mr. Moz."

When they got out of sight and listening distance, Curtis said, "Why didn't one of you mothers holler and wake me up? I hadn't planned to go to sleep sitting on the throne. I didn't have to shit. I didn't even pull my pants down. It took that bastard so long to come back with that asshole guard when they came back and approached the door to the shit stool, I saw their feet, and as soon as they snatched the door open, I jumped up off the stool, said 'Amen,' did the sign of the cross, and began cursing their asses."

We told Curtis we tried to alert him by calling his name. He said, "Shit, I was tired. It felt so good sitting on that shit stool. I didn't intend to go to sleep. It just happened."

We asked him if he heard the foreman come in the first time. He said, "Sorta, but I thought it was one of you fuckers fuckin' with me." The word got around our crew what Curtis had done. What a laugh we had. Later, in the evening, Mr. Mosby came around. Curtis told him what had happened, but not the whole story. We all laughed and told him what the foreman and the guard had done. Mr. Mosby asked Curtis if he wanted to "grieve what happened."

Curtis told Mr. Mosby, "Hell no, Mr. Moz, I told you to just stand back of me and go along for the ride. I'll be all right. I'll leave when I get ready. I might be here when all those bastards are gone."

At Ford, I Began to Explore My Career Options, 1952

After almost two years at Ford, I didn't foresee any change for the better for those of us who were Black. And I now was a father of a one-year-old. Although Ford had a multimillion-dollar contract with the Feds to build bomber wings, the rights of Black workers were far from a reality. I really didn't go to Ford looking for a future. Even though I was just twenty, I had enough experience to know the limitations for Blacks, no matter how prepared we were.

But I intended to keep moving forward with my education. I really didn't know where it was going to take me, but I knew that, over the long term, Ford was not where I wanted to go. After Ronall was born, Carol and I were discussing our future together. We talked about me graduating from college and going to law school.

Before I tell you about my big career move to the police department, I want to relate the story of my son's life. He will appear again in this memoir, but next you will learn the main events.

Chapter 2

MY SON, RONALL

Ronall's Early Years—From Day Care to Kindergarten

When Ronall was three or four years old, we enrolled him in the Catholic day care on 25th Street between Garfield and Euclid. Directly across the street was a small Catholic mission, Holy Spirit Catholic Church, 2008 East 25th Street. In the fall of 1956, when Ronall was five, we enrolled him in kindergarten at St. Monica Catholic School. For him to be eligible, we had to take catechism class and attend 9:00 a.m. Mass at St. Joseph Catholic Church at 19th and Harrison where Father Alvin Deen was the priest. St. Monica School at 17th and Lydia was six or seven blocks from the church. The students had to walk to the church regardless of the weather conditions.

Ronall attended St. Monica School until we moved from 2632 Park to 3336 Agnes on October 13, 1960. Then he attended Annunciation Catholic School across the driveway from the church at Linwood Boulevard and Benton. Ronall was nine years old when we moved into Annunciation Parish when we changed our membership from St. Joseph.

I remember getting a call from Ronall's teacher, a Catholic nun, who said that Ronall was having difficulty reading. She thought it was because he needed glasses. He was about nine years old, in the third grade. I knew that wasn't true because he read at home with his sisters, Estelle and Carrie, who came along in 1953 and 1954.

I went to school one day and had Ronall stand at the place where the school nurse checked students' eyes. A nurse gave him the eye exam, placing the instrument over one eye and then the other and changing the size of the letters to be read. As the nurse looked on, I placed my glasses on Ronall—and lo and behold, he could read. But I knew he could not see through my glasses. So, I asked, "Son, do you want to wear glasses?" He said, "Yes, just like yours!" That was the answer. Ronall wanted to wear glasses like me. He was satisfied when I told him that when he was older, I would buy him some, should he need them. Ronall was probably in his forties before he really needed glasses.

Another incident occurred when Ronall was in the fifth or sixth grade at Annunciation. I got an emergency call from his teacher, Sister Fredrick, while I was in the office of the police department's youth unit where I was a detective. Ronall's teacher said it was an emergency and that I should come to the school as soon as possible. I really got scared. Several days prior, I had taken several pieces of porn material from someone when I made an arrest. I was holding the porn material until the court date. Officers did that in those days. I thought, *My God! I bet Ronall found where I had placed the porn stuff and had taken it to school.*

I caught the police elevator and could hardly wait until it reached the garage. My police car was parked across the street on 12th Street. Without using my siren, I drove like hell to get to the school. When I arrived and approached Ronall's room, I peeped in the door's window, and the students got the nun's attention to see that I was outside. She came to the door with Ronall. She had an envelope in her hand, and we went across the hall to the nurse's office. I realized that the envelope she had was not large enough to hold the porn books—unless Ronall had torn some pages out of the book. She closed the door. My heart was still beating fast.

I think I broke out into a cold sweat when sister told Ronall, "Tell your father why he was asked to come to school this morning because of the emergency." Ronall told me that he had used a razor blade to cut a large rubber eraser into small pieces and was throwing them at certain persons in class. After he told me what he had done, I wanted to hug him, kiss him, tell him how much I loved him.

And I wanted to cuss his teacher. But I did what I was supposed to do first. I scolded him and made him apologize to Sister Fredrick. Then I asked Sister Fredrick if it was permissible for him to apologize to his classmates. But that was not approved. I then asked Sister Fredrick if he could go back to class. She approved, but I asked if she could stay a moment so I could talk to her alone. She agreed.

Short of cussing her under my breath, I told her, exaggerating slightly for effect, that she had made me use the red light and siren to get from police headquarters to school because she told me there was an emergency involving Ronall and that I should come as soon as possible. I could have had an accident or killed myself or someone else. Should there be a next time, please use different language, unless it really was an emergency. She didn't agree with me. To her, throwing small pieces from a rubber eraser was an emergency because Ronall could have put some student's eye out. I got up and walked out, thanking her as I left. But I was highly pissed, to say the least.

From Annunciation Catholic School to Central Junior and Central Senior

Ronall had a change in behavior in seventh grade at Annunciation. He was running the nuns crazy and they seemed to be running him crazy. He shut down doing his work in class and became the class clown. He did his homework but at times would not even turn it in.

This was driving everyone up the wall. I thought, *Well, maybe there are too many women in his life.* Nuns, mother, two sisters. Since he was flunking in most subjects, I thought that if he could make it through the seventh grade, we would enroll him in Central Junior High School next fall.

A longtime friend and former teacher of mine, Dr. Edward Fields, was the principal there. I took Ronall to meet him and ran down for him why I wanted to make the change. He and Ronall had a long conversation regarding "dos and don'ts," what was expected from him at Central Junior, what Dr. Fields expected of him, and what he would not tolerate. Dr. Fields pulled a paddle and told Ronall, "This, Ronall: I call this 'the board of education.' You understand? I never had to use this on your daddy out at Dunbar and don't plan to use it on you unless I have to. But I want you to know it's available. Right here in this drawer. You read me?"

Ronall told him, "Yes, sir."

Ronall was an altar boy at Annunciation. He also worked for a newspaper deliveryman, throwing papers at 4:00 a.m. He had an alarm clock, set it to wake him up, got up on his own, got dressed, and waited for the paper man to pick him up. He got back home about two hours later and took a shower. When he had to serve as an altar boy, he stayed up, walked to Annunciation, and served early morning Mass, then came back home. Carol fixed his breakfast along with the girls', and off to school he went. He did well his last year at Central Junior and through the second semester of his junior year at Central Senior. Boy, did that surprise the nuns! I think he succeeded as an altar boy just to prove that he was not as stupid as they had labeled him.

Just before the end of the first semester of his junior year, he had talked to an Air Force recruiter. But before that, he got one of his sister's friends, Jessica Elizabeth Roundtree, pregnant. She was fifteen. Ronall's son, Stephon Maurice Roundtree, was born August 9, 1968. Ronall denied to all of us that "Jessica's baby" was his. His sisters sort of took Jessica under their wing, put her in some of their clothes, and did her hair. They kept her looking nice. Eventually, after Stephon was born, Ronall accepted the fact that Stephon was his son.

Ronall Joins the Air Force

Ronall enlisted in the United States Air Force in December of 1968. Since he would not turn eighteen until January 12, 1969, I had to sign for him. Ronall went off to Lackland Military Training Center at Lackland Air Force Base, Texas. In July 1969, he completed his training, earned one stripe, and was assigned to security police. I'll never forget the kids on the block (33rd and Agnes), including his sisters, constructing a large banner that read

"Captain Jack." Carol and I didn't know until later that the phrase was not complete. The kids were respectful. It was really meant to say, "Captain Jack Ass!"

After being home for a while, Ronall was sent to Bitburg, Germany. While there, according to him, a racist superior disrespected him while he was on guard duty. He accused the officer of being racist. He was sent to the "brig."

Later during his stationing in Bitburg, he was selected with others to represent their base against another base in boxing. I never knew Ronall to fight, much less box. He wrote about his successes. He even sent back photos. Then there was his last fight. He hit his opponent and threw his own shoulder out. He was sent to the service hospital, and from that point on, his left shoulder never healed right. Never. He was later discharged from the Air Force with an honorable discharge and full medical coverage with a 20 percent disability.

Drug and Alcohol Abuse

Ronall was not able to work. Despite all the operations, his shoulder had worsened. He began to turn to drugs and alcohol. Most of his money each month was going for drugs, which meant he was continuing to abuse his body and mind with drugs and alcohol. He once told me that he had used every kind of drug that money would buy. He was admitted to almost every treatment center in the metropolitan area—Atchison, Kansas; somewhere near Warrensburg, Missouri; the VA Hospital in Topeka, Kansas; and several in Kansas City.

Everyone knew him as Al Brooks's son. And everyone in the treatment field knew him, as did the other drug addicts—those in recovery as well as those on the street. And all the dope dealers and the police knew him, along with his two sons and one daughter in Kansas City—and I can't forget his sisters who lived in the city.

Ronall's Final Hospital Trip

Now I must fast-forward to Sunday, January 5, 2003. According to Ronall's wife, Lueretta, as they were sitting at home watching television, Ronall seemed to be getting ill. She called an ambulance. Ronall, like me, suffers from claustrophobia. He told the ambulance folks that he could not ride in the back of the ambulance, so he switched seats with the EMT in the passenger seat, and off they went to Research Medical Center. Lueretta called and told us Ronall was on his way to the hospital.

When Carol and I got to Research, Ronall had already been placed in a private room. But while we were there, he began to act somewhat erratic. He became worse to the point they had to strap him down. The nurse came in and gave him an injection.

Whatever they gave him quieted him down. We all left. For the next several days they seemed to have Ronall heavily sedated, but then he turned for the worse and went into a coma.

He was moved to the ICU with all the tubes and machines hooked up to him. We were told that his body seemed to be shutting down, especially his kidneys. We thought Ronall was drug clean, but apparently the episode on Sunday was withdrawal symptoms. As the days passed, Ronall was not getting any better. His body was not giving off any measurable amount of urine. Numerous specialists were called in. We were told by the kidney specialist that if Ronall's kidneys completely shut down, ammonia from his urine would get to his brain with a massive stroke imminent.

Ronall had told us that he had learned that his heart was functioning only partially. The alcohol and the impurities in the street drugs were clogging his liver.

Ronall's condition worsened. All the kids came into town. Carrie and her daughter Carre, Rosalind from Germany, Ronall's daughter Ronika from Atlanta. Our friends from many faiths came to visit and pray for Ronall and us. Ronall was in a coma for his birthday on Sunday, January 12. He was fifty-two. Since he was not breathing on his own, all the medical personnel suggested we take Ronall off the support machines. They said that as soon as the support machines were removed, Ronall would expire.

The social worker and the chaplain asked to meet with Carol and me to discuss what we wanted to do. I wanted all family members, especially Ronall's sisters and two kids, Damon and Ronika, who were present, to be in on the decision. We all met. Ronall's condition was laid before us. We asked questions and got responses. Then we asked the social worker and chaplain to excuse themselves. We concluded to have Ronall taken off life support before his kidneys shut completely down and he had a stroke.

The next morning, the family was at Ronall's bedside. Father Philip Egan, our pastor at St. Monica Catholic Church, gathered everyone around Ronall's bed. We joined hands and prayed. The moment had come to remove the life support, Friday, January 17, about 11:00 a.m. No one but me wanted to be in the room when this happened. The curtain was closed, and the technician removed the breathing tube from Ronall's throat. As soon as it was removed, Ronall hollered, "Daddy! Daddy!" He was breathing on his own but was still in a coma. He was far from making his transition.

The hospital staff were shocked and, of course, so were we. Ronall was moved from ICU to the fourth floor, where RN Detrice Green was on duty. Detrice and family were also members of St. Monica. Ronall had only the morphine tube connected to him because he was in so much pain. We were told we would know when the pain became too intense and he needed more because Ronall would quiver and jerk. We would then push the button at the end of the tube, and his quivering and jerking would subside. For the rest of the day, we sat with Ronall and followed the instructions regarding the morphine. After midnight, Ronall's pain became more intense.

I began to whisper into Ronall's ear his whole life's history, beginning with his birth and everything I could remember through his going into the Air Force. Early Saturday morning, the morphine was not doing any good. The kids had been playing church music in his ear. It was close to 6:00 a.m. I leaned over Ronall's bed and began to tell him, "Go ahead, son, let go. Go to God, we'll see you on the other side. Go ahead. Let go." I sat back down in the chair next to his bed. There was a small table in the corner next to the chair. I turned and laid my head on my crossed arms on the table. I heard Ronall take a deep breath and let it out, and that was it. He made his transition.

Ronall's transition service was held on Saturday, January 25, 2003, at St. Monica Catholic Church with the Reverend Philip Egan officiating. Ronall's service was beautiful. His sisters and my nephew, Donell Nolan, put the order of service together. Donell got the guest artist. The girls, with Father Egan's help, put the rest of the service together.

Chapter 3

MY POLICE CAREER

"Why in the Hell Do You Want to Get Involved in That Police Mess? You Know How They Treat Us!"—1953

One day when my dad was visiting with Carol and me, I mentioned that I was considering joining the police department. I hadn't gotten the words out of my mouth before my dad responded, "Why in the hell do you want to get involved in that police mess? You know how they treat us!"

Several days later, Dad came by as he often did around dinnertime. This day was no different. We all sat down and ate together. I brought up the subject of my joining the police department. I approached it a little bit at a time. "Daddy, you know a couple of weeks ago when I was out to your house and I told you that I was considering going on the police department? Carol and I believe if we just let white folks define who we are, where we go to school, live, work, and who we vote for, we're giving them the authority and superiority that they believe is theirs. I'm convinced there are times when you get inside and let others press from the outside. That's the way I think you bring about change.

"I remember what Momma would tell me: 'Baby, you've got to do better than them because they'll have an edge on you because you're colored. Getting your education in the long run will make the difference.' I don't believe God intended for us to always be last and victims of racism. But we will never be what God made us to be if we don't challenge things that are wrong. I've decided to join the police department and do what I can to change those things that we agree are against us. I don't think things will change, Daddy, unless we become involved."

Daddy said, "Now that you've made that decision, I'd much rather hire you a lawyer if you have to kill someone defending yourself than pay Watkins Funeral Home to bury you!"

Well, that was the end of the discussion about my joining the police department.

I still did not tell my dad that I had already made an application and taken the various tests and was waiting to hear back from the police department.

When I was notified that I passed all the requirements and was assigned to the 1954 January class, I was midway through my sophomore year of college and wanted to finish with an associate of arts degree. I went to the personnel department and asked if I could defer the January class because I wanted to complete my sophomore year. They approved my request and assigned me to the June class of 1954. I received my degree and entered the 44th Cadet Class on June 1, 1954. I was the only Black cadet out of twenty-nine in my class at the police academy.

It didn't take long before I encountered what Carol, my father, and I had discussed about the police department. There was very little regard for the Supreme Court decision of *Brown v. Board of Education*, handed down May 17, 1954, the decision that provided for equal protection under the law (the Fourteenth Amendment to the US Constitution) for Black students in public schools.

I got along well with my white colleagues, although racism showed its dirty head occasionally. I always thought before I spoke on this issue. I gained all their respect, and I respected them, and I respected myself.

The police academy was on the fourth floor of police headquarters. The room was organized like a school classroom. There was a desk where the sergeant sat. We were seated alphabetically, so I sat in the front row: Harold Antrim, Raymond Beall, Robert Birt, me, Robert Culver, and John Darr.

As a police cadet, I began to see my city from a whole new vantage point. I began to clearly see racism far more than I had experienced it in my twenty-two years of living. I began to see and hear the racism in the department—not only among the rank-and-file but also among the command staff. The person in charge of the academy was Sgt. James Canaday. He had a son, William "Bill" Canaday, who was a captain. Sergeant Canaday was an honorable man. At least he treated me with respect and sometimes cautioned my colleagues in class when racial slurs were thrown around. Despite the racism, I began to bond with my classmates. The highest-ranking Black officer was Lt. Clifford Warren. I met Mr. Warren through Mr. Leon Jordan. Both Mr. Jordan and Mr. Warren had joined the department about the same time in the 1940s.

Mr. Jordan was in the department for a number of years and was given leave to train police officers and airplane pilots for Liberia, West Africa. When he returned to the KCPD, he was offered a promotion to lieutenant to command the all-Black station known as the Flora Avenue Station at 20th and Flora. Mr. Jordan turned the promotion down. He thought he was a good enough cop to serve more than Blacks as a station commander.

When it came to choosing a partner for a particular exercise, I rarely got left out— mainly because the choosing usually began with the front row! It didn't take long before my fellow recruits knew where I stood with things like "nigger" or "colored" jokes.

But there were always Irish, Italian, and gay jokes. No one called check on these kinds of racist, ethnic, and homophobic slurs. I didn't laugh at any of them, and when they were said in my presence, I would say, "Someone's getting out of line." If Sergeant Canaday heard them, he would agree.

I didn't play the "goosing game" either. That was when someone used his hand, finger, or an object to play around with another's ass. No, I didn't play the game, and let it be known that I did not want it played on me. There was also the game of walking past another recruit and with the back of your hand hitting the head of his penis. I established early on that I didn't play that way either. I said loudly, "These are my family jewels, and they are off limits to anyone else except my wife!" Sometimes thumbtacks were placed under the thin seat cushions on which several of the new recruits sat. I had to call them out on that. I was respected most of the time. I was called a few names, but none that was racial—at least none that I heard.

We went through the curriculum and finally got through the firearms training, which was not one of my strengths. I did pass—barely—but, like some others, didn't get any medal or recognition for my passing.

Our firearms instructor told us once, "It's not as important to hit your human target the first shot. Just get the first shot off. By the time the suspect checks to see if he's been hit, you can then focus more on the second shot. These .357s make enough noise that he'll think he's been hit."

I always managed to get the first shot off. But the second was not much better.

In 1954 (and until 1964), the only place downtown where Black folks could eat was Kresge's on the northeast corner of 12th and Main. My experiences twelve years earlier when I was a kid going to Kresge's still resonated with me. Never again would I stand up and eat a segregated hot dog and drink a segregated Coke—now that I was old enough to understand racism, segregation, and discrimination. No more.

So, I would bring my lunch to the academy. My twenty-eight fellow white cadets could fan out downtown and eat where their money would take them, if they were able to eat and get back to class by 1:00 p.m. Sometimes others would also bring their lunches. Many times when I was eating in the classroom by myself, Sergeant Canaday would join me.

"Can I Arrest Anyone?"

When I came on the department in 1954, a Black officer could arrest a white person, but just a few years earlier, that couldn't happen.

(When Lloyd DeGraffenreid Sr. joined the police department as a patrolman on September 1, 1948, he was one of the few officers, Black or white, who had earned a college degree. In fact, Black officers with college degrees outnumbered white officers with college degrees. I was the first Black officer who earned a college degree (1959) while a full-time police officer and, at the time, one of the few officers, Black or white, with a college degree.)

Lloyd tells the story that when he had met all the qualifications to enter the police academy, the final step was to be interviewed by the Board of Police Commissioners. At the conclusion of the interview, one of the board members asked him, "Lloyd, anything you want to ask us?"

Lloyd responded, "Yes. Can I arrest anybody?"

Lloyd said they looked shocked. They looked at each other and then looked back at him and said, "Lloyd, excuse us for a few minutes."

The sergeant who had escorted him in now escorted him out and offered him a seat in the adjoining office. About fifteen minutes later, the phone on the sergeant's desk rang. The sergeant responded to the voice on the phone: "Yes, sir!" Then he turned to DeGraffenreid and said, "The commissioners will see you again now."

The sergeant opened the door for DeGraffenreid, and he entered and sat down again.

The same commissioner said, "Lloyd, yes, you can arrest anyone. Have a great career."

Before Lloyd's question, Blacks could not arrest whites, as I mentioned. From all indications, Lloyd's question changed at least that phase of the race culture for Black officers who were on the department at the time and then for me and for others that followed. I wonder how long that racist tradition would have existed if Lloyd hadn't raised his question. Sometimes you have to raise a question, even if there is a refusal to answer. Fortunately, this time the question was answered fairly, and a bit of progress was made.

DeGraffenreid graduated from Benedict College in South Carolina in 1941. He enlisted in the United States Army and served from 1941 to 1945 and shortly afterward joined the Kansas City Police Department. He became the first African American detective sergeant. DeGraffenreid—"D," as he was affectionately called—was assigned to the vice unit. He was promoted to detective and the next year, after I left the department, to the rank of detective sergeant and assigned to the vice unit. He also was a supervisor in the homicide section. In July 1970, DeGraffenreid was the lead investigator in the assassination of Leon Jordan. Jordan was a founding member of the powerful Black organization Freedom, Inc., a political club. I had several conversations with "D" regarding the Jordan assassination case and told him who I had heard were Jordan's assassins, and not one had been charged by Jackson County Prosecutor Joe Teasdale.

"D" retired from the police department and was appointed director of the Jackson County Jail. He retired from that position after several years.

I had a chance to ride with "D" while I was in the academy. He was very bright, an all-around good cop. He didn't play white cops' games, like telling Black or ethnic jokes. And he warned me not to get caught up in those games. He said, "If you get close enough to be joking about race issues, name-calling, and so on, whites don't know when to stop and will leave the door open, intentionally or unintentionally, to say things to you anywhere and everywhere. Don't give them the option. Nigger jokes will be right around the corner."

He also warned me, more importantly, "Don't be a follower of the crowd and get messed up. The department needs you. It needs us. This department can't stay this racist way forever. It just might be your generation that takes us just a little closer to where we ought to be."

March 23, 2010, "D," although suffering from failing health issues, at my invitation, did attend and witnessed, along with his wife, Cleo, my swearing-in as police commissioner. DeGraffenreid passed in May of 2013. At the invitation of his wife, I spoke at his funeral service.

I wonder how long Black officers would have been unable to arrest whites who violated the law if Lloyd had not raised that question when he began his police career. Lloyd made it possible for me and other Black officers who came after me to continue to challenge the department's age-old racism and discrimination practices. On another occasion, "D" told me, "Don't give up on finishing your education. Remember, it's the road to progress here in the department and elsewhere." Yes, we all stand on the shoulders of those who've come before us. Even today we stand on Lloyd DeGraffenreid's shoulders.

"He's the Colored Boy Who Robbed Me!"

An interesting thing happened while I was still in the academy, maybe in the sixth week of training. One day, after our classes resumed after lunch, we were being given a lecture—I don't remember the subject or the officer lecturing. Sergeant Canaday was sitting by the door and someone knocked. A white officer in plain clothes whispered something to him. They both stepped outside the door. When Sergeant Canaday reopened the door, he beckoned for someone to join them outside the room. I responded along with several others seated with me in the front row: "Me?"

Sergeant Canaday narrowed the *me?*s down to me, so I joined him and the plainclothes detective. Sergeant Canaday introduced me to the detective and said the detective wanted me to assist in a downtown lunch hour situation.

The detective explained I could help in the investigation of a strong-arm robbery that had just occurred. A white woman was knocked down and robbed of her purse at 12th and Main by a young Negro male. The Negro was about my age, complexion, and build. He stated they had picked up a suspect and had two other Negro males in custody for other charges, and they were going to be used in a lineup with the suspect. They, too, were about the same age, complexion, and build as the suspect and me.

The detective asked me if I would join the other three for the lineup. He said the victim indicated she could positively identify the suspect from a lineup. Sergeant Canaday gave his approval if I wanted to do it. He asked if it was okay with me to be out of the class for fifteen or twenty minutes.

I said, "Yes, I'll do it." I thought this was a good opportunity for me to become known by folks in the various police units—this was the robbery unit. Plus, I thought it would be fun.

The detective and I took the stairs down from the fourth floor to the second. He engaged in small talk on the way down. "How do you like the academy? When does your class get out? Do you want to make a career of police work?"

Before I could completely answer his questions, we were on the second floor. Another detective met us just outside the "show-up room," and I was introduced. They prepped me on what I would be asked when I entered the show-up stage. The second detective escorted me to the holding cell just outside the show-up room and I joined the other three Black men.

All four of us were near the same age. I was twenty-two. I had the feeling that we all knew each other; if not personally, we had at least seen each other around. There were only two Black high schools in Kansas City, Missouri, so if you went to high school in Kansas City, you had pretty much seen everybody somewhere. These three whom I joined in the holding cell thought I had done something even though I had not been in jail on the eighth floor with them.

The two non-suspects were not told why they were in the lineup. Only the suspect and I knew why we were there. The suspect was mumbling to us that he was accused of "robbing some old white lady downtown at noon today. I was just walking. They stopped me in the alley and jumped on me for nothing."

Finally, the moment had come. We were marched out on stage together, standing almost at attention, under incredibly bright, nearly blinding lights. You could not see anyone, although you knew they were out there looking at you. (An earlier tour of the headquarters for the cadets included the show-up room, but I was now experiencing it from quite a different vantage.)

We were told, "Number One, step forward. Say your name. Your age. Turn to the right. Face the wall. Turn left. Face the front. Step back." Numbers Two, Three, and Four went through the same routine. I was Number Three.

We were then ordered back into the holding cell. I can't recall whether the others were taken to an elevator or what, but the same detective came and got me out of the holding cell. I think the other two thought I was the suspect. He guided me into an interrogation room. On the way, he asked, "Alvin, where were you during the noon hour?"

I told him, "I was eating my lunch in our classroom with Sergeant Canaday."

He looked a little startled. He said, "Sit here. I'll be right back." He left and closed the door. In about fifteen minutes, he returned. He said, "Come with me."

We went into the show-up room. When I walked in ahead of the detective, the woman began screaming, "That's him! He's the one who knocked me down and stole my pocketbook!" She was screaming hysterically and crying.

She had run to a corner opposite me, all drawn up as though I was going to attack her in the room with at least three white police officers present. The detective placed his hand on my chest, indicating for me to stand where I was. He walked over to the woman and tried to quiet her.

I was still standing near the door, thinking, *What the hell? What are all these white detectives thinking?* I was scared now. Then I thought back real quick. "Thank God! I was in the classroom eating lunch with a white sergeant!"

The detective told her, "Ma'am, this is police cadet Alvin Brooks. It couldn't have been him. He was in the building eating his lunch with his sergeant all during the lunch hour."

The woman looked as though she had seen a ghost. She began to cry again hysterically. She kept trying to say she was sorry. The woman tried to walk toward me but hesitated and backed up. I was glad she did. I really didn't want to hear her or see her anymore.

The lead detective thanked me for helping. I took the stairs back to the fourth floor. I walked in the hallway for a minute, then went to the toilet and looked in the mirror and saw tears in my eyes. I washed my face. I stood before the mirror for a minute or two. Exhaled. Thanked God.

As I was leaving the restroom, several of my classmates were coming in. They were on break.

I started back to the classroom but was stopped by Sergeant Canady and the officer who had been lecturing when I had left. Sergeant Canaday must have told the other officer why I was out of class. They both asked me what happened. I told them, "That woman down there identified me in show-up!"

Sergeant Canaday said that the detective "came up here and asked if I knew where you were during the lunch hour, and I told him you were sitting there eating your lunch at your desk while I sat at my desk eating mine. And that we were talking as we ate. He said the victim had identified you as the one who knocked her down and snatched her purse. I told him no way. And if he wanted me to come down and tell her, I would."

I told him the detective brought me back into the show-up room and she "tried to apologize through tears." I told the sergeant, "Thanks, Sergeant."

The rest of my day was not good. I almost asked Sergeant Canady if I could check out for the day. In fact, he asked me if I would be okay. He said, "Alvin, I know how you feel.

I'm pissed like you are." I'm sure he saw the expression on my face when I had come back to class and was approached by our instructor and him.

I said to myself, "No, Sergeant, you don't know how I feel, because if I hadn't been with you, I'd be in jail with those other three brothers."

The next day, Sergeant Canady mentioned this incident in class. Most of my classmates laughed. Sergeant Canady halted the laughter. He told the class, "What happened to Alvin is not a laughing matter. That's the way sometimes folks get accused and go to prison when someone claims to 'give positive ID.'"

During the break, several of my classmates came up and apologized. Others wanted to know more about what happened. I told them I didn't want to discuss it any more at this time. Maybe later.

While Still a Recruit, I'm Assigned to a Court-Ordered Newly Integrated Swope Park Swimming Pool

In 1951, a lawsuit brought by three African Americans, Esther Williams, Joseph Moore, and Lena Smith, challenged the segregation of Kansas City's Swope Park swimming pool. The park board argued that the Paseo Park pool for the Black community, 17th and Paseo Boulevard, called the Bath House, was equal to the Swope Park pool. It closed the Swope Park pool in 1952 to avoid integration.

Thurgood Marshall, then chief attorney for the NAACP, who won *Brown v. Board of Education* of Topeka in 1954 and who in 1967 became the first Black US Supreme Court justice, came here to argue the case.

The Fourteenth Amendment to the US Constitution was the deciding factor that led Federal District Judge Albert Ridge to rule in favor of the three plaintiffs. Howard Sachs, who later became federal district judge for the Western District of Missouri, was then Judge Ridge's clerk and did considerable background research on the case. The judge ruled that the Black swimming pool at 17th and Paseo was not equal to the Swope Park pool under the Fourteenth Amendment requiring equal protection under the law.

Judge Ridge's ruling was handed down in June 1954. The Swope Park pool reopened. Fearing violence between white and Black swimmers, the police department placed a large contingent of police officers at the opening of the pool. Since there was no violence or disturbance through the month of June, it was decided to withdraw the contingency of officers from the pool until after the Fourth of July. It was thought that just one Black officer could manage the swimming pool for the rest of the summer through Labor Day.

It must have been the middle of July when my class had completed firearms training. Sergeant Canaday approached me just before the other officers were relieved of duty at the pool. He said that Lieutenant Warren, who handled the assignments at the pool, told him he would like to assign me to the Swope Park pool duty for the balance of the Sundays and Labor Day, when the pool was closed for the season. Sergeant Canaday noted that everyone in my class had passed the firearms training and were carrying our weapons and had their police ID. He said I would have to go to the supply room and be fitted for my uniform. He would assign me a car with a special radio number. My hours on Sundays would be from 4:00 p.m. to the closing of the pool at 9:00 p.m. I would still be responsible for attending all classes at the academy until graduation in September. Sergeant Canaday told me to see Lieutenant Warren for further instructions. That I did.

Lieutenant Warren said he had followed me through the academy and his impression of my demeanor and maturity was corroborated by Sergeant Canaday. Both felt I would do a good job at the Swope pool. He further said that I would fit in better with both Black and white youth because of my youth. Although the other Black officers were experienced, the age gap between them and the pool patrons was a concern. He also said he didn't think any of the older Negro officers would accept the assignment. Lieutenant Warren also said that I would not have a supervisor—that I'd be on my own—but if I ever needed advice or assistance, I could call the dispatcher for a sergeant or call him. He gave me his radio number and home phone number.

I started my assignment Sunday, August 1. I spent most of the five hours of my assignment at the swimming pool. But Blacks still could not rent boats at the lagoon—or horses or bicycles—because Judge Ridge's decision did not go beyond the swimming pool. Other parts of the park were not included and were still segregated. Groups of white youths would attack Black youths on the "Swinging Bridge," which spanned the Little Blue River if the Black young people were outnumbered by the white young people. Blacks could picnic and congregate at only one of the many shelter houses: Shelter House #5, which somebody named "Watermelon Hill." So, my patrol area was officially limited.

But I took advantage of the assignment and patrolled over to Shelter House #5, just across from the zoo. There was lots of food, drinking, and gambling. Folks were glad to see me. They didn't know I was still in the academy.

I was greeted by those I knew and those I didn't know with surprise, delight, and respect. They were startled to see a Black officer patrolling out of the Black area and in what was still a white park.

When I drove up, I always responded to such reception with, "Thank you, brothers! I appreciate that!" Everyone would laugh. If anyone really got out of line (like cursing) while I was there, someone would caution them, "Hey, you'all, respect Brooks! Check yourselves!"

Detective Sylvester Young was working vice. He heard that there was a young Black officer assigned to the swimming pool. He came out and introduced himself. Man, he was a sharp dresser, from head to feet! I imagined myself becoming a detective one day and dressing like Detective Young. He asked me to call him just "Syl," not "Detective Young" or "Mr. Young."

Sometimes he would get into the car with me and have me drive through other parts of the park. We'd see the all-white park rangers. Most of the time they wouldn't speak, even when they came by the pool. They looked at us in a very strange way when we rode around the white shelter houses.

I was apprehensive. I knew my assignment and what Lieutenant Warren had told me. Syl said, "Don't worry about those white asses. If they say anything, I'll handle it. They know better than to fuck with me—and you're with me. That means you, too."

Syl had been on the force, I believe he said, since 1948. I wasn't even out of the academy. I respected him, but I told him that I didn't want to go into the all-white areas just for that reason, and I remembered what the lieutenant had told me. Syl understood. Syl shared with me a great many of the "dos and don'ts" as they related to the department because of racism. But he always said, "Keep yourself clean. Do your job and don't let anyone lure you into some bullshit, whether they be Black or white. Fuck 'em when you're right."

On Labor Day, the last day for the pool to be open, I reported to Swope Park at noon and stayed until closing.

I never had to make an arrest, although there were numerous fights and arguments; but if I happened on the scene, I was always given respect. I was a "kid" to many older adults. I never tried to prove it different but accepted it as a compliment.

I did call for the police car that rode Swope Park when there were auto accidents. A couple times, I called the dispatcher for the district car and an ambulance for serious injuries. Most were caused by white drivers. Interestingly, I never saw police cars in and around the swimming pool area except when I called the dispatcher regarding an automobile accident.

My colleagues at the academy always questioned me every Monday when I returned to the academy.

Someone recently sent me a newspaper clipping from the *Kansas City Star* during my assignment at the Swope Park swimming pool. It stated that "Negro police officer Alvin Brooks was the only police assigned to the Swope Park swimming pool through Labor Day," and noted that there were no reports of any confrontation between the races.

This is true, but it is also true that the Black kids and the white kids didn't mix. The Black youths gathered at one end of the pool and the white youths at the opposite end. When a member of either group dived from the diving board, they would swim back to their respective group. They were in the same pool, but they didn't socialize together.

They could not ignore each other, but they did their best to avoid each other. Near Labor Day both groups grew, but there was still obvious separation. Both Black and white parents and other adults often outnumbered the youths.

Blacks did not come in large numbers; some probably didn't know they could now come to the pool. But maybe the main reason was that their parents didn't let them come. They may have thought, *If the whites don't want us, then we don't wanna be there.*

"Be Careful, Son, Allowing Someone to Come into Your Life. You Never Know Their Intentions"

In August 1954, I was still in the police academy and received an envelope addressed to me from the Kansas City School District with another envelope and letter inside with this inquiry: "I'm trying to locate a young man named Alvin Lee Brooks, born May 3, 1932. I hope you can help me."

The letter was dated and signed: Thomascine Davis, #9 Josiah, San Francisco, California. My last known address was 2632 Park, where I lived my two years as a student at the all-Black Lincoln Junior College (remember there were two junior colleges and both the Black and the white junior colleges were under the Kansas City School District, as I recall).

Whoever received the letter at the school district just looked up my address and forwarded the letter on to me at my last known address. Several days later, I decided to write to Mrs. Davis. Shortly after she received my letter, she wrote me back, telling me how happy she was that I had received her letter and replied. She then went on to make inquiries about "Mr. and Mrs. Brooks. How were they?" She made some other inquiries about my parents. I told her I didn't have answers to some of her questions. After three or four letters back and forth, I approached my father at his home in October and told him about this woman in San Francisco who had written the school district and someone at the district office had forwarded her letter to me. I told him this woman was asking a lot of questions about him and mother and I didn't know what she was talking about. My dad asked me her name. I told him, "Thomascine Davis."

My dad jumped. He looked shocked and almost broke into tears. He looked as though he had seen a ghost. I could see his eyes well up. Kinda choked up, he immediately responded, "You know, son, you never know what folks' intentions are. People want to meddle in your family. I wouldn't continue to write them."

I told him okay, I understood. But I saw and heard my dad and it troubled me. I left. When I got home, I told Carol what I had told my father and how he reacted when I mentioned the woman's name and that I felt something was wrong.

Neither of us could figure why my father reacted as he did when he heard the name Thomascine Davis.

I took my dad's advice for about a month, although I continued to get letters from Mrs. Davis. Then I began to receive letters inquiring about me. Was I married? Did I have children? What kind of work did I do?

Carol and I, over my dad's suggestions, answered her questions. That I was married. My wife's name was Carol. We wrote her that we had three children and gave their names and ages and that I was a police officer. This was October 1954.

In the next letter from Mrs. Davis she wrote, "I hope I'll know my grandchildren better than I know my son." Carol and I read her letter over and over again. What did all this mean? That Estelle Brooks was not my mother? What about my dad, Cluster Brooks? Carol and I wrestled with whether we should say something to my dad. Should I respond to Mrs. Davis and get some clarification on what she said and what she meant?

We decided not to say anything to Dad. At least until Mrs. Davis, who was claiming to be my mother, gave some further explanation. As I remember, I didn't respond to Mrs. Davis's last letter right away. I had told her early on that my mother, Estelle Brooks, had passed in 1950.

Thomascine said in one of her November letters, or an early December letter, that she was married to a James H. Davis, that he owned his own business and she was an independent hairdresser. She went on to say in another letter that she hoped to come to Kansas City, to see me, Carol, and "my grandchildren sometime soon."

We still hadn't said anything to my father. Carol and I did wonder just how old Mrs. Davis was in relationship to my father, Cluster. God, we had so many questions!

The first part of December, we talked to her on the telephone—Carol, me, and Mrs. Davis. Carol and I shared the one phone between us. We didn't really know what questions to ask although it seemed as though we had thousands.

Again, Mrs. Davis said she would "love to come to Kansas City before the end of the year." She asked if that was okay. She couldn't see the expression on Carol's face and on my face when she asked that question. We paused for a minute, looked at one other, nodded, and said yes. She said that she would get back with me soon.

The last question was about the weather. We explained it was December and it was cold. Sometimes snow, sleet, and freezing rain. She described what clothes she would have to buy because they didn't have too much cold weather, far from what I had described in Kansas City. She said San Francisco was mostly fog and dampness in the morning. But it cleared up midmorning, and then the fog returned later in the day. It was cool enough to wear a light coat or a sweater.

It's Graduation Time—Time to Play Cops and Robbers, 1954

It was graduation time for the 44th Recruit School Police Academy of the Kansas City, Missouri, Police Department. The ceremony was held at the KMBC Playhouse, 11th and Central Street, on Monday, September 20, 1954. Of course, I was the only Black out of twenty-nine to graduate.

I had received my assignment after sixteen weeks of training. I also had been observing problems of segregation, discrimination, and the root of it all, racism. Of all the members in my recruit class, I was the only one who knew where I was going to be assigned. The only thing I didn't know was what shift. As it turned out, I was assigned the dogwatch shift (midnight to 8:00 a.m.).

I rode relief. I was on the black-colored wagon called the "Black Mariah." Other police departments around the country also called their black wagons "Black Mariah." I read that the history of the name related to a Black woman in New York City who was into gambling and prostitution. Her name was Mariah, and because she was arrested so much, the black wagon that was used to cart her to jail was called Mariah, eventually being called the Black Mariah.

On numerous occasions, two Black officers were assigned to ride together in each of the two districts and the wagon on the same shifts. One interesting note: if the lieutenant in charge of a particular shift had more than the required number of Black officers to cover the two districts and the wagon, the extra Black officers were sent home—rather than having Black officers riding with a white officer or a Black officer riding in a white district. But there were times when a white officer was assigned to ride with a Black officer. Remember there were three patrol stations at the time: Headquarters (downtown), Sheffield Station, and 63rd Street Station. Black officers were allowed to work only from Headquarters.

I consider it an honor that while I was still a "rookie" cop or year or two beyond that, these men were assigned to me for training: William Bumpus, Leroy Swift, William Hayes, Lester Duke, and Henry Scott.

Now a Police Officer, I Witness Police Brutality, 1954

I had only been out of the academy for about sixty days and I was riding the wagon—and riding the midnight shift—when I encountered an act of police brutality. I was dispatched on a call to Patrol District 125 as backup.

I was to investigate an alarm at a clothing store called the Store Without a Name, on the southwest corner of Truman Road and Prospect. I got there before the District car. I was driving the wagon. I got out of my wagon, and as I looked through the window, I could see that a portion of the ceiling was hanging, indicating someone had come down from the roof to enter the building.

I shined my flashlight across the store from the outside. There were numerous places a person or persons could stay out of sight from someone outside. As I shined my flashlight across the store, I spotted a figure, a Black male, running across the rear of the store just for a flickering second. I notified the police dispatcher that I had seen a subject inside. About that time the District officer arrived, and almost at the same time, an ADT (American District Telegraph) company security guard also arrived. The security guard was able to open the front door. He tried to find the light switch and he deactivated the alarm system. The sergeant appeared. He indicated he would stand by the door. Rather than wait until the ADT security person found the light switch, my fellow officer, who was white, decided to begin his search. Just as the suspect disappeared behind several clothing racks, he shouted, "There's the bastard!" and fired two shots. I heard glass break.

Almost as if orchestrated, the lights came on all over the store. Another voice hollered, "Don't shoot! I'm coming out with my hands up!" A young Black male came in sight with his hands in the air walking toward me. He saw me and said, "Mr. Brooks, please don't shoot me. I ain't got nothing. My hands are up." I ordered him to back up to me. The sergeant heard the shots and could see me and the burglar. He held his gun on the suspect while I handcuffed him. About that time the District officer appeared, gun in hand, and ran up to the handcuffed burglar. He struck him across the head with the butt of his revolver and cursed him, "You Black son of a bitch!"

The sergeant hollered at him, saying, "What are you doing? What the hell's wrong with you?" I think he spoke that way only because I was present.

The District officer was angry—and embarrassed, too—because he had seen his own reflection in a full-length mirror and mistaken it for seeing the burglar. I wanted to laugh so bad in his face and tell him a few things, but since I was driving, I headed toward the wagon with my prisoner and told the sergeant that I was taking him to General Hospital #2, the "colored hospital."

My prisoner had sustained a bad cut and blood was everywhere. I had snatched a couple pieces of clothing off one of the racks and held them up to his head. The District officer and the sergeant back inside the store with the ADT security officer were watching and laughing.

I took the handcuffs off the suspect and had him hold the pieces of clothing to his head. The blood was not stopping. The sergeant came out and told me, "Al, get the hell out of here and take him to the hospital."

I helped the suspect into the rear of the wagon.

By that time, the officer and the ADT person were at the rear of the wagon. The District officer asked, with a small notebook in hand, "What's your fuckin' name?" The suspect mumbled his name. I repeated it to the officer, closed the door, got into the wagon, and headed with siren blaring to General Hospital #2. The prisoner was crying and moaning. I stopped a few blocks away from the scene and let the prisoner sit in the front seat with me. Occasionally, I would turn off the siren and address the suspect by name. "I've only got a few more blocks to go."

He responded, "I'm doing okay, Mr. Brooks, just hurt a little and still bleeding."

I turned on the siren again and in about ten minutes I was at the emergency entrance to the hospital. I got out, opened the door, and helped him as we went into the hospital's emergency room. There were several other patients there, but none seemed to have life-threatening conditions. A nurse, two orderlies, and a doctor approached my prisoner. The pieces of clothing were blood-soaked, as were his clothes. The nurse asked what happened. He said, "A police officer hit me with his gun."

They sat him in a chair. He was still bleeding profusely, with blood running into his eyes and mouth. The clothes were removed, and a stack of large compresses were pressed against his forehead and the left side of his head. The police officer on duty came and I turned the suspect over to him. I told him the suspect was to be held for the burglary detectives, but I thought the District officer would probably be over to the hospital to question him. I found out from one of the orderlies that the suspect was twenty years old and lived around the corner from the store he attempted to burglarize. I told him, "Young brother, you could have been killed back there by a bullet or beaten to death. I'll check on you."

He said, "Thank you, Mr. Brooks. Could you go to my house and tell my mother what happened and where I am? We don't have a phone and she's there by herself, probably waiting up for me." He started crying as they were still trying to stop the bleeding. When they removed the gauze to see if the bleeding had stopped, I could see two large gashes above his eye and on the side of his head. He gave me his mother's name and address.

Just as I was driving out of the emergency entrance, the other officer drove up with the sergeant following behind him. I didn't say anything to either of them. I headed to the young man's residence. It was about three in the morning. I knocked on the door and said, "Police officer." His mother came and opened the door. I identified myself and told her what had happened and where her son was. She started crying, saying, "I knew something was wrong. He stays home most of the time and he's never out this late. I just knew something was wrong. He left walking his girlfriend home 'round on Benton. I expected him to come right back like he always does."

I told her to call the burglary unit in the morning and they could tell her what he was going to be officially charged with. I also told her she probably would not be able to see him at the hospital, but she could after he had been charged and taken to the county jail. I also told her if she or her son wished to file a complaint regarding the officer striking him while he was handcuffed, she should go to police headquarters and ask to speak to the captain. She thanked me and I left.

What happened worried me as a young Black man. I was just a couple of years older than the burglar. Why would my colleague strike a handcuffed suspect? Because he was Black. I understood why the white officer shot twice from his gun because in the dark he saw himself reflected in the mirror and thought it was the suspect with a gun in his hand. At roll call the next night, our sergeant made mention of what happened the night before when the officer shot up the mirror in the store. Everyone had a big laugh. Nothing was mentioned about the District officer's behavior and the handcuffed suspect.

The Blind Leading the Blind, 1954

It must have been early December 1954 when I got a call from Sergeant Canaday. He told me, "Al, there's a colored recruit named William Bumpus in the 45th recruit class who wants to meet you and ride out with you some weekends. Is that okay with you? His class has gone through firearms training, so he's allowed to carry a firearm."

I said, "Sure, Sarge, that's fine with me."

"Okay, I see you're working third shift this weekend. I'll have him give you a call about seven o'clock from the garage. That'll give him a chance to go home and eat a little something. I might let him out a little earlier. You can pick him up there. Thanks, Al."

"You're welcome, Sarge."

When I got to the police garage about 6:45, Bumpus was there. We introduced ourselves and hit it off right then—a relationship that would last thirty-five years.

First, we had to decide what to call each other. Me: "Al. Alvin. Or Brooks." He: "William. Bill. Or Bumpus."

I came to find out that it was not Bumpus who asked about riding out with me. It was Sergeant Canaday who suggested he ride out with me after describing me to Bumpus, mentioning my age, demeanor, and how I had gained the respect of my classmates. I had some real concerns, though, because I had myself just come out of the academy only ninety days earlier. But I was happy to have Bumpus ride out with me. We were the same age. I was born May 3, 1932; Bumpus was born May 24, 1932. May 24 was the birthday of my wife, Carol, but her birth year was 1935.

Bumpus didn't have any parts of a police uniform because they had not yet been issued to his class. The other few officers who rode along with experienced officers wore their own clothes. Bumpus wanted to look like a police officer when he rode with me, so he borrowed my second uniform, since he and I were close to the same size at that time. I even lent him an old second holster for the .357 Magnum weapon that he also was assigned.

It wasn't long before all the Black officers knew Bumpus by name. They made fun of his last name. Some called him Bill. Some called him Bumpus. After several rides with me, the Black officers referred to Bumpus and me as "the blind leading the blind," meaning neither one of us knew what we were doing. But it became more interesting.

Bumpus not only rode weekends but also began to ride out with me almost every evening after class was over. He'd go home and eat, and I would pick him up, and he would ride with me from about 6:00 p.m. until midnight, and then he'd be in class the next morning at eight.

After a while, when I got a call from the dispatcher in my district where two one-man cars were to be dispatched, and the dispatcher would ask if I was a two-man crew, I'd respond yes. Then they would give us the call rather than send another car. During the several weeks Bumpus rode with me, we made several "good arrests," as they were called. "Robbery in progress," the dispatcher would say. We were, most times, near the scene of the robbery and caught the suspect in the act. We managed to disarm suspects just by saying, "Police! Drop the gun! You're under arrest!" It worked more than once.

I remember the sandwich shop, Agnos, at 12th and Forest, that was shaped something like a bus. Only whites were permitted to eat inside. Blacks could only order from the service window on the sidewalk. That included Black police officers. One evening, a white patron inside was robbing the place. Of course, there were no cell phones, but there was a pay phone outside at the corner of the business. A patron inside eased outside and called the police.

Bumpus and I were at the Gateway Boxing Center at 22nd and Tracy and got the call: "Holdup in progress. The sandwich shop, 12th and Forest. Calling car 123." The dispatcher described the suspect as a white male, armed with a gun. I used the siren until I got to about 13th and Tracy, then no siren, no red lights. The caller was still standing by the outdoor pay phone and saw us with the lights out. He pointed inside. We could see the back of one of the employees with his hands in the air. Bumpus took the shotgun out of the rack. We both left the car and made it to the corner of the shop just as the suspect exited the door with gun in hand. There was a car parked right at the corner where I took cover.

Bumpus was at the corner of the building by the pay phone, and I yelled, "Police! Drop the gun now!" He could partially see both of us. I again said, "Drop the gun now!" He had the gun in one hand and a brown paper bag with money in the other hand. I hollered, "Bumpus, don't shoot him!"

The suspect yelled, "Please, don't shoot, don't shoot!" and dropped the gun and the bag with the money. I ordered him against the building. Bumpus picked up the suspect's gun, a .32-caliber revolver. Bumpus handcuffed him with my handcuffs.

Because he took the time to rob several patrons in addition to the two employees, we were luckily able to get there before he left.

The sergeant and several other cars came to the scene after we had made the arrest. I was afraid that was the last time Bumpus would be able to ride with me because he was not officially out of the academy. Plus, I thought I would be reprimanded for allowing Bumpus to become involved in the holdup call. When the sergeant walked over to the police car where Bumpus was standing with a shotgun still in hand, he looked in and said something to the suspect as I was talking to the robbery victims. The sergeant then walked up to me and said, "Good catch, Al. The robbery detectives are on the way."

The next night at roll call, the lieutenant came and congratulated me. He never mentioned Bumpus. I don't think he even knew Bumpus was on the arrest with me. I told Bumpus not to tell Sergeant Canaday and his classmates what had happened the night before.

"Alvin, This Is Your Mother. Can You Come Get Me?"

Let me return to Christmas Day 1954. I was working what we called the "dogwatch" shift, midnight to 8:00 a.m. I had worked Christmas Eve or Saturday, Christmas morning. As I recall, it was cold that Christmas morning—clear, but cold. But after my relief brought me home, Carol, Ronall, and Estelle were up and waiting for me upstairs. The baby, Carrie Lynn, was still asleep. Carol wouldn't let Ronall and Estelle come downstairs until I got home. When I opened the door, they hollered like a duet, "Daddy!"

I went upstairs and hugged and kissed them along with Carol. "Merry Christmas! I love you!"

They responded, now as a trio. "I love you!" Ronall was three years old, soon to be four January 12. Estelle was two, soon to be three May 11. And Carrie Lynn was five weeks old, born November 17. Carol said, "Now that Daddy's home, let's go down and see what Santa Claus brought you." I had taken all of my police uniform off except my pants and slipped into my house shoes.

Downstairs we went. WOW! Ronall went directly to his tricycle. Estelle to her doll. Carol was carrying baby Carrie Lynn. Thanking God, I prayed. Carol and I exchanged gifts. What we gave each other, I don't remember. But we never missed a Christmas exchanging gifts until her illness in 2011. The phone rang constantly—family and friends wishing us Merry Christmas. Carol and I made some calls in between calls to us.

Then there was THAT CALL! The phone rang. I answered, "Merry Christmas. Brooks residence." Before the person on the other end could say anything, I heard in the background, "TWA flight . . . United flight . . . Braniff . . ." Then the voice responded,

"Merry Christmas to you! This is your mother. I'm at the airport. Can you come and get me?"

I responded, "Yes! I'm on the way! Be there shortly!"

Carol asked, "Who was that?"

I said, "My mother, Thomascine. She's at the airport." We were both ecstatic. I slipped on a pair of jeans, dressed quick but warm. I told Ronall and Estelle that I was going to the airport and would be back with a surprise. That didn't mean too much to them. The tricycle and doll had their attention.

So off I went to the Kansas City Municipal Airport just across the Broadway Bridge in Clay County, but the Kansas City part. I parked in front of the terminal and left my blinkers on. As I got out of my car, I said to myself, "God, I don't know what my mother looks like." As I entered, I began to scan the crowd. Thank God, there weren't too many Black folks traveling by plane that Christmas.

There she was! Fur hat, fur coat to match across her arm. A red two-piece suit, jacket and skirt, and a white blouse with a long red scarf tied into a bow hanging down to her waist.

I knew that was my mother. She looked like me. Or I looked like her. I ran to her and her toward me. We both cried. I don't remember what we said to each other while we were embracing there in the middle of the airport terminal. I grabbed her luggage, took her by the arm and led her to my car, opened the door for her, and placed her luggage in the trunk. Small talk and pleasantries occupied the time until we reached my home. When we arrived, Carol must have been looking out for us because she was standing in the front door holding Carrie. Estelle was standing beside Carol with her doll. I led the way with luggage in hand and Carol opened the door. I stepped aside so Thomascine could go in first.

She said to Carol, "Well, Carol, I'm Thomascine. And this cute little girl is Estelle?" Carol and Thomascine embraced each other. Thomascine stooped down and picked Estelle up, doll and all. Ronall was on his tricycle riding through the house. Carol called Ronall. I took Thomascine's fur piece and her luggage upstairs to our bedroom. We were giving up our bed to her. We were going to sleep with the children. When I returned downstairs, the questions were already in progress. Thomascine was now holding Carrie, who was wide awake. There were no questions about adoption or about my father, Cluster. Carol and I were very careful for some reason with just what to ask.

Thomascine wasn't. She asked about my mother, Estelle, and my daddy, Cluster. Carol announced that she had begun cooking Christmas dinner, turkey and all the dressing, plus everything else that was on the menu. Carol said, "We are expecting Mr. Brooks over near dinner time."

I said, "Don't be surprised if he's in his sin." That meant if he had been drinking, he might say anything.

Thomascine wanted to go to church if it wasn't too late in the day. "Alvin, is there a Catholic church near here? I would like to attend a Christmas Day Mass if there's one near and it's not too late." I said, "Holy Spirit Catholic Church, a little mission church, is just across the street from where Ronall attends Garfield Circle Day Care. It's just five minutes from here. Come on, I'll drive you around there. I've never been there. We go to St. Joseph Catholic Church, which is about fifteen minutes from here. But they have a 9:00 a.m. Mass."

Thomascine went upstairs and changed her clothes. Carol said she would go with us except it would take too much time to get the kids dressed. Plus, she had food cooking on the stove. Thomascine told her she would come back and help her. When we got to church, there was a small group of people just arriving. Mass started at 11:00 a.m.

When we were back home, Thomascine kept her word. She changed clothes again and pitched in and helped Carol in the kitchen. I sat there in the kitchen and we talked about everything, including my mother Estelle's death and our young marriage. My attending college. My being a police officer. Thomascine talked about how she got from Memphis to San Francisco and her marriage to Jimmy Davis. She did tell us that her birthday was August 6, 1917.

She asked if we could hold off telling Mr. Brooks who she was until she felt the time was right. I had told her how Dad reacted when I mentioned her name to him last fall. She asked if I could introduce her just as "Davis," no need to say "Mrs.," just a friend of mine and Carol's. "Sometime after dinner, I'll ask Mr. Brooks if he knows who I am. I know he won't. I'll tell him." Carol and I agreed.

The cooking was on with Thomascine helping but mostly talking to Ronall and Estelle and holding the bottle for Carrie, "baby talking" as she held her.

Carol said to me, "Honey, why don't you go up and take a nap? I'll send the kids to wake you up when dinner is ready. You have to go to work tonight, don't you? Mr. Brooks will be here in time to eat with us. I told him what time we were having dinner when I went out to see him yesterday."

Thomascine said, "I'll be here with you, if you don't mind, until New Year's Eve." We all laughed. "So, there's plenty time for us to play catch-up. What—at least twenty years or more?" We laughed. I excused myself and headed upstairs.

My Mother, Thomascine, Asked My Dad, "Mister Brooks, Do You Know Who I Am?"

Carol sent Ronall upstairs to wake me up. I was not asleep. More like nodding. I had Thomascine on my mind. How was she my mother? And what about my mother, Estelle? And Daddy? So many questions. I told Ronall to tell his mother I would be down shortly.

Thomascine was setting the table. Carol was placing the food on the table including the turkey, chitterlings, and ham. And all else. Just as we sat down, the front door opened and what do you think? There stood Cluster Brooks. Yes! In his sin. He spoke loudly. "Merry Christmas." The three of us said, "Merry Christmas to you!"

Ronall wanted Daddy to see his tricycle. Daddy asked him to let him see him ride. Carol played along as Thomascine had asked.

"Mr. Brooks, this is a friend of ours, Miss Davis, who stopped by for dinner."

My dad responded in his alcohol slur. "Hello there, Miss Davis. Happy to see you." Carol told my dad he had just come in time and we were ready to sit down and have dinner. Dad said he wasn't too hungry, but he would take "some of those chitterlings and corn on the cob."

We all sat down. I asked Thomascine if she would offer the prayer. She did. Carol took a plate and began to place on it what Dad had requested. She asked him if he wasn't going to wash his hands. He said, "My hands ain't dirty. I washed them before I left home." Carol kind of insisted. She walked to the kitchen sink. Turned on the water and told Daddy to "come on here, take this bar of soap. Mr. Brooks, your hands don't look clean to me. Looks like you've been working on your car." He didn't respond one way or the other but got up, walked to the sink, and took the soap from Carol while she turned the water on. Daddy barely washed his hands and reached for the towel she had in her hand. Carol wasn't ready for him to use the towel yet. There was still soap on his hands because he hadn't really washed them. He managed to get hold of the towel Carol was holding back. When he wiped on the towel, the towel turned oil-greasy black. Carol called him back to the sink.

We were ready to eat. Ronall was sitting on two telephone books so he could be high enough to eat at the table. Estelle was in her high chair. Finally, Carol and Daddy sat down. We all started eating. We talked about everything except who Miss Davis really was. Carol was dishing out the dessert to the kids, who had eaten their main course. Thomascine was holding Carrie. She turned to Daddy and said, "Mr. Brooks, do you know who I am?"

Daddy said in his alcohol voice, "Yeah! The boy said you were . . . mmmm, Davis."

She said, "Yes, Mr. Brooks. Alvin didn't tell you my first name. I'm Thomascine."

My dad kinda screamed. He literally jumped up and went up to his room upstairs that was his when he wanted to stay all night or when the weather was too bad to stay at the home where I grew up. He slammed the door behind him. He was crying loud enough that you could hear him from where we were sitting at the dining room table.

Thomascine followed him upstairs. When she opened the door where he was, he was crying so hard and desperately. We could hear Thomascine talking to him. Trying to quiet him down. After about an hour, Thomascine came out and back downstairs. Dad stayed up in his room for a while.

Ronall asked Thomascine, "What is wrong with Grandpa?" She didn't know what to say. The three of us looked at each other. I told Ronall that his grandpa was tired and went up to his room to rest. It was dark before Dad came out of his room and went straight to his car and drove off.

It was the kids' bedtime. Carol and Thomascine took them upstairs. Shortly afterward, Thomascine came back down. She said that my dad had told her that he and my mother, Estelle, had hoped they both would have been dead before I found out that they weren't my real parents. Before he said that, he asked her not to tell me that he wasn't my father, that he didn't have much more time to live, to wait until he was dead before she told him. She said she told him she couldn't do that because if I asked, she'd have to tell me. So, I asked her. "Well, who, then, is my father?" She said, "Your father is Wilbur Herring. I got pregnant while staying with my great-aunt in Miami, Florida. I was fourteen. He was seventeen. To this day I don't know whether he knows he has a son or that I got pregnant. I got sent to live with my other sister, Mozella, and brother-in-law, Willie, in North Little Rock, Arkansas, across from Mr. and Mrs. Brooks. I left you with them and returned to Memphis, where I was born. I needed to finish school."

For the next six days we talked about everything and everybody. But for some strange reason, we never got into details about my adoption. What relationship did she have with the Brookses? Had she talked to or seen my father since I was born?

I gave Thomascine a tour of Kansas City. She insisted that she and I should have our photo taken together. So, on December 27, we put on our Sunday best and went to the photography studio and had our photo taken together.

My dad was nervous when the three us were together three or four times before she left. He didn't know whether Thomascine had told me that he wasn't my birth father. I asked her a couple of days earlier what she wished for me to call her, Thomascine or Mother. She left that decision with me. The last day or two before she left, I called her "Mother." She cried. Carol called her Thomascine. She promised to try to locate my father for me when she got back home. I was anxious to know him.

It was New Year's Eve. My mother had an early morning flight, but after getting off work, I still had time to drive her to the airport. All of us piled in my car. When we got to the airport, I let them out and I went to park the car. I met them inside. Thomascine went to check in. We all sat and talked and talked about the beautiful week we had together. They announced her TWA flight. We all hugged and kissed. My mother and I cried as we did six days ago, almost in the same spot as when we met.

On the way back home Carol asked me, "What do you feel about Thomascine, now that she's come into your life?" I told Carol I accepted her to be my mother and understood as a fourteen-year-old, she was not capable of taking care of me. I believe she made the right decision since she wasn't accepted by Uncle Willie. Especially since she was not sure my father, Wilbur Herring, ever really knew that she was pregnant, much less that he had a son.

Carol asked if I felt comfortable calling her Mother. I said, "YES!" I reminded her we were just a year older than Thomascine and Wilbur when she got pregnant. We were fortunate and God blessed us. "First, because I knew you were pregnant, and I could take full responsibility as a father when you were fourteen and I was still seventeen. [I thought I would have to be twenty-one to be married without a parent's signature.] And that we had decided, without anyone's suggestion, that we were going to get married if your mother and my father would sign for you since you were underage. And we had lots of support, especially from your grandmother."

Carol reached over and took my hand and squeezed it as she was holding Carrie and said, "I love you, Alvin Brooks Gilder Herring." We both laughed. Ronall and Estelle were in the backseat giggling about something but didn't know what was going on or what we were talking about.

We had promised Mother that we would try to make it to San Francisco and see her and meet her husband, Jimmy Davis. Later that evening, Mother called and said she had made it home safely and thanked us for the best Christmas she had ever had.

"Let's Go! I Got the Stuff!"

Most of the officers didn't like to work the dogwatch shift, so I volunteered to work my rotation not only in December but also in January. Bumpus wanted to ride with me, and I agreed.

New Year's Day, about 2 a.m. we had an interesting incident. It was cold, sleeting, snow on the ground. We were just a few blocks south of Agnos Sandwich Shop and had turned into one of the alleys, behind one of the grocery stores. All of a sudden, a fellow jumped from behind the trash cans, opened the rear door of our police car, and got into the back seat of the police car. He said, "Let's go! Let's go! I got the stuff!" Bumpus jumped out and opened the back door of the car. When the dome light came on, the fellow looked up. "Oh shit," he said. "Man, I get caught every time I fuck up and steal something."

Bumpus and I looked at each other. The brother in the back seat had a money bag in his hand, some liquor, and some cigarettes. He admitted that he had burglarized the store we were in back of and that his getaway driver was supposed to come back and pick him up behind the store. He got so cold waiting he was trying to keep warm behind the trash cans until his ride came back. Bumpus searched him and I looked in the money bag. There were a couple hundred dollars there. The brother explained that he had just gotten out of prison for burglary a week ago. He had done three years. He was in prison over

Christmas and was not able to get anything for his wife and kids. He went out every day looking for work but had no luck. Bumpus and I went to Headquarters and booked him for burglary and he was to be held for the burglary unit. He asked Bumpus and me if we would go by his house and tell his wife what had happened. We did. We woke up his wife and teenage daughter. When we told her what had occurred, and what he was booked for, she said she knew something had happened because every day he went out looking for a job but was only able to find work with the farmers unloading their trucks at the City Market about four in the morning. She and her daughter began to cry. We asked if she had food in the house and if utilities and rent were paid. She said yes, that she and her daughter had part-time jobs. But the four other kids were too small to work. They were in school, as was the teenage daughter.

Several weeks later, after Bumpus had graduated from the academy, we followed the case together and approached a Black attorney, Joe Moore, to look into the husband's case. Sometime later, Joe reported back to me that he had talked to the prosecutor and mentioned that Bumpus and I were interested in helping this man. After pleading guilty, he was given probation. Brumpus and I were able to get him a job at the Sinclair Service Station at 18th and Brooklyn. We followed his affairs for a while and saw that he was still working at the service station.

The Pendergast and Mafia Days Were Not Over

I'll never forget—I was out of the academy and assigned to ride with 6'5", 270-pound veteran officer Omar Brown. We rode as a two-man crew. In other words, if we got a call that called for two cars with one officer each, Omar and I would handle the call without the second car. One Sunday we stopped at the delicatessen called Smokey Joe's at 9th and Brooklyn, several blocks from our District 123. We parked right in front of the business. Omar was driving. As I got out of the car, I saw a lot of people coming and going. People were leaving with beer in the open—some in sacks, but you could tell it was beer. Some had bottles of whiskey.

I thought a few minutes. Isn't today Sunday? No alcohol is sold on Sunday. That's the law. Folks were walking out of this place like it was New Year's Eve. I waited and let Omar go in first, and I followed.

"Good Sunday afternoon, Smokey," Omar said, as he walked past the cashier counter where a large-build white man was checking people out.

"Good afternoon, Officer Brown, how are you?" he said in broken English. By this time, Omar had reached a huge galvanized tank that was filled with watermelons and water and chunks of ice.

"I'm fine, Smokey. How much are your watermelons?" Omar said in one stretched-out breath.

"Oh, Officer Brown, go ahead and help yourself."

"How about this young cop, Smokey?" Omar asked.

"Yeah, Officer Brown. Sure, him, too."

I had my eyes on him and his steady line of customers who were buying beer, other liquors, cigarettes, and bread, but mostly beer. Some folks had their kids with them. Smokey never looked in our direction. Omar hollered, "Smokey, do you plug 'em?"

"Go ahead and help yourself, Officer Brown, and the young officer, too."

Omar pulled a knife out of the side of a wooden post beside the watermelon tank, fished down in the tank, and turned the watermelons over and over. He pulled one from under several others, brought it to the surface, and placed it on a small table where you could see others had plugged watermelons.

Omar took the big knife and dug into the melon he had picked out. He sunk the knife in the watermelon and made the shape of triangle, took the tip of the knife, and pulled the plug out. The plug was still on the tip of the knife. He took a bite. "Mmm, that's pretty damn good. Get you one of those big ones and plug it," Omar told me. I did as he did. We put the plugs back in place in the watermelons and headed for the door.

Oops, I was too far ahead of Omar. He was at the beer cooler. With a watermelon in one hand and two six-packs in the other, he caught up with me. "Thanks, Smokey," Omar said as we walked past him.

Smokey looked up at us as a customer was standing with several items on the counter in front of him, including a stack of six-packs. "Thank you, Officer Brown. Any time. You too, Officer," he said, looking directly at me.

I didn't say a word.

Omar said, "Hold on, let's put this stuff in the trunk." He unlocked the trunk after setting the beer down. I put my watermelon in the trunk, as did Omar. There was a blanket in the trunk. He told me, "Spread that blanket over those melons so they won't roll around back there." I did as he said.

We headed back to our district. As we turned the corner and headed south on Brooklyn, I asked Omar a question. "Omar, this is Sunday. How do those folks back there get away with selling liquor on Sunday when it's against the law?"

Omar replied, "Smokey is paying off the captain or somebody at Headquarters to sell on Sundays. It happens all over. So, we can't let the white folks get ahead of us now, can we?"

I said, "But they are so open with it. Our police car was parked right in front and people were coming and going like it was a weekday."

Omar headed right to his apartment in the 2400 block of Tracy on the southern edge of District 123. He said, "You're a young, clean, bright Black copper. You're educated. Stay clean, apply yourself. There won't be much change during my generation of cops, but with pressure from our community, the white folks will have to make some concessions. There's a good chance your generation just might begin to see some changes. It certainly hasn't happened during my time, except now we can arrest 'crackers,' like I give a goddamn."

We were now in front of Omar's apartment building. He owned the four-unit building. He got out and went to the trunk and took his watermelon and two six-packs out, slammed the trunk down, and said, "I'll be right back. Catch the radio if they call us."

I began to think about what had occurred an hour ago. I had participated in a "payoff situation," turning my head to law violations because someone up the chain of command was getting a big payoff. But I hadn't been on the force for more than six months. Who am I at the early stages of my police career to be another Serpico?

Omar returned to the car. I felt I had to ask Omar some further questions about what had gone on at Smokey's. "Omar, how widespread is the kind of activity like what's going on at Smokey's?"

"That shit's bothering you, ain't it?" Omar said.

Omar had been one of my training officers. *Oh shit,* I thought, *is Omar deep into this kind of illegal activity?* I was cautious with my response, not knowing where Omar stood.

"A little bit, Omar."

Omar interrupted me. "Church people know what's going on. Some of them are the first ones to go to Smokey's when they get out of church. The damn nigger ministers are saying nothing and doing nothing. What few Negro politicians there are can't or won't do anything. So where does that leave us Negro cops? So, let's ride the gravy train with these racist motherfuckers. They won't dare say anything to us because they think we got connections with the Negro power structure. We don't, but let them think it. Shit, Mick [one of the older officers, Detective Laymon Walker, gave several of us nicknames; mine was Mick], in one respect, I've exposed you to that shit, but on the other hand, I'd rather have done that than you trying to arrest folks in your district because there are Negroes paying some motherfucker up the ladder. At least you know now. You'll have to decide how you do police work in this environment. Those damn dagos damn near run our community. They're in with those fuckers downtown. . . . This is the shit we Negro coppers have to deal with. Certain places in our community are off-limits. You can't arrest certain people. If you do, they'll be out before you get back on the streets or out before your shift ends. That kind of shit makes you want to get what you can, like they do, and retire and take off to the lake like these motherfuckers do. But not you and your generation of Negro cops. You're smart enough to methodically outsmart these bastards. And your generation will outlive them and reap the benefits."

I thought, *Damn, what have I gotten myself into?* When I was just thinking about becoming a cop, my daddy said to me, "Why do you want to get involved in that mess? You know how they treat us." He was talking about how white cops treated us. And it was true. I found that out beginning with the academy. But he also might have been warning me about what was happening inside the department. My dad probably knew about bootlegging on Sundays and other illegal and criminal activity.

I understood very clearly what Omar was saying about having second thoughts about my witnessing Smokey Joe, who was Italian, and his operation. He didn't want me to be ignorant of what I would be facing when I was riding solo and how would I react.

Thanks, Omar. I needed all of what you said and did. It made me a better cop—and less naive.

New Year's Day, 1955

On New Year's Day, Dad came over to the house for dinner to enjoy one of his favorite meals—chitterlings, hog maws, black-eyed peas (an African American tradition for good luck for the coming year), collard greens, cabbage greens, candied yams, corn bread, rice pudding, and strawberry Kool-Aid. During dinner I approached the subject of Thomascine, Mother Estelle, and him. Dad told me the same thing he said to Thomascine: that he and mother were hopeful that they would have been dead before I ever found out they were not my "real" parents. They were afraid that I would not accept it well because all these years they had never told me the truth, that I wouldn't feel good about them.

I told my father that I could never forget how he and Mother had loved me as though I was their blood child, that I would always love and respect them both, although Mother was not here for me to tell her. "No one could ever say or do anything, Daddy, to keep me from loving you two."

Carol chimed in and said, "Mr. Brooks, the kids will always love you and know you as their Grandpa. I just wish Mrs. Brooks could have lived to see her grandkids and seen Alvin and me getting married, as you did."

Dad got so emotional he had to get up from the table before he finished eating and went to his room. We cleared the table, washed everything and put the food away, and covered Dad's plate and left it on the kitchen table. We knew sometimes during the evening he would come back and finish eating.

Officer Down—Detective William "Dirty Bill" Kenner, May 6, 1955

By now, Bumpus had graduated from the academy and was assigned to relief driving, mostly the wagon. We were on different shifts, but we had really bonded. Bumpus had gotten his own apartment at 27th and Benton, but he still didn't have a car.

Neighborhoods were so restrictive because of segregation that we lived near each other. We stopped by each other's houses and took each other to work in the police car. Most times, we picked up whoever was our relief, but if by chance that District car was tied up on a call, the other one picked him up.

Just short of completing my probationary period, I was faced with my biggest challenge during my ten years as a cop. It was Friday night around 11:30, May 6, 1955. My brother-in-law, Maurice Green, was to meet me at 17th and Paseo Boulevard and follow me to the station and give me a ride home. I left him at that location and headed southbound. Just as I got to the corner of Paseo Boulevard and 18th, I heard a loud noise followed by a weaker one. I thought, *Who's shooting firecrackers in May?*

I turned my red lights on, hit the siren one time, and turned right onto 18th Street headed west. Just as I neared 18th and Lydia, in front of the Lincoln Theater, I saw two white officers in uniform trying to steady a heavyset African American male in plain clothes. His right shoulder seemed to have been shot off. I could see the blood flowing out of the wound. I tried to get on the air, but some other car had gotten in and reported the shooting.

Just as I was preparing to exit my police car, a man approached my vehicle with a pistol in his hand—holding it by the butt. He threw it in the front seat and said, "Brooks, that's Detective Dirty Bill Kenner who's been shot. This is his gun." (Although I had met him, I always called him "Mr. Kenner." I could not see who the victim was.)

The man continued, "The man who shot Dirty Bill is in that car with his lights out going down Lydia."

I notified the police dispatcher. "Emergency car 123. I'm pursuing the suspect that shot the officer in a dark-colored car northbound on Lydia from 18th with his lights out."

The dispatcher repeated to "all cars" what I had said. The suspect turned off Lydia into the alley behind Virginia Liquors at 16th and Virginia. Just as I approached the corner of a garage on foot carrying my shotgun, I could see that the suspect had driven up to a fence behind the liquor store and was exiting his car.

I yelled, "Police! Come out with your hands up!" I saw the suspect move again along the passenger side of the car. I fired one shotgun blast into the rear fender of the car and yelled again, "Police! Come out with your hands up!"

Right at that moment, the suspect was running for the fence. My spotlight was on him. Two plainclothes officers from Headquarters emptied their revolvers at the suspect as he was trying to climb the fence. I could see his hands. He had no gun. Neither officer hit him.

I leveled my shotgun at the suspect as he was trying to climb the fence after the two officers had emptied their revolvers at him.

They hollered, "Shoot the bastard, shoot him!"

I didn't shoot. I returned to my car and gave the dispatcher a description of the suspect and told the direction he was last seen. By that time, police were swarming all over the area. I checked the suspect's car. There was a shotgun across the front seat.

The detective who later came to the scene took charge of the suspect's shotgun. I gave them Detective Kenner's revolver, which had been in the front seat of my car. I stayed with the suspect's vehicle and ordered a tow truck. My police car was blocked in, so while waiting for the tow, I walked to the middle of 16th Street, where a number of officers were staging. I could hear the information I had given the dispatcher being broadcast repeatedly over the police radios.

As I walked toward several officers who were sort of huddling in the middle of 16th Street between Lydia and Virginia, I heard the plainclothes officer say, "Where is the son of a bitch?" At first, I thought he was talking about the suspect, then I realized he meant me.

The plainclothes officer walked up to me with five or six other officers in uniform trailing behind him, along with the two plainclothes officers who had shot at the suspect.

Major Pond, who was in plain clothes, walked right up to me and began talking to me like he was crazy. "You bastard, why didn't you kill that bastard? What in the fuck do you think that shotgun is made for? To kill a no-good son of a bitch like the one who shot Bill Kenner."

He poked me in the chest with his finger as hard as he could. He was probably about 5'6", maybe 160 to 170 pounds. He said, "You're no better than that no-good son of a bitch who pulled the trigger on Bill."

He kept poking me in the chest and cursing me. "You're out of this police department, I promise you that, you goddamned coward." I stood my ground amid the verbal and physical abuse. Unbelievable.

After he stood in front of me huffing and puffing, staring, I looked him back, eyeball to eyeball.

I said, "Major, are you finished?" He didn't respond, but I could tell he was still very angry. He didn't take his eyes off me. I said, "Major, not you nor anyone can tell me when to kill someone."

The other officers heard me because they had gathered around when he was cursing and poking me. I turned around and walked down the alley to my car, where the red light was still on and the motor was running. I waited for the detective, lab crew, and tow truck to come for the suspect's car. After the tow truck came, I backed down the alley and drove back to the crime scene at the Lincoln Theater. I sat there and was reflecting on what had occurred: seeing the two officers helping Detective Kenner, me chasing the suspect, and me placing my spotlight on him, seeing him trying to climb the fence as my two plainclothes officers emptied their guns at him.

(These two officers in plain clothes who worked out of Headquarters were not detectives. They were brought out from Patrol Division, where they wore police uniforms, to the plainclothes unit, where they were allowed to wear their own clothes like detectives and perform some of the duties like detectives, but under the direction of the captain of the station. Some officers described them as the captain's "favorites" and the positions as plums.)

I had the chance to shoot him in the back and kill him with my shotgun, but with my spotlight on him, I could see he had no gun in his hand.

Even though my two fellow officers were shouting, "Shoot the bastard, shoot the bastard," I did not. I didn't freeze; I just couldn't kill someone who was unarmed and not a threat to anyone at the time. The police dispatcher announced on the police radio that "Officer William Kenner was pronounced deceased at General Hospital." I don't think I would have shot the suspect even if I had heard the announcement before I had the confrontation with him.

While I was sitting at the crime scene in my police car, I heard the dispatcher announce that the suspect was believed to be Hershall Williams and gave his last known address. I knew most of the Williams family. His brother, Horace, was a former police officer who left the department just before I came on. We often talked when I was in the academy. Horace had returned to the department after serving a tour in the Korean War. I was told that he was a second lieutenant and a jet pilot. He came home an alcoholic, which got him fired.

I got the feeling that if I had killed Hershall, I would have been a hero. Probably would have been honored by my peers, and the entire department would have bragged about my actions and given me an award for bravery. I thought, *Damn, I'm one month before going off my probation. I'm not going to make it now.* I knew I was going to be fired because Major Pond told me I would.

I was finally headed to Headquarters. I had never gotten into service. I needed to turn my car over to my relief officer. When I drove up to the station, my relief waved at me. He was a white officer whom I did not recognize. He said, "You had a rough night out there, didn't you? Better you than me. I hope it'll be a quiet morning out there for me." I snatched my activity sheet off the clipboard and turned to my relief and said, "My district is waiting for you. Have a good one. By the way, I didn't have time to fill her up for you, you mind?" He responded, "Thanks, I can handle it. Good morning."

Maurice walked up to the garage door. "Hey, Huss, I'm parked across the street. I'll wait in the car." I told him I'd be back as soon as I ran my activity sheet upstairs. I went upstairs. It was quiet. There was a white corporal who was the acting sergeant. I handed my activity sheet to him. He said, "You all had a helluva night out there tonight. I understand the officer who was killed was a good cop, treated everybody the same."

I said, "Yeah, Mr. Kenner was quite an officer. Please put my activity sheet with my shifts."

"You got it. Good night, get some rest." I asked if it was okay to use the phone. He said, "Go ahead."

I called Carol and gave her a brief on what had occurred and why I was late. She asked me if I was okay, and I told her yes and that I would tell her more when I got home. I told her I'd be there in about an hour, but I needed to go back where it all happened. Maurice had come to pick me up.

I walked down the stairs and out of the garage door and across the street to Maurice's car. "You wanna drive?" Maurice asked.

"No, but let's go by 18th and Lydia." When we got to 18th and Lydia, there was still a group of folks milling around in front of the Lincoln Theater. I got out, and Maurice followed. I approached pretty much the spot where both Kenner and another victim were shot. There was still a large puddle of blood on the sidewalk.

A fellow from the crowd approached me and said, "Hey, Brooks, I'm the one who gave you Dirty Bill's gun. We heard that Hershall Williams was the one who shot Dirty Bill. That was him who left in that car you chased. Did you catch him?"

I said, "Yes." I later learned he had been arrested.

Others chimed in on the discussion. One man said, "Everyone knows that Dirty Bill had helped Hershall as he grew up, even helped his family at times. If anybody knew that, surely Hershall did."

Someone else said, "I don't think Hershall intended to kill Dirty Bill. In fact, I don't think he knew it was Dirty Bill when he happened upon him. I just think Dirty Bill scared Hershall. I think he just turned and shot, scared. I bet if he's been told that it was Dirty Bill that he killed, he's as sorry as any of us."

Someone asked me, "Brooks, do you know whether Mrs. Kenner has been contacted?"

I said that I was sure she had. Someone from the department probably picked her up and took her to the hospital. After about an hour, Maurice took me home. I asked him if he wanted to come in for a minute, that I knew Carol was waiting up. He said, "Okay."

We both got out of the car and I unlocked the front door. Carol was sitting at the kitchen table with Ronall in her lap. She was rocking him. He was wide awake. I hugged and kissed both. Maurice hugged Carol. I took Ronall off her lap and asked, "What are you doing awake, little fellow?"

He said, "Mama woke me up."

Carol told him, "Don't you tell your daddy such a story. The telephone woke you up."

I said to Ronall, "You need to go back to bed. You want to tell your Uncle Maurice good night?"

"Good night, Uncle Maurice," he said.

Maurice sat down. I took Ronall upstairs and laid him down in our bed. "You wanna lie here until we come to bed?"

He said, "Un-huh."

I told him, "Daddy loves you."

"Love you," he said back to me. I covered him up and kissed him.

He said, "Leave the light on." I said okay and left the room.

Downstairs, I told Carol what had happened about what Major Pond had said and done. I had already told Maurice bits and pieces. I told both, "I think I'm going to get fired today."

Carol said, "Maybe not. Why would they want you to kill someone who was not trying to kill any of you?"

I told her that I knew what she was saying, but the major wanted Hershall dead, and I didn't carry out what he wanted me to do—and he's the head of the investigative division.

Maurice said, "I agree with Carol." I walked Maurice to the door. We agreed we'd talk later in the day before I went to work. "That is, if I still have a job," I said.

Maurice said, "Good night, Sis. Or should I say, 'Good morning'?"

We all laughed.

Officer Down—My Prayer, 1955

I began undressing. I really wanted to take a bath, but I was too tired, both mentally and physically. Ronall was asleep. Carol had gotten into bed on her side facing the wall. I know she was worried, maybe even scared, too. I went to the bathroom, washed my face and hands and brushed my teeth. I held a cold washcloth to my face. I looked into the mirror and saw some relief but lots of fear. I kind of shrugged my shoulders and thought, *Oh well.*

I went to Carol's side of the bed and got down on my knees as I always did when we went to sleep together. I took her hand. She joined me on the floor. As always, we held hands. Carol always squeezed my hand so tight—as though she was scared of something. She did the same this time. Maybe even harder. I kissed her. I began to pray.

"Oh God, we thank you for another day, your day. We want to pray for Mrs. Kenner in the loss of her husband tonight. Please comfort her and her family and Hershall and his family. Thank you, God, for our family whom you've blessed, the two of us and our children. Help us to keep the faith and trust in you and help us to pass that on to our children.

"God, I pray I did the right and just thing tonight by not killing the man who killed Officer Kenner. I believe you were there with both of us. Only you know what my future is as a police officer. Continue to guide me that I may do the things that are just and pleasing to you."

All the time I was praying, Carol was squeezing my hand so hard and she was crying. I could feel tears running down across our hands.

I ended our prayer. "God, what I face today is in your hands. Let your will be done. In Jesus's name we pray."

Both of us said "amen" and held hands for a minute or two before we got up, kissed, and got into bed.

Officer Down—Continuing "Dirty Bill" Tragedy

The next day, just as I was preparing for work, I got a call from Laymon Walker, an officer who lived in the 2700 block on Park, just south of me. "Hello, Mick. How are you doing? Speck [DeGraffenreid's nickname because he had freckles on his face] called me this morning and told me about what had happened to you. I went over to the hospital earlier this morning shortly after they had pronounced Bill dead. That was a damn shame. All of us knew the Williamses, and especially Horace, Lee, and Hershall. Bill was a damn good cop. He and I used to ride together years ago, that same area. One helluva loss. Mick, have you been to back to work yet?"

"No, sir, I was getting ready for work now and waiting for Bumpus or Officer Tommy Soils to pick me up."

"Listen, don't let those racist bastards get to you. It would have been okay if you had killed Hershall because he had killed a Black cop. They'll be madder with themselves that they didn't get a chance to kill Hershall and therefore mad at you because you didn't carry out what they wanted to do. Mick, you did the right thing. You can sleep at night with that. Fuck them! Call me when you hit the field this evening if you have a chance. Hold your head up to those damn critics. You did the right thing."

At around 3:15, I heard Bumpus blow his horn. I kissed Carol and the kids and said goodbye. As I sat in the car, Bumpus said, "Dirty Bill's death was the talk at Headquarters today, how great an officer he was. Some of them wished you had killed his killer. I never heard anyone criticize you, but I'm sure there were some, especially on your shift. You want me to come back and ride with you? You can pick me up after I eat a little bite. I don't have anything to do tonight and I'm off for the next two days."

"Hey, man, I can handle it," I said. "I'm prepared for anything. If I can feel good after the confrontation with the major, I feel I can handle any of the others."

"Pick me up about six just in case some of the white boys act shitty with you and take their time backing you up. Not that we need them, but you never know. You just might get a call in their district, and you could get caught in a situation with one of those white drunks out there. Just pick me up at six and we'll go as a two-man crew. See you at six."

I got out of the car, and Bumpus drove off. Unless he got tied up on a call, he'd be off in about half an hour.

I said a little prayer as I walked into the garage at Headquarters and into our roll call room. Only about a half dozen of my colleagues were in there. Some were standing outside the west garage door. I had entered through the east door. As I walked into the squad room, I spoke to everyone. Two or three responded. I walked up to the makeshift desk against the west wall just under the window. I began reading the latest teletype information for suspects, stolen cars, etc. It was about ten minutes before 4:00 p.m., the beginning of my shift. I could sense the room filling up behind me. My back was to the door.

One of my classmates walked up beside me and spoke: "Al, how are you doing, man? Sounds like you had one helluva night last night."

"Thanks," I said. "I didn't get much sleep. I hadn't known Mr. Kenner but about a year when I met him while I was riding out before I hit the streets. He was a great cop, I've heard."

"I've been off for the past three days," he said, "but I heard about it on the radio this morning and I think there was a small article in the *Star* this morning. I heard about your involvement when I went upstairs earlier. They were saying you chased the killer's car and cornered him and he was later arrested."

"Yeah," I said. "The sad thing is I've been told that Mr. Kenner helped Hershall Williams, the killer, when he was a kid. And helped his large family."

Ivy Wharton, the second of three Black officers on the p.m. shift, walked up and put his hand on my shoulder and said, "Brooks, you had a heck of a night last night. Bill Kenner was well liked around here and will really be missed, especially in the burglary unit of the investigative division. I'll miss my cigar-smoking friend. There was none better in his unit."

The other officer walked away as Ivy continued, "Dirty Bill didn't take no shit off any of those prejudiced white boys up there in his unit. They couldn't hardly do anything in our community regarding crime without involving Dirty Bill, especially if it was of a violent nature. Bill knew our community, the good and the bad."

"Roll call," Lieutenant Mullens bellowed out. "Let's fall in." He began to call the roll. There were about twenty officers on the p.m. shift out of Headquarters. Three of us (including me) came out of the 44th graduating class. Roll call was called by the district numbers, beginning with car 101 and so on.

"Car 123, Brooks." The lieutenant paused a minute after calling my name and said, "That was a damn good piece of police work, Al, with the tragic shooting of Bill Kenner."

I was surprised but managed to respond, "Thanks, Lieutenant." The squad broke out into applause. The lieutenant continued talking about Mr. Kenner, almost like he was eulogizing him.

Roll call was over. I met Soils at our car. Soils told me he was glad I didn't kill Hershall. He said all day in our district and in District 124, the word had gotten around that I could have killed Hershall running, but I didn't, and that I might be fired for not killing him. "The folks out here are sorry about Dirty Bill being killed, but, Al, they see you as a hero. I'm gone. Do you work tomorrow?"

I said, "Yes."

Soils said, "Okay, I'll see you tomorrow. You need me to pick you up?"

I told him yes because Bumpus said he was off Sunday. I got in service and headed east of 12th Street to my district.

Saturday night was, as usual, a busy night for the two Black districts. Arthur Williamson was riding his regular District 124. Most of the calls were in either my district or his. Most of our calls were disturbances. I made several arrests. All suspects were sent in via the wagon, which Ivy Wharton was driving.

When I wasn't on a call, I just parked at the corner of 18th and Lydia, by the Lincoln Theater; 18th and Tracy, in front of Powell's Pool Hall; or 12th and Vine, at the dead end by the Orchid Room, which was actually in Arthur's District 124. A couple of times, during the night between calls, Arthur and I met there.

Almost every place I went, people were talking about Dirty Bill and Hershall, at times mentioning my role in all of it.

Midway through the evening, I got a call at DeLuxe Café. The owner was Flossie, a man who was a good friend of Dirty Bill's.

In fact, Dirty Bill had been standing outside the DeLuxe to meet a man for information when a woman approached him and told him there was a shooting down by the Lincoln Theater.

Now Flossie was sitting at the far end of the counter. He began to talk about his relationship with Dirty Bill over the years and his relationship with Hershall's family—especially his relationship with Hershall.

"Hershall couldn't have known it was Dirty Bill who came upon him," Flossie said. "He and Bill were just too close. Damn, he helped raise Hershall, Brooks! And everybody down here's talking about you, man, a young Negro cop who was not out to make a name for yourself for the white folks. My hat's off to you, Brooks."

I told Flossie thanks, and after about twenty to twenty-five minutes, I got back in service. I knew that Flossie did some bootlegging out of his place on Sundays and after midnight Saturday nights. I was going to ask Omar about Flossie. He certainly would know. If I was right, Flossie was probably on someone's payroll, but not mine. Nor would he or anyone else ever be.

Who's Riding the "Queer" Mall Tonight?—1956

The Liberty Memorial Mall was known as the place where gay men frequented and cruised, slowly driving the circle. Many of my police colleagues had "pet names" for the gay men: fags, queers, misfits, and gays.

Many who frequented the mall were arrested repeatedly, but those who sought them out never were. Before roll call one evening, when the mall and its after-dark frequenters were being discussed, I said, "I wonder what would happen if we started arresting those who are looking for gays on the mall. I suspect there are more so-called straight men searching for gay men than gay men searching for other gay men. You can't sell if you don't have a buyer."

"Leave it to Brooks to throw water on your hot coals," responded the lieutenant. There was a burst of loud laughter.

"Okay, men, it's roll call time." End of the discussion for that evening.

This was the same group of officers who made derogatory remarks about the Italian residents who lived in the area then called the North End between Missouri Avenue and Independence Avenue—the area we now call Columbus Park. Comments were made that if you "catch them south of Independence Avenue, they're free game." So Black males, gay males, and men and boys of Italian ancestry were "free game" for the racists and homophobes.

I recall asking a similar question when I was in the academy when one of our lecturers discussed with us the role of the vice unit and who was targeted. The detective from the vice unit didn't appreciate my question, "When do you arrest the buyers?"

At the break, the detective left and a group of us were in a huddle. Someone said, "Al, why do you always ask questions that piss off our visitors?" Everybody laughed.

My response was, "We need to know the answer to these kinds of issues. We'll be out there among all of this in just a few weeks. We need to have answers."

End of discussion.

I Deliver My First Baby as Officer Brooks, M.D.

It was a night of snow, sleet, and ice. I received a call. "Investigate a call for an ambulance at 2127 Flora, the Flora Apartments, second floor."

Upon arrival, I saw a couple of women standing just inside the door on the first floor. As I stepped inside, one of the women asked me, "Where's the ambulance?"

I asked, "Who needs an ambulance and for what purpose?"

They said someone was having a baby. "She's on the second floor. She is dilating. That baby is coming anytime now." I asked if they would take me upstairs to the apartment.

There must have been at least a half dozen women standing just outside the door of an apartment near the end of the hall. As I got closer, I could hear a woman's voice screaming, "Oh, it's hurting, it's hurting so much." It got louder as I stepped inside the apartment.

I knew several of the women. Two of them were sitting on either side of the bed where the woman, who was in her early twenties, was screaming. One of the women said, "Brooks, where's the ambulance?" I asked for a phone but was told there was only a pay phone in the hallway.

The mother-to-be continued to scream and cry. One of the women sitting on the side of the bed was the woman's mother. She said, "Alvin Brooks, my daughter needs to get over to General Hospital. They have her file there. She's been going back and forth there ever since she got pregnant."

I said, "Let me make a call and see if an ambulance is on the way." I stepped into the hallway and I walked over to the pay phone.

One of the women who had been at the door downstairs was standing at the top of the stairs. She yelled to me down the hall and asked, "Is the ambulance coming or ain't it?"

I said I was going to check.

A woman standing by the telephone said she called some number and a police officer answered and said the ambulance was on the way. The screams were getting more frequent and louder. I got the dispatcher and asked about the ambulance. He told me to hold on. I could hear him talking to the emergency room at General Hospital #2.

He came back to me and said, "The folks at the hospital said the weather is too bad for them to get out. Give me the phone number that you're speaking from, and they'll call you." I gave the dispatcher the pay phone number. As I stood waiting for the phone call from the hospital, the mother-to-be was still crying out. There must have been a dozen or more people in the hallway now.

Finally, the phone rang. When I answered, the Black male doctor on the other end said, "Is this Officer Brooks?"

I said, "Yes, sir." The doctor said the weather was too bad for the ambulance driver and the intern to get out. He asked me a series of questions about the expectant mother and then gave me a set of instructions. He then told me to put someone else on the phone who could take instructions and relay them to me. The mother-to-be's sister came and took the phone. I told everyone what the doctor said about why the ambulance could not come.

I began to do what the doctor had told me to do. I asked one of the women if she would put some water on the stove, another to get a clean white sheet. We were all moving around like in a delivery room. I asked if someone had some sharp scissors. I asked for several clean bath towels. We needed several pillows. I told the sister on the phone to tell the doctor what we had done.

He asked how far apart the pain was. He told the sister to tell me to be sure the water was boiling hot and have someone place the scissors over an open flame until they turned dark but not red. If the scissors turned red, they might become misshapen.

With the help of the woman's mother, we propped her legs up on pillows and turned back all the covers. We covered her with the clean white sheet. All of this was being relayed between the doctor and the sister. The woman was still in pain, and the pain was becoming more frequent.

I was told to wash my hands several times really good and look at the mother to see if I could see the baby's head. If not, I was told to feel around and see if I could feel it and not the feet. Someone brought a standing lamp so I could see.

Everyone inside the room and those standing outside the door were women. All had children, but no one wanted to do what I was being told to do. At times there were as many as four persons relaying instructions to me from the doctor.

As the expectant mother's pain intensified, her birthing area enlarged. I could see more head. The white sheets were stacked up. It seemed like everyone brought two or three sheets.

I told the woman nearest to the door that the head was coming. The mother was screaming. Word came back to help her to push and push as though she was trying to have a bowel movement. There it was. The head coming out. Following the doctor's instructions, I didn't pull, just kind of guided the baby toward me. The mother was pushing and screaming. She pushed, and I gently guided the baby out. Blood was oozing out, too.

The mother's mother was praying and was stroking her daughter's forehead and face with a warm, damp towel. Sweat was rolling down her daughter's face—and I was sweating also!

I had taken my uniform jacket off. It was hot in the small studio apartment with all the burners on the gas stove on and the water boiling.

Several voices in the hallway were repeating what the doctor was telling the sister to tell me. I said, "The baby is out!" The message was passed back up the line to the doctor.

The mother asked, "Is my baby all right? Is the baby breathing?" He wasn't, and I sent word to the doctor that the baby was not breathing.

The word came back from the doctor: "Hold him upside down. Spank him gently." I did all that and the baby let out a loud scream.

I told the mother, "Yes, he's all right. It's a boy." I could see his little penis. That message went up the hallway and was passed on to the doctor.

His next instructions were, "Wipe the baby off all over with a piece of the clean sheet. Then lay the baby on the mother's stomach. Tear several pieces of the sheet. Dip them in the hot water but let them cool until they are just warm. Take a wide enough piece of the sheet, wrap it around your hand and pull the umbilical cord gently and see if you can pull a larger piece out."

I did, but the mother screamed too loud. The doctor then sent back another message: "Take two torn pieces of sheet. Dip them in the hot water. Make sure the sheet pieces are just warm. Make two strips. Tie them around the umbilical cord very tight, about six inches apart. Dip the scissors into the hot water. Wipe them with a clean sheet. Cut the cord in the middle [which I had learned in my first aid class].

"Is the baby moving its hand around its mouth? If the mother's milk has come, tell the mother to let the baby nurse her."

The mother followed the instructions, and the baby began nursing. Several of the women came up, some laughed. The older women prayed. Some were saying, "Thank you, Jesus!"

I wrapped the one part of the umbilical cord in another piece of the clean sheet as instructed—to save for when the mother was able to get to the hospital. The bed, of course, was soaked with blood, although we had placed several towels under the mother. More sheets were brought from several apartments. Several of us maneuvered the mother around to get the towels and sheets from under her and padded the bed, trying to make the mother as comfortable as we could.

The doctor gave instructions to take towels after dipping in the hot water and cooling them off to try to clean the mother up. Her mother and two other ladies did that, as they held the baby up and began to clean him.

Someone suggested the mother name the baby after me, "Alvin." They all called the baby "Baby Alvin." We all laughed.

The grandmother, whose name I don't recall, said, "No, you don't want to do that." She called her daughter's name and said that her husband-to-be was supposed to be there so they could get married. He was a soldier at Fort Leonard Wood but could not get here because the buses could not run in the bad weather. "But he'll be here as soon as the weather clears."

I left the mother and baby to go to the phone and talk to the doctor. I thanked him for helping me. He said, "You did well, Dr. Brooks." We both laughed. "As soon as the city is able to plow the streets and salt them down, I'll send an ambulance over there and get the mother and child over here." He said he hated to leave the other part of the birth sack in her, but tonight he had no choice. We exchanged names again and said that we looked forward to meeting each other.

I called the dispatcher on the phone and told him what had occurred and that I would be in service shortly. The dispatcher was all the "ten questions" about the baby. I answered them all and could hear some comments from others in the background.

I went back into the room—which was still hot—and now full of about a dozen persons marveling over the mother and baby. All the burners on the stove were still on and water was still boiling. I walked over and turned the burners off.

Before I left, I asked if someone could offer a prayer. An elderly woman who said she was one of the "evangelists" from Barker Temple (Barker Temple Church of God and Christ, down the street at 17th and Highland) was suggested by the group. We all joined hands. After about fifteen minutes of prayer and praising the Lord and specifically mentioning my name, everyone said, *"Amen!"*

I walked over, kissed the young mother on the forehead, congratulated her, and patted the baby boy on his back as he nursed frantically.

I had the number of the pay phone in the hall and told the grandmother that I would call in the morning and hopefully someone would answer and let me know how mother and baby were. I said I hoped the ambulance would have already been there and both would be in the hospital and that I would drop by to look in on them.

They thanked me for everything. I thanked everyone and started down the hall toward the stairs. There were a couple men standing in one of the doorways. They had heard everything that was going on but did not come down the hall to the apartment. One of them said, "You did it, Dr. Brooks." They both laughed, as did I. Just as I approached the stairs, the same man hollered, "Give policeman Dr. Brooks a big hand." The hall was full of applause. I thanked everyone, shook the two gentlemen's hands, and trotted down the stairs.

The second baby I delivered, in 1957, was born in a taxi cab, and when the cab driver and I finally got the mother and baby boy to the hospital, one of the older nurses looked at me and said, "Dr. Brooks, you again?"

My Friend Gene Buie Decided to Join the Department

During these years in Kansas City, as all over the country, it was well known that school segregation had ended only on paper, in the case of *Brown v. Board of Education*, May 1954. Out of ten high schools, Kansas City had two Black segregated high schools, Lincoln and

R. T. Coles. If you attended either of them, you likely knew most of the Black students at both schools.

Well, Gene Buie, who attended Lincoln, and I had met because I, who attended Coles, was dating Carol and *somehow* often found my way to Lincoln where she attended. Plus, I played in the Coles band and orchestra, and those of us in the orchestra were pretty popular because we played at dances at Coles and let Lincoln folks slip in. And Buie was a track star at Lincoln, so everybody knew him. Buie earned a full-ride scholarship to Pittsburg State University in Pittsburg, Kansas, where he set all kinds of track records. He returned home to Kansas City and married his high school sweetheart, Marlene Mayberry, of the Lincoln class of 1953. Buie's class was 1951.

Before joining the department, Buie was employed by the Manor Bread Company as a truck driver. Buie often would stop by my house just to talk. But it was early 1956 when Buie made some overtures about joining the police department. He would question me about being Black as a cop—about treatment by white officers, promotions, racism, discrimination, and segregation.

I couldn't paint a beautiful picture in response. After almost two years, I was able to witness and assess the situation and answer his questions fairly. But I told Buie I was an optimist, that we just might be the generation of Black cops to get real changes started. Some of us might not survive, but we would have left it better than we came on.

I shared with him what the older Black officers were sharing with me—and the other two young Black officers, William Bumpus and Thomas Soils, who graduated from the 45th Cadet Class in January 1955. I hoped if he decided to join with us, he'd get a chance to meet with us. I explained that older Black officers told us that the Mafia and Pendergast days of control were not completely over, especially in the Black community, and that Black men, and on occasion Black women, were used to conduct illegal activities within the community. So, when the "shit hit the fan" and arrests were made, Blacks went to jail and did time, but seldom were the white bosses touched.

The "old-timers" advised us, "Don't get out there and try to save the world and try to make names for yourselves. You might get hurt by some of our own people, paid to do it by the white bastards who want to continue to stay in control of the Black community. Reprisals could come from inside—the racist department officers paid off to look the other way."

They went on to tell us, "These white motherfuckers are getting something out of our community at our expense. It's bad enough just doing your job. Don't bring additional bullshit down on you."

I told Buie that I didn't want to discourage him, but Bumpus, Soils, and I had already witnessed what our elder Black officers were telling us. But we were just bold enough to believe we could stay clean and still survive, despite what our elders warned us about. We were committed and loyal to our community and to the ideals of the department by doing the right thing. I told Buie that Bumpus and I had become very close. I also mentioned that both Bumpus and Soils had recently come out of the army. I said, "Come on, join us. We need another young Black cop." We both laughed.

None of the other Black officers were near our ages, the early twenties. Buie said he'd give it some further thought, talk to his wife, and let me know. I told Bumpus and Soils about Buie. We all were hopeful!

In the first week in May, Buie called to see if I was home. He asked if he could stop by for a few minutes. I told him, "Come on by." In about twenty minutes, Manor truck and all, Buie arrived and seemed happy.

"Well," he started, "I talked to my wife, Marlene, and she had talked to Carol, your wife, and Marlene said she was fine with it if I really wanted to join the department. So I did it! I've taken everything they threw at me and I'm to start in the 48th Cadet Class on May 16!"

I congratulated him and suggested he let me set up a meeting with him and the other two young Black officers, Bumpus and Soils, who were in the 45th Cadet Class. I did, and we all hit it off together.

After Buie got into the academy, he rode out with me many times as an observer, although he was not assigned to me as his training officer as Bumpus had been. He also rode out occasionally with Bumpus. Soils rode relief but eventually was assigned a district relieving Bumpus. Buie and I were on the same shift. Bumpus relieved Buie. Soils relieved Bumpus, who was assigned to District 124. (Remember, District 123 and District 124 were the two Black districts. Black officers could ride with white officers in the two Black districts, but not in the white districts with or without a white officer.) When Buie rode with me, as when he rode with Bumpus and sometimes Soils, we rode as a "two-man crew." Buie graduated from the academy August 20, 1956.

After Buie, Bumpus, Soils, and I hit the street, a special burglary squad was assembled, headed by DeGraffenreid, who became the first Black detective sergeant. And Omar and Laymon were transferred from the patrol division to the investigation division. Several of the other older Black officers were also reassigned.

Buie, Bumpus, and I had been on long enough to see the gambling houses, prostitution, where "fencing" was going on, bootlegging, and drug-dealing, rarely checked by cops on the streets. We saw Black men and women being used and fronting for the Mafia and Pendergast. We saw that when the shit hit the fan, Blacks were identified as the known offenders and were sent to jail or prison, and the whites involved were not charged.

The "3Bs" Began Our Crusade

Bumpus, Buie, and I became close. Soils by his own choice was sort of a loner and was not too fond of the "disruptions" the three of us planned. So that left us as the 3Bs. Bumpus was born May 24, 1932, Buie was born May 3, 1933, and I was born May 3, 1932. The 3Bs—all born the same month!

We decided to start our crusade. We became known in our community among the Black criminal element as three young "nigga cops" trying to make a name for ourselves. And from within the department, we were called "the 3Bs"—Brooks, Bumpus, and Buie. We took advantage of the moment and started our crusade, interfering with the final stages of Mafia and Pendergast power in the Black community. And we disrupted some of the illegal activities some of our fellow white officers were involved in. But it seemed folks got too scared to say or do anything about what we had begun to do. Remember, both the Mafia and the Pendergast machine were on their way out, politically and criminally. Some of the Black police officers we followed allowed those who worked for Mafia and Pendergast members in the Black community to skate by when they committed minor offenses, like prohibited parking, because they were in on some of the illegal stuff, too.

The 3Bs began to write traffic tickets, sometimes requiring towed cars, and made arrests if someone came out and tried to intimidate us when the traffic ticket was torn up and thrown back at us. We made unprecedented numbers of arrests for both minor and criminal offenses. Most of these confrontations over traffic tickets came in the No Parking zones, 7:00 a.m. to 9:00 a.m. and evenings 4:00 to 6:00 p.m. We continued our crusade and even got help from some of the Black old-timers, without any interruption from our sergeants or commanding officers.

"Brooks, I Ain't Dead!"—1957

I was working the day shift that spring of 1957, cruising east on 13th Street approaching Lydia. There were apartments on the south side of the street and Yates Elementary School was across the street facing Lydia. Just as I approached the apartments, Harris came stumbling out. High as a kite, he leaned against the building. "Coasting" is an effect of heroin. I got out of service on a pedestrian check.

When I approached, Harris barely knew who I was. After focusing on me, he said, "Hey, Brooks. How are you?"

I said, "What's going on in the building, Harris? Where'd you get your stuff?"

He said, "Upstairs, Brooks. Those niggers up there are shooting up and letting Boudreaux die. Boudreaux is dying up there. He's got some straight shit."

"Come on, show me," I said. I turned him around and began to search him . . . and ran my right hand into a hypodermic needle still on a syringe. It must have gone almost a half inch into my hand. I cursed and pulled it out and placed it in the glove box of the police car.

Harris could hardly walk, but I pushed him up the apartment steps. At the top, he pointed to the first door on the left. I pushed him to the door. I tried the doorknob. It was locked. I could hear voices. I knocked and told him what to say: "Hey, let me in. This is Harris. Let me in!"

Someone inside said, "Let that nigga in before he wakes up the building." The door opened. I pushed Harris in. He fell in the bed almost next to Boudreaux.

There were four Black males sitting around. The fifth, who opened the door, hollered, "That's Brooks!"

He ran through the kitchen to the back door. Out the back door all five went. At least two jumped over the rail. I heard one of them holler, "My leg's broken!"

Across the bed was Boudreaux. High. Taking long, deep breaths. His face had turned gray. I called his name and shook him. No response. I yelled to Harris, "Come on, man! Help me get him downstairs." Harris was still lying across the bed. I said to Harris, "Come on, man; you've got to help me get Boudreaux down to the police car." He wasn't much help, but we made it down to the car.

I managed to get Boudreaux into the back seat with Harris in the front—and got out of service with, "to General Hospital #2 with a possible OD." I used the red light and siren.

When I arrived at the emergency room entrance, several medical personnel met me with a gurney. It took several of us to lift Boudreaux onto the gurney. Inside the ER, I sat Harris down in a chair.

Boudreaux was nodding off and finally stopped breathing altogether. The medical personnel cut off his shirt and tried to revive him. A Haitian doctor (with an accent) was in charge of the emergency room. He inserted a long needle filled with a fluid or medication around the heart area. They tried a defibrillator to get him breathing and to get his heart beating. Everything failed.

The doctor said, "He's gone; we've done all we can. He's gone." He looked at the clock and gave the time of death. He told the nurses to unplug the various lines they had going into Boudreaux's body.

For some strange reason, I didn't think Boudreaux was dead. Like everyone else, I saw them make every attempt to revive him. I said, "Doc, I don't think he's dead. Could you work on him, try just a little longer?"

He responded, "No, sir, Officer, he's gone. There's nothing else I can do. I'm sorry. I've done all I can. He's gone." He pulled the sheet over Boudreaux and walked away.

Harris was sitting in a chair "coasting." He had overheard what the doctor had said. He pulled himself up and staggered to the gurney and turned the sheet back and began to call Boudreaux by name. "Wake up, man! Come on, wake up! Don't do this to me! Wake up!"

I was still standing next to the gurney. I bent over and pressed my fingers to Boudreaux's neck. I could swear I felt a pulse. An intern was standing close by. I said, "Come on, man, this brother isn't dead! Let's do something."

I told Harris to sit back down. He was still high and could hardly stand. The intern and I, on either side of the gurney, sat Boudreaux up to a sitting position. I began striking him in the back. I don't know why. I just knew he was alive, and striking him in the back was the first thing that came to my mind. I must have struck him as hard as I could several times with the palm of my hand. Suddenly, as we were holding him up and as I was striking him, he shook his head and coughed.

"Hey, man, whatchall doing?" He opened his eyes. The ER personnel came back, laughing. An older nurse that I knew said, "My God, Brooks, what did you do? Get the doctor in here quick!"

I said, "Boudreaux, this is Brooks! Do you know where you are?"

He said, "Brooks? Cop Brooks?"

I said, "Yes, man. We thought you were done!"

"I'm hurting all over, man. I need some help. I'm hurting!"

The doctor came in, and his eyes "bucked." "Mawn [in his Jamaican dialect], I thought you were dead. Here, lie back down. Let's get some IVs going and ready him for pumping his stomach. Mawn, we need to keep you overnight. You hear?" Boudreaux didn't answer him. They strapped him down and began to start the IVs again and gave him several shots. He was breathing normally—far better than the short breaths he was taking when I first brought him in and, of course, from when he stopped breathing altogether.

I thanked everybody and they came back with, "Thank you!"

The doctor said, "Officer, you are a good mawn. This mawn owes you a great debt. He'll thank you, I'm sure, when he's sober, all those drugs pumped out of him. Thank you, Officer."

Harris was standing. I told him, "Let's go, Harris, unless you want to stay over here with Boudreaux."

Harris said, "I'm ready. Take me back to 12th Street." I stopped at Paseo Park and lectured Harris. I knew it wasn't going to do any good because he was still pretty high, but I had to get it off my chest. I went over what we had gone through the last two hours. And he had almost lost one of his best friends. He didn't argue with me, agreed with everything I said. I dropped him off at 12th and Paseo by the cannon.

When I came to work the next day, a couple hours after patrolling my district, I got out of service at General Hospital #2. I went in to check on Boudreaux. I talked to the hospital switchboard operator who said, "Officer Brooks, Mr. Boudreaux was released about two hours ago."

I told her the story about what had happened the previous morning. "Praise the Lord!" she shouted. I left and got back in service.

Coincidence or Divine Intervention?

As I was working to complete my memoir in March 2017, I remembered Jules Boudreaux and his wife, Beverly. I could remember seeing Boudreaux and Beverly (one of the most beautiful women you've ever seen) standing on the corner of 12th and Troost, with other drug addicts, men and women, "coasting" in a stupor, in their own worlds, and the women disappearing for short periods of time to turn tricks with their white clients.

Often when other officers and I worked the night shifts, we would interrupt their sex acts. I rarely arrested "ladies of the evening" because they were my best source of information for crime suspects. But on several occasions, I did arrest both the woman and the man. The men were always white, but the sergeant at the booking desk would always release them, saying, "We don't want to interfere with his family and his job."

Taking what the sergeant said into account, I'd just break up the activity in my district, send the woman on her way after a lecture, and detain and interrogate the white male. I'd take down his name, birth date, Social Security number, address, and where he worked. I'd call the dispatcher on the man and his car to check for warrants. Sometimes there were warrants for arrest. When booking them, I didn't mention anything about the sex act, but only the warrant. I'd tow the car.

When my white counterparts caught a white male and a Black prostitute in the act, or when decoys were used, the Black prostitute was always arrested and the white male released, sometimes without even getting their names to determine if warrants were outstanding.

As I was writing about Jules and Beverly, I wondered what happened to the two of them. The last time I saw Boudreaux, he was with his mother at Annunciation Catholic Church at the morning service. After the service I talked to them. He told me he had gotten his life together and was a contract painter. He and his mother thanked me for all the help I had given him when I was a police officer. I never saw Boudreaux again, but often wondered where and how he was. Then it happened.

I was in an automobile accident in December 2017. Since it was the other driver's fault, his insurance offered to pay to repair the damages to my car. I asked if I could take it to the Hendrick Collision Center and my request was approved. The day I was notified that I could bring in my car, that the parts were in, I took my car there. The insurance provided a rental car until the repairs to mine were complete.

I headed upstairs to Enterprise Rent-A-Car. The associate told me that my car was being cleaned and would be ready in ten to fifteen minutes. He took a photo of my driver's license. As I was about to sit down, a young African American male entered. We spoke and shook hands. I said, "My name is Al Brooks."

The young man responded, "I know who you are, Mr. Brooks. Glad to meet you."

He turned to the Enterprise associate, who asked, "Yes, sir, what can I do for you?"

The young man responded, "I have a car reserved." The associate asked for his name. I didn't hear the first name but heard the last name "Boudreaux."

I said, "Pardon me, young brother, what did you say your last name was?"

He said, "Boudreaux." I asked how he spelled it. He said "Boudreaux, Jules Boudreaux. Jules Boudreaux II."

I said that I had saved a man's life in the late '50s when I was in the police department, and his name was Boudreaux, but I didn't think he spelled it that way.

The young man said, "That was my dad, Mr. Brooks. He told me all about how you saved his life." He walked over to me and opened his cell phone and showed me a picture of his dad. It definitely was the Boudreaux whom I had brought back from overdosing.

Jules told me that the woman I had known was his dad's first wife, Beverly, and that both she and his dad had passed. His mother was Lavern. I asked him if I could call him and learn more about him and his mother. He said yes and gave me his phone number and forwarded the photo of his father to my cell phone. About a week later, I called Jules and asked if I could take him to lunch and wondered if his mother would join us.

He said he was sure she would like to meet me and hear more about his dad during the earlier time when I knew him and Beverly. I set the date for February 23 at the Peachtree Restaurant.

We met and shared stories. Jules has seven children. He has a sister from the marriage of his mother and his father and half sisters and brothers from his dad and Beverly. Jules II is forty-three years old. His father died in 1995, just short of his seventieth birthday. Jules said his dad's offspring—counting his children, his brothers and sisters, and their kids and grandkids—number nearly 100. He also said, "If you hadn't saved my dad's life, none of us would have been born."

Was it a coincidence or divine intervention that some sixty years after my involvement with Boudreaux Senior that I would meet his son in the office of a rental car company? I believe it was divine intervention.

The 3Bs Continue Our Crusade—and Save an Informant from a "Hit"

Remember the junkie, Harris, heroin addict? He was a junkie who hung around 12th Street, day and night. We became friends and respected each other. He often gave information to me as a district cop. Most of the time, the info was good.

But one day he slipped and told me, "Brooks, I've got some good info to send a lot of niggers to jail, but I can't tell you. My FBI folks have to handle this. Oh shit, maybe I shouldn't have told you that. Well, as long as you don't put the word out here on the street or tell any of those crackers downtown, I can still help you, I promise."

I told Harris, "If you are as loose-mouthed as you seemed to be, the word eventually would get out and someone will give you some 'hot-shot shit' or I'll find your ass in an alley somewhere shot up with battery acid."

He thanked me and said, "The not-so-big stuff I'll pass on to you, Brooks. I promise. But I've got to deliver every once in a while. Otherwise, I'll find myself in jail—or exposed to these niggers on the streets. You know how the white racist Feds are. Like the white cops you work with. You're a good nigger informant, but when you don't deliver, they'll let some of those crooked white cops arrest you and they'll play crazy that they never heard of you."

A combined squad of Feds and KCPD officers brought on a sweep of heroin dealers and junkies. The word on the street was that Harris set everyone up. Every junkie on 12th Street between Harrison and Woodland was arrested on numerous charges from city to state to federal. Harris was left out on the street alone.

The word now was that a contract had been taken out on him. One afternoon I was sitting in the police car at 12th and Lydia when I saw Harris walking hurriedly west on Paseo toward me. When he got to me, he was out of breath. He opened the back door and slumped down on the floor. "Please, Brooks, drive me up on Tracy about 25th." He was sober. Talked straight talk. The first time I had seen him that clean—ever.

I started down south on Paseo, driving slow. "What the hell's going on, man?" I asked.

"Brooks, just like you warned me, those crackers hung me out to dry. I gave them all the information, names and all. I begged them to arrest me when they were arresting the junkies at 12th and Woodland yesterday. They refused. The eight or ten folks who got arrested were standing with me. Everyone got arrested except me. Everyone began to mock me and curse me and called me a snitch. You told me those fuckers were going to do that to me. Those rotten sons of bitches. Now there's a contract on me from someone. I don't know who put the money up, but I do know who's supposed to carry it out."

He named two crooks known on the streets and some dope dealers. I knew them. As I rode past 14th and Paseo, I thought about the five cops who had been killed there by the Bell brothers in 1948 when I was in high school, three white and two Black officers.

I drove Harris around, talking to him. He was sweating and shaking. He had a cigarette in his mouth, but he didn't smoke. His lips were quivering. He climbed over and sat in the front seat when we got to 19th and Troost. I pulled over just east of Troost on 25th Street.

"Brooks, you and Buie got to help me. I don't want these niggers to kill me for a couple hundred dollars. I'd rather hot-shot myself, but everything is dried up out here. I couldn't buy anything anyway. I don't have a fuckin' dime."

I asked him where was he going on Tracy. He said to his aunt's house. "Maybe I can borrow five dollars from her, but she knows I'm on that shit and probably won't give no more than a meal and a place to sleep." Maybe he'd stay there for the night. And if his aunt gave him the five dollars, he'd get out and see if he could find a hit. Mix it with some battery acid and kill himself.

I told him to hold off a couple of days and let me see what Buie, Bumpus, and I could do with the two crooks he had named with the contract.

When I let him out at the house, I realized it was up the street from where Bumpus's aunt lived. Bumpus had lived with her after he got out of the service and for his first several months with the department.

I also knew Harris's aunt. Harris gave me her phone number. I told him to tell her that I dropped him off and that I would call her.

Buie was off. Bumpus was scheduled to come on his shift on his car 124 at the end of my shift. I went by Buie's house on Olive. I saw his car. I blew my horn. He came out. I told him about Harris. I told him that he and Bumpus and I had to do something. I didn't want to see Harris murdered by those two bastards. He agreed because Harris had helped all three of us and was just a victim of the streets and drugs. We decided that if we talked to any of the white detectives in the vice or narcotic units, they would just tell us, "Fuck Harris. He'd be just one less 12th Street junkie."

Buie said he was off, but that if Bumpus and I decided on something, he was in. I told him that when Bumpus came on, I'd share what we'd talked about with him and maybe the three of us could get together later somewhere in their district.

About 8:00 p.m., the three of us met at Vivian's Restaurant, 12th and Paseo. Bumpus got out of service on an "e call" (a time to eat). I picked up Buie. I was still living at 2632 Park. Bumpus now had his own apartment in the 2700 block of Benton.

We decided we would find the "hit men." We knew the car they drove. Only one had a car, a 1948 Lincoln. Bumpus used the phone in Vivian's and checked the records on both. One of them had a pickup order on him for assault. He was to be held for investigation for the plainclothes unit.

After drinking coffee, Buie and I joined Bumpus and rode with Bumpus until he got a call. It was a vehicular accident. No injuries. He dropped us back at Vivian's and was to come back after he took the vehicular report.

It was after 9:00 p.m., so Buie and I decided to go home. But if Bumpus ran across the Lincoln, he'd call us, and we'd meet him. Bumpus would arrest the one, with us there, and try to find out where the other crook was. We didn't hear anything from Bumpus.

The next day, Buie and I were at work. I called Harris from the police station. His aunt answered the phone. I told her who I was and apologized for not calling her as I promised Harris that I would. I told her I just got busy and when the calls finally lightened up, it was just too late to call. She said she understood.

She said Harris was "asleep in there on the couch. Alvin, is he in some trouble again? I haven't seen him this sober in years. It's like he's scared of something or someone."

I told her that she had been around him long enough to know that something was always happening when you're on the streets and fooling around with that drug culture. I told her if he were in any kind of trouble, there were a couple of us who would try to find out what it is. I asked her to have him call the station number I had given him when I dropped him off last evening but asked her to tell him not to give his real name. They would call me from the station and relay the information.

When Buie and I hit the streets, our number one job was to locate that Lincoln, and hopefully both crooks would be together, as they always were. Nothing before noon.

Harris did call, and both Buie and I went by to talk to him. We told him to lie low until we could locate the two "hit men." He told us where they hung out—at a girlfriend's house at 23rd and Highland. He gave us her name and a description of her car. (The other girlfriend lived at 12th and Harrison.) We headed toward Highland. I parked on Vine. Buie drove by the Highland address. He met me back on Vine. He didn't see either car.

That afternoon I was returning to the district shortly after I had made an arrest. And there they were: the two cars, parked bumper-to-bumper on Harrison between 12th and 13th. The Lincoln and the girlfriend's car, parked right behind it.

I called Buie to meet me at 13th and Tracy. I told him where I saw the two cars. But I didn't want to get out of service on a car check because I didn't want vice, the FBI, or our white officers to know we were working that case—because they would interfere with our plan, and the white officer who was riding District 109 would come in on the assist. (Harrison was in District 109, and a District 109 boundary was one block west of Troost. Troost was the dividing line between 123 and 109. Remember, Black officers didn't patrol west of Troost.)

So I went and sat in my car and observed the two cars for about a half hour, hoping that neither Buie nor I would get a call. The plan was that I would get out of service on two unoccupied cars and report the info on both to the dispatcher. As soon as the dispatcher asked, "Do you want a second car, 123?" I'd say, "Yes." Buie would immediately respond and say, "124's at 12th and Troost. I'll make that with 123."

As I sat right at 13th and Harrison looking north, the girlfriend came out of her apartment to her car, carrying a basket of clothes as though she was going somewhere to wash.

I radioed the dispatcher, "123 to the dispatcher," as I drove up beside the car where the girlfriend was placing the basket of clothes in the back seat.

"Come in, 123."

"123 out of service on two car checks and a Negro female."

I gave the dispatcher the address and the description of both cars and their license numbers.

"Do you want a second car?"

"Yes, thank you."

"Come in, 124?"

"124 is at 13th and Troost. I'll make that call with 123."

"123 and 124 out of service on two car checks and a Negro female at 1221 Harrison."

Buie was there before the dispatcher's transmission was completed. He was out of his car and talking to the young woman. She was digging in her purse for her driver's license. I got out of my car. The dispatcher began to give registration information on the two cars. The car the woman was getting ready to drive off in was registered to a woman in the 2300 block of Highland. There were three traffic tickets on the license. We had our outside speakers on, and when the dispatcher came back with the information, the whole block could hear.

The license on the Lincoln was not registered to the car.

Then two dudes came down the steps and one asked, "Hey, officers, what's going on with my girl?"

Then the district officer drove up but didn't get out of his car. *Good,* I thought.

Buie ordered both men against the car and searched them as I watched them and the girl. Buie asked both for some ID. One was reluctant. "We ain't done nothing. We just want to know why you stopped her."

I spoke up and said, "The officer asked for your ID. We need to see it."

The two men handed their IDs to Buie. The woman found hers after digging in her purse and handed it to me. Both Buie and I kept our eyes wide open on the two men. Buie handed me the two men's driver's licenses. I walked back to my car and flipped the outside speaker switch off after I gave the dispatcher information on the three to check their records.

Shortly, we learned the woman was clean. But one of the men was wanted for investigation for assault, as we already knew. And the other had several traffic warrants.

I ordered a tow truck. I got out of the car and told both men, "You're under arrest," and told each one what the charges were.

Buie handcuffed both with my cuffs and his. Then wagon 115, which happened to be in the area, came up with Joe Trabon. The district officer was still double-parked and sitting in his car.

Joe got out and asked, "You need me, fellows?"

Buie told him, "Joe, thanks; we got it covered."

"I just heard all the activity. Thought you might need the wagon. I'm gone."

I asked the woman who it was who owned the car that she was getting ready to drive off.

She said, "It's my auntie's," and gave her aunt's name and address.

I said, "You heard the dispatcher say there are traffic warrants issued to that license. Did you get the tickets?"

She said, "Yes, sir."

One of the men said, "Hey, Brooks, please don't book her. I'll take care of the tickets for her auntie. Please don't arrest her and tow the car."

I said, "What do you think, Gene; should we give these folks a break?" I winked at him.

"Yeah. We can always arrest the aunt if we have to. That's my district anyway. Why don't you go on and finish your day, lady? But tell your aunt you got those traffic tickets on her car and she needs to get her car properly licensed."

She kissed the one fellow who had the investigation pickup order on him, got in the car, and drove off.

The tow truck was there hooking up the Lincoln. I sat one of the men in my car and Buie sat the other one in his car. Buie and I searched through the Lincoln and the truck. There was a box of .38-caliber bullets in the glove box. Gene found a homemade sawed-off double-barreled shotgun in the truck, nothing in it.

After I signed the tow report, the driver took off with the Lincoln. I told Buie we needed to talk to these two before we got downtown. The district officer was still double-parked but never got out of his car. I went over and shook his hand and thanked him for standing by. He said, "You're welcome. Anytime." And he drove off.

Buie and I decided to follow our game plan for talking to them individually and maybe together about Harris. About half an hour later, we met outside our cars and exchanged the conversation we each had with the two men. The man I had in my car was on ten-year paper (parole) for murder in Kansas. He did seven years of a fifteen-year sentence. He begged me not to tell the other man that he told me that. Yes, they had been approached by someone (he gave me a name), and they had agreed to do the hit on Harris for $1500—but had not planned to carry it out. The man who put out the hit and gave the money was going down with the Feds and would be gone for a long time.

I shared this with Buie. Buie's man denied any such hit given to them.

I suggested we talk to them together and "read the riot act" to them. Although my man had admitted it, we would play the game on through.

Buie agreed and got the man out of his car. He sat him in the front seat with me and got in the back seat with the one I had. We cussed and threatened, and in the final analysis we made it clear that "if anything happens to Harris at all by anyone, we're coming after the two of you, whether you had anything to do with it or not."

Buie told them, "Every Black officer, those patrolling the districts and the detectives, know about this 'hit' that the two of you were supposed to carry out. Some of us will come up with something that will put both of you away for a long, long time. You understand? Do you hear us?"

Both said they did and would put the word out when they got past their charges. The man I was questioning loudly said, "We understand. Although we don't know anything about the hit on Harris, we'll try to find out who has it and try to discourage it and get back to you. We promise." He winked at me.

Buie took the man he questioned back to his car. I had the one I questioned in the front seat with me. I radioed the dispatcher, "123 and 124 out of service, Headquarters with two arrests."

The dispatcher responded, "Cars 123 and 124 out of service, the station with two arrests. KAA359."

Buie delivered his suspect to the plainclothes unit. And who was there to receive him on the investigation of assault? Yep, one of the most racist cops!

I took my man upstairs and booked him on the traffic tickets. He thanked me because he knew I could have booked him for investigation to "check on recent activities," using a phony charge if I wanted to just hold him for twenty hours. That would really mess with him since he was on paper.

Harris got his life together for a while but ended up getting back on that stuff and was arrested "in possession." He was sent to Lexington, Kentucky, for a period for the offense and for treatment. I don't know what happened to him after that.

There were a lot of situations Bumpus, Buie, and I carried out until we were transferred out of our two all-Black patrol divisions and were reassigned to the Sheffield Station.

It's Police Circus Time

Each year, I think in the fall, the Hamid-Morton Police Circus came to town. I'm not sure how it was all put together, but it was a benefit for the police department. It was called the Police Circus, perhaps more fully called the Police Officers' Benefit Association. All police officers were encouraged by some sergeants—and ordered by others—to sell a minimum of 100 tickets at a dollar each. There were twenty to a book. My desk sergeant, who handled roll call, distributed the tickets and gave the "pep talk" on the importance of selling the tickets. He "strongly suggested" each officer on our shift at Headquarters sell 100 tickets.

To understand this incident, you need to know that a "houseman" is on the payroll of someone in the vice unit or someone else who's higher up downtown, or the North End Italians, to protect the operation from law enforcement. The houseman collects the proceeds from illegal gambling and is given his cut, a pittance. But most of the money goes to the white man outside the community.

The three of us met at Vivian's Restaurant at 12th and Paseo. Buie and I were on duty, working days. Bumpus relieved Buie on car 124. Buie's scheme was that he and I would get out of service at the Monarch Bowling Alley at 1822 Vine for a building check. The "off-limits" gambling game was upstairs, above the bowling alley. The plan was to take 1500 circus tickets (500 each), go up there three strong, argue our way in, and sell the tickets to the gamblers.

Our plan was to leave the 1500 tickets (valued at a dollar each) with the houseman and to tell him we'd be back the next day, same time, for the $1500, and to remind him of our request to give the circus tickets to some worthy kids.

Since it was Buie's idea and his and Bumpus's district, hell, I was game. The day we decided to carry out the scheme, Buie and I got out of service as planned at the bowling alley for the building check. Bumpus was riding with Buie. Bumpus was the only one of us off-duty but in uniform. He was Buie's relief. He and Buie had "rendezvoused" somewhere before joining me. (By the way, we were encouraged to sell tickets off-duty wearing our uniforms.)

We headed up the flight of stairs to the second floor to the gambling room, bypassing the Monarch Bowl. Buie knocked on the door with his nightstick really hard. The slot in the door slid open. The doorman peeped through the opening and said, "Yeah, what you want?"

Buie said, "Police! Open the damn door, man!" The doorman could see Buie's badge and uniform. He looked a little closer and recognized all three of us.

The doorman said, "Buie, you know I can't let you in."

Buie said, "You want me to shoot the lock off the fuckin' door? Call the houseman to come open this door and tell him what I said. Hurry up!"

We could hear the doorman telling the houseman what Buie said but the houseman added, "He's with two other little punk cops. I can see them in the background."

The houseman came to the hole in the door. He started to say something and Buie cut him off.

"Open the fuckin' door now, nigger!"

The houseman just stared at Buie.

I said, "Don't ask him anymore, Buie. I'm going down to get my shotgun and call the wagon. That asshole thinks we're playing."

Bumpus said, "This .357 Magnum is more powerful than that shotgun. It'll blow the lock off plus it'll hit three or four people inside, go through the wall, and hit somebody down on 18th Street. Here, step aside in there."

The houseman said, "You young niggers are crazy and trying to make names for yourselves. Here, I'm opening the door. Come on in."

All three of us stepped in with guns drawn but not pointed at anyone. The houseman was begging, "Man, don't do this to us. You're going to fuck me up and you all, too. If you take all our money, what you think I'm to tell the pickup folks?"

Buie said, "Shut the fuck up crying like a damn baby."

Bumpus said, "Everybody move back from the table against the wall! Let me see your hands. And leave your money where it is."

The houseman, close to really crying, said, "You all really going to rob all of us in front of our own eyes?" Everyone laughed.

But Buie told him to shut up and said he sounded like a baby. "We're not here to rob nobody, I don't think!" We laughed.

The houseman named two old Black cops that came by occasionally. He would give them a couple of dollars and "they'd go on their way and never asked to come inside and we ain't never been robbed."

Buie walked over to the large pool table where there were stacks of dice and money in front of about twenty men and one woman. Buie told the houseman, "The three of us know everyone here, and you know us. We're not thieves. We're not on the take. And you can tell anyone downtown you want to; we don't give a shit. You understand?"

Like a choir, everyone said, "Yeah!"

"Now," Buie said, "it's Police Circus time." Everyone, again like a choir, laughed. "All of you got kids or know some kids. We're selling Police Circus tickets. They are $1 a ticket. We're leaving circus tickets here with you." He called the houseman's name again. "There's 500 from me, 500 from Brooks, and 500 from Bumpus. Now, everybody here can count. Three times 500 is 1500. We'll be back tomorrow around the same time. We don't want any circus tickets back, but $1500 in three stacks of $500 each. Is everybody on board?"

The houseman said, "Yeah. We'll have it. We can do that. I really thought you young brothers were breaking in on the white folks' hussle."

Buie said, "We are. This is our community that we patrol. So put the word out. You can tell the crackers you're workin' for."

Bumpus spoke up, "Anyone have any complaints about what Officer Buie has said?"

Several persons mumbled. Some said out loud, "No!"

The houseman said, "We're straight. It'll be here for you."

I had to say something. "We don't want any food stamps, personal checks, or money orders. It's got to be greenbacks. Cash. You can mark 'em if you want to."

Everybody laughed.

The houseman responded, "You are some bold nigger cops, but we'll have you $1500 tomorrow. Now get the hell out of here so we can continue our friendly game."

Everybody laughed.

Bumpus said, "Oh yeah, there are more circus tickets where those come from in the event you want to buy more than 1500. We'll have more tickets with us."

I said, "Just a dollar a ticket, no more, no less."

Buie said, "Good day, gentlemen, and lady."

We laughed and left. Buie and I got in service and drove around to 17th Terrace and The Paseo in the parking lot of Papa Lou's restaurant where Bumpus had parked his own car. Bumpus and I got into Buie's car. We had a good laugh on what we had done.

But there was some concern about the information getting back to the folks downtown. We agreed that they couldn't afford to fire all three of us. And the money wasn't for us. It was for the Police Officers' Benefit Association and to make kids happy at the circus.

The next day, just about an hour before Buie and I were to end our shift, Bumpus met us, and Buie and I got out of service to check the bowling alley. Up the steps we went. Buie banged on the door with his nightstick.

The same doorman peeped out at us. The houseman appeared. He handed Buie $1650 and said, "Keep the change."

I said, "Bullshit! How many tickets you got, Buie? How many you got, Bumpus?"

Buie said, "Mine are in the car, only about twenty-five." Bumpus reached in his inside jacket pocket and said he only had sixteen. I had twenty in my jacket pocket. All together we only had sixty-one tickets. We needed eighty-nine more tickets to take the other $150.

Buie said, "Here, take the extra money back. We'll come back later with additional tickets. You'll be here. We appreciate you helping out the Police Association and the kids."

Bumpus suggested all three of us keep the tickets we had and he would get another 150 from his sergeant when he got to work. We divided the $1500 equally as agreed and gave Bumpus the go-ahead to pick up the additional 150 tickets. Buie said he would ride back out with Bumpus after he relieved him and go back to the gambling place and give the houseman the tickets and pick up the additional $150.

Later, in the evening, Buie stopped by my house and gave me $50 of the $150 the houseman had given him. At the end of the circus ticket sales period, I turned in the highest amount of the three of us and the highest of my squad.

No, we never got any "blowback."

We had this pact among the three of us, that we would never do anything illegal or unethical. Occasionally, some of the older Black officers cautioned us about what we were doing. We made sure that if we were ever confronted with discipline, it wouldn't be because we had done anything wrong. We only confronted the illegal activity that was in our predominately Black district.

I said we never got any backlash, but we did get a warning.

One afternoon after the circus ticket move, three of the "old-timers," Detective Sergeant DeGraffeinreid, Detective Omar Brown, and Detective Laymon Walker, met with Buie and me (Bumpus had the day off) at Paseo Park near the bathhouse (now the Gregg/Klice Community Center). I had received a call from Omar that he, DeGraffenreid, and Walker wanted to meet with Bumpus, Buie, and me. I tried to reach Bumpus, but my message didn't get to him in time for him to make the meeting.

Sergeant DeGraffenreid started the conversation. "We've wanted to meet with you three young officers for your own safety while on this racist department in this racist city. What you're doing out here in our community is so necessary, but it's going to have to be another move like in the '30s when this department went from city to state control. There still are remnants of both the Mafia and the Pendergast machine in the community. We don't want the three of you to get hurt. The way you hit the crap house up there on Vine was like a movie! Everybody's talking about how clever it was—and it was clean.

"But you made a lot of folks mad, inside and outside the department. I imagine, after lauding you for it, some are saying behind your backs, 'Who do those young rookies, nigger cops, think they are?' We just want you to be careful."

Omar said, "DeGraffenreid has five of us working for him. Although the bastards want us to just work burglaries, we're working everything. You need backup on some of this shit, give us a heads-up ahead of time. We'll back you up! No shit!"

Buie and I thanked them and told them we'd pass the conversation on to Bumpus. We knew they took our safety and future seriously.

After we both got off, we went by Bumpus's house and told him about our meeting with DeGraffenreid, Brown, and Walker. We knew we had to take their words of caution seriously. But we decided we would continue without asking for backup because they knew more about what was going on than we did; they might be compromised by knowing more of the actors than we did, and they might not agree with certain places or persons we were targeting. We thought the fewer who knew what and when we were going to hit, the better off we would be.

So, we continued, but nothing drew the attention like the gambling house on Vine. That was "cool," if we had to say so ourselves.

As we began to draw a lot of heat, I suggested to Bumpus and Buie that we should share with some of the leadership in our community what we were doing, just in case something went down. Bumpus and Buie thought it was a good idea, and since it was my idea, they "commissioned" me to make the contacts. We sat down and drew up a list of persons who should be approached. Those on our list were: Dr. Girard Bryant, my Lincoln Junior College professor; Miss Lucile Bluford, of the *Kansas City Call*, a Black weekly newspaper; Mr. Thomas Webster, executive director of the Urban League; the Reverend Dr. John W. Williams, pastor at St. Stephen Baptist Church; Mr. Carl Johnson, president of the NAACP and who later became the first Black Kansas City municipal court judge; and Mr. Leon Jordan, former Kansas City police officer and the first Black lieutenant (who resigned the appointment when he found his charge was over only Black officers). I met personally with each of them over a week. They all appreciated what we were trying to do and why, but like the "old-timers," cautioned us . . . not to fear being reprimanded or fired. They assured us that wouldn't happen as long as we didn't break the law. But cleaning up our community— that was a different thing.

Mr. Jordan was very angry. He said what we were doing was just the tip of the iceberg. He said, "Those are the most corrupt and racist bunch of bastards that you've ever seen. It's going to take the Feds to come in and break that shit up." He called the names of several people; among those was a chief and a high-ranking officer: Bernard Brannon and Lieutenant Kenneth Layne. He predicted they and others would be indicted. And later on, they were.

Miss Bluford was the last person whom I talked with and she summed it up for the group. She said, "Brooksie, I'm not worried about them firing either one of you down at that police department where that racist cop is. He's a terror in our community and the chief won't do anything about it. I am concerned about the safety of you all. So, watch yourselves. That's my concern. Tell Officers Buie and Bumpus what I said. You all be careful."

I thanked each of them on behalf of the three of us. And as I reflect, our safety was our least concern. Maybe because we were young and somewhat naive—and were out to save our community by ourselves. Our safety never ran across our minds—at least, we never discussed it.

After having so much success without anyone complaining, somehow the word got out to those on the take—especially the higher-ups—that we had contacted a broad cross section of the Black community leadership. And it wouldn't take much to prove that many of the places we were hitting were paying some cops and politicians off or someone from the North End, even those in administrative positions.

For example, after the three of us had hit a couple big illegal gambling places, Captain Canaday came to roll call one evening and said, "When you do your job out there on the street and someone says that they are going to call me about it, forget it. Put their asses in jail. You'll damn sure have my support and the support of all the sergeants and lieutenants under my command." Most of the Black officers knew that Captain Canaday was really talking to Bumpus, Buie, and me because no other officers, Black or white, were doing this except for one of the most racist cops.

Canady was the owner of a tavern out on Troost and frequently called out there because of trouble.

After the captain made that statement, we intensified our efforts and had great success. We conducted these three-man attacks on lawbreakers in the two Black districts, both Black and white owned.

And we dropped Captain Canaday's name on the street on numerous occasions. We might say, "Captain Canaday will hear about this." (There was a feeling on the street that Captain Canaday was on the take and close to the hoodlums on the north end of town.)

Even when we stopped certain Black men on traffic violations, we'd be told, "I'll get your job." On many occasions, they would tear up the citation in front of us and throw it on the ground. So, we got together with a certain city prosecutor who prosecuted those who tore up the citations. We arrested them for "careless driving." Sometimes, if they were driving, we had their cars towed.

Years Later, a Familiar Face Joined My Shift, 1957

Earlier, I mentioned that my cousin Raymond and three of my friends and I were approached by two white cops when we were with our horses at 35th and Elmwood. Well, lo and behold! The left-handed cop—who so many years ago wore a leather glove on his left hand, cursed us, called us niggers, and choked Raymond almost to death—joined my shift. Now it was nine years later, and I was an established police officer. We were working the "dogwatch" shift (midnight to 8:00 a.m.). I didn't say anything that first night, but I knew that I had to eventually let him know who I was and that I knew who he was. It was about the fourth or fifth day, still on the evening shift, when I had made up my mind that I would find the right time, one on one, to confront him.

It was just before roll call time and I went into the roll call room to read over some of the old pickup sheets that were on the makeshift shelf against the west wall. Some of my colleagues began to come in. We engaged in small talk about what had occurred during our duty the night before and so on.

In walked my colleague from the past. I introduced myself, shook his hand, looked him dead in the eyes, and welcomed him to our shift. He said, "Okay, thanks. I guess I'm the only newcomer. When I was introduced about a week ago, no one said shit to me, except the one who I relieved."

I said, "Yes, as you can probably tell, I was off three days. But do you remember me?"

He stared at me for a minute or two and said, "No. Should I?"

I said, "Maybe not, but let me share with you why I remember you. In 1948, did you ride the district around 35th and Elmwood and had a partner who was older and obese?"

He answered, "Yes." He remembered and spoke his partner's name.

"Do you remember driving upon maybe five or six Black boys who had three horses, and you approached them and asked, 'Where'd you niggers steal these horses?' And they told you the horses belonged to them. Then you asked for identification, and one of the boys had just turned eighteen, according to his driver's license, and you asked for his draft card. He told you he had just turned eighteen and had a number of days left to register.

"You grabbed him by his shirt collar. You twisted it and choked him until he almost passed out. You held your billy club in your left hand with a glove on it, with your hat cocked to the left, just as you are wearing it now. And you told him if he didn't have the card the next time you saw his nigger ass, you would kick his nigger ass with the club?

"I know it's been nine years, but do you remember any of what I've said?"

He said, "Hell, no! That wasn't me."

I said, addressing him by his name, "It was you. I was one of the Black teens. I was sixteen. The eighteen-year-old you almost choked to unconsciousness was my cousin Raymond. You have a glove now on your left hand. No hard feelings. But I did want you to know that what you did to innocent young Black males left a lasting impression of you and the police department. But don't worry about me; I got your back out there on the street."

He turned and walked away.

He and I were patrolling adjoining districts. He was west of Troost; I was east of Troost. We had received a number of calls together, most in my district east of Troost, which meant we were occasionally called as a backup to each other. We patrolled adjoining districts for two or three nights after I confronted him. He had asked the sergeant to be transferred to another district. I don't know what excuse he gave, but he rode the district farther southwest, and we never made calls together again. We were still on the same shift and assigned to the same squad.

I spoke to him every evening when we both reported for work. He never acknowledged his racist behavior nine years earlier or said he was sorry about what he had done. I really didn't expect him to. Racists rarely admit their racism, except the KKK with their hoods on.

A One-Man Terror

While in the police academy, we frequently heard of a white officer whom some called "a one-man terror." We heard he had been promoted and demoted many times. Some said that he had a "hard-on" for Italians and Blacks. He often had three or four henchmen. He was known for a sawed-off cue stick that he used many ways—to punch an individual in the gut, to go into the after-hour clubs or cafés and rake the counter of everything in sight.

When I rode out with my training officers, I heard about this officer's reputation, and it was echoed throughout the Black community. After I hit the streets, my first car assignment was on the police wagon, used usually for transporting those arrested. I made numerous calls to locations where this officer and his henchmen were making arrests. Sometimes, men and women from the Italian and Black communities were crammed into the back of my wagon.

Here is a humorous example. I received a call from the police dispatcher to meet the officers at Parker's Show Bar at 18th and Highland. Its owner was Mr. Obster Parker, a well-known and respected businessman, operating a legitimate club. Mr. Parker served food and drinks and had live entertainment, often with national artists. The club was frequented by Black professionals. Most of the Black police officers and their wives or significant others were regular weekend patrons. My wife, Carol, and I also frequently attended.

Some whites folks also patronized the club. This was before the passage of the public accommodation laws, so while Blacks could not attend white establishments, whites could and did frequent Black establishments.

On this occasion, when I arrived at the club, this officer and several of his henchmen had a dozen or so Black men and women lined up against two police cars. I learned that officers had seen one man coming out of the club with a drink in his hand, a liquor violation. But when they arrested the man, other folks began to complain. Everyone the officers identified as protesters, correctly or incorrectly, was arrested.

One of the officers opened the rear door of my wagon and began to file the men and women into the wagon. There was a lot of mumbling and some loud voices calling the lead officer by his name and mentioning how wrong he and his henchmen were.

This officer hollered back, "What son of a bitch called my name and had something to say? I'll put your ass in with these asses on their way downtown." Of course, no one responded.

After everyone was crammed into the wagon, one of the officers said, "You can go. We'll meet you at Headquarters."

I took off. When I stopped for the red light at an intersection busy on a weekend night, persons from the back of the wagon were hollering out the small side vent, "Open the back door. Let us out." All of a sudden someone opened the back door and all of my "prisoners," women and men, jumped out.

Someone closed the wagon door, banged on the side of the wagon, and yelled, "You can go, Brooks. You got the green light."

The crowd applauded and laughed. I drove a couple of blocks and radioed the officer and told him, "Someone opened the wagon door while I was stopped at the light at 12th and Troost, and everyone escaped." He cursed loudly over the police radio and the catcalls from the crowd went over the police radio, too.

At the end of my shift, officers who heard about the incident gave me thumbs-up or said in a low voice, "Good job, Al," and laughed.

Comradery Grew among the Younger Black Officers—and Our Wives

The department hired a couple more Black officers in our age group. We decided to reach out to them. They were open to our invitation. Our wives had started a "wives' club" to give us support. With the addition of a couple more young Black officers and their wives or significant others, we were really brought close together. These new women became members of the wives' club. The wives' club proposed that we would take turns hosting the get-togethers at different homes centered around the once-a-month paydays of the husbands. A main course meal would be served by the host couple. Others would bring desserts, salads, and drinks—both soft and hard.

We adopted the idea. The next payday, Carol and I hosted the first Friday night session. It went well. We talked about everything and everybody. It started about eight o'clock and ended a little after ten.

It then took on a life of its own. Almost all the young Black officers and their wives or significant others looked forward to our monthly get-togethers. For the second get-together we prepared an agenda. We talked about the police department, promotions, recruitment of Black officers, the dos and don'ts of dealing with racism, and our obligation to our community.

These sessions brought us as officers yet closer together, bonding, looking out for each other. Our numbers grew. After sharing a meal together and discussing our agenda, about 9:30, we socialized, sometimes as late as two or three in the morning. So, what did the women do? Bingo, Pokeno, Old Maid, Spades, bid whist. The men? Gamblers! Shot craps, poker, dominoes (rise and fly), blackjack . . . everything for money. Sometimes, folks lost quite a bit of money but came back the next time and tried to get even. Sometimes they did—and sometimes they got further in the hole.

After a while, all of us officers tried to get the Saturdays following our meetings off because our get-togethers lasted so late.

We had a great time. The comradery grew strong among us officers and our wives. I don't remember what ended our get-togethers, but it was great for everyone while it lasted.

Our wives became close—Bumpus's wife, MayJuana, Buie's wife, Marlean, and my wife, Carol. All were about the same age as Bumpus, Buie, and me.

I have more to tell but let me pause and reflect. Here I am, at eighty-eight, the first and last of the 3Bs, still here. The other two Bs and our wives made their transitions years ago. What's shared herein is only part of the many things we did as the 3Bs. I won't tell all. The statute of limitations has long expired! But I am proud to say we never violated any laws or police regulations (well, maybe a few that didn't apply to a particular situation). We never mistreated anyone. Maybe some of the things we did and how we did them were a little imaginative, creative, out of the ordinary, and even scary, but we never got a rap for what we did; we were never reprimanded, although we developed quite a reputation!

"Robeson Found Guilty of Second-Degree Murder," 1957

It was a Sunday evening when I received a call to meet a woman for information about young kids playing on the roof of an old garage. It was in an apartment building on East 10th or 11th Street right off Paseo Boulevard. The dispatcher gave the apartment number, and I knocked on the door. The lady who called welcomed me. Another woman was sitting on the sofa. The caller said that several small kids were playing on the roof of an old garage in the back of the apartment.

She asked me to follow her to the kitchen. Looking out the back door, I saw the kids. I went out on the porch and hollered to them to be careful and come down off the roof. They all did. I told them it was near dark and they should be going home. One or two said, "Thank you." I watched them go in several different directions. The woman said that she warned them all the time, but they keep coming back. This time she thought she would call the police.

I thanked the woman for calling and told her that I was going to drive around the block and see if any of the kids were still out on the street. Both women thanked me. When I was walking out the door, I noticed a copy of the *Kansas City Call*, the Black weekly newspaper, sitting on the end table. I glanced at the headline, which said something about a man convicted of second-degree murder and gave the victim's name. I knew the victim, Eugene

Russell, and the alleged murderer, Alex Robeson, and their friend Denver Parlor. All three frequented my patrol area.

I made some comment and read the headline aloud and started out the door. The woman who had called said, "Yes, but he's not the killer."

Standing in the doorway, I asked, "How do you know?"

She said, "We just know."

I said, "What do you mean, 'We just know'?"

She said, "We know who the real killer is."

The woman who had made the call regarding the kids said, "It's her husband!"

I said, "You mind if I come back in and ask some questions and take notes?"

They said, "No. It's okay with us."

I was offered a seat. I then asked about the other woman's husband. The two women proceeded to fill me in on the details. The woman's husband was Denver Parlor. The couple lived in Wayne Miner Court on Woodland. Alex Robeson and Eugene Russell had been involved in a fight at 14th and Troost in front of the apartment building. People had been watching. Denver pretended to separate the two men when Russell seemed to be getting the best of the fight. When Denver pushed them apart, he stabbed Russell in the side, just below the armpit. Russell hollered, "Hey, man, you stabbed me," talking to Alex.

Denver grabbed Alex by the arm and ran around the corner somewhere. Russell fell to the ground and yelled, "I've been stabbed. I'm bleeding. You all saw Alex stab me." The police came and ordered an ambulance to take Russell over to the hospital.

Some of Russell's friends followed the ambulance and went into the emergency room. Alex and Denver came back to the scene. The police arrested Alex. The people who were willing to tell what happened had already named Alex as the one who stabbed Russell. Someone whispered, "That's him." The officer who was at the scene questioning people placed Alex under arrest. He left the scene with Alex and took him to General Hospital #2.

When the officer and Alex walked in, the doctors had begun working on Russell. The women told me, "Russell raised up off the gurney and said, 'That's him, that's Alex. He's the one who stabbed me.'" Russell later died from stab wounds. Both women said that Alex had been writing everyone—the judge, the prosecutor, and the police—about his innocence. No one would respond. I asked the women if they would be willing to talk to me again about this and hang in there with me while I checked a few things out. Both said they would.

I asked the woman who made the call if I could have her phone number. She gave it to me, but Mrs. Parlor said I couldn't call her because her husband came home on occasion.

I went and bought a *Call* paper. On Monday, I came in earlier than usual and went to talk to Captain Canaday, who was head captain over the patrol division at Headquarters and the plainclothes unit.

Plainclothes units were like the playpen for the station captains. They called up uniformed officers from the streets and allowed them to wear their civilian clothes and let them play detective. All those who were in the plainclothes unit were favorites of the captains. I never knew any Black officers to be in the plainclothes unit.

The captain was in his office—with the door open. I knocked and said, "Captain Canaday, good afternoon. Can I come in and speak with you a couple minutes?" I had already walked in and had my hand on the doorknob and was slowly closing the door.

The captain stood up and said, "Yeah, Alvin, come on in." I thanked him, and he told me to have a seat.

I mentioned the case of Alex Robeson and Eugene Russell. Before he could respond, I rolled out my scheme to him and told him the two women, one of whom was Parlor's wife, would help. I told the captain that I didn't know why Mrs. Parlor was obsessed about Robeson being in prison and his innocence. I made my case, telling him, "Captain, I'm not as much concerned about Parlor getting charged as I am about an innocent man down there at the state penitentiary."

The captain said, "Al, I'm reluctant to go along with your scheme, but I want to talk to these two women first. Get them down here and let me talk to them."

I said, "Thanks, Captain. Can we keep this just between the two of us at this time?"

He thought a minute and said, "Okay, I'll play along with you." I thanked him again and left.

I called my contact, who said that she and Mrs. Parlor were at her apartment. I asked if I could pick them up for the purpose of meeting my captain to plan what we were going to do. I told them that the captain may want to ask them to go over some of what they had gone over with me. They told me they didn't want me to come by their apartment anymore but they would meet me at 11th and Forest. I told her I would be in my own car. She said, "Okay, come on by then."

I picked the two women up, and after meeting with Captain Canaday, our strategy was set. The next day, I located Denver Parlor at 16th and Troost, after checking for him at his home. Denver had quite a police record, so I told him that the detectives wanted to talk to him about something but I didn't know exactly what it was. He said he hadn't been involved in anything except gambling. I told him that if he hadn't done anything, he wouldn't need to worry and would be back on the street in no time.

After I drove into the garage at Headquarters, I took Denver to the first floor. Captain Canaday came, and I introduced them. Canaday told him to have a seat and that he'd be with him in a little while. I had made arrangements for Denver's wife and the other woman to come to Headquarters. We waited for almost an hour until the women got there.

As planned, I asked the women what they wanted. Mrs. Parlor said she had got a call that Denver had been arrested, and she and her friend came downtown to see what was going to happen to him. The captain allowed them to sit in his office while we were checking to see why the detectives wanted to talk to Denver. The captain and I took our positions in the hallway between the two offices where we could hear the conversation between the three.

Denver led the conversation wondering why the detectives had me pick him up. After some back and forth, the other woman said, "Denver, you don't think this has anything to do with Eugene Russell's death, do you? Most folks around 16th Street thought Alex had stabbed Gene, but then they found out that you did. Maybe someone snitched."

Parlor said, "Those folks on 16th Street don't know nut'n but a lot a talk. Anyway, Alex is in prison for Gene's kill'n. Let him do the time. He won't do but a couple years, then he'll be out. Nobody can prove I did it, and the only two that really knows is you two. And you better not say shit."

Both women said they weren't going to say anything. After we had heard Parlor admitting that he was the one who stabbed Russell, Canaday and I entered the office. The captain said the detective who wanted talk to Denver was off and told me to book him for investigation and hold him for one of his plainclothes officers. He told Denver that one of his officers would talk to him the next morning and, if there was nothing, he would be back on the street by noon.

Denver's wife kissed him and told him she'd be back in the morning. I took Denver upstairs to the jail and booked him for investigation. On the elevator on the way up to jail, Parlor said, "This is bullshit, Brooks. I ain't done a damn thing. They're just fuckin' with me because I have a record." I told him that I suspected he'd be out before noon tomorrow, like the captain said. Parlor said, "If my wife is still down there, tell her to call my lawyer and tell him about this shit." I told him I would.

When I got downstairs, the women were still talking to Canaday. I told Parlor's wife what he said. Canaday thanked both women. Mrs. Parlor asked what would happen to Denver. Canaday said he didn't know yet. After the women had left, the captain congratulated me. He said, "Alvin, I think we heard enough that we can talk to the prosecutor and the judge and get Alex free. How long that'll take, I don't know, but the word ought to get to him that we're working on it."

Canaday said he would have Parlor booked for the murder but was sure it wouldn't go anywhere because of the way we got the confession. But at least Alex would be set free. That was all I wanted anyway. In about ten days, Alex was on his way back to Kansas City, and Denver was back on the streets. There was a write-up in the *Kansas City Star*, mostly about Captain Canaday. He was promoted to major and went on to become lieutenant colonel. I only received a letter of commendation.

Alex found me months later and thanked me. Unfortunately, I don't remember whether I was on the department or not, when I got word that someone tried to rob Alex at 19th and Woodland and beat him to death with a rock.

"Officer Brooks Is Inside. Everything's Okay"

As I've mentioned previously, my earlier years on the police department were the final stages of the Pendergast era, with "payoff" practices to either police or politicians or both with Sunday sales of liquor, businesses that fenced stolen merchandise, policy games, and gambling houses.

I was sitting in my patrol car about 2:00 a.m. one Saturday morning at 19th and Vine. It was fall. I saw a woman walking toward me with no sweater or coat on, wearing a sleeveless dress. She approached my police car and tapped on the window on the passenger side. I rolled the window down and said, "Yes, ma'am. Can I help you?"

She began telling me about her husband who was around the corner at a gambling house. She had been there trying to get him to come home. I asked her to have a seat. She continued to tell me that her husband was a good man. Worked hard on construction in Kansas, but almost every Friday after he got paid, he stopped at the gambling house and came home broke about daybreak. They were parents of seven children. They were members of Bethel African Methodist Episcopal (AME) Church. Her husband stopped attending months ago because of the guilt of gambling. But she said, "The first of the month is right around the corner, and we got everything due. My husband works hard for what little money he gets. He rarely wins. And when he does, it does not make up for all he's lost." She told me their address on Highland.

I had a plan. I didn't have anything better to do at 2:00 a.m. I told the woman that I would go back around to the gambling house with her, that I would knock on the door. She would call her husband by name and tell him he'd better come out and go home with her. When the houseman would answer as before that her husband was not in there, she would say, "There's a police car up the street, and I'm going up there and tell the officer what's going on in there."

We rehearsed a couple of times. She was shaking. I didn't know whether it was the weather or what I had asked her to do. Some of these gambling houses were owned and operated by whites; some white owners had Blacks run them. This house was one of many in our two patrol districts. And I knew of at least two that were Black owned and run.

I knew that gambling house. Of course, they, too, were paying someone off to keep from being hit by the vice unit.

Thomas Thomascine Gilder, my birth mother, about age sixteen.

My maternal grandpa, Thomas Gilder. His parents were slaves.

Cluster Brooks, my adoptive father.

Me, twelve to fifteen months old, with my adoptive mother, Estelle, and my Aunt Mittie McDonald.

My adoptive mother and me, three or four years old.

My adoptive mother and me (about nine years old) in our backyard.

Me and my dog, Midnight.

The infamous Brighton hill . . . "Run, nigger, run!"

Carol's eighth-grade class, 1947–1948. Carol is standing in the last row, fourth from right.

My high school graduation class, April 1950. I'm in the back row, third from left.

The Rich/McCoy family home, 2632 Park. Carol and I were married here. A new police station stands in its place today.

rol and me with our two-month-old son Ronall Laverne. Ronall was born January 12, 1951, and weighed
: pounds, four ounces.

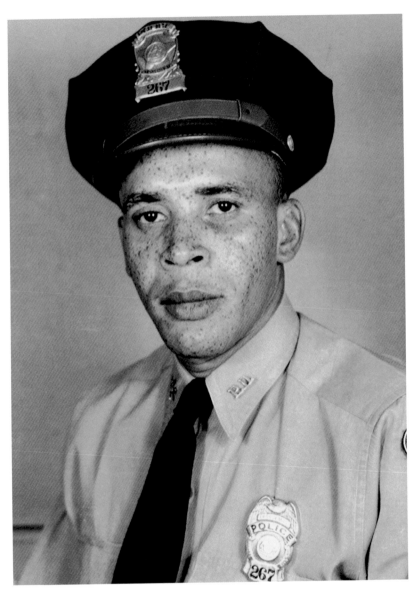

Detective sergeant Lloyd DeGraffenreid.

Forty-fourth KCPD graduation class of twenty-nine cadets, 1954.

In foreground, F. Ratliff; Sgt. Clyde Davidson. From left first row, N. Lecuru; A. Brooks; J. Peterson; F. Kenney; W. Salmon; G. Bramble; E. Scovill. Second row, M. Long; A. Allen; H. Chase; E. Felts; W. Clark; J. Russell.

My first assignment, first platoon, dogwatch (midnight to 8:00 a.m.), 1954.

Christmas morning, 1954.
Thomascine (mother)
holding Carrie Lynn, Estelle
Louise, and Ronall.

My biological mother and me, 1954.

The 3Bs: (top) Brooks, (center) Bumpus, and
(bottom) Buie.

Jules Boudreaux: "Brooks, I ain't dead," 1957.

Coincidence or divine intervention? Jules
Boudreaux II and his mother, Lavern.

Ronall; my son joins the Air Force.

Wilbur Lamar Herring, my biological father, 1963.

Negroes Still Angry at Police

THE police treated all Negroes as if they were hoodlums and rioters."

"Before, people had mixed notions about the police department, but not now."

"It is clearly out in the open the police don't like Negroes, and we don't like them."

The Negro community, following the disturbances here, has never been more united in its opposition to the police.

While the police are a constant point of friction in almost every lower income Black community, police-community relations in the inner-city area here have suffered immeasurably.

Angered by Gas

Several Negro parents said they doubt if they could ever forget or forgive the police for its incidents at a church and central and Lincoln high schools.

Many middle-class Negroes who formerly had little reason to dislike the police report they now are bitter.

One mother said some of the incidents have resulted in a negative attitude on the part of many.

"We felt we were all being contained to destroy ourselves," said Mrs. Samantha Cunningham, 3809 Benton boulevard. "Aren't the police supposed to protect me, too?"

She said many teenagers are bitter after the gas incidents, stating they feel they are afforded no protection by the police. Parents, she said, are frightened because they don't know whom to turn to.

Herman Johnson, president of the Greater Kansas City chapter of the National Association for the Advancement of Colored People, said the police could have shown more compassion for those not involved in the rioting.

whatever the police did was right.

Elige Martin, brother of "Shugg" Martin, a fatality victim of the disturbances, said many Negroes had supported Hearnes because he was from a rural area and they thought he would be for the poor people, but that they have no use for him now.

Others felt the governor had been misinformed as to the chain of events.

a long time and it is just natural for them to do what they did because they have been taught that.

"Negroes are only paying back some of the things whites have done to them."

Parnell said he felt the white community now would make promises, but would not do anything. Many Negroes expressed this view, that everything will be the same.

William Russell, a member

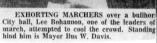

EXHORTING MARCHERS over a bullhorn City hall, Lee Bohannon, one of the leaders of march, attempted to cool the crowd. Standing hind him is Mayor Ilus W. Davis.

a deaf ear. They don't have to do anything because there won't be any reprisals. But when people bring pressure to bear through riots and destruction, those in power are ready to sit and listen and try to work out a solution."

He said anyone who thinks the riots served no useful purpose is out of touch with reality. He pointed to the passage of the civil rights bill, adding, "many congressmen were going to slash it to pieces until the riots.

"I believe the riots did some good because it made the white man aware of what can happen in Kansas City," said James Anderson, 1321 East Thirty-first street. "But, if the white man forgets the riots—that Negroes are tired of being down-trodden—there will be more riots and on a larger scale."

Anderson directed most of his anger at the police.

"The police," he said, "often stop and question Negroes entering white neighborhoods but ignore white persons entering Negro neighborhoods." He said the continued presence in Negro communities of police only adds to the tension and creates animosity toward the police.

Anderson said the black man is bitter because he has been a second-class citizen too long and he is tired of the indignities forced upon him by the white community.

"If the white community does not change its attitude," he said, "the black man will force a change."

Need for Tact

Miss Carolyn McMillian, a clerk at Drumm's cleaners

Tuesday, April 9, 1968. Speakers at city hall following the student march: Mayor Ilus "Ike" Davis and community activist Lee Bohannan.

Police throw tear gas at students.

The crowd listening to speakers at the top of the City Hall Steps.

Black Panthers

Early formation of the
Kansas City Black Panthers.

My swearing-in ceremony administered by City Clerk Edwin Byrd. I became the first
African American city director, 1968.

The twentieth anniversary of AdHoc: Don and Adele Hall (Hallmark Cards, honorary co-chairs), and me and my wife, Carol Brooks. The Halls raised $160,000 for AdHoc.

Michael Carter, general manager of Carter Broadcasting Group, Inc. (oldest Black-owned radio station west of the Mississippi) and me.

Man Gives Up 27-Hour Siege

Human Relations Director Successful In Ending Crisis

A 37-year-old Kansas City man ended a 27-hour hostage situation on Wednesday afternoon at about 1:30, after a city official persuaded him to surrender to police.

Albert Abdul Harbin ended the siege and surrendered to authorities at his duplex, 4213 E. Linwood Blvd., after talking with Alvin Brooks, director of the City's Human Relations department.

Harbin kept his month-old son, Hakeem and his common-law wife's two other children, Tiuana, 12 and Felisa, 6, in the duplex

after a fight on Tuesday morning with the woman who has been identified as Bridget Bryant, 32.

The couple had been arguing Tuesday morning. The woman escaped from the duplex at around 5 a.m. Tuesday and told police that Harbin had beaten her with a baseball bat and shot her in the foot with a handgun and also told them that Harbin was in the home with her children.

When police arrived, Harbin refused to let police enter and an Operation 100—a hostage situation

where the police department's special tactics squad is called—began at about 10 a.m. on Tuesday.

Communications Problem

It was reported that Harbin had asked to speak with Brooks on Tuesday, but Brooks did not get to talk to him because of what he termed a "communications problem" with police.

However on Wednesday, Brooks was called upon by Police Chief Larry Joiner to negotiate with Harbin. Using a bull horn from an adjacent duplex, Brooks said he told Harbin that he

understood he wanted to talk to him and that he was there to help.

Brooks, in an interview with THE CALL in his office on the fourth floor of City Hall on Wednesday, said Harbin told him he wasn't worried about the children.

Power and gas had been cut off in the duplex throughout Tuesday and Wednesday at interval periods.

"I told him to send the children out and to put their coats on because it

was cold outside," Brooks said.

"He was concerned about being beaten because he said he had been beaten

before," Brooks said.

Brooks added that he talked to Harbin about possible charges that would be filed against him,

but also assured him that he would not be beaten or killed by the police.

Harbin stuck his head out the door, holding the baby,

and stuck his head back in before handing the baby to Brooks. The eldest child ran across Linwood Blvd.

Continued on page 2.

THE CALL
Southwest's Leading Weekly

(USPS 585-260)

VOL. 65, NO. 36   KANSAS CITY, MO., WEEK OF FEBRUARY 8 TO FEBRUARY 14, 1985   Price 35 Cents

CITY OFFICIAL ENDS 27-HOUR SIEGE. . .Alvin Brooks, director of the City's Human Relations department, carries out the four-week old son of Albert Abdul Harbin from the duplex at 4213 E. Linwood Blvd, ending a 27-hour Operation 100 on Wednesday afternoon at

ending the police department's longest hostage situation in it's history. The Operation 100 began on Tuesday morning at about 10 a.m. after Harbin had an argument with his common-law wife, who escaped from the duplex a few hours earlier and reported the

Successor To Holliday To Be Chosen Monday Night

The Jackson County legislature will select a successor to Harold L. "Doc" Holliday of the fifth legislative district Monday night, Feb. 11, at its meeting to be held in the Independence, Mo., City Hall. The session begins at 6 p.m.

Holliday, a member of the county body since its organization 12 years ago, resigned his position January 25 in the midst of a Circuit Court hearing at which his ouster was being sought because of his handling of the Leon Jordan scholarship fund.

The 14 remaining members of the legislature will pick one of three nominees submitted by the Democratic county committee members from the fifth district which Holliday represented.

The committeemen and committeewomen of the Holliday's seat but he failed to get a second, so his

downtown courthouse to pick a panel of three nominees.

The three persons chosen, all members of Freedom, Inc., are: Mrs. Carol Coe, an assistant city attorney; Thabit Murarah, an officer with the Jackson County Juvenile court; and Ms. Byther Williams, Democratic committeewoman from the 18th ward.

Of the eight wards in the fifth legislative district, seven are considered controlled by Freedom, Inc., since all of the committee persons from those wards are members of the inner city political organization. Only the 19th ward is not a Freedom ward.

At the county committee meeting Monday night, Joe Nickel, committeeman from the 19th, nominated himself as a candidate for

placed in nomination by Mrs. Aretha Welch, wife of Archie Welch, newly-elected president of Freedom, Inc. Her nomination was seconded by Mrs. Lisa Hughes.

Mr. Murarah was nominated by Rob Hollinger. John Toombs seconded the nomination.

Ms. Williams was nominated by George Coates with Mrs. Hughes seconding the nomination.

The meeting, held in the Jackson County legislative chambers on the second floor of the downtown courthouse, was presided over by Bill Baker, chairman of the Democratic county committee.

The meeting lasted less than 10 minutes.

Each of the three nominees will be interviewed by the legislators Monday night before the choice is made.

Speculation around the

Twenty-seven-hour police standoff, 1985.

THE NATION'S NEWSPAPER

USA TODAY

Pushers meet their match
Neighbors are uniting to reclaim streets

ANTI-DRUG WARRIORS: Members of the Ad Hoc group against crime have helped shut down 54 crack houses in Kansas City, Mo since February including the one behind them. From left, they are Ricky B. Bell, Stephen Newman, Clifford Sargeon, **Alvin Brooks,** Aasim Baheyadeen, Ron Monroe and Calvin Neal. On weekends they go door-to-door.

AdHoc's Black Men Together front page of *USA Today* (Tuesday, May 23, 1989). From left to right: Rick Bell, Stephen Newman, Clifford Sargeon, me, Aasim Baheyadeen, Ron Monroe, and Calvin Neal.

To Alvin Brooks
With best wishes, a gratitude. Sincerely
Gy Bush

Officially appointed to the president's Drug Advisory Council, 1989. White House: William Moss, council chair; me; President Bush; William Bennett, drug czar.

President Bush and a Washington delegation meets with AdHoc, Kansas City, 1990.

To Alvin Brooks
with best wishes, Geo Bush

The president and me at the Music Hall just before he addressed metro law enforcement officers.

Miller Nichols, civic leader and a supporter of AdHoc Group Against Crime.

Torchbearer, running in the torch relay in the 1996 Olympics.

Me with President Clinton at the White House.

Brooks will run for mayor

Fund raising will help gauge candidacy

By STEVE KRASKE
The Kansas City Star

Ending months of uncertainty, Alvin Brooks, mayor pro tem of the Kansas City Council and a longtime anti-crime crusader, said Wednesday that he is running for mayor in 2007.

"I don't want to do it for ego," Brooks said. "I don't want to do it for show and tell. I want to do it to continue the progress of the city and build on what's been done and continue to try to build bridges and narrow the gap between north and south and various ethnic groups."

One likely opponent, Councilwoman Becky Nace, acknowledged that Brooks would be the best-known candidate for the office. If elected at age 74, he also would be the oldest mayor in city history. The record-holder is James Cowgill, who was 70 when he began serving in 1918.

Brooks said age should not be a factor.

"I feel good," he said. "There's nothing more important than feeling good about yourself and others and wanting to serve and wanting to help."

Brooks said he wanted to raise $50,000 in the next 90 days to "see if people will put their money where their mouths are." If he falls short of that mark, he might reverse course.

"I won't run for the sake of running," he said.

Brooks

Besides Brooks and Nace, other potential candidates to succeed outgoing Mayor Kay Barnes include 1999 mayoral candidate Janice Ellis; Councilmen Jim Glover, John Fairfield and Chuck Eddy; and lawyer Mike Burke. Barnes is barred by city charter from seeking a third consecutive term.

Ellis said Wednesday that Brooks' entry would have no effect on her decision and hinted that she was likely to enter.

"It looks very, very good," she said. "I don't see why I wouldn't do this."

Nace said she welcomed Brooks into the field.

"It'll give the public a choice, which they should have for mayor," she said.

Brooks is the president of MoveUp, a grass-roots crime-fighting group formerly known as the Ad Hoc Group Against Crime. He is a former Kansas City police officer and assistant city manager and was the first director of the city's Human Relations Department.

He is known as something of an unofficial inner-city minister, the person grieving families call even in the middle of the night after violent crimes.

Brooks said he expected to campaign on a portfolio of issues, including improvements in basic city services, race relations and city infrastructure.

"I don't think there's one single thing at this point," he said.

He described himself as a big fan of City Manager Wayne Cauthen, who recently received a new three-year contract from the council with Brooks' support.

One longtime Kansas City political observer, Jim Bergfalk, said Brooks and Nace rank as the race's early front-runners. "But having said that, there's still a whole bunch of unknown factors yet," including Brooks' ability to raise money and secure a political base.

The city already has elected an African-American as mayor in Emanuel Cleaver, so race may not be a major factor. "Even in places where race lies below the surface, he has something of a Buck O'Neil quality," Bergfalk said.

Brooks' age may not be decisive either. Bergfalk said a lot of likely voters in Kansas City are in their 70s. "It's less of an issue than it may have been in the past.

"But is he formidable? Without question."

To reach Steve Kraske, call **(816) 234-4312** *or send e-mail to* *skraske@kcstar.com.*

News spreads fast about my decision to run for mayor.

PUTTING THE FOCUS ON MAYOR'S RACE

Brooks and Funkhouser are both determined to lead the city, but they reached this campaign from different backgrounds.

Candidates Alvin Brooks (left) and Mark Funkhouser on trail. Recently they sat together for a portrait b

Funkhouser . . . 6'8" to my 5'11" (with four telephone books under my butt!).

Funkhouser becomes mayor. My concession speech with Carol, and grandchildren Cierra, Mylin, and Mariah, 2007.

3-28-07   SHANE KEYSER | THE KANSAS CITY STAR

Accompanied by his wife, Carol, and grandchildren, Alvin Brooks conceded the election to Mark Funkhouser at Brooks' election night party at the Westin Crown Center hotel.

Spokesperson for the Obama campaign for the Western District of Missouri.

Alvin Brooks & Barak Obama

January 2008

Alvin Brooks - Police Commissioner
March 23, 2010

Swearing-in ceremony, Kansas City Board of Police Commissioners. Left to right: Attorney Mischa Buford Epps, secretary to the board; attorney Karl Zobrist, board president; James Wilson, retiring board member; Carol Brooks, wife; daughters Estelle Brooks, Carrie Brooks Brown, Rosalind Brooks Wesley, Diana Brooks Lloyd, and Tameisha Brooks Jenkins. I was sworn in by Judge Thomas H. Newton, Missouri Court of Appeals, Western District.

Our sixtieth wedding anniversary with family, Branson, Missouri, 2010.

Receiving the Harry S. Truman Public Service Award. Left to right: Naomi Holt, sister-in-law; Shanita Pardue, granddaughter; Estelle Brooks, daughter; Diana Brooks Lloyd, daughter; Paula Holt Nix, niece; and Avery Pardue, great-grandson.

My queen . . . from age thirteen (1948 until 2013) . . . and after.

In fondest memory, Carol Lavern Rich Brooks.

IN FONDEST MEMORY
Carol Lavern Rich Brooks
MAY 24, 1935 - JULY 21, 2013

Loving, devoted and meaningful...
a life well lived.

My five queens and me, Las Vegas. Left to right in order of age: Estelle, Carrie, Rosalind, Dianna, and Tameisha.

The African American officers, Buie, Bumpus, and I, knew what gambling houses or places were paying someone off in our two districts. We were among the youngest and newest Black officers on the force, and we developed a scheme to invade when necessary.

How did we know? Because if we got out of service for a building or a house check, and it was one of the places that was paying off to run, the dispatcher would order us to call the dispatcher.

For example, my radio number was 123. I would say, "123 to the dispatcher."

The dispatcher would come back, "Come in, 123."

I would say, "123 out of service on a building check," and give the address.

If it were one of "those" buildings or houses, the dispatcher would come back, "Car 123, call the dispatcher before getting out of service at that location."

So, I would call the dispatcher from a pay phone. When one of them answered, they would call us by name and tell us, "Al, that location is under surveillance. They don't want district cars interfering." We had no choice but to get back in service.

So, we employed our scheme. We wouldn't get out of service at the address. Instead, we would get out on a pedestrian check near the gambling house. So, that's what I did.

One of my crusade partners, Buie, car 124, was off duty. There was a young white officer driving relief on car 124 who really didn't know the streets, and I was afraid to involve him anyway. In a situation like this, the one-man car procedure was to call a second car. So, I'd have to violate the procedure and go into this crowd without any backup. "Oh, what the hell!"

I drove up to the corner a half block away from the gambling house. "123 to the dispatcher."

"Come in, 123."

"123 on a pedestrian check at 19th and Highland. Black female, light complexion, in her forties, dark, sleeveless dress."

"123 out of service, pedestrian 19th and Highland, 2:53 a.m. [call numbers]."

We got out of my police car and headed down the hill to the gambling house. There were several such houses in that block, but I knew the right one. I knew who the houseman was. We stepped on the porch. I asked the woman if she was ready.

She said in a quiet voice, "Yes, sir. I'm ready."

I said, "Remember now, when you say that you're going up the street to tell the police officer, I believe he's going to tell your husband that he has to leave. As soon as the door opens, you step behind me and follow me on in. But stay close to me. You identify your husband for me if he's not the one who comes to the door."

I knocked on the door hard. I said, "Call your husband." She called him as I knocked again and again. The houseman hollered. "I told you awhile ago, your husband is not in here tonight."

The woman spoke the lines about the police car up the street. The houseman, as I had predicted, said, "Hey, man, you'd better go out there with your woman. I don't want no cop coming down here. See you next Friday."

The door opened, but it wasn't her husband. It was the doorman. I stepped in with gun in hand and ordered the doorman to get against the wall. There were about two dozen gamblers around a pool table. The houseman was at the head of the table facing me. I ordered everyone back off the table. "Leave your money where it is; keep your hands in sight."

"That's my husband," the woman said, pointing.

The houseman, in his early fifties, was speaking to me from the time I stepped inside. "Hey, Brooks, you're a young rookie cop. Man, don't mess with these white folks' money and get fired. You and those other two young nigger cops. The word has gotten around. You'all gonna get fired. The white folks downtown know what you'all are doing out here."

I called the houseman by his name and told him, "Open the damn back door. Now! Holler out there real loud: 'Brooks is inside. He's okay.'"

I still had my gun out but not pointed toward anyone. The money was in front of each gambler. I ordered the houseman again to open the back door and holler outside as I had told him. The houseman finally opened the door and asked, "Why am I hollering that out the back door?"

I told him again, "Just holler out there real loud, and say, 'Brooks is inside; he's okay!'" He said, "Say what?"

I said, "Just say real loud what I told you to say. 'Brooks is inside; he's okay.'"

He said what I told him to say. The dogs were barking loud. I said, "Shut the door. Thank you." I told the houseman to go around the table and take $5 off of every pile, beginning with his—but take $10 off of his.

He said, "Brooks, you're a bright young nigger cop, man. Don't be on the take like some of these other cops. These white folks gonna get your gun and badge before daybreak. And that goes for Buie and Bumpus, too. You'all trying to make a name for yourselves out here in the Negro community. You'all still rookies. Come on, man."

I told him, "Thanks for worrying about me and my job and Bumpus and Buie. But nobody in here's gonna tell what happened tonight. Hurry up, man, pick up the money before daybreak."

I kinda smiled. I told the woman's husband to go get his money and come over and give it to his wife. He had certainly been losing again. He only gave his wife about $17.

She had told me that his paycheck every Friday was about $90 a week if the weather was good because his construction work was all outside.

I said to both, "I want you to go and sit in the police car, but hold just a minute." I told the houseman to give the money he had collected to the woman. "Count it out to her," I told him. "Count out loud." He did. It was $105. Some of the persons seemed to be spectators, and not at the table. Others were mumbling about losing their $5. Some didn't have much more than $5 showing. Which meant, as always, the house was the winner.

I told the woman to go over to the houseman and get the money. And thank everyone. She did. I told everyone, "Don't blame this woman and her husband for taking your money. Blame yourselves for being in here." I told the woman and her husband to go and wait in my police car.

The houseman continued to look after my welfare. I told him to open the back door again and holler loud. "'Brooks is coming out. Everything's okay.' Say it again, loud, over those dogs barking back there." I told him holler again louder and closed the door.

He did. "Brooks is coming out. Everything's okay." I told him real loud a third time. I then told the houseman that if he allowed the woman's husband to come in here again, Buie, Bumpus, and I and other Black officers would put him out of a job. "And the rest of you can find another gambling hole." I told the houseman, "Now test us." I had holstered my gun. I left, closing the door behind me. The couple were standing by the police car because I had locked it. I unlocked it and they both got in. The husband sat in the front seat and the wife in the back. He asked, "Where are the other cops you had the houseman hollering out the back door to?"

I said, "They left down the alley back there." None of them knew there actually were no police behind the house.

I took the couple home. I told the wife that she could go inside, but I wanted to talk to the husband.

I got back in service as soon as I got back in my car. I was out for about a half hour, but I hadn't received a call inquiring if I needed another car, or if the dispatcher felt I had been out of service on a pedestrian check too long and I might have been in some kind of trouble.

After the woman got out of the police car, I began to lecture her husband. I told him all the good things his wife said about him. Also, about his gambling habit and how most of the time he lost and that she had to borrow money to pay bills and buy food. He admitted everything his wife had told me. I suggested strongly that he start going back to church— "this Sunday." He thanked me and promised he was going to surprise his wife and kids and walk the two blocks to church with them.

I asked when he had to go to work. He said he caught the streetcar a little after 5:00 a.m. and got to the West Bottoms, where the construction foreman would pick him up with two other workers and drive to the Eudora, Kansas, construction site. He normally got to work about 7:00 a.m.

I took his phone number and told him I was working midnight to 8:00 a.m. and if I wasn't on a call, I would call him and pick him up and drop him off in the West Bottoms. That Monday I did take him to meet his ride. And several days after that. When I changed shifts to evenings, I couldn't pick him up.

A month or so later, I saw him one evening on Vine Street. He thanked me. He said he had not been gambling since the night I came and got him, that he had been working steady somewhere in Kansas and the job had been completed. He was now working in Independence, Missouri. He said none of the family members had missed a Sunday at church. He asked if we could pray together. I said, "Yes!" He led a prayer and we went our separate ways. I saw him and his wife individually and together many times after that. We always spoke and inquired how each was doing.

Six Black Officers Transferred to Sheffield Station as an Experiment, February 1958, and the Dissolving of the 3Bs

In early February 1958, six Black officers—Bumpus, Buie, Jethro Jones, Williams Hayes, Lester Duke, and I—were ordered to report to Chief Brannon's office. Buie, Bumpus, and I wondered if it was discipline time for us—but why would Jones, Hayes, and Duke also be called in? Well, we decided we were prepared to defend our honest manner of policing and everything we'd done. Lieutenant Clifford Warren, the highest-ranking Black officer who worked out of the chief's office, sat in on the meeting but didn't say anything.

To our surprise the subject was: "I want to try something here, gentlemen. I've selected the six of you to leave your assignments here at Headquarters and reassigned you to the Sheffield Station and to two predominantly all-white districts. I want to see how you all are accepted in these two districts working from the Sheffield Station. Officers Buie, Bumpus, and Duke, you'll be assigned around the clock around Central High School, District 306. Jones, Brooks, and Hayes, you'll be assigned to District 301 over in the northeast around the clock. Captain Hastings is the commander out there, a good captain. He's expecting you. Sergeant Warren here will give you your letters of transfer with your shifts. I'm depending on you gentlemen to represent the department out there as you have down here. Any questions?"

I waited to see if anyone was going to say anything. Just as I saw he was going to dismiss us, I said, "Yes, Chief Brannon, I do have a question. When are some of the Black officers going to be assigned out to the Country Club Station?" (This is the station that served the all-white, affluent neighborhoods, known as the south-west, where the mayor and the police chief lived.) He looked shocked. My brothers looked at me and then at the chief. I caught him off guard. Warren seemed embarrassed.

"Not yet," he responded. "That's it, gentlemen." Sergeant Warren gave us our reassignment letters and we all caught the elevator together. We all laughed.

Jones said, "Did you see how red the chief turned when you asked him that question? That's why you're being sent to the boondocks with Hayes and me." We all laughed.

But I said, "I gave him something to think about, even if he never makes the change."

District 306 was mostly a working-class white area that was slowly experiencing white flight because of the Supreme Court's 1954 school desegregation decision. District 301's residents were first- and second-generation Italian, Croatian, Belgian, and other poor whites.

There wasn't much for us officers to do in the far eastern part of our patrol district. It was all industrialized. The residential area was on the western side of the district. The only "action" in District 301 was the drag strip, where dragsters came from all over to show off their cars and race each other. That went all night long.

I want to take just a few moments to reflect on the importance of the crusades of the 3B's. Fresh and perhaps a bit idealistic, these three Black officers, all in their early twenties, were, like all Black officers at that time, relegated to just two of the city's patrol districts, the districts with most of the illegal drugs, gambling, bootlegging, fencing, and prostitution. While some of these enterprises were owned and run by Blacks, most were owned by whites who did not live in the community, and they used Blacks to operate them. The whites had immunity from arrest because someone inside the police department ruled them "untouchable."

So three rookie Black cops set out to change this. One of us was just out of the police academy and on probation, and the other two had hardly completed their probation period. We decided to do our best to arrest and close down, or at least harass, those who were involved in criminal activity who had been "off limits," protected by corruption within the department. We made these criminals vulnerable as they had not been before.

It wasn't until the mid-sixties—after a new police chief, officer retirements, and actual indictments—that the untouchables were eventually put out of business. The 3Bs crusade had made this officially unacknowledged criminal activity so visible, it had to be addressed. The 3Bs created a vanguard legacy for the Black community in just eighteen months.

The story does not end. Three young Black men with a burning desire to spread justice made a difference despite constant opposition. We were able to be examples of encouragement for future policemen of color. We worked extra hours without pay to ensure each other's backs were protected. Bumpus became the first Black field sergeant and the first Black helicopter pilot, and he had two sons follow in his footsteps: William and Christopher. Buie also had two sons who joined the police force: Gene Jr. and Marlon. Christopher and Marlon both recently retired. I often wonder what my partners would say about me coming full circle from a beat cop who experienced a lot of adversity to police commissioner. We each made a difference together and individually. In the end, we were all blessed with legacies of good family and friends. The mark of the 3Bs lives on!

"Alvin Brooks, Nigger, Go Home!"

I had a few interesting incidents occur while at Sheffield. I got a call that was out of my district to "investigate a possible suicide, a person hanging from the flagpole in front of Northeast High School." That was really an all-white residential area, heavily Italian American and working class. There were various businesses, liquor stores, and what we called "fruit stands" or delicatessens, which were owned and operated by Italian Americans, especially along Independence Avenue.

I used red lights and sirens to make the call. It was "dusk dark." When I arrived at the school, I could see what looked like a man in uniform hanging from the flagpole rope and what looked like blood all over him. I notified the dispatcher of the situation and ordered an ambulance and the fire department, which was just down the street at Independence Avenue and Van Brunt Boulevard. The fire department arrived first. I had my spotlight on the flagpole. The fire department used a ladder to reach the man hanging by the flag rope. The firefighter who reached the top yelled, "This ain't no damn person. This is one of those things you see in department store windows. It's a dummy with ketchup all over it."

He lowered the mannequin as he came down the ladder. But there was an interesting note attached to the ketchup-covered uniform (which was the same color as our police uniforms). Someone had hung me in effigy. The note read: "ALVIN BROOKS NIGGER GO HOME." Some folks laughed when the mannequin neared the ground but became mum when they saw the note attached to it. I thanked everyone for responding, including the ambulance, and notified the dispatcher what had happened.

The sergeant of that district and the district officer who had gotten into service both came to the scene after I had placed the mannequin in the trunk of my car. The sergeant asked me to let him see. I did. He and the district officer held it up. The sergeant said, "I'll be damned. I know this was done by some of those little 'peckerwoods' around here. They need their little asses kicked." I knew the sergeant made that comment to appease me because he had made racial and ethnic slurs when I had overheard him talking to other white officers. "Why don't you take this up to the station, Al? Leave it upstairs."

I did. Someone sat it in a chair, and it became the joke of the station among my white colleagues. Not among the six of us who were Black.

After a couple days, I took the mannequin from upstairs at the station and threw it in the trunk of the police car. Bumpus, Duke, and Buie, and of course Hayes and Jones, had seen the mannequin. Only the six of us knew what had happened to the mannequin. People asked about the mannequin's whereabouts numerous times on all three shifts, but none of us Black officers ever said what had happened to it. After a while I threw it in the city dump that was in the east end of my district.

The officer in whose district this occurred told me he would help me locate the little bastards who were probably "dagos." I thanked him for his help but told him I didn't engage in ethnic or racial slurs toward any group, and I hoped he understood what I meant. I told him that too often people who use such slurs about one group more than likely do the same toward other groups.

As he was walking away, he said, "I've been working out here at Sheffield with these Mafia bastards for too many years. All the officers out here feel the way I do. And you should feel that way too because it's their Mafia kids that hung you from that damn flagpole." He got in his car and drove off. These kinds of comments toward Italian Americans were not new since I had been at the Sheffield Station. It was the same as the feeling toward Italian Americans who lived in the North End.

Although Northeast High School was not in my district, I spent a lot of time driving to it and talking to kids. They were all respectful. About two weeks later I stopped and talked to a group of kids at St. Anthony's Catholic Church on Benton Boulevard and Lexington. They were no more than thirteen years old. One of the kids asked, "Are you the colored cop that some kids put you up on the flagpole at Northeast?"

I said, "Yes, I'm the one."

Two or three of them said in unison, "We know who did it to you."

I said, "Oh, you do? I got an idea who did it and some names, too." But I really didn't have any names.

They said, "Was it . . . ?" and began to rattle off four names.

I said, "Yeah, and they all go to Northeast."

They said, "Yeah, yeah, and they're all brothers. And Italians. Some of us are Italians, but we don't do stuff like that. That's wrong. Are you going to arrest them? We know where they live. We'll take you there if you give us a ride in the police car."

"Fellows," I said, "I appreciate your help, but I already know who did it, and I need to talk to them and their parents." (This wasn't true either.)

One kid said, "Their family runs the fruit store down on Independence Avenue. You want us to take you down there?"

I said, "No. Do you know the street it's near on the Avenue?" The kids told me the street, and I said, "Listen, you want to ride with me, if I promise not to take you to jail?" They said yes, so all five or six of them piled into the police car, two of the smaller ones in the front, the others in the back.

They asked me to turn on the siren. I drove up on Cliff Drive away from the residences and hit the siren two or three times. I scared the hell out of those whose cars were parked overlooking the East Bottoms. Like kids, they asked if they could hit the siren. So, I pulled over where there were no other cars and gave each one a chance to hit the siren.

The kids had the windows down and were yelling out of them. It was almost dark. I circled around and took them back near the church and let them out. They asked if I would take them for a ride again. I told them yes. They all hollered as I drove off, "Thank you, Officer Brooks."

I had what I needed. I decided to wait until the next evening before I went to the delicatessen and talked to the owner.

Several days after the mannequin incident, I decided to call on the father or grandfather of the four boys whose names—and the location of their family's business—had been given to me by my little friends.

I knew exactly which delicatessen on Independence Avenue it was. It was just a few blocks from the police station. I drove right in front of the business and got out. I approached an elderly gentleman who was wearing an apron and picking out fruit that was rotten and throwing it in a bucket.

He looked a little surprised to see a Black cop. I introduced myself and asked if he was the grandfather of the four youth. I called their names. In broken English he asked, "What have they done?" I asked again if these boys were his grandsons. Before he could respond, a younger man who overheard my questions identified himself as the father of three boys and called their names and named the fourth boy as his nephew, his brother's son. I thought he was going to ask who identified them. Instead, the father said something to his dad in Italian, walked back just inside the deli, and dialed a phone number. He spoke in Italian on the phone.

He came back to me and said the boys were on their way and would be with us in about fifteen minutes. While we were waiting, I asked if the two of them would accompany me out to my police car. They did. I opened the trunk and showed them the mannequin that had been taken down from the flagpole by the firefighter with the note addressed to me. The father apologized. And said something to his dad in Italian.

The grandfather asked me if I wanted some fruit "or anything you see you want."

I said, "No, sir. But thank you." The father went back to the phone and again spoke to someone in Italian.

The father came back and said, "They're on the way." He mentioned the name of the woman bringing them. About ten minutes after the father's call, the four boys arrived with a woman.

The grandfather talked to them in Italian. They answered in English: "NO!" I told the four that numerous persons told me they were the ones who had put the mannequin on the pole with the note and that they had been bragging about it throughout the area. I told the grandfather, the father, and the woman who brought them (who identified herself as their aunt) that I didn't come there to arrest them but just to bring it to the attention of their parents.

The grandfather grabbed one of the boys, who looked to be the oldest, maybe sixteen or seventeen. He walked him into the store by the arm. I just stood outside with the father and aunt and the three other teens. The father began to interrogate the three. He was rough with them. The grandfather came back. "Yes, these are the little dagos that put that damn thing up there."

He slapped each about the head and said something again in Italian. They all apologized. The father asked what these "asses who know better" could do to make things right. He apologized to me and went on to say, "What would my colored customers at the liquor store down the avenue say?" The father said he was a close friend of Capt. Bill Canaday and that Bill knew his family well since he was a boy and could vouch for him that their family was not prejudiced.

"He knows; he'll tell you my family won't stand for anything like this from our kids. Our family has businesses all over the colored community. Many of our best friends are colored, even some of the colored cops."

The grandfather said, "What can we do to make this up to you, Officer Brooks?"

I said, "Summer is here, and school is out. Do they have access to brooms, rakes, and a lawn mower?" Both the grandfather and the parents said yes.

"How about having them cut some of the elderly folks' yards? I'll identify the yards and contact the homeowners."

All three of the adults thought that was a good idea. I said to the boys, "What do you fellows think?"

Before they could respond, the grandfather said, "It's not their decision. Yes, they're going to do it, and you let us know if the yards are done right! When do you want them to start?" I told them that this area is not my district and that I would have to talk to the field sergeant and the district officer first. They knew the field sergeant and called him by name. I told them I would get back with them.

I called the district officer and asked him to meet me. I told him I found the four boys and talked to their parents and told him of my proposal. I then asked him if he would assist in locating elderly homeowners for whom these boys could do yard work at least twice this summer. He said, "The little Mafia bastards. All of them ought to be in prison. Yeah, I'll help you."

I wanted to ask him why he was so down on Italians, but I needed these kids to carry out my proposal, and it was his district. He and the sergeant could have gotten together and headed it off. But the father of the boys had said he knew the sergeant well. Then I thought he might tell me not to follow through because they were friends, that the kids didn't commit any crime, that I was out of my district. So, I had to "hold my peace."

In about a week, we had some thirty yards identified. The elderly homeowners were pleased. They wrote a letter to my captain, Captain Hasting, thanking me and commending me for taking time with these youths and helping the elderly of the area. The father and the uncle of the boys co-authored a letter to the captain praising me for what I had done with their sons.

I Earned My Bachelor's Degree, May 1959

As I mentioned before, I didn't come on as a cadet in the January 1954 class because I wanted to complete my sophomore year in college. I completed my associate of arts degree in May 1954 and joined the 44th Cadet Class on June 1, 1954. I started working on my bachelor's degree in the fall of 1956. I was one of only three who had ever completed a college degree while working as a full-time cop. One other of the three was Norman Caron, who rose through the ranks and became chief in 1978.

Chief Brannon wrote me a letter that appeared in my personnel file:

June 4, 1959
Dear Officer Brooks:
May I extend my personal and hearty congratulations to you for your outstanding achievement in completing the work necessary for your Baccalaureate Degree.
From a personal experience viewpoint, I know of the tremendous effort and determination that must be put forth to accomplish such an honor, particularly when a person has concurrent responsibilities to his family.
I have every wish and expectation that you shall apply your capabilities as a professional police officer to the credit of yourself and our Department. You should have a fine future in police work.
Most sincerely,
Bernard C. Brannon

I truly believe if Brannon had not gotten indicted in June of 1961 (to the best of my knowledge he was not brought to trial) and had remained chief, I would have risen in the department earlier than other Blacks who were promoted later, and I probably would have retired as a police officer. I found Brannon to be fair; he realized that change for

Black officers was due. I believe that his assigning the "fearless" six to the Sheffield Station demonstrated the direction he was going.

I completed my last three years of college while facing opposition from my lieutenant. When I asked to work only the p.m. and midnight shifts so I could finish my college degree, he responded, "What'ya want to do, Brooksie Boy, be a cop or become an educator?"

I asked, "Lieutenant, can't I do both?" Nothing was said after that.

He did write an Interdepartmental Communication recommending that I be promoted from Class B to Class A patrolman. Sometimes at roll call, he would make little remarks about my report writing. I'll never forget when the dispatcher asked me to "investigate a call for an ambulance at 13th and Troost; a passenger has fallen getting off the streetcar." I arrived and ordered an ambulance. The man was conscious but bleeding "profusely after falling and striking the occipital region of his head."

The lieutenant brought my report to roll call the next evening. After calling roll and giving car assignments, he said, "Listen up, men. Here's what one of your fellow officers, who made a very simple call for an ambulance yesterday, wrote in a simple accident report where one of our elderly citizens had fallen getting off a streetcar."

He read the narrative portion of my report as I had written it. "That's the kinda bullshit you learn in school. Hasn't got a damn thing to do with police work, catching the bad guys." It was interesting because I was taking chemistry and just that day, we had used that terminology regarding a frog that we were individually dissecting. Just three hours before I came to work! So, I thought I'd use what I had just learned and transfer it to the situation. Everyone laughed.

The lieutenant never mentioned my name, but everyone knew whose report he was reading. As he was dismissing us, he said, "Get out there, men, and write good reports that can be understood. Dismissed." I asked Sergeant Gore, my sergeant, about what the lieutenant had said about my going to school and working just the two shifts. He told me it was fine with him, but I might want to tell the lieutenant that I would like to speak to the captain regarding my request.

I told the lieutenant that I would like to see if the captain would permit me to work just the two shifts. The lieutenant said, "Shoot your best shot, Brooksie Boy!"

I told him, "Thanks, Lieutenant," and did what he said. There had been a change in the commanders: Captain Canaday had replaced Captain Bishop, and Captain Canaday approved my request.

I Was Transferred to the Juvenile Unit, May 1, 1960

On May 1, 1960, I was reassigned to the juvenile unit at the request and insistence of Mrs. Genevieve Allen. Although she was not a commissioned officer, Mrs. Allen was the first African American woman to work in an investigative capacity with the department, and she had worked in the juvenile unit for a number of years. Mrs. Allen's coworker had been Det. Sylvester Young. Young was transferred to the homicide unit, and Mrs. Allen was able to pick Young's replacement. She selected me and convinced the captain of the unit, Capt. William Burch, to bring me in.

Mrs. Allen knew me before I became a police officer. We furthered our relationship when I was working numerous juvenile cases with her and Young, when I was assigned to the district. Our assignment was working with juveniles up to age seventeen who were abused, incorrigible, runaways, truants, members of gangs, or committed other juvenile offenses.

"Drop the Gun, You're Under Arrest," 1960

In August 1960, Carol was pregnant with our fifth child, Diana. About 9:30 or 10:00 p.m., Carol asked me to go to Leo's Drug Store at 18th and Brooklyn to get her a half pint of black walnut ice cream. Grudgingly, I said yes. I was dressed in a T-shirt, jeans, and house shoes. I took $5 from our dresser top and the keys to my dad's '39 Buick. Dad was living with us off and on at the time.

As I traveled northbound on Brooklyn, I passed the Municipal Stadium, home of the Kansas City Athletics baseball team. The game was just letting out. When I stopped at the four-way stop sign at 19th and Brooklyn, a woman walked up to my car and said, "Mister, those three men are robbing a bunch of white people over there against the church." She made eye contact with me and said, "Oh, Officer Brooks, it's you!" She further described what she had seen as she pointed toward the church. From the streetlight, I could see eight to ten white women and men with their hands on the wall of the church, two Black males moving from one to the other, and the third Black male standing a few feet back. I could not see a gun.

I asked her, "Ma'am, would you walk down to Leo's and tell someone there that Officer Brooks is up here in plain clothes, that there's a robbery, and to please call the police for him?" She said she would and left trotting downhill toward the drugstore. I was without a weapon, identification, or badge. I drove the old '39 Buick over the sidewalk, hit the light switch on the floor, and the sealed high beam. It lit up the whole side of the church, including, of course, the victims and the two men collecting money, watches, billfolds, and pocketbooks.

I exited the car quickly, standing behind the car door. I could see that the man standing back was holding a gun. I shouted, "Police officer! Drop the gun now! All three of you, get on your knees. Put your hands up high. Now!" All three did as I said. "Don't any of you move or I'll shoot you. Keep your hands where I can see them." I walked up to the man who had dropped the gun and picked it up. A crowd was gathering. Police sirens could be heard coming to the scene.

The first officer to the scene said, "Brooks, whatcha got?"

I said, "Three holdup men."

He said, "I'll take it from here."

By that time, a half dozen or more police officers were on the scene. A crowd from the game had now formed on the sidewalk. Officers handcuffed the three suspects. I knew all three of them. I knew Robert Strong, who had the gun, quite well. I asked him, "Strong, what the hell's wrong with you, man? You've got a family. I know you know better than this, man."

He said, "Yeah, Brooks, I know. I'll be all right. Thanks for not shooting me." I walked over and gave the gun to the first officer. He asked me, "Where's your gun?"

I told him, "I don't have one."

I was far enough away so Strong couldn't hear what my response was. I had known Strong ever since I had been on the department. He had never done anything as serious as this. The onlookers heard some of the conversation. Some began to laugh, and someone said, "That man there made a citizen's arrest without a gun. Boy, that took a lot of guts. He should get a medal." Hearing that, people began to applaud. I thanked them, but I didn't say I was a police officer.

The officers began to question the victims. The sergeant came over to me and said, "Alvin, that took lot of guts, boy. Glad it turned out the way it did."

I said, "Thanks, Sarge. My wife, who is pregnant, sent me to Leo's for some ice cream. I need to get it before they close. May I use your pen and a piece of paper? I'll leave you with my phone number and address in case the detectives want to talk to me tonight. I'm working days and will be in the office at eight in the morning." He said, "Go, go, man. Get that ice cream."

When I got to Leo's, they had locked the door but recognized me and let me in. There were three or four persons still in the store. I thanked them for calling the police. They wanted to know "blow by blow" what occurred. I told them. I asked to use the phone to call Carol. I had been gone about an hour or more now. She answered the phone.

Before I was able to say anything, she said, "What happened? Where are you? You've been gone almost two hours." I finally got a word in and told her what had happened and that I would be home in about ten minutes with her ice cream.

Her response was, "I've lost my ice cream appetite now. But come home with it."

Leo was there and wouldn't let me pay for the pint of black walnut. He gave me a half gallon and sent his best wishes to Carol.

About midnight, two robbery unit detectives came to my house and took a statement from me. They had Strong's gun. As Carol listened, they said, "Man, you sure took a chance. Strong is a known criminal."

Then Carol chimed in. "I won't be sending you out anymore for nothing at night. You'd go out there and get yourself killed and leave me and these kids here by ourselves." They laughed and left. Dad woke up, and I had to hear from him, too. It went on and on until about 2:00 a.m.

The next morning, the head of the juvenile unit said, "Well, Brooksie Boy, you did it last night."

I said, "Thank you, Captain."

He said, "You need to write me a memo for downstairs about why you didn't have your gun. One of the officers reported you didn't assist him in the arrest because you didn't have your gun."

I said, "Captain, you're kidding!" I wondered who complained. [All three suspects had been placed under arrest and on their knees when the first officer arrived. Other officers handcuffed them.] The complaint must have come from the first officer to assist me because he asked me about my gun, and I told him I didn't have one.

The captain said, "Well, Brooksie, put that in your 100 Report [a formal department report]."

I was pissed and cursing to myself. "That no-good son of a bitch! That bastard!" I said over and over to myself as I was writing the "100 Report." Then I had a thought—what do the "Rules and Regulations" (we referred to it as our "Bible") say about an off-duty officer carrying a gun? I reached into my desk drawer, and there it was, something to the effect that "an officer may carry a firearm while off duty." It did not say "shall carry" or "must carry." Oh! Got your ass now! You rotten fucker! In my "100 Report," I cited the chapter and wrote verbatim what was in the book of "Rules and Regulations." In about fifteen minutes I handed my response to the captain.

I stood before his desk as he read it. When he finished, I asked, "Is that okay, Captain?"

He smiled and said, "Brooksie Boy, that's it. I'll get it downstairs."

I said, "Thank you, Captain." I expected him to make some comment regarding my response to the allegation, but his smile told the story.

A couple days passed. I asked the captain about the outcome of the complaint against me. He said, "Someone wanted you fired, Brooksie Boy. But you just go ahead and keep up the good police work that you've always done since I've known you. Let it go. It's over. Okay?"

"Okay, Captain, if you say so," I replied.

He came back with, "I say so!"

But it wasn't over.

Sometime later, I got a notice of the preliminary hearing for all three robbery suspects. I believe all three were bound over for trial.

By the time Strong's case was scheduled for trial, the other two defendants had pleaded guilty. Strong had a jury trial. In discovery, both Strong and his attorney found out that I didn't have a weapon when I interrupted the robbery and made the arrest. The early part of the defense's case and questioning centered around whether the arrest was legal since I yelled, "Police officer, you're under arrest! Drop the gun, on your knees." I was grilled and drilled. But after a day-long trial, the jury went out and came back late afternoon with a guilty verdict. I believe Strong got ten years.

There's more to this story. My birth father, Wilbur Herring, had left Kansas City for New Brunswick, New Jersey, with his wife and five children. He gave me a quitclaim deed to the house at 3604 South Benton. I put the house up for rent. My name and phone number were on the homemade sign. Carol got a call from a woman who was interested in seeing the house. Carol made the appointment, and I met the woman at the house. She liked it, gave me a deposit, and planned to move in the beginning of the next month.

She moved in as scheduled. For the next several months, she paid her rent on time. She had told me that she was married and that her husband was out of town (well, she could have been more specific, as you'll learn below) but would be joining the family in a few months. She always brought the rent by my house on or near the first of the month, when it was due. Anything beyond five days late, there was a $5 penalty. She never was late.

This month, I happened to have been home when she paid the rent. I answered the door, and the woman was there—but this time with a man. The man was Robert Strong.

Robert spoke first. He asked me if I remembered him. Sure, I did! I remembered him before and after the arrest and the time he was convicted based on my testimony. The woman who had rented the house never mentioned her husband's name to Carol or me. She had used her maiden name. I invited both in and suggested they have a seat. Robert started telling about when I had arrested him with no gun. He made a joke out of it. We all laughed. Robert said he had done some years in prison but was out on "paper" (parole) and gave the date when he would be off parole.

He thanked me again, saying, "Mr. Brooks, I'm glad you didn't shoot me 'with your gun.' Man, that was slick. But seriously, I appreciate you. You're one helluva cop. Seriously."

I thanked him. The woman was not his wife, but they were living together before he went to prison. Both he and the woman were working. She had children. I rented the house to Strong.

Robert stayed in my dad's house for about two or three years. He paid the rent and utility bills on time all the while he was there.

Years later, I think it was after I started AdHoc, Strong became known as a big-time dope dealer. He owned a house in the 4000 block of Prospect with steel doors back and front, one-way windows, and a large pit bull in the backyard. He became known on the street and by law enforcement as "Red Strong."

One Sunday morning, as my family was preparing for church service, I got a call from a homicide detective who knew about my past with Strong. He also knew that I had been made aware of Strong's drug operation by some street folks, the KCPD drug unit, and the Feds.

The detective said, "Well, Brooks, you don't have to worry about 'Red Strong' anymore. He went out to get the morning paper in his robe and house shoes and someone was waiting on the side of the house over on 40th and Paseo and blew his head off." The end of Robert Strong.

I Was Promoted to Corporal, October 1, 1960

I was promoted to corporal in October just before Mrs. Allen retired. Now the head of the juvenile unit was my former captain at the Sheffield Station, Captain Hastings. Hastings (shortly thereafter promoted to major) asked me, "Alvin, which one of the Negro officers do you want to bring up here with you?" I asked him to let me give it some thought. A relatively new officer named Willie Walton came to the department with a background as a physical education teacher and coach. Since the unit was working with juveniles, I thought Walton would work well with Rosie Mason (one of the unit's investigators who later became the first sworn woman police officer for the department) and me.

I requested Walton over several other Black officers whom I had known longer. I had worked with these other officers and we had formed sort of a fraternity. They didn't accept my decision too well. They didn't feel Walton socialized with us. And that was somewhat true. Walton and I talked about that before I recommended him to the captain. He acknowledged that he was somewhat unsociable with the Black officers.

I held Captain Hasting off for a while to give Walton a chance to try to relate more to the "brothers." He did. Not as much as I thought he should, but Walton was Walton. He was still a good cop. After a while, Walton was accepted, but with reservation. The general feeling was that he had made minimal change because I had talked to him. I talked to Rosie about Walton. She also had reservations but said she thought I was right about his background and experience. And maybe he would understand that because there were so few of us, we needed each other.

It was about a month after Captain Hasting had asked me about "bringing another Negro officer in the unit" that I approached him to suggest Walton. About a month later,

Walton joined Rosie and me in the unit. I had started working on my master's degree at the University of Missouri–Kansas City, and I asked to work the shift from 4:00 p.m. to midnight. Sometimes I even worked from midnight to 8:00 a.m., a shift most of the officers didn't want.

My Father's Death: Cluster Brooks, 1891–1961

On Thursday, June 8, 1961, I was in my office at Headquarters when I got a call from the police that my father had had an accident in the backyard of his home at 3240 Quincy and that I should come to the scene as soon as possible. When I got there, my father had already expired.

He had been with a man calling himself Laron Bens. Both my dad and Bens said they were cousins. I doubted it, but I accepted it. They were drinking buddies. I never knew how they were cousins or became friends.

My dad had a bruise over his right eye and was lying flat on his back when I arrived. This cousin had been drinking with him. Bens had apparently called the police but left the scene. No one was there with my dad when the police arrived.

It was only sometime later that I learned that this so-called cousin had been there. He couldn't explain what happened to Dad except that they were drinking together and "Brooks just died." That was his statement. I had the detective talk to him, but that was all they got out of him.

I ordered an autopsy. Deputy Coroner L. M. Tillman performed the autopsy at his office at 1618 Lydia. Dr. Tillman was Black. My dad's death certificate listed the immediate cause of death as pulmonary edema due to cerebral thrombosis and atherosclerosis. He was sixty-nine years old. Therefore, Dr. Tillman found no signs of foul play.

Watkins Brothers Funeral Home had moved from the 1700 block of Lydia (when my mother died) to 18th and Benton Boulevard. My dad's funeral was held at 11:00 a.m. Tuesday, June 13, at Watkins Brothers Funeral Home. My dad was not Catholic. In fact, neither of my parents belonged to any church. Annunciation Catholic Church was my family's congregation. The priest, the Reverend Victor Moser, officiated. My dad was buried at Lincoln Cemetery, the colored cemetery, Record Grave 12, Lot 22, Section G 5345.

I've mentioned that the Kansas City VA Medical Center now stands on a 48-acre tract between Linwood Boulevard and 35th Street and between Elmwood and Van Brunt Boulevard. Prior to 1949, that property was nothing but a field and wooded area. My dad farmed some of it. He often told people, "You see all that? That belongs to the Brookses."

When my dad died, the folks who heard him tell that story thought I had inherited a large sum of money from the sale of the land because the hospital had been built and was fully operating when my dad passed in 1961. The funny part of all this is that I was a detective on the Kansas City Police Department, earning $532 per month with a $10-a-month clothing allowance. It took me close to five years to pay Watkins for my dad's funeral service.

Request to Chief Kelley to Review My Personnel Record for Promotion, 1961

I wrote a memo to my captain, William Burch, January 14, 1963.

"Attention: Chief Clarence M. Kelley, requesting a review of my personnel record for the purpose of promotion."

Before my Interdepartmental Communication (IC) got to Chief Kelley, Lieutenant Colonel Canaday reviewed my personnel file and made the following comments at the bottom of my IC.

"To: Chief Clarence M. Kelley

"In checking the officer's file with the Personnel Bureau, I find where he made a grade of 85.22 on the written phase of the Sgt's examination; a grade of 81 on Supervisory Training and Organization and Management given at the University of Kansas City; a grade of 93 on Human Relations; and a grade of 88 on Police Operations and Methods. His Sergeants gave him an evaluation of 80 and his Commanding Officer rated him above average.

Signed Lt. Col. Wm. M. Canaday
Commanding Operations Division

My IC then went to Chief Kelley with my grades and the evaluations from my sergeants and my commanding officer. This was the result of the sergeant examination I had taken in 1961.

After Chief Kelley received my memo, I asked to meet with him to discuss the concerns mentioned in my IC. I didn't know that there had been a review of my personnel file by Canaday submitted to the chief until I received a copy to integrate into my autobiography. Chief Kelley granted me the meeting with him. He told me I was doing a good job in the Juvenile Bureau.

"Keep up the good work," he said. "You are well thought of in your community and by the folks you work with and your supervisors. You are one of the few officers in the department who has a degree. We need to use your talent." In conclusion, he told me, "If you pass the next sergeant exam coming up in a couple of months and you're in the top twenty-five, I'll make you a sergeant." I told Kelley that I was now on the list and in the top twenty-five and that I had been passed over for the second time. He told me he's not making any more sergeants off that list.

I took the test again and was in the top twenty-five. Kelley picked number twenty-six. When I confronted him, he told me that he had been told by my supervisors up and down the ladder that I was too valuable to the juvenile unit and that they couldn't afford to lose me.

I said, "Chief Kelley, that doesn't make sense, and you and anyone else who made those comments know it. If I'm so valuable, make me a sergeant in the juvenile unit. Two of the sergeants are planning to retire."

"It'll be considered, Al." End of conversation.

Although I was never promoted to sergeant, my best friend William Bumpus was promoted to sergeant in July 1962 and became the first Black field sergeant (supervisor over a squad of officers). In March of 1969, Bumpus was assigned to the helicopter unit and became the first Black helicopter pilot.

Resurrected KCPD Explorer Scout Post No. 700 and Organized a Cadet Program, 1962

One day I approached Clifford Warren, who I believe had been promoted to lieutenant colonel and was still the highest-ranking Black police officer (followed by Leroy Swift), about resurrecting the department's Explorer Scout Post No. 700 and forming a police cadet program. I told him I wanted to try to get some Black youth interested in the department.

He said, "Al, that's a great idea, but you know if you do, you've got to include whites, too. The old post was all white, and I think the reason it died was someone did not want to include Negro boys."

I said, "I know, Colonel. If I get it approved, there'll be some whites in it, too." I told him I just wanted to run it past him before I talked to my captain about it. I got it approved after submitting some paperwork about why we should resurrect the post, how I would select the boys, whether this would be done on or off duty, who would be selected, and who would do the selecting. I apparently answered all questions satisfactorily because I was given the green light.

In the juvenile unit, some kids really needed a lot of help, but the majority of the kids were on the right track in the Black community. So, I set out to mix those who were headed in the right direction and were going to make it regardless with several others whose odds of making it were not as good. I came up with about twenty young males, twelve to sixteen years old, from different junior and senior high schools. There were sixteen Blacks and four whites.

I cut off the age at sixteen because the sixteen-year-old kids were mostly sophomores and a couple were juniors, which meant, I hoped, the youth would spend at least two to three years in the organization. Seniors would be trying to graduate in the spring. I was able to get good cooperation from the various bureaus and units. I mainly approached everyone with, "My captain suggested I approach you to see if you would permit a group of members from the department's Explorer Scout Post No. 700, etc., etc."

We held monthly meetings. The kids were really interested. I picked them up in the police car and returned them home. They had to get signed permission. I met every parent or guardian at their home.

They spent many nights and weekends watching and listening as they sat in the eighth-floor jail. We had every unit commander, captain, and sergeant take time to explain the function and role of their respective work. The kids saw how the polygraph machine worked and were given polygraph tests. (This worried me. Beforehand, I got with the polygraphist and asked that only certain questions be asked. I was worried about being told, "This kid has lied about this or that.") We visited the lab and the coroner's office at the hospital—but only talked to the coroner. They did not see any autopsies, but most of them wanted to. We visited the county jail. They often saw relatives and friends there.

The father of two of the white kids had a brother who had a farm in Nevada, Missouri, about 90 miles south of Kansas City on 71 Highway. He asked me if I thought the boys would like to visit it. He outlined activities for the boys. He said he took his boys down there twice a month year-round. He stated further that groups from both Kansas and Missouri brought kids to his brother's farm but charged them a "pretty penny." Still, he was sure he wouldn't charge us if the weekend was available.

At our next monthly meeting, I had him give a rundown on the activities offered to the boys. His two sons told way more than their dad had. The boys were excited and ready to go. The father said he would give his brother a call and ask him what weekend the boys could come down. He called me a couple of days later and told me his mother and sister-in-law were excited about the idea. He planned for me to take a load of boys down for the weekend, from Friday evening until Sunday afternoon. The father was going to drive his truck and I would drive the police car.

It was in the summer, but only eight of the kids were able to go. When the weekend arrived, I took five in the police car and he took three in his truck. His twelve-year-old son, the youngest of the boys, wanted to ride with me and his brother with his dad and two other Black kids. So, on a Friday evening in mid-August, about 6:00 p.m., after the rush hour traffic, we struck out to Nevada. I followed the father. We were to have dinner prepared by his brother and sister-in-law and two neighbors.

It was late when we arrived at the farm, but the couple and their neighbors had dinner ready for us outdoors in the bunkhouse. Really not a house. It was called a bunkhouse, but it didn't have sides—just screen-in to keep some of the flies and other flying creatures out that were now attracted by the lights.

The boys were ready to eat before washing up, but I insisted they wash. After I blessed the food, here it comes, being passed around . . . extra-large cheese hamburgers, baked beans, potato salad, tomatoes, onions, and, of course, bread. And quart jars of iced tea. And that's not all! Dessert: cherry pie and vanilla ice cream!

The youngsters ate like it was the Last Supper! There was enough food prepared for about a dozen, but there was not enough left to feed the multitude. We were served on paper plates so there were no dishes to be washed. I had the boys go around and tell something "interesting" about themselves. The things they said were interesting!

I suggested we take a couple of lanterns and do a fifteen-minute or so walk before we turned in. The bunk beds were in a bunkhouse adjoining the one where dinner was served. One of the kids asked if there were snakes out there. The host told him, "Yes. But you'll scare him away when you step on him."

The hostess cleared the question up. "He is not telling the truth. There're no snakes around here. The hogs that run out here eat them or chase them away."

Well, I won't go into how long that discussion lasted. But I still made them walk the fifteen minutes. Then to bed on those army cots, the ones made of canvas that sink down just a little in the middle, and bunk beds. Oh! The two toilets—men's and women's—were outdoors. But unlike the ones I grew up with in Leeds, they flushed!

At about daybreak, there were several roosters crowing. They woke me up, but not a boy stirred. At six, the cowbell was ringing in the hands of our host. Still, not a boy stirred. A couple pulled the sheet over their heads. I never went back to sleep after the roosters started crowing.

We had been told the night before that there were two shower stalls. One male, one female, both outside, neither with hot water. I got up, talked to our host, and headed to the shower. At first the water was a little warm because it was hooked up to a hose and the day's heat left it warm. But the warm water ran out quick. I took a quick shower. Since there were no females in our group, we were able to use both toilets and showers. I know several of the boys just ran in and ran out because the water was so cold. Everyone was given a towel to be used all the time we were there.

We had our chores to do before breakfast. That didn't go over too well, but the boys survived. Chores included feeding the hogs, letting the horses out to another pasture with a large lake, feeding the chickens, and changing their water pans. Learning how to milk the three cows brought lots of laughs. Of course, I knew how, and the two boys whose aunt and uncle were our hosts knew; but if we had waited on the others, we'd never have had breakfast—or lunch or dinner! The neighbor man came over to help instruct. I tried to give some instruction, but my patience ran out. I milked my cow by myself—about three gallons of milk. After the boys made a game of it, our host brought out the electric milking machine!

We finally had breakfast, a cowboy kind of breakfast. Then we all went fishing. Everyone had a pole. The boys had to dig worms out of a big tub inside one of the horse sheds. Then we rode the horses. In the heat of the day, we pitched hay. Our hostess rang the cowbell for lunch. Then a lot of after-lunch fun.

Dinnertime came, bedtime, and Sunday morning. Another neighbor farmer, a deacon in the small Baptist church up the road, stopped by to meet and greet us, joined us for breakfast, and asked permission to hold a little Sunday School. The boys weren't too enthusiastic about it, but I gave him permission. All the boys got into reading and responding to the deacon's questions. Both our hosts and the deacon were surprised, and so was I. But I felt good that these six Black boys did come from churchgoing families, or at least the Bible was taught in the home.

Well, we enjoyed another full day of farm activity, including shoveling manure, picking strawberries and blackberries, and digging up sweet potatoes and washing them. We had lunch in between and then our last meal, dinner!

We were supposed to leave from Nevada before dark on Sunday. The last we heard from the father of the two boys was when he left us after eating dinner with us in the bunkhouse. He was to return after dinner and take half the boys back to Kansas City. Just before dark, after we ate dinner, a couple of us got to ride the two horses for the last time before we left for home.

The older boy whose aunt and uncle owned the farm rode the horses well. It seemed like the horses knew him. He knew when to holler at them or yank the reins one way or the other. When the four of us returned to the house to pick up another two boys, our host told me he had some bad news for me. His brother had called and said he wouldn't be back for us because the starter had gone out on his truck and it being Sunday, he would not be able to get it repaired until Monday. Our host said he would take us, but he couldn't drive at night. He could get us back to Kansas City, but it would be dark by the time he headed back home. His wife did not drive.

I said, "Oh my God, I've got to get these kids back to Kansas City tonight."

All the kids like a choir said, "Great, Mr. Brooks, let's stay another night!"

I said, "I've got to get you kids back some way tonight!"

One of boys suggested, "Why don't two or three of us, the smallest ones, ride in the trunk and hold the trunk lid open enough so we can breathe?"

A couple of the fellows spoke up and said they would ride in the trunk. "That ought to be a lot of fun," said one of the kids who volunteered to ride in the trunk.

I told the kids, "That's a crazy idea. Throw it out of your mind." Our host and his wife laughed at the idea. So, I was stuck with getting back home with eight kids. What the hell! Since the trunk of the police car was out of the question, I had to figure something out. Eight kids in a five-seater car with the driver. I said, "Okay, let's see how this can work."

I had two larger boys get in the front seat with my smallest little fellow sitting on one boy's lap. Then, by size, I got the other five in the back seat. Somehow. Our host had to help me close the rear doors. He was on one side pushing, and I was on the other. The kids were being kids, "Help, Mr. Brooks, I can't breathe!" Everyone was laughing. For them it was fun.

One of the kids who was being sat on hollered, "Mr. Brooks, this boy smells funky! He didn't mix any soap with water this morning!" Someone else called one of the kids by name, "Hey, stop farting!" Everyone laughed, including our hostess. Then there was the farting contest. I had to have everyone in the back seat get out until the breeze took the odor out. I scolded them and told them we had to get back home and they had to stop fooling around.

Before they got back in, one of the boys hugged our hosts and thanked them. They had just shaken hands and told them thanks earlier, but one of the boys started it and all eight got their chance. Both of our hosts thanked them and said, "Thanks, Officer Brooks, for bringing them down. You boys can come back anytime Officer Brooks can bring you." My little fellow hollered, "Next weekend?" I immediately said, "NO!" Everyone laughed.

Our hostess actually shed tears during the hugging. She said, "Kids from all around down here come for the 'roundup,' but none are as sweet and well mannered as you boys. You didn't break anything, and you didn't misuse any of the livestock or our dogs. We love you boys." The kids responded in unison, "We love you, too!" We got loaded again with the same hollering and the same complaints. This time, they positioned themselves to be as comfortable as possible, but still complaining. We were off.

The old 1954 Ford had almost 200,000 miles on it, and the rear was almost touching the tires. I still had a little more than a half tank of gas. All the noise the kids made and the fun they were having was unbelievable. When a car passed us, they hollered everything at them, but no obscenities. We were trucking right along, but I decided to stop at a small town called Archie. I had watched the highway signs and Archie was about halfway home. The boys needed to stretch, as did I.

When we drove up to the truck stop, I could tell the folks weren't used to seeing that many Black folks too often, especially all piled up in one car with two white kids. Some of the boys had money, but I told them I was going in with two at a time. I didn't want anyone accusing them of taking anything. "Remember who you are. Who are you?" They responded loudly, "Explorers. Members of Explorer Post 700 of the Kansas City, Missouri, Police Department!" Boy, did we draw attention by the way they hollered and who they were. They were proud.

The toilet facility was outside, which was good. I told them that no more than two could go in together. I took my little Explorer and the younger one in with me first. Neither had money, so I paid for theirs. The young female cashier was very friendly. She asked where we were going. My little fellow said, "Home!" I sent him out to tell two more to come in. After everyone had used the restroom, they got some snacks. I think I spent about $20. I had to remind them that they couldn't buy everything in the store—that the money they were spending was my money, not theirs.

So, we started loading up again with the same arguing about who was sitting where. I had to go around to the two rear doors and close them. There was an old woman who was talking with the young female cashier who had come outside to see us off. "Who are they?" the old woman asked. The young cashier was trying to explain to her what the boys had told her. I saw the expression on the old woman's face and saw her walking toward the pay phone, digging in her pocketbook. I said to myself, "She's going to call the police."

When I got on the highway again, I told the boys, "Fellows, I believe we're going to get stopped by the police. There's a sheriff or state patrol up ahead soon." In unison they said, "For what? We didn't do anything wrong." I said, "I know that, and I appreciate that. As I told you back there, I'm proud of the way you conducted yourselves. It's in violation of the law for me to have as many of you as I have piled up in one car. The max should be six. So, I want you to understand that. I just might get a ticket or get arrested."

They didn't understand the latter comment, so I had to explain that the law applied to everyone, even police officers. I went on to tell them, "When we're stopped, I want you all to do what you're told to do, and don't say anything unless you are individually asked. Let me do the talking. Does everyone understand?" Again, in unison, "Yes, sir, Mr. Brooks." I also cautioned them about hollering out the car and waving at cars that passed us.

City Kids from the Farm: "Where in the Hell Are You Going with This Overload of Kids?"—1962

Just as we passed a weigh station outside of Peculiar, there was a state trooper and a Cass County Sheriff's car parked alongside each other. I told the boys, "Get ready, fellows, we're going to get stopped just as I told you." No sooner than I got the words out of my mouth, the red lights flashed behind me. I eased over and turned off the engine. I told the boys, "No one get out unless you're ordered to. And if so, don't utter a word. Just follow whatever instructions are given."

The state trooper came up on my side and the sheriff on the passenger side. His flashlight was on and he was shining it in the car. All our windows were down, of course. As soon as they got in hearing distance, I said, "Good evening, officers."

The state trooper said, "Where in the hell are you going with all these damn kids? This is against the law. Do you know that? All you kids get out on the ground. Now! You get out over here and let me see your driver's license."

The kids didn't say a word and lined up against the police car, almost like at attention with hands in sight. The trooper and the sheriff conversed with each other somewhat sarcastically, as I was getting my driver's license out. As he shined his flashlight on my hands and billfold, he happened to see my badge. "What kind of a badge is that? You an officer or something?" I said, "Yes, sir. I'm Corporal Brooks with the Juvenile Bureau of the Kansas City Police Department."

"Well, you ought to know better," he said. "We put police officers in jail when they break the law." The sheriff backed him up. "We put wrongdoing police in jail as quick as any other criminal." I handed the trooper my driver's license. He took my billfold and examined my badge and ID. "You big-city coppers think you can come down here and break the law and nothing is going to happen to you. Is that what you think?" I said, "No, sir. I don't think that. May I tell you why I have all these young Explorers, advanced Boy Scouts, piled up in this one police car?"

The trooper responded, "Try me."

I explained the whole nine yards as to why eight kids were in a five- or six-passenger police car. On the other side of the car, I overheard the sheriff asking the boys if they were wanted for anything. "Don't lie. If you do, your asses are going to jail, and you may never get out. Do you understand English?"

All my boys answered in unison, "Yes, sir." The trooper walked around the car and gestured for the sheriff (I saw that he was a deputy) to come to the side and talk to him. In about five minutes, they called me to join them.

The trooper told me, "We discussed this high tale of yours with all these kids driving with five too many in a vehicle, but since you're police like us, and we do try to cooperate when possible, we're going to let you get these kids back to Kansas City. We hope you appreciate what we're doing for you 'cause if you were anyone else, we'd tell you to call someone to take half of these kids—or leave them here and come back and get the other half."

I told them that I appreciated their consideration and extended my hand to shake theirs. The sheriff seemed a little reluctant at first, but he did. I asked for another consideration. "Would you be willing to shake the hands of my boys before we leave? I'm trying to teach them to be respectful of law enforcement officers regardless of who they are or where they are. I think it would be a good gesture on their part to have that happen, if you don't mind." They agreed. I called the trooper and the deputy sheriff by their names, and I told my boys to thank them. Which they did, almost in unison.

The highway became jammed both north- and southbound—to see what was going on and what the outcome was. My boys piled back in the car. Both the trooper and deputy sheriff laughed as I went on both sides of the car to close the doors. Well, I made it home with each boy and got myself home about midnight. What an experience!

Police Stop Sociology Class, 1963

While I was a police corporal, I was stopped one day by a police officer. On occasion, one of my professors at UMKC would have our class at a local pub on Troost called Boots. There were about fifteen students in Dr. Ed Tomich's sociology class. Depending where we were parked, we would pile into whoever's car was closest to Haig Hall. This occasion, I rode in the car with three white females and one white male, the driver. His car was a convertible, and the top was down. One of the females was sitting in the front seat with the driver, and I was sitting in the back seat between the other two females. Just as we cleared the intersection northbound on Troost and Volker Boulevard, we were stopped by a white police officer. He demanded that everyone get out of the car.

The driver asked why we were stopped. He was told to "shut up and get against the car." He told the three women to stand at the rear of the car. He told me to get against the car also. His backup pulled up. The first officer searched the driver and put his hand on my shoulder.

I said, "Officer, I'm a KC police officer and I'm armed."

He quickly stepped back and drew his gun and ordered the driver to step aside. The backup officer drew his gun. All kinds of thoughts were going through my head. What were the officers going to do? It appears they were afraid and didn't know what to do. I didn't know what they were afraid of: my saying I was an armed police officer or that I was just a Black man with a gun. I was afraid to move.

Finally, the first officer told me to turn around. I said, "Are you sure, Officer? I don't want to make any kind of move that may cause either of you to think I'm going for my gun. My name is Alvin Brooks. I'm a detective on the same department that you're on. Might I suggest you call your sergeant? I'd rather stay just like this until he arrives."

One of the officers said, "Turn around." I did. I could see the faces of the three women at the rear of the car. The driver had moved to the front. The number two officer went to the first officer's car. I could see he was on the police radio. The outside speaker was on. I heard who I believed to be the sergeant say, "I'm on the way."

The driver of the car I was in asked again, "Officer, why did you stop us?" The officer didn't answer. The sergeant drove up. I couldn't see whether the one officer still had his gun out. The second officer, who had called the sergeant, didn't have his gun out when he went to the car to call the sergeant. When the sergeant walked to the side of the first police car, I turned and looked at him.

He said, "Alvin?" Then to the first officer, "Holster your gun." He walked up to me. I then turned around. He kind of whispered, "What the hell's going on here, Alvin?"

I said, "I don't know except the officer there pulled us over. I think it's because he saw me sitting in the back seat between two white women." I explained what had occurred, that I told the officer that I had a gun, and that I was a detective on the KCPD. By that time, the driver of the car I was riding in walked up and finished my response.

"That officer there pulled me over. We're leaving the university and were meeting with other class members and our instructor down the street there at the pub."

The sergeant asked him to excuse us and told everyone to get back into the car and go on to the meeting. "I'll bring Alvin down there in a few minutes." The sergeant had been in my graduating class of 1954. He had been promoted to that rank and was assigned to the Country Club Station.

The sergeant told the backup to get back in service. He walked to the other officer with his hand on my shoulder. He said to the officer, "What the shit is wrong with you? You had no reason to stop their car. Then after Alvin told you he was a KCPD detective, why didn't you ask for his ID, apologize, and let them be on their way?"

The officer didn't respond. He just dropped his head. The sergeant told the officer, "Alvin and I were in the same recruit class and graduated together. You owe Alvin an apology." The officer did apologize with his head down and extended his hand to shake mine.

I shook his hand and told him I accepted his apology. But I said to him while holding his hand, "Officer, I don't know where you came from or how you feel about Negroes, but if you keep up what you did this evening, you're not going to last long. Again, I accept your apology."

The sergeant told the officer to "write a report on what happened here this evening and call me when you have it ready. Don't get back into service yet. Call me when you're done.

"Come on, Alvin, I'll run you down to Boots. I'll handle that stupid ass. By the way, how have you been? I'm sorry about what happened to you tonight. I can remember when you brought this kind of thing up during our recruit days, and many of our classmates came close to booing you."

I said, "Sergeant, you're looking good, man. I'm glad you were this cat's sergeant. He really had me scared when he pulled his gun when I told him I was a KCPD officer and had a weapon."

We sat in the police car for a brief minute and shook hands, and then I joined my class. Rather than dealing with the chapters that we were assigned to read, my encounter became the classwork for the next hour or so. Dr. Tomich, who was quite a "cussa," did that for a few minutes after I told him what happened after my classmates had left.

The "N-word" was occasionally used by some of these white officers that I answered calls with. Afterward, they would say, "Al, I didn't mean you, what I said back there."

I always responded, "Yes, you did. Your prejudice is showing how you feel." After I said that, I always lost a "friend." I was often told by the brothers who were frequently arrested, sometimes on legitimate charges, sometimes not, that they were called "nigger." Especially by the vice unit detectives.

My Biological Father, Wilbur Lamar Herring, 1915–1984

In January 1963, I received a call from my biological father. As my mother promised, when she returned home from visiting us in KC, she began to try to locate Wilbur Herring. Although it took nine years, somehow the message got to my father, who still lived in Miami, Florida, that Thomascine Gilder was trying to locate him regarding their son, who lived in Kansas City, Missouri. My father called my mother; they talked, and she told him that they had a son named Alvin Lee Brooks who was anxious to get in touch with him and gave him my phone number. She said, "Wilbur was so surprised to hear from me after thirty years. And more surprised—and happier—that he had a grown son who had a family in Kansas City."

I am sure he was crying. We talked a long time. He wanted to talk to Carol. Afterward he said he would like to visit us in Kansas City if that was okay with us. I told him yes, it was okay.

In March, he drove up to our house at 3336 Agnes. It was amazing how much he resembled my adoptive dad, Cluster. My God, did he love me! I could feel it. Carol could sense it also. She and my dad hit it off immediately. The kids, Ronall, Estelle, Carrie, and Rosalind, had some difficulty dealing with the two grandpas—Cluster Brooks and now Wilbur Herring. But my father Cluster had passed in 1961, and really it was just Ronall, Estelle, and Carrie who could identify closely with Cluster. Of course, my mother Estelle had passed in 1951 before any of them were born, when Carol and I were not yet married.

My biological father, Wilbur Lamar Herring Sr., was born in Miami, Florida, on September 26, 1915. My dad told me it was rumored in Miami that he had gotten Thomascine pregnant, so she was sent from Miami to North Little Rock, where she gave birth to a boy—namely, me. "As you know, we were just teenagers," he said.

While my dad was here, he got a job at Parkview Drug Store on State Line just off 75th Street.

I should reflect on our telephone conversations before he came to Kansas City. He wanted me and the family to come to Miami, Florida, to live there. He said he would build us a house in Carver Ranches. Carol and I declined the offer. Unknown to me—but Carol knew—my dad began looking for a house in Kansas City, near where we lived. It was supposed to be a surprise to me.

My dad found a house just three blocks from us and began to make plans to dispose of everything in Miami and move his family to Kansas City. He had married his wife, Florence, in 1949 in Miami. They had five children near the same ages as our kids. I'm mentioning them oldest to youngest: Ella, Wilbur Jr., Lamar, Julia, and Tomette. William, their sixth, was born in New Jersey after they left Kansas City.

Disposing of everything in Miami almost caused a divorce, he told me later. Carol and I told him we could understand why Florence was at the brink of telling him, "Go to Kansas City with your grown son and his family! We'll stay here in Miami!" But Florence relented, and near the end of 1963, they moved into the house my dad found in the 3300 block of South Benton. Dad and Florence left behind in Florida several businesses: a kiddie school, an ice cream parlor, apartments, a theater, a laundromat, and a house in Carver Ranches. They also had investments in land, hotels, and motels. He was an Eisenhower Republican.

Carol bawled out my dad many times, but Florence opened up to Carol. Florence adjusted to life in Kansas City somewhat; but several years later, Dad moved the family to New Brunswick, New Jersey. Dad was a World War II veteran and served under General George Patton and was the bugler. I have the bugle. My dad died in September 1984 and Florence in 2007. Both died in New Jersey.

I should mention that on one occasion, my mother visited me while my dad and his family were in Kansas City, and the three of us met and as a result, became close. My mother also met my dad's wife, Florence.

I Was Promoted to Detective, June 1, 1964

After being promoted to detective, I was asked by Captain Hastings if I wanted to try to get into another investigative unit. I told him no. I told him that I enjoyed working with the children and youth and their families and working with members of several gangs, specifically the 31st Street and the 23rd Street gangs. I also told him that I liked his management style. Which I did. All of this was true, but there was another reason.

I was still an optimist and wanted to make a career of police work. I wanted to move up the promotional ladder. I knew the limitations for Black officers in the department. Discrimination and segregation based on racism persisted. Yes, Chief Brannon had taken a bold step and used six of us to test the behavior and attitudes of white folks in two other sections of the city. I believe if Brannon had remained chief, he would have been fairer toward Black officers. It was under his watch that the special Black unit was organized and headed by Lloyd DeGraffenreid, who was promoted to detective sergeant.

As I recall, there were older Black officers who were promoted to detectives and who worked burglaries. So, I thought if I was promoted to sergeant, I would become a field sergeant. There was but one Black sergeant as I recall, and that was Detective Sergeant DeGraffenreid. Then there was Lt. Col. Clifford Warren, aide to Chief Kelley.

Several years earlier, four of us Black officers decided to take the sergeant's exam. I had just become eligible. I was the youngest and had the least time on the force. The other officers were Ivy Wharton, Arthur Williamson (who made the highest score), and Jethro Jones. Jethro was very angry because each of them had been on the eligible list before and had been passed over, even for detective.

It happened again. None of us was selected to become sergeant. I didn't expect to get it, but I did expect one of us to be selected. Arthur was number two or three on the list. He suggested we all boycott taking the test the next time. Arthur's rationale was that if Black officers didn't take the test, it would prick the conscience of the chief and other high-ranking officers.

The word got around that none of us was going to take the sergeant exam when it came up next time. Sometime later, after another test had been given, Chief Kelley was requested to attend a meeting with a group of Black community leaders at the YWCA at 1901 Paseo Boulevard to discuss the actions of the white officer that the Black community complained about. The chief was told that no one had called "check" on this officer. Kelley still defended him, although he put out an order that only police-issued batons would be carried and that the K-9 dogs would not go into residences and businesses.

Then the chief was asked why there were no Black sergeants and why the only Black officers above detective were Lloyd DeGraffenreid and Clifford Warren. Warren, who was brought to the meeting by Kelley, did not advocate for the Black officers. Kelley responded, "None of them took the test." So, I made up my mind and shared my thoughts with the Black officers who had stood firm to not take the test again. I urged all the younger officers to take the sergeant exam when they became eligible.

Several of us took the sergeant exam the next time around in 1961. Wharton, Williamson, and Jones did not take the test, but I did. I was on the list again in March of 1961 and in the top twenty-five with a score of 85.22, the only Black officer in the first twenty-five. By the time the eligible list had been exhausted again, none of us was appointed. Although several white officers with scores in the 70s were appointed, I was again passed over. The only excuse I was given was, "You're a damn good cop and doing such a great job in the Juvenile Bureau. It's hard to find a replacement for you."

"Bullshit." That's what I said to one of my sergeants when he told me that, although he had given me an excellent evaluation. He immediately took the "disclaimer" position. "Al, don't give up, my boy. It'll come to you in due time. I hope you know I'll help all I can. You believe me, don't you?"

"Sarge, all I know is that this is the second time I've been passed over. I'm not willing to accept the bullshit any more than you would—if you were told the reason you're not promoted is because you're too valuable and no one can replace you. This was a good bureau before I got here and it'll be a good bureau when I'm gone, one way or the other. That excuse is unacceptable. And Sarge, whoever is passing that down to you—I know it's not the major—please pass on my feelings of displeasure and tell them it's a matter of race."

The sergeant said, "Alvin, you don't want that kind of word to get around. Some folks will have a problem with that." My response was, "So be it, Sarge. Please pass it on and let the chips fall where they may. And if there's anyone who would like to take me up on the issues, I'm here waiting." That was the end of the conversation. I'm sure that the sergeant passed it on because some folks outside of our bureau who had been friendly when our paths crossed now rarely spoke to me. Some were lower in rank, some the same, and others higher.

My Letter of Resignation: October 9, 1964; Effective October 31, 1964

3336 Agnes
Kansas City, Missouri
October 9, 1964

Chief Clarence Kelley
1125 Locust Street
Kansas City, Missouri

Sir:
This letter is not addressed to you to minimize or criticize the Juvenile Bureau in which I serve; nor is it meant to express dissatisfaction with supervisors, superior officers, or other

coworkers, but rather, once again, to call to your attention my personal dissatisfaction with promotional procedures.

No longer can I accept the commendations, letters, and conversations of civic appreciation as being the only form in which my value to the police department can be rewarded.

My record will attest to my loyal and conscientious service to the department since becoming a member in June 1954. My Qualification and Evaluation reports will show that I have proven to be an asset to all the areas to which I have been assigned and to the police department as a whole. My length of service, ten years, proves an honest desire to make law enforcement my career.

As you know, and my personnel record shows, I have completed my undergraduate studies at the University of Missouri at Kansas City, in a social science field, history and government, and have completed twenty-one hours toward my master's degree in still another social science field, sociology. The fact alone that I have accomplished this while maintaining a full-time status in the department should cause one to have faith in my perseverance.

I have involved myself in special training that would enable me to be more valuable to the department, such as the training course in Delinquency and Control taken at the University of Wisconsin campus at Madison, Wisconsin. I have also had special courses in supervisory training and seminars designated and approved by this police department, courses which were held on the campus of the University of Missouri at Kansas City.

During my service with the department, I have attempted to promote a better understanding between the community and the police by speaking before church groups, parent-teacher organizations, community councils, and school groups on the functions, principles, and policies of our department.

I have attempted to incorporate the high ideals of our department into my personal life by becoming civic-minded and participating in community affairs. I will not utilize space to set down in detail these involvements inasmuch as they were set down in detail in the inter-department communication that I addressed to you on January 14, 1963.

I asked at that time that my personnel record be reviewed in terms of consideration for promotion to the rank of sergeant, a rank that I might remind you, Chief Kelley, I successfully passed the examination for in 1961 and in 1963.

In your reply you stated: "I assure you, however, I will keep you in mind for promotion in other bureaus and divisions of our department where it appears your background, capabilities, and experience indicate you would be qualified for a sergeant rank." Am I to believe that in the twenty months that have elapsed since you made that statement that no such opportunities have presented themselves? In my heart, I cannot believe this, for I can see around me many who have been made sergeant without myself being given even so much consideration as to warrant a personnel review board interview.

Why should outside forces have to come into our department and dictate departmental changes, which should be commonplace, and thus place our department in an embarrassing position similar to that recently endured by the Coffeyville, Kansas, police department (note clipping attached herein). In this instance, the Negro officer in question, having grown tired of existing conditions of racial discrimination, which I believe also exist in our department, was forced to file a complaint against his department with an outside influence (the Kansas Commission on Civil Rights) that forced his department to grant him the promotion he was deserving of and more than capable of handling.

I hope and pray that our department will see need for a change in regard to the hiring and promotional opportunities for the Negroes (including the clerical field where there are no Negroes) so they might be in keeping with those of the whites. Only one set of rules should be applied: all should be judged according to the rules, race notwithstanding.

I hope that in the immediate future our department will undergo a complete change in promotional policies and opportunities, whereby a qualified Negro applicant can become a part of our department with the feeling that he will be judged for promotion (after meeting all requirements) by the content of his character and ability rather than by the color of his skin. I have in mind my thirteen-year-old son, who has shown a desire to follow in the career example set by his father. Should this desire remain for the next eight years, and if through his ability he is appointed to the department, he can have a feeling that the "ceiling" is as high as the potentials of his character and qualifications.

I can no longer keep faith with this belief nor with our departmental promotional procedure, nor can I wait any longer to make some attempt to secure the future that I feel my family and myself are deserving of; hence, it is with regret that I must tender my resignation from the department, which I would like to become effective October 31, 1964.

Respectfully,
Det. Alvin L. Brooks

Chapter 4

SCHOOLWORK—AND THE RIOT

From the Police Department to the KC School District, 1964

When I knew things weren't going to improve for me at the police department, I began to explore other employment possibilities. I submitted my letter of resignation to the department on October 9 and officially left the police department on October 31, 1964—Halloween. The following week, I started with the Kansas City Public Schools as a home school coordinator. Years earlier, they were called "truant officers."

Here's the background. Mrs. Eugea Parker was a home school coordinator. She and I and most all the Black home school coordinators had worked family cases together when I was in the Juvenile Bureau. When Mrs. Parker heard from one of her coworkers that I had given notice to the police department, she contacted me.

"Alvin, there's a spot waiting for you over here at the school district as a home school coordinator. The principals know you. If you want to join us over here, I'll pass the word to the principals, and they will request you. I'll handle it here on the inside. The families and kids who need our services know you. And the folks at the juvenile court know you. This job was made for you since you're leaving the police department. If you say you'll take it if it's offered, I'll talk to the director of the department, Mrs. Belguard. She'll hire you. I know she will. Send me a résumé and do it right away."

I knew Mrs. Parker's husband, Mr. Obster Parker, who was the owner of Parker's Show Bar on 18th Street (I mentioned Mr. Parker earlier when his place was raided). I told Mrs. Parker I would get her my résumé. Several days later, I was to meet with Mrs. Belguard in her office at nine in the morning. Mrs. Parker was to meet me there. When I arrived on the ninth floor of the Board of Education building, I introduced myself and said I was there to meet Mrs. Belguard and Mrs. Eugea Parker. The secretary said Mrs. Belguard was expecting me and ushered me into a conference room where there was a meeting in session with all the home school coordinators.

Mrs. Belguard walked up to me, introduced herself, and welcomed me to the meeting. Mrs. Belguard asked Mrs. Parker, "Eugea, will you introduce our guest?" which Mrs. Parker did. Mrs. Belguard went through my résumé without really looking at it. When she finished, Mrs. Parker talked for fifteen minutes about my past and bragged about my relationship with the school principals, teachers, parents, and students and about the resources I had in the community.

She then said, "That's my friend, Alvin Brooks."

Mrs. Belguard said, "Thank you, Eugea. Alvin, welcome to this wonderful staff of dedicated people." She shook my hand, and everyone applauded. I was shocked; I really didn't know what to say. I never heard of anyone being hired on the spot and being presented to all his coworkers before he even said he accepted the appointment. But I went along with what was happening and gave my "acceptance speech," which lasted for about five minutes. When I finished, I got a standing ovation. All within a little over a half hour. The meeting was adjourned.

Each "colleague" came up and congratulated and welcomed me aboard. I thanked Mrs. Belguard and Mrs. Parker. No one asked me, but I was still on the police department's payroll. As I remember, I still had a week to go before clearing out my desk. Mrs. Parker pulled me to the side and said, "Didn't I tell you you had a job waiting for you over here? Come on, let's go to personnel so you can complete the necessary paperwork." I said, "Mrs. Parker, I have another week before I leave the police department." She responded, "That's okay. Let's get this done—then all you need to do is come to work."

I followed Mrs. Parker to the personnel office. She introduced me to a woman who greeted me and welcomed me to the school district staff. She handed me some papers, explained them to me, and said I could complete them there or take them with me and bring them back the day I start work. I thanked her and said I'd bring them back when I reported to work and gave her a date. She said that was fine and placed the personnel papers in an envelope. She had a copy of my résumé on her desk.

Mrs. Parker and I left. She said she had some reports to complete in her office. She shook my hand and said, "Welcome aboard, coworker. I'll see you on Monday." I thanked her again and left.

Now that was the damndest thing I'd ever heard of. Hired in front of a couple of dozen people. No interview or reference check. Nothing!

Well, the rest is history. I stayed until Bob Wheeler, assistant superintendent of the Division of Urban Education for the school district, asked me to join him and Dr. A. Leedy Campbell in their division.

From the Department of Home School Coordinators to the Division of Urban Education, 1964

Dr. A. Leedy Campbell, former school principal and now director for the Division of Urban Education, called me and asked me to stop by his office the next time I was in the Board building. "Alvin," he said, "I have something I want to run past you that you might be interested in." I told him I would be in that afternoon.

I went to Dr. Campbell's office, and he closed the door and invited me to have a seat. After pleasantries, Dr. Campbell asked, "Alvin, how would you like to join Bob Wheeler and me here in the Division of Urban Education? You know Bob is the assistant superintendent in charge of the division. Well, we've been talking, and we need someone who has the skills to deal with folks in the schools under the Division of Urban Education and bring our patrons into the loop. We thought you would be a natural for that position. Think you'd be interested?"

I said, "Yes, sir, Dr. Campbell. I feel honored that you and Bob would consider me for the position. What is it called?"

Dr. Campbell said, "If you're really interested, we need to meet with Bob. It will have a new title, but the pay will probably be just under the director's pay scale."

I said, "I'm seriously interested, Dr. Campbell."

We met with Bob Wheeler several days later. The conversation went well, and I accepted the job, "Coordinator of Parent and Student Relations and Community Interpretation." The position had a considerable increase in salary. I started the summer of 1965 and had the opportunity to participate in the first Head Start program, working out of W. W. Yates Elementary School at the 1200 block of Lydia. At the beginning of the school year, I was given an office in the Board building on the ninth floor, just down the hall from Dr. Campbell. I believe Bob was also at that end of the hall on the ninth floor.

Civil Rights: The Congress of Racial Equality (CORE), 1965

Dr. Howard Nelson Jr., local Black dentist, was chair of the local Congress of Racial Equality (CORE). Many of their meetings were held at our house. Carol was a very active member. From marches to sit-ins, ideas and strategies were planned on our dining room table. The public accommodations ordinance was passed by the city council in 1964. We then planned strategies to test if those public places covered by the ordinance were in fact obeying the law.

Fairyland Park, an amusement park at 75th and Prospect, was a major target and got all kinds of publicity after the passage of the city's public accommodations law. Arrests were made even before the ordinance was passed. Blacks could only go to Fairyland Park one day a year, in July. We could be seen waiting for the streetcar going south from 12th Street to our southern boundary, which had been extended to about 39th Street. As I reflect, that entire corridor looked like a bunch of Black folks going to the plantation to pick cotton for the white man.

I don't know when we stopped the annual Fairyland Park event, but it was before the city's public accommodations ordinance. Even after passage, the owners of Fairyland Park still refused to allow Black citizens to enter the park. CORE was in the forefront of the protest. CORE filed complaints with Kansas City's Mayor's Commission on Human Relations, which was assigned the responsibility of administering the ordinance. The commission's main objective was to try to mediate complaints. Those efforts failed. The matter was then turned over to the city prosecutor. Those in violation were to be prosecuted.

Fairyland Park was found numerous times to be in violation of the ordinance. CORE organized sit-ins, blocking the entrance to the park. The owners had the protestors arrested for trespassing. I was still on the police department, a detective, prior to the passage of the ordinance, when my wife, Carol, and many others were arrested. I happened to be on duty and in my car when some officer riding the area of Fairyland Park went on the air without identifying himself and said, "Al Brooks, your wife just got arrested at Fairyland Park. Thought you ought to know." Officers all over the city began to make comments and catcalls, which put me at odds with some of my fellow white officers.

The CORE members did get arrested. They were brought to Headquarters but were not booked. After numerous complaints were filed by CORE members and the city, the park owners turned Fairyland Park into a "private club." That meant "whites only." Several of our white members made application and were allowed to join. Although Blacks could make application for membership, none were ever accepted. Eventually that "private club," specifically formed to avoid admitting Blacks, finally closed.

CORE members tested restaurants and nightclubs all over the city. One of our white members was beaten at a club on Blue Parkway where the Swope Park Health Center now stands. David Stupple, a multiple sclerosis victim who walked with metal crutches, was beaten with a club, while Carol and others were held at gunpoint and threatened by a Doberman pinscher. David ended up in the hospital, but fortunately his injuries were not serious. Although the police were called, no one was arrested. To the police, it was a "civil matter." We organized numerous marches against the police department for acts of police brutality. Complaints were filed by the victims, but I don't recall any disciplinary actions ever being taken against an officer.

Several CORE members were attorneys. Gwendolyn Wells, one of the CORE chairs who preceded me, was an attorney. She later became a member of the Board of Police Commissioners. Leonard Hughes Jr., who became a county judge and then a city judge, was a CORE member, and both he and Gwen investigated all cases of alleged police misconduct before having the alleged victim file a complaint. Dr. Robert Farnsworth, a white man, was the first CORE chair, which was formed nationally in 1961 by James Foreman. The Kansas City chapter became affiliated with the national organization the same year it was formed. Farnsworth was succeeded by Gwen, then Dr. Nelson, and then me. And I was succeeded by Bervin Fisher when I resigned as CORE chair and was appointed director of the city's Human Relations Department on May 27, 1968.

Panel Discussion with Mayors and Civil Rights Leaders: "Can We Have a Riot?"—1968

About two weeks before Kansas City's riot of April 9, 1968, I was one of six persons on a panel at the Jewish Community Center at 82nd and Holmes. The panelists, including local mayors and members of NAACP and CORE, discussed the recent riots in cities around the nation. The panelists were Mayor Ilus Davis, KCMO; Mayor Joe McDowell, KCK; Andy Rollins, KCK NAACP; Lee Vertis Swinton, KCMO NAACP; Carl Randolph, chair of the KCK CORE; and me, chair of the KCMO CORE.

Lena Rivers Smith, a reporter for the *Kansas City Call*, the Black weekly newspaper, was the moderator. (Lena became the first African American to serve as a reporter for an all-white television station, Kansas City's WDAF-TV 4, an NBC affiliate.) The event was open to the public.

Each panelist had about three minutes to share insights.

I was the last to speak.

I began, "A riot will not occur except where there is a long history of social tensions which have festered over time. A spark, especially involving the police, can ignite into a full-blown riot. Both Kansas City, Kansas, and Kansas City, Missouri, are vulnerable. They have the same ingredients that all the other urban communities that have had riots do. A number of unmet needs have not been addressed."

The auditorium was packed—standing room only. Some booed me. The other two Black panelists also expressed their feelings, although theirs were not as strong as mine. Most of the questions and comments were directed at me. I held my own, if I say so myself. The question and answer period got heated, but near the end of the two-hour session, Lena and the six panelists were almost all on the same page.

The mayors were reluctant to use the word "racism." They used the word "indifference." It was a lively discussion. Lena did a masterful job moderating, although it got loud, and she was heckled at times. But I was proud of her.

After the meeting, people were standing in line to express their opinion. As I recall, the lights began to blink, notifying everyone it was time to leave.

About two weeks later, as I predicted, Kansas City, Missouri, had its own homegrown riot. Kansas City, Kansas, also had disturbances.

The Assassination of Dr. Martin Luther King Jr., April 4, 1968

It was just before 7:00 p.m. on Thursday evening, April 4, 1968, when I received a call from an FBI agent assigned to Kansas City to monitor the tension and possible violence. He said, "Dr. King was shot and killed just moments ago in Memphis, Tennessee. No one has been arrested yet."

I said, "Say what? Dr. King what?" He repeated that Dr. King has been shot to death in Memphis, but no one had been arrested. He said, "The media probably have it now, but the Memphis field office notified me."

I asked, "Are you sure he's deceased?" Carol overheard what I was saying and turned on the television. All the stations were carrying the story. I told the agent and Carol at the same time, "All hell is going to break lose now. Probably right here in KC."

The agent said, "You're probably right, but I hope not. If you hear anything, will you let me know?"

I told him I would. My phone began to ring off the hook, call after call after call . . . the *Kansas City Star*, radio stations, and TV stations wanted a comment.

Kansas City was quiet during the night and early Friday morning. Reactions and disturbances all over the world were reported. As I hit the streets on the way to my office at the school district, horns were blowing nonstop. A couple of TV stations caught me for comments as I entered the school district building. Each wanted to know if I thought there would be violence in Kansas City.

I was cautiously honest. "I hope not, but the least spark could set something off. There's already a lot of angry people here; and if the police overreact, that'll be the spark to set something off."

The weekend was quiet. It was announced that Mrs. King would be in Memphis Monday to speak, and there would be a symbolic march as Dr. King and others were there in support of the city's sanitation workers.

I had been away from the police department for four years when Dr. King was assassinated on the balcony of the Lorraine Motel in Memphis, Tennessee, on that dreadful evening.

My son, Ronall, and I went to Memphis on Monday, April 8, and heard Coretta Scott King speak, and we participated in the symbolic march to show support for Memphis garbage workers. I had planned to go to Atlanta—where Dr. King lay in state on the campus of Morehouse College, his alma mater—but we couldn't get a flight, so we returned to Kansas City early Monday evening.

When we got home, Carol told me that Bob Wheeler had called and that school superintendent Jim Hazlett was calling a meeting that evening at the Board building to discuss whether the schools should open the next day. Bob wanted me there. I went to the meeting.

From a phone at a conference in Washington, DC, Superintendent Hazlett summoned administrators to the meeting including Wheeler, Dr. Campbell, and me. Because of the weekend, the discussion was to reconsider whether the schools should be open on Tuesday, April 9, the day memorial services were scheduled. At an earlier meeting when Hazlett and other school officials had met with some Black community leaders, they decided that the schools should be open on the day of the memorial services. Bob Wheeler, Dr. Campbell, and I tried to impress upon those old white men and Superintendent Hazlett that our schools should be closed. We told them that if they were open and the Kansas City, Kansas, schools were closed, their students would come to our schools. If our schools were open, it would be easy to form impromptu marches without any adult involvement, plus if schools were not in session, our students would feel able to attend memorial services or other appropriate activities. If school was in session, our kids might gravitate toward leaders with "loud, clear voices" who might also be immature, rather than organizing and selecting leaders who are respectful and obedient and, most important, nonviolent. We were not heard.

Hazlett overruled our suggestion and said we would name the new junior high school at 42nd on Indiana Martin Luther King Junior High School and that flags would be flown at half-mast but that schools would remain open. We tried as hard as we could to impress on Hazlett and his all-white male team that his Black team didn't think it was a good idea to keep schools open. In fact, Bob told the group, with Hazlett still on the phone, "It's crazy for us to open school tomorrow. If you do, we can predict that all hell is going to break loose. You might as well get ready for it if you have school."

I tried to point out that Kansas City, like many cities and small towns where Black folks lived, as well as many white communities, was mourning the assassination of Dr. King. They could relate to his August 1963 "I Have a Dream" speech in the nation's capital. Anyone—Black or white—with any cultural knowledge and sense of Black folks should have known that there would be memorial marches and memorial ceremonies being held across the nation. Kansas City was no exception. They didn't listen.

The word got out that Kansas City schools would be open.

Later that evening and night, a group of ministers and neighborhood folks met at the Congress of Racial Equality (CORE) office at 12th and Paseo. They mapped out a strategy for the area in case violence occurred. I joined the group after my meeting at the board of education, and I shared with them what the "white folks" had decided.

There was outrage. I also told them that some Black folks were in favor of the district keeping the schools open and naming the middle school on Indiana after Dr. King, holding minutes of silence at all schools, and flying flags on all schools at half-mast. I reported that Bob Wheeler, Dr. Campbell, and I predicted that our kids would walk out, justifiably so, and we needed to be there with them. The group wanted to give Superintendent Hazlett a call at home. I told them that Hazlett was out of the city, and that Dr. Glen Hanks was acting superintendent. We finally decided to meet the following morning at 7:30 at Bethel AME Church at 24th and Flora, where the Reverend Dr. E. Woody Hall was pastor.

This infamous morning began with local media discussing the assassination of Dr. King and listing memorial services being held and school closings, as well as those schools where classes would go on as usual—among them the Kansas City School District.

The 7:30 a.m. meeting was well attended, some fifty to sixty in number, with broad community participation, men and women of all ages. The decision was that we would begin this morning patrolling and monitoring each school that has a predominate Black student population: Lincoln, Central senior and junior, East, Southeast, Manual, and Westport. There would be four persons in each car. Other than the driver, the other three would have pencils and notepads to record any abusive behavior. It had been reported that the police were seen around Central in unusual numbers. The meeting was adjourned, and people began to load up as planned.

I had three ministers with me, including the Reverend E. Woody Hall. I informed my team that I was going to bring them back to Bethel about nine o'clock because I was going to attend the memorial services at the Episcopal Cathedral downtown. I said I would return to Bethel after the service and join whoever was there and wanted to go out on "patrol."

Our first stop was Lincoln High School. Although the bell had rung, there were large groups of students milling around the flagpole in front. It just so happened as we turned left on Woodland from 22nd Street, we found ourselves behind a marked police car occupied by two police officers. They stopped in front of the school for no reason at all. I pulled up behind them. The driver of the police car waved his arm for me to come around him. I ignored his gesture. They finally moved on. The students waved at us.

We then went to Manual and East, then to Central, where students were also milling around outside although school had begun. There was a police presence around the area. I took the ministers back to Bethel Church and headed downtown to Grace and Holy Trinity Episcopal Cathedral.

When I reached the cathedral, it was almost filled. I managed to get a seat near the rear door. The local media since early morning had been discussing the assassination of Dr. King, his funeral, where memorial services were being held, and the schools' closings and noting schools that were open, including the Kansas City School District.

By the time the memorial service started, the church was full beyond capacity. As the service progressed, a woman walked up to the person then speaking and handed him a piece of paper. It was a note. The speaker looked at it and asked, "Is there a Mr. Alvin Brooks in the audience?"

I responded, "Yes."

He said, "You have an emergency call. The young lady will show you to the phone." I met the woman just outside the door. I introduced myself and she walked me to the phone. The voice on the other end was Bob Wheeler's.

"Al, all hell has broken out with our kids. They're coming from all schools and, at present, are at Troost Lake. I don't know what you can do, but head out that way and let me know where they're headed and if there's anything we need to be doing. I'd hate like hell for this thing to get out of hand—and some of our kids get hurt. We told them last night that this was going to happen, but no one wanted to listen. See what you can do, Al."

I headed toward Vine Street.

The Black-owned radio stations KPRS-FM and KPRT-AM began receiving calls that the students at Lincoln High School were walking out and marching to Central High School. Students at Lincoln and Manual High School refused to go to class. Some of the Manual students marched to Lincoln, and then students from both schools marched toward Central.

It was suggested that a representative from these three schools march to Paseo and then find a suitable place to have a memorial service. Another group wanted to march downtown to the board of education to protest the schools being open. The largest group of students from four or five schools had gathered at Central. Someone in the crowd suggested that they march to city hall, but as they started, police tried to get them to return to Central.

The students refused and were determined to march to city hall to report the actions of the police. About 10:00 a.m., it was announced that schools in Kansas City, Missouri, were closed. The students, who had grown in number, now decided to march toward the stores at 31st and Troost. Community activist Vernon Thompson, who had been marching with the students from Central and advising them of their rights to march and protest, was arrested and charged with interfering with the police. Police again used tear gas to disperse them. The majority of the students regrouped at Troost Lake. At each stop in between, they picked up more students and more momentum and more determination to go to city hall with their grievances and make Mayor Davis aware of what the police had done to them.

The marchers, who now had grown to several hundred, began marching from Troost Lake north to Vine Street. I believe that Councilman Bruce Watkins joined the students at Troost Lake. They were detained until the message got to the police that the mayor had agreed to meet the students at 17th Terrace and Vine in front of Gregg Community Center. When I arrived at 21st and Vine, there must have been nearly a thousand school kids, as later reported, marching north on Vine approaching 22nd Street.

Kansas City Chiefs football players Otis Taylor and Curtis McClinton, the Reverend Kenneth Ray (my boyhood friend), and I joined the kids. We marched on the front line with the students to meet Mayor Davis at 17th Terrace and Paseo.

In his remarks, the mayor seemed as though he didn't want the students to march to city hall—but wanted them detained in the Black part of the city. The students told the mayor that they wanted to go downtown to city hall for a rally. The mayor joined us, the adults, and began walking north on Paseo with the students. When we got to Truman Road and Paseo, a line of police officers was blocking both northbound and southbound lanes on Truman Road. The officer in charge told the mayor that he and the students could not go any farther.

The mayor was placed in a police car and taken away. Seeing this, the students headed up the embankment to Interstate 70 and arrived in the eastbound lane. After a while, traffic stood still. We four adults were still on the front line with the youth and headed west toward the 13th Street exit. A state trooper placed a round in the chamber of his shotgun. I told him, "Officer, you really don't want to stand in the way of these kids. They are peaceful."

The trooper stepped aside and got back into his patrol car, and we continued down 13th Street to Locust and up to city hall. When we got there, the crowd had grown to more than a thousand. The mayor was already there with a bullhorn. Then I went inside city hall and asked the woman at the information desk if I could use a phone. She handed me the phone and I called Mr. J. D. Williams. He owned the Consolidated Cab Company with whom the school district had a busing contract. I got Mr. Williams on the phone.

I gave him a brief background of what had happened and what was happening at city hall. I told him that with the heavy police presence and what had already occurred at 31st and Indiana and at 31st and Troost, I was afraid for our kids to be walking back to their respective neighborhoods. I asked him if he could send buses downtown to city hall to transport some of our kids back to the community. Mr. Williams asked, "How many buses do you think you need, Brooks?" I said five or six. He said, "I'll have to call my drivers in from their cabs, but I'll get them to you as soon as I can."

The police were everywhere and were supported by the state troopers. The mood was very tense. I just felt something could happen at any moment. The students were restless. They were milling around on the lawn and steps of city hall. One student tried to get between police cars, and a state trooper stepped out of formation and struck the student with his baton. A police officer pulled the trooper back. The students were yelling for Vernon Thompson, who had been arrested earlier, to be released.

The mayor, community activist Lee Bohannan, and I spoke at the students' request about the King assignation and the situation that followed. I talked about non-violent protests for human rights and justice and King's vision of the "beloved community." For anyone or any group to commit any violent act toward anyone would dishonor Dr. King's plea and vision.

Then Mayor Davis, Bruce Watkins, and several others went to police headquarters to meet Chief Kelley to seek the release of Vernon Thompson. Police sirens went off downtown. You could hear glass breaking and alarms going off at some of the businesses. The K-9 officers with their dogs were blocking the front doors just inside of city hall.

John L. Frazer, a KPRS radio disc jockey, took the bullhorn and announced that he had contacted Father Timothy Gibbons at Holy Name Catholic Church at 23rd and Benton, who was opening the church hall for the students. The church provided "Teen Town" for youth on weekends. There was a jukebox, bowling alley, and snack bar. They could dance. Frazer said buses were on the way to "take you to your respective schools or to the church."

In a short time, the buses began to arrive. I told the kids to board the buses to be taken to Holy Name.

The buses were filling up. The drivers knew where to take the kids. A bottle was hurled into the street. No officer was hit, but then all hell broke loose.

The police began to hurl canisters of tear gas from several different points. The students who had boarded the first bus, along with the driver, abandoned the bus because of the tear gas. Others thought it was safer staying on the other buses.

Police officers began chasing the kids east on 12th Street. Several of us were just below the front doors to city hall and were catching some of the tear gas. A white male and I fell to the concrete. The K-9 officers would not let us in the city hall doors. As we were facedown and I was lying next to that white male, he said to me, "I like the way you addressed those kids, telling them not to do anything that would bring dishonor to themselves, their families, their school, and their community—to remember what their marching down here was all about, the memory of Dr. King. They seemed to listen to you. I'm impressed."

I said, "Thank you. I'm Al Brooks."

He said, "I'm happy to meet you, Al Brooks. I'm John Taylor, city manager. I work in the building behind us."

Still facedown to avoid the heavy tear gas cloud, Taylor asked, "What do you do?" I told him I worked for the Kansas City School District, just across the street. We finally got up, with burning, watery eyes.

The captain in charge of the K-9 officers recognized Taylor and allowed him to enter through the doors. Taylor said I was with him, and we both went to the water fountain to rinse our eyes. John told me to contact him when "this stuff is over. I'd like to talk to you further." He gave me his card. We shook hands, and he caught an elevator.

As I was starting to leave, several ministers and others, about a dozen in all, began to meet in the lobby to discuss what had happened and the conduct of the police. They were writing up demands to present to the mayor and the police chief. A woman came in and said that the police had thrown a tear gas "bomb" into one of the buses and that the kids and the driver had to abandon the bus. It was blocking traffic on the 12th Street side of police headquarters. They were talking about how brutal the police were toward the students, using tear gas and chasing them with nightsticks.

I went outside in time to see two Episcopal priests, one Black and one white, beaten by the police for nothing—even though they had their collars on. The Black priest was Father Ed Warner, pastor at St. Augustine Episcopal Church on Benton Boulevard. The white priest was suffering from the tear gas and was lying on the lawn for a while. There was blood on both priests' heads and faces.

I went up to the ninth floor of the Board of Education Building, where my office was, to see Bob Wheeler. I found Bob, Dr. Campbell, and two others in Bob's office talking about our meeting the night before in the superintendent's office. I told Bob and Dr. Campbell what I had done across the street at city hall and how I thought I might go to the church. The staff in the Board building were watching out of the window overlooking the activity.

I drove out to Holy Name Catholic Church. Bruce Watkins was already there. The kids were coughing from tear gas that the police had thrown into the basement of the church. Bruce was cursing furiously. I understood why. People from the neighborhood were helping the kids with water, rinsing the gas from their faces and their eyes. Bruce and I walked into the church basement. Tear gas canisters were lying on the floor. Several police cars were parked on the side streets with officers observing everything. Bruce wanted to go and talk to them. I discouraged him from doing that. He said he was going to get to a phone and call the mayor, Chief Kelley, and Cliff Warren. He left. I hung around with other adults trying to help the students and watching the police until they were able to get rides. Youths in cars with Kansas licenses circled the area. They mocked the police, but the police did not move against them. I believe they would have if a dozen or so adults hadn't been there.

After the incidents at city hall and Holy Name Church, the word had spread throughout the Black community—and in fact, all over the city—as the media carried continuing coverage of what was occurring, "blow by blow." There were lootings and fires. Superintendent Hazlett returned to the city from Washington and after several meetings announced that the schools would be open on Wednesday. Bob Wheeler and Dr. Campbell were now doubly angered, as was I. Remember, the three of us had tried to encourage Hazlett and others the night before to not open the schools. We were convinced that had our suggestion been followed, there would not have been the incidents at City Hall, at Holy Name, and around the community. We felt that the worst was yet to come. And we were right. Before the day was over, it was reported that a Black man was shot to death by a white police officer as he ran away after looting a liquor store at 19th and Vine Street. The mayor issued a curfew. By the end of the night there were countless fires and property damage.

On Wednesday morning, April 10, the group of ministers and other residents who had met to develop a strategy for such occurrences again met following a meeting at Central Christian Church with civil rights leaders. The strategy adopted involved persons being assigned to certain schools. The governor had sent in the Missouri National Guard, who were riding four deep with police officers. Our group again met at Bethel African Methodist Episcopal Church. The same three ministers riding with me suggested we go to Lincoln again.

This time we came from the north. Cars of parents and youth were parked headed southbound and westbound down 21st Street. I parked just behind one of the southbound cars with several adults in it. Some students were milling outside as they were the day before. Coming from the south on Woodland was a police car with two police officers and two national guardsmen.

Just as they approached the front of the school, they stopped. We could see the back-and-forth hollering between the students and those in the police car. Shortly after that, the students were looking for objects to throw at the police car. Then the police officer drove almost even with my car. I saw the officer talking on his radio. I told the ministers, "He's calling for assistance and it's the police who started this whole thing. All they had to do is keep on going. The students are on school grounds."

One of the ministers began to curse—and apologized—and we all laughed. One of them said, "Pastor! I didn't know you still had it in you, but I feel the same way!"

In three to four minutes four or five other police cars were on the scene. I said, "Didn't somebody tell you?" All the other cars had police and guardsmen in them. The students then really began to throw whatever they could find. Mostly wooden chips and small rocks. The students were on the school grounds in front of the school, just above the stone wall. As their number grew, the police responded with tear gas. A group of teachers came out and talked to the officers and asked them to leave. The teachers told them that they could handle the kids.

Instead of leaving, there were now more officers—and more national guardsmen. The crowd of kids grew even larger, still on the school grounds in front of the school. There seemed to be a standoff between the teachers and the officers.

Then the officers came up the steps and confronted the teachers and the students. Still more officers and guardsmen arrived. Then we witnessed the second round of tear gas. This time it was thrown into the front doors of the school as the students and teachers ran into the building. One officer threw a canister of tear gas into a window open in the girls' restroom.

A lieutenant arrived and the three ministers and I began walking toward the lieutenant to tell him what we had witnessed. As soon as we got close, he saw us and hollered out, "Get out of here! This doesn't concern you all."

Pastor Hall hollered back, "It does concern us! These are our kids." I told Pastor Hall to cool it before they gassed and arrested us. "Just write the numbers on the police cars down."

There were several cars of parents watching from across the street. Because the tear gas was now throughout the school, it emptied of both students and teachers. We could see them running on the north and east sides of the building. The four of us and several of the parents watching from their cars headed to the rear of the school. The students, the teachers and the other adults assembled on the football field. Some students and teachers were coughing, having problems breathing because of the tear gas.

The police and national guardsmen had followed them and already surrounded them on the football field. The lieutenant, the principal, and several teachers huddled. The lieutenant was asked to please remove all the police and the national guardsmen. The lieutenant hollered out something to the officers and guardsmen and they followed him back to their cars. Pastor Hall and another minister tried to get to the lieutenant, but some of the officers ordered them back behind the school. There was not one Black officer or Black guardsman in the entire group.

I am convinced if there had not been some dozen or so parents and ministers with the kids, and every adult that had been in the building, more tear gas would have been thrown.

We heard later that teachers and parents took several students to the hospital where they were admitted because the tear gas had made them seriously ill.

City Manager John Taylor Kept His Promise to Call Me, 1968

Shortly after the riot, my secretary, Carol Johnson, gave me a message that City Manager John Taylor had called and asked that I call him. I had intended to return his call, but I forgot about it.

One morning I was at one of the schools. Carol called me. She said, "You have a visitor, Mr. Taylor, the city manager. You never returned his call, did you?"

I said, "No. I forgot. You know all what's been happening."

She said, "He's sitting in the outer office. What should I tell him?"

I said, "Put him on the phone."

After we each said hello, I said, "John, I apologize for not getting back to you sooner, but those of us in the Division of Urban Education have been extremely busy in the aftermath of the riot a few days ago, trying to work with our students here at Lincoln who are still so very angry—and justifiably so. But can you wait there about ten minutes for me?"

He said, "Sure, I'll wait."

Carol came back to the phone, and I told her, "I'll be there in about ten minutes. Keep him company."

In just a little over ten minutes, I was back at the Board building. I welcomed John into my office and closed the door. I again apologized. We shook hands and I asked him to have a seat. I took the chair in front of my desk. (I had a thing about talking to people from behind my desk.) John said, "I suspect you'll remember where and how we met. Facedown in front of the doors at city hall trying to dodge the tear gas the police had thrown everywhere, unnecessarily."

"Oh, yes! I do remember. In fact, I'll never forget that or that week of death and destruction in our city. And the actions of the police. John, I can't forget that. As I told you just a few minutes ago on the phone from Lincoln, those students and teachers are so angry with the police. I don't know how long it'll take for that to heal. If it ever will with this generation."

John said, "That's what I want to talk to you about. I don't know whether you've been keeping up with what's been coming out of the mayor's office. The Mayor's Human Relations Commission has not functioned for at least a year. Councilmen Thomas and Watkins brought that to the attention of the mayor and me. The mayor, through his chief of staff, Peter Newquist, has stated he plans to resurrect the commission and hire a staff person, an executive secretary, to run the office for the commission. I came over here from across the street, wondering if you might be interested in becoming a candidate."

I laughed and then apologized. I said, "John, is the mayor the appointing authority for this position? It is his commission. And although the commission is defunct, what role would the commission play in the selection? Because I would assume the commissioners are still legally the commission."

John said, "That's true, but I'll have something to say about who's appointed. The mayor and I have agreed on that. And the mayor and I haven't yet discussed potential candidates at all. He's waiting for me to say when. But I wanted to talk to you before the mayor and I met, to see if by chance you might be interested."

I said, "John, you apparently don't know my status in the minds of the police, the mayor, and many white folks in this city. I'm seen as a 'radical'—some say 'militant.'" I told John about what had happened a couple of weeks before the riot when I was one of six on a panel at the Jewish Community Center. Mayor Davis was one of the panelists. I was the only one of the six who said Kansas City, Missouri, and Kansas City, Kansas, could have a riot, that the same ingredients were present in these two cities that existed in those cities that had riots, like, for example, Newark, New Jersey. I was booed. But before that, in fact last year, when Dr. Thomas and Bruce Watkins mentioned my name as a possible candidate for that position, the mayor's response was, "As long as I'm mayor, Brooks will never be on any staff in city hall."

I said further, "I don't know whether you know it or not: I spent ten years with the police department and resigned October 1964, just short of four years ago, because I couldn't get a promotion although I meet all the qualifications. Clarence Kelley was the chief then, and Chief Kelley is the chief now. Kelley, I suspect, feels the same as the mayor. Both are members of Country Club Christian Church, south on Ward Parkway. I bet they've had some discussion about Al Brooks." I continued, "John, you just got here to our fair city. Don't waste your capital on me. This city is not ready for a Black person in a responsible position—although we've had a riot that was the Black community versus the police and at least some of the white Powers That Be. A Black man? No way! Dr. Thomas and Bruce can tell you whether I'm blowing smoke or not. Of course, Dr. Thomas will probably see it a little differently than Bruce, but they won't be too far apart."

John said, "Okay, I hear you. But suppose'n the mayor changed his mind. The chief doesn't have anything to do with appointments over here. And now just might be the right time to bring somebody Black into a responsible position in Kansas City's city government. And I'm willing to move on that. So, if Al Brooks is the best candidate for the job, let's go with him. Let's appoint him. I'm speaking out of school, but I think you're the best of the candidates for this time and this city."

"John, let me run something by you. Since the mayor is the appointing authority for his commission, why don't you strongly consider establishing a department of human relations where you are the appointing authority, as with all other city departments? If that occurs, I think I would give more consideration of joining you over there in that mess."

John said, "Well, if that would help you make a decision, I'll strongly consider that."

We both laughed. "You've made a good point and raised several relevant questions," John said. "And now that I talked with you, I'm more interested than ever that you become a candidate. I hope I've answered some of your questions about me."

I said, "Ummm. Maybe so!" We had another laugh.

John stood up and said, "Don't close the door on the idea. Give me a couple of days to feel people out and I'll get back to you."

We shook hands and I said, "Okay, John. I'll look for your getting back to me." I walked him to the elevators. As the door opened, we shook hands, and his parting words were, "You'll hear from me soon." And the elevator doors closed.

As I walked back to my office, I said to myself, "Ummm." When I got back, Carol asked me what the city manager wanted. I responded, "Candidates for a position in city hall."

When I got home that evening I told my wife, Carol, about the conversation I had with John Taylor for about an hour and a half that afternoon when he asked me to consider entering my name into the mix for the position of executive secretary to the Mayor's Human Relations Commission. Carol said, "Does he know about your relationship with the police department? And Mayor Davis? You remember when we were preparing a big march from the CORE office to the police department protesting two white police officers who had beaten two Black teenagers and threw their bikes in the weeds because they were riding their bikes in the street rather than on the sidewalk? And in broad, open daylight. And the bus driver saw the whole incident. But Chief Kelley refused to meet with the parents and no one from the police department would talk to the bus driver or the kids' parents. You were to call the police dispatcher and tell them that we were marching in a nonviolent manner straight down 12th Street to Headquarters and the dispatcher called you a turncoat and a Judas and said that you should be run out of town. The words out at that police department were anti-Brooks! Taylor apparently has not done his homework trying to bring you into city hall. Does he know what Mayor Davis told Dr. Thomas and Bruce? Probably not. So, whatya gonna do? Challenge them, or tell Taylor you're not interested and tell him why? Whatever you decide is fine with me. I'll support your decision."

I told her I had shared with Taylor some of the attitudes of some folks at the police department and why. "And the mayor. And some white folks in the city, like those who booed after my comments at that panel discussion at the Jewish Community Center on the possibility of a riot here. But John made some of what he called 'out of school' comments to me. I heard a kind of seriousness and urgency from John. I can read white folks pretty good. I have this feeling he's serious and will urge the mayor to go along with his suggestion relative to me. We'll see. He asked me to give him some time to make some inquiries and he would get back to me. He said he was more interested after we talked about me being an applicant than before he approached me. You know me. I was straight down the middle with him. I don't think he went away wondering who Al Brooks is and what kind of Black man I am. Well, we'll see how this whole thing plays out."

Unbeknownst to me, someone hand-carried a copy of my résumé to the mayor's office and handed it to Peter Newquist, the mayor's chief of staff, in December 1967, after Newquist had announced in the *Kansas City Star* that they were recruiting candidates to fill the position of executive secretary to the Mayor's Commission on Human Relations. But here's how I found about the résumé.

About a week after John Taylor and I met in my office at the Board of Education Building, Carol Johnson got a call from Joan Starcher, John's secretary, asking, "Would it be possible for Mr. Brooks to come to city hall and meet with Mr. Taylor this week?" I was in the office at the time and Carol had Joan on hold and told me what she was asking. I picked up the phone and asked Joan when John wanted to meet, that I had my calendar before me.

I could hear John in the background saying, "Ask Al if he can come over now."

I told Joan, "Tell John I'm on my way now."

John in the background, said "Thank you."

A short time later I arrived at John's office. He apologized for asking to meet at such short notice, but he wanted to follow up on our conversation. He said he was a little surprised that I didn't tell him that I had sent the mayor a copy of my résumé back in December. He said, "You must have been just pulling my leg, weren't you?"

I said, "John, I haven't sent my résumé over here." He said there was a list of the names on the front of the folder with the résumés of all the candidates. The list was alphabetical; my name was first on the list and the first résumé in the folder.

I began to laugh. John said, "What wrong? Why are you laughing?"

I said, "Because my résumé was not in any folder in the mayor's office. I haven't submitted a résumé and wouldn't, based on what we talked about when you were in my office." He called Joan. She came to the door.

He said, "Would you step over to the mayor's office and bring me that folder of résumés? They should be on the table nearest the door." Joan came back a couple of minutes later with the folder and handed it to John. I could see that there was nothing on the front of the folder. He began to thumb through the résumés. There must have been a half dozen. Then he looked strange. He called Joan again. "Joan, was there anyone in the mayor's office?"

She said, "No, sir."

"Would you go back over there and look on the mayor's desk and see if you see Al's résumé? Last evening, I happened to go over to the mayor's office to leave something on his desk. He was there. And as I was walking past one of the tables in his office, I saw this folder with the list on the front with Al's name first and the first résumé inside." Turning to me, John said, "I stood there and looked through all of them. Yours was first."

Joan came back and said, "Excuse me, but Mr. Brooks's résumé isn't over there anywhere. I looked all over the mayor's desk and in the various baskets. It wasn't anywhere."

I gave a halfhearted laugh and said, "John, I don't think my résumé was in that folder because I never sent it over. I think that's wishful thinking." John didn't crack a smile. He looked a little bewildered.

Joan was still standing beside John's desk. She added that she asked the mayor's secretary if she had seen Mr. Brooks's résumé, that it seemed that the others were in the folder. She said she didn't know what happened to it, but she had seen it among the others in the folder she gave to the mayor several days ago.

John said, "Well, I just be damned!" He said, "I'm sorry I can't produce your résumé, but everybody up here knows it was here. I'll find out what happened. By the way, you should know that I had a long discussion with the mayor yesterday about his feelings toward you. He's talked to Dr. Thomas and Bruce and told them and me that he has the highest regard for you since the riot."

I said, "Well, thanks to everyone." John asked me if I could get him another résumé to take over to the mayor. I told him I would. I left John at the elevator looking kinda "What the hell!"

When I got back to the office, Carol Johnson asked me what had happened at the meeting with the city manager. I told her he had called me over to ask why I hadn't mentioned that I had submitted my résumé to the mayor when we met in my office about the Human Relations Commission job. Everyone over there seemed to have seen a copy of my résumé, but when I got over there, the résumé had disappeared. I just laughed because I know I didn't send any résumé over there. I knew I wouldn't be seriously considered. I don't doubt now that my résumé was over there, but how, and what happened to it, is a mystery. Maybe a ghost did it all. Carol and I laughed.

But I did notice Carol looked a little strange when I asked about how my résumé got to the mayor's office. I didn't say anything to her then; I decided to wait awhile. But I sensed there was a conspiracy somewhere and Carol was at the bottom of it. She was the only one who had access to my résumé. And I had an idea who else was involved in the conspiracy. I asked Carol if she would either take or send a copy of my résumé over to the mayor's office. She assured me she would.

As the saga of the missing résumé continued, Carol Johnson came to me and said, "Mr. Brooks, you won't believe this, but I hand-delivered a copy of your résumé to the mayor's office last week as you told me to. I handed it to a rather large white gentleman and asked if he would see to it that the mayor got it. He said he would. But earlier today, I got a call from Joan Starcher, Mr. Taylor's secretary, asking if she could come over and get a copy of your résumé. I told her that I had personally hand-delivered a copy to the mayor's office and described the person I gave it to. She said, 'That sounds like Peter Newquist, the mayor's chief of staff. But Carol, I looked in the folder on the table in the mayor's office, and it was not there. That's why I'm calling. Just between us, and I hope, Carol, it is just between us, someone over next door doesn't want Mr. Brooks in competition for the commission position. I thought maybe Mr. Brooks had forgotten to tell you to send another copy of his résumé. Carol, could I come over and get another copy of Mr. Brooks's résumé? I'll let Mr. Taylor deal with the vanishing of Mr. Brooks's résumés.'"

Carol said Joan had come over this morning and she handed her a copy of my résumé.

I told Carol, "I agree with Joan Starcher that someone over there doesn't want me to be in the competition for the commission position."

For some time, a group of Black men had been meeting for breakfast almost every morning, except maybe Sunday, at Mooney's Restaurant on Prospect. The restaurant became known as "Black city hall." These men met to discuss and solve "all of the community's problems." Sometimes women joined us. You can believe everything was discussed! Often, directions from those breakfast meetings were given to our elected representatives in city, county, and state governments.

On this morning when I was present, the discussion focused on the riot aftermath since four of the six Black men were killed by the police just one block north of the restaurant.

Bruce was there and mentioned the mayor's Human Relations Commission. He said that several persons had applied for the staff position and that the mayor would be making the decision on that appointment. He added, "In fact, I believe all the candidates have been interviewed already by the commission and will be submitting three candidates for the mayor to select one. The city manager, I believe, will sit with the mayor and make the decision. Dr. Thomas and I have pushed for Alvin to be appointed."

Bruce turned to me. "Alvin, have you been interviewed?"

I said, "No."

Bruce said, "I'm going to check on this right away. There is some pushback against you, but it's not cut-and-dried. They still ought to interview you. We are still on the mayor about the appointment because the commission hasn't been functioning for more than a year."

I knew that Joan Starcher had submitted my résumé for the third time to the mayor and it should have been in the group of résumés for the interviews. I thought, *Well, I'll just be damned. They're interviewing candidates and I haven't been contacted.* So, I decided to add some mess to the interviewing process. I told the group that I would file an Equal Employment Opportunity Commission complaint if I didn't get an interview. I said this strategically because there was one among us who I knew would relay my comment to the white folks.

Our session at Mooney's then adjourned.

The person I suspected who would take my message to the white folks left shortly after our meeting adjourned. So, I decided to hang around at least for an hour to see if my trick worked.

And lo and behold! It did. Just short of an hour, the phone rang and one of the waitresses answered and hollered, "Alvin Brooks, you have a call. You can take it at the phone over there." She pointed to a phone on the wall close to where our meetings were held.

I answered, "This is Al Brooks." The voice at the other end said, "Good morning, Al Brooks. This is Jim Doran, chair of the Mayor's Commission on Human Relations." (Now how did Doran know that I was at Mooney's?)

I said, "Good morning, Jim Doran. What can I do for you?"

He said, "We've been trying to reach you. You're one of the candidates for the position of executive secretary to the commission. I need to set up a time for you to be interviewed by the commission. Are you still interested in being considered for the position?"

I hadn't told City Manager John Taylor one way or the other, so I considered how to answer Doran. I said, "Yes, I am still interested, Jim. How soon is my interview scheduled?"

He responded, "Tomorrow morning at nine o'clock in my office." He gave me the floor and room number in the Federal Building.

"Jim, I'm looking forward to the interview. I'll see you at nine o'clock tomorrow morning." I knew he was pressing me, thinking that since it was an eleventh-hour request, I wouldn't be able make it.

But that was trick number two.

Later, that evening, I got a call from Bruce Watkins informing me that the commission had interviewed nine candidates and had selected the top three to forward to the mayor. He said that he would call Dr. Thomas now and set up a meeting with the mayor and city manager tomorrow morning.

I told Bruce to hold off because I had received a call from Jim Doran, chair of the mayor's commission. He said the commission wanted to interview me tomorrow for the position. I told Bruce that I had planned to keep the interview, although we knew the interview was only because I had threatened to file an EEOC complaint. I just wanted to see how they responded to me, knowing that they had already interviewed everyone and had forwarded their selection of the top candidates to the mayor.

After Bruce finally let up his swearing and name-calling, I said, "Just hold on, let me go through the interviewing process. I will then see if the city manager is aware of what occurred and get his position on it. If he knew this was happening without saying anything to me, then I'm pissed. My faith and trust in him will be shot. Particularly since he literally begged me to become a candidate."

Bruce agreed to wait until he heard back from me.

Carol had overheard most of the conversation with Bruce. She asked, "Why in the shit are you going down there, messin' with those white folks, when you know they don't want you and they're not goin' to hire you? Why are you wasting your time and allowing them to make you angry and you end up saying some things that further piss you off—and them, too?"

I said, "Thank you, Miss Brooks, my Number One Supporter. But sometimes there are certain things that you must do and say. And for me, this is the time." End of conversation.

Remembering everything that Carol and Bruce had said, at 8:50 a.m., I appeared at the Federal Building and went directly to Jim Doran's office for my nine o'clock meeting. The receptionist greeted me and asked me to have a seat. While I was still standing, Mr. Herman Johnson, a member of the mayor's commission, came out of a conference room where I assumed my interview was being held. "Mr. Johnson, are you leaving? You're going to miss my interview." He responded, "Yeah, I've got to go and earn some money. I can't earn any money sitting in here," pointing to the conference room where other commission members were. I knew that Mr. Johnson and Mrs. Margaret Holiday were the only two Black members of the commission. I suspected at least she was there.

A white man came out of the same conference room and said, "Alvin Brooks, welcome. I'm Jim Doran, chair of the Mayor's Commission on Human Relations. Glad you were able to interview with us this morning. Please come in."

I shook his hand, grasping it tightly. "I'm Alvin Brooks. Good to meet you, Jim." I stood until all had introduced themselves. Then I introduced myself and added, "Good morning to you, Mrs. Holiday." (She was the wife of the famous civil rights lawyer.)

Doran opened the interview with an excuse. "I'm sorry that you're our last candidate, but these are all busy people, and sometimes, it's hard to get a quorum, but we're here to hear from you."

I thanked them for the opportunity to be interviewed. I almost told Doran that I knew they had already sent their three top candidates to the mayor and city manager. But I didn't. I was there to have some fun. I felt good. And since I had a job that I enjoyed doing, this interview didn't mean much to me.

There were nine members on the commission. Six were present. The one Black member present was Mrs. Margaret Holiday, as I recall. Each member looked down to review my résumé. Jim asked the first question. "Alvin, why do you want employment with the city?" I rolled out some response. It sounded good to me. A middle-aged white female asked about the riot. "What are your thoughts about our riot a couple of days ago?"

"I think it sends a message loud and clear to the city—of which each of you is a part—that there's a lot to be done in the area of Black and white relations. Black and white. Those of us east of Troost and those of you west of Troost. The riot should have been a wake-up call for all of us."

One of the women asked me, "How do you think you can perform in this position as a militant?"

"How are you defining 'militant'?" I responded. "I'm one of a number of Black men and women who just want our community to come into its own, and the white community west of Troost should join in that effort. But I must ask, what kind of Super Negro are you looking for to take this position?"

No one answered, and Jim Doran let me know that the interview was over. "Alvin, thanks again for coming in. We'll be making our decision, and all of the candidates will be notified by mail." I came close to saying, "I know you have already interviewed all the candidates except me and even submitted to the mayor your three top choices for the commission position. But I decided I'm going to play this out."

Instead I said, "Thank you, Jim and commission members, for taking the time to interview me. I await your letter, hopefully, naming me as your next staff person."

I went around the room and shook each member's hand. I knew that was the last of that. I knew I would not be considered for the position and probably wouldn't even receive a rejection letter.

After I left, I wondered if John Taylor knew the commission had interviewed the candidates and had submitted three to the mayor. I headed across the street to Taylor's office. Good for the both of us, he wasn't in. But I asked Joan to have him call me. And did he know that they had already decided on three candidates and had submitted them to the mayor? I thought I'd wait awhile to see if John would get back to me as he promised.

Chapter 5

CITY HALL APPOINTMENTS

Mayor Davis Appoints Commission on Civil Disorder, 1968

It wasn't quite a month after the riot when Mayor Ilus Davis appointed a five-member Commission on Civil Disorders to study the riot in Kansas City. It was modeled pretty much after the President's National Advisory Commission on Civil Disorders (also called the Kerner Report) following series of riots across the nation. It concluded that "our nation is moving toward two societies; one black, one white—separate and unequal."

The members of the commission were chairman Robert Ingram, attorney David Hardy, attorney Arthur Mag, Mrs. Malcolm Smith, and the fifth member, the only Black member, Dr. Charles Wilkinson, a brilliant psychiatrist.

It should be remembered that the riot started April 9, 1968. It left six Black males dead. They were George McKinney; his sixteen-year-old son, George McKinney Jr.; Charles (Shugg) Martin; Julius Hamilton; Maynard Gough; and Albert Miller Jr. None of the six victims were armed.

The Mayor's Final Report was released August 15, 1968. I do have some knowledge about the riot, having been in the midst of it. I can in the strongest voice say that the report did not reflect the accurate role and conduct of many of the police officers. The report avoided criticizing the police department, the school superintendent, or other racist institutions. It was at best a "make you feel good" report.

I was one of over 200 persons representing the commission's attempt at surveying a broad cross section of the city. I do feel that the report's recommendations were a fair assessment of the racism in institutions such as the police department and the school district. In fact, racism was not identified as a problem in many areas of some of our institutions. There has been a failure to enact the recommendations, including local control of the police department. What the report called for in 1968 is still needed as I write these memoirs, more than fifty years later.

An Offer I Didn't Refuse, 1968

On Thursday, May 9, 1968, the Brooks family was having dinner together when the phone rang. Carol got up from the dinner table and answered. She came back and said, "It's for you. It's John Taylor, the city manager." We looked at each other. I got up and picked up the phone.

"Hi, John."

"Alvin Brooks, how would you like to be the first Black department head in Kansas City government?"

"You've got to be kidding."

"If you accept the appointment, you'll be director of the Human Relations Department and the first Black director in the history of this city."

I said, "John, hold on just a minute, okay?" I turned to Carol and the kids and told them, "John Taylor offered me the job as director of the city's Human Relations Department."

Carol said, "Okay!"

"John, are you there? I accept."

John told me that a short time ago he had announced at the city council meeting that he was going to offer me the job and that no one dissented. "So, when can you start and be sworn in?"

Looking at the calendar on the wall I said, "Two weeks from Monday, May 27."

John said, "Great! Why don't you come in next week and let's talk?"

I said, "Fine. I'll see you next week. John, thank you. I appreciate you."

Carol said, "Well, Mr. First Black City Department Head, congratulations!"

The next morning, I told Dr. Campbell and Bob Wheeler that I had been offered the position with the city as director of the newly formed Human Relations Department and that I had accepted and would be resigning from my position. Bob called Dr. Campbell to his office and closed the door.

I had great respect for both educational giants. Two giants, Black men. We had known each other since I was a kid at R. T. Coles High School in the late 1940s. "Al, you're making history, boy. Do you realize that?" Bob said.

Dr. Campbell chimed in, "You'll do a great job representing us over there. Just take your time. Know who your friends are and, most of all, who your enemies are. You'll have lots of them just because you're Black."

I thanked them and told them how much I appreciated them bringing me on in the Division of Urban Education. I told Carol Johnson that I would be leaving in two weeks. The first thing she said was, "Can I go with you?" I told her that I was going to talk to Taylor next week about a host of things, among those would be staff. I told her I would like to take her with me.

Either the city manager or the mayor's office had sent out a press release that I had been named director of the city's new Human Relations Department. I attended a community meeting at St. Augustine's Episcopal Church in the Santa Fe area. The place was crowded, but there was a vacant seat by Mr. Herman Johnson, who, you may recall, was a member of the Mayor's Commission on Human Relations. I slid in and sat beside Mr. Johnson and extended my hand, but he refused to shake my hand. I whispered to him, "What's wrong, Mr. Johnson, that you won't shake my hand?"

He said that John Taylor had the commission go through all those interviews for someone to fill the executive secretary position and had even selected three top candidates and submitted them to the mayor, and "the city manager persuaded the mayor to disregard the three candidates and allowed the city manager to appoint you."

I said, "Mr. Johnson, I didn't have anything to do with that decision, and I'm sorry you feel the way you do because I was appointed, but I thank you anyway."

On Monday, May 27, 1968, I was scheduled to be sworn in by City Clerk Edwin Byrd. My mother, Thomascine Davis, flew in from San Francisco. Carol and the kids, all except Ronall, were there. Ronall couldn't make it because he had joined the Air Force in January. My mother-in-law, Ruby Robinson, was there—along with Dr. Thomas and Bruce Watkins.

Also being sworn in was Thomas Lewinsohn, the new director of the Personnel Department. Tom and I became friends throughout our respective careers, and we still are.

The City Manager, Mayor, and I Talk about Our Expectations, 1968

John and I met and covered a multitude of subjects. I also reviewed the list of members of the Human Relations Commission. As I recall, there were nine members. I said to John that I would like to sit down with him and the mayor since the mayor was the appointing authority for the commission.

The day of my meeting with John and the mayor, I went to John's office. John told me to follow him. He led me through the back door where the manager's office connects to the mayor's office. He knocked on the opened door and said, "Knock, knock."

I couldn't see the mayor, but I heard him say, "Yeah, John, come on in."

John and I walked in and the mayor stood up from his desk. "Al, welcome aboard. I remember we met at the Jewish Community Center about two weeks before the riot when you and I were panelists. You upset all of us when you told us that we had the same ingredients in Kansas City, Missouri, and Kansas City, Kansas, that they had in other cities that had riots. You said all that was needed was a wrongful act from the police—and that would set it off. How can we ever forget that? Then I saw you and the two police chiefs marching the kids down here to city hall and heard you speak to them on the steps outside. But it's good meeting you formally and without the violence."

As we were shaking hands, I told the mayor, "Mr. Mayor, it's my pleasure meeting you also, sir. And without the tension and violence that our city experienced several weeks ago. The city manager and I have talked, and I believe John and I have developed in a short period of time a respect for each other. I want to thank you and John for allowing me to meet with the two of you."

"Well, come, let's sit down," the mayor said. "You wanted to talk about the Human Relations Commission?"

I told the mayor that John had given me the roster of the members and minutes of previous meetings from over a year ago. I told him I was a little surprised that the commission had not met since the spring of 1967. I also noted that all the members—except Mr. Herman Johnson and Mrs. Margaret Holiday—lived almost within walking distance of each other.

"Mayor, I would like to suggest that the commission be expanded at least by six members to get more diversity that's representative of all parts of the city—Negro and Mexican American representation. And you might want to ask whether all nine want to continue to serve under the new structure, a commission that's responsible to you and a director who's responsible to the city manager."

The mayor said, "I don't have a problem with your suggestions. Based on where we are as a city after a terrible riot, whatever we can do to bring the community together makes sense to me. Do you agree, John?"

John told the mayor, "Alvin and I have discussed the changes in the size of the commission and in the responsibility for administering the public accommodation ordinance. Both of the changes will, of course, need council approval."

"There'll be no problem with that," the mayor said. "Is there anything else, Al? John?"

I said, "Not at this time, Mayor. I look forward to working very closely with you and the commission—and calling on you for advice, if you don't mind."

"That fine, Al, and I'll be calling on you," the mayor said. "But the election is next year, and I'm leaving at the end of my term. So, you and John will have a new mayor, several new council members, and a new team on the city council. But let's get as much done as we can while I'm here."

I thanked the mayor and we shook hands.

As John and I walked back to his office, Joan and another woman on staff in the office congratulated me and offered whatever help they could give. Joan said, "I know Mr. Taylor is glad you agreed to join his team. Are you going to bring Carol over with you? She seems like a nice, personable woman—loyal and efficient."

I said, "Yes, I plan to bring her over with me."

Joan said, "Please tell her she's got a friend in the manager's office."

John had heard Joan's question and came out of his office. "It's your call," John said. "All directors can choose their personal secretaries. Why don't you have her get in touch with Joan and she can take Carol down to personnel and work out the particulars."

I said, "Thank you. You've helped and I'm not even on the payroll yet. But thanks to both of you."

I asked John where my office would be located, and he told me there was some space on the twenty-sixth floor right behind the council chambers. I asked him if I could get some help tidying up the place before I started on Monday, and he said, "Joan can handle that. She runs things around here." We all laughed.

I shook John's hand and told him, "Thanks again. I'm looking forward to the challenges that this office brings."

John said, "Great! See you next Monday morning. Joan will get with the city clerk and schedule the swearing-in ceremony. Don't forget you can invite whomever you wish to witness the ceremony."

Joan took me to the office space. We got off the elevator on the twenty-sixth floor. The two rooms were used for storage and were full of old Steelcase furniture. Almost in unison, we said, "My God!" Joan told me she would have the maintenance people move the stuff out before Carol and I cleaned it up that weekend unless there was other office furniture elsewhere.

Sure enough, the extra furniture had been removed, and Carol and I cleaned the office and made the most of a bad situation.

All Power to the People: The Formation of the KC Chapter of the Black Panther Party, 1969

After being sworn in as the director of the newly organized Human Relations Department after the 1968 riot, I faced numerous challenges, both outside city hall and within. Several grassroots organizations began to emerge. These groups were well organized—each different but with common threads woven through them: the self-determination and community control of the Black community.

One of the most active groups after the riot was the community-based Kansas City chapter of the Black Panther Party. Pete O'Neal announced its formation in January 1969. "All Power to the People!" was its rallying cry. When the Black Panther Party began to display guns to protect themselves and the Black community, fear arose in the white community, and particularly in the Kansas City Police Department under the leadership of Chief Clarence Kelley.

The department and the FBI spent a great deal of money trying to keep up with the Black Panthers. All the members were local folks. They espoused unity in the Black community. At local churches, with food from local businesses, they fed kids breakfast—at one time including nearly a thousand children. They also organized free health clinics. The Kansas City Black Panther Party had several other successes, among them the mobilization of the Black community.

Many Black leaders resented the Panthers and Pete O'Neal because they advocated violence if they were approached with violence. There was a continuous display of weapons. I assigned one of my staff members, Jesse Greer, as liaison to work with the Panthers. On one occasion, Jesse told me that Pete wanted to talk to me and asked if I would come to their meeting place in the 2200 block of Lydia. I agreed.

I asked Pete if he wanted me to alert the police ahead of time. He said he "didn't need any police pigs to protect them or our community."

I thought that if I alerted John, the mayor, and the chief, there would be less chance of confrontation. Again, Pete said, "We don't need no police pigs to protect our community. You can tell them that."

When Jesse and I arrived, a helicopter hovered over us, and the KC police and the FBI were up the street watching. They attempted to use a system to pick up the discussion when Panther members came out to meet me. The members who met me used sheets of plywood held high to shield us from the authorities picking up our discussion. Inside, I met Pete and other members and saw the weapons they had amassed on a table. I got a chance to hear more about the vision of the Party and Pete, its leader.

There was a march on city hall planned for the following day. I alerted the police about the march and told them that it would be peaceful. I also told Mayor Davis and City Manager John Taylor. The mayor called Chief Kelley to alert his officers of what I had said—that the march would be Panther members and other organizations and individuals and that I would be marching with them.

Several hundred people, mostly men and young boys, marched without police interruption. They went into city hall peacefully. I asked the elevator starter to hold the elevators for the marchers. She did. The marchers were directed into one of the council committee rooms, which I believe was on the twenty-fourth floor. I had scheduled City Manager Taylor to speak. The marchers wanted all the department directors there. I told Taylor about the request and he had several city department heads present.

Pete and others spoke of police actions in the Black community. They told how the Panthers were feeding poor Black kids breakfast and providing tutoring programs. These concepts were further developed in the future and some say were the basis for Head Start programs. The term "pigs" was used for everyone who was white throughout the discussion.

The major subject was that police brutality must stop. They said that the Panthers would protect their community from the police and from anyone who would take advantage of those in the Black community. The meeting ended after an hour or so, and the marchers left and marched back to the Black community without incident.

Several days later, I was asked by the same groups to set up a meeting at the Catholic Charities office at 11th and Forest with the mayor, city manager, and police chief so that further grievances could be aired and the three leaders could respond. I met with City Manager Taylor first and told him of the request and informed him of the importance of the meeting. I asked him to go with me to meet with Mayor Davis and to ask the mayor to get the chief to have a "pre-meeting" with just the four of us. I also suggested he encourage Chief Kelley to be at both meetings.

I was told that the chief was reluctant to meet and wanted to send Lt. Col. Clifford Warren, the highest-ranking Black officer. I told the mayor and the city manager that the chief needed to be there. A couple of days later, the city manager told me that the mayor had talked the chief into attending both meetings. I contacted Father McNamera, director of Catholic Charities, and he gave me permission for the meeting to be held at Catholic Charities.

It was a hot August day when different groups packed into the meeting space at Catholic Charities. Even though the room was air-conditioned, because of the number of persons there, you could not tell that the air-conditioning was working. The mayor, city manager, and police chief took quite a verbal beating, but as I had suggested to them in our pre-meeting, they should take notes, ask questions, and not become defensive or argue. They accepted the verbal abuse well. After almost two hours, the group began to dwindle because of the heat. I thanked everybody for coming and adjourned the meeting.

On October 30, 1969, Pete O'Neal was arrested and charged for transporting a gun across state lines. Later, Pete fled the country to live in Tanzania, in eastern Africa. He is one of the last Americans in exile from this period.

"Alvin, I Want to Apologize to You and to Your Mother"

One Sunday evening—I believe it was in the fall of 1971—a little more than three years after I had been appointed as director of the Kansas City Human Relations Department, I was asked to speak at a church in Overland Park, Kansas. I believe it was a Presbyterian church. It was a dinner and my topic for my speech was "Race Relations after Kansas City's Riot." Some 200 church members attended. Carol accompanied me. During my remarks after dinner, I shared an example of how white people could, consciously or unconsciously, make racist remarks that affect their kids. I used grandkids as an example.

I told of my mother working for a white woman who was caring for three of her grandkids, one a baby, the other two twins about my age, about ten. My mother worked for this woman a half day on Saturdays. My mother would bring me along. I would help my mother by sweeping the porch and sidewalk and wash the one window on the front. Depending on the time of year, I would mow the front lawn.

As soon as my mother got to work, she and the woman would have a cup of coffee and make small talk. As usual the twins and I were given a glass of milk and a sweet roll. The twin boy had a habit after he finished his milk to go to either his mother's cup of coffee or my mother's, take a spoon, and begin, spoon by spoon, to put coffee in his glass and drink it. This morning, his grandmother, calling him by his name, said, "You keep drinking that coffee, you're going to turn the color of Alvin."

My mother looked shocked. What the woman said was appalling to my mother. She immediately said, "Come on, baby, let's get to work. It'll be noon before we know it."

When we were waiting for the streetcar to go home, I asked my mother what the woman meant by what she said earlier. My mother never responded, but she began to cry silently. Tears began to run down her cheeks. I worried that something was peculiar with my color, that the woman's grandson's color was okay. My mother sensed what was bothering me but never really addressed it, even when we got home. She only said a familiar prayer to God: "Dear God, please help my baby become the kind of man you want him to be." (You'll remember, I talked about her practice of responding to incidents like this earlier in this memoir.)

After the question and answer period, the pastor thanked me for coming. He gave me a card with $25 in it. He asked everyone to stand for the benediction. As people began to stand, they also began to put their coats on. There was a Q&A mike in the middle of the aisle. A woman spoke to the pastor after the prayer.

He spoke her name and asked everyone to sit back down, that she had something to say before we adjourned. The woman approached the mike with an elderly lady holding onto her arm and tapped on the mike to determine if it was still on. She apologized for the interruption but said her grandma had something she wanted to share with Alvin.

I had come down off the stage with the pastor. Carol had sat in the front row with the pastor's wife. So, I stayed standing several feet from the two women and the mike. The elderly woman was given the mike by the younger woman. The elderly woman began to speak in a very weak voice. She didn't hold the mike to her mouth. The younger woman held the mike up to the elderly woman's lips.

She spoke. "Alvin, I want to thank you and your wife for speaking to us this evening." I responded with a smile. Folks applauded. But she had more to say. "Alvin, the white woman you were talking about in your presentation is me." She introduced herself, and then her granddaughter. "Please forgive me. And I wish your mother Estelle were still living so I could ask for her forgiveness. I've hurt you all these years. And your mother died probably hating me because my words hurt her so."

There wasn't a dry eye anywhere. I walked up to her and hugged her. I took the mike from her granddaughter and spoke so all could hear me. I spoke to her using her name. "I forgive you. And I can say on behalf of my mother, she forgives you, too. She probably did long ago. She was very fond of you," I said, using her name again. "For my mother, my wife here, Carol, and me again, we forgive you."

The pastor offered prayer again. We stayed almost another hour with her, reminiscing about my mother and their relationship. Also, I reminded her that she called me to say she had a gift for me for graduating from high school and asked me to drive over to her house to pick it up, a red polka dot tie.

The pastor of the church said he was sorry to interrupt us, but it was "close up" time. We all—about thirty or forty of us—hugged each other as we stood outside the church.

On the way home, Carol said, "Aren't you glad you didn't mention the name of the woman your mother worked for during your speech? It would've very hard to clean it up."

As if we were singing a duet, we both said, "Thank God!"

From Director of the Department of Human Relations to Assistant City Manager, 1972

Around mid-June 1972, the city manager asked me if I had a minute to come up to his office. I said, "Yes!"

Joan said, "Go on in, Mr. Brooks. Mr. Taylor is waiting for you."

John said, "Come on in, Al. Have a seat. I have a proposition for you. How would you like to join the assistant city manager staff up here?"

I said, "Great!"

"Well, if we make that move, whom do you suggest I appoint as your successor?"

In 1969, I had brought Mack Warner on staff as my assistant director. Mack left to join Cesar Chavez in California just prior to John's offer, so I told John, "I think Mary Hayes can run the department. She knows and gets along well with the staff. They'll work well for her as they have for me. Plus, Mary knows the ordinances and the investigative processes. Mary will do well. Let me suggest that I be the liaison with Human Relations for a while."

John said, "Okay, let's get her up here and see what she says."

I used John's phone to call her. While we were waiting for Mary, we discussed what departments other than Human Relations I would be the liaison for. John assigned me to the Police Department, the Fire Department, the Community Services Department, and, I believe, the Health Department.

Mary walked in and John said, "Ms. Hayes, Al and I have been talking about your performance in the Human Relations Department. Your performance is far from what it should be."

I caught what John was doing. It shocked me at first because of the expression on Mary's face.

"So, Ms. Hayes, what excuse can you offer?"

Mary said, "There's no excuse, Mr. Taylor, because your perception of the performance of the department is not factual. The Human Relations Department is performing at an all-time high."

She went on seemingly without taking a breath, rattling off all the things the department was doing. Both John and I were fighting back laughing.

Mary was serious. Her faced tightened up and her lips were quivering. I said to myself, "He'd better let her know he was putting her on before she starts cursing both of us and wondering why I allowed John to come up with these false accusations."

Seeing that Mary was taking his comments seriously and was about to explode on him, John said, "Mary, just kidding. Y'all are doing a great job. You were worked up, weren't you?" We all laughed.

Mary said, "We don't let anyone talk about us when we know that if we're not the best in the business—we're at least in the top ten in the nation."

John said, "I agree. But now to what we really called you up here for. Alvin is coming up here as an assistant city manager. His position as director of the Human Relations Department will become vacant. Alvin tells me he thinks you can handle the department. What do you think?"

Mary gave us a big grin and said, "Sure, I can handle it. And I want to thank Alvin for suggesting me to you for the opportunity. You can be sure I will continue the hard work to make sure the Human Relations Department continues to provide the services that we are mandated to provide."

I broke out with applause and laughing at the same time. John said, "Let's keep this under wraps for a couple of days until I get with Tom Lewinsohn about these changes."

After the announcement was made public and I moved to the twenty-ninth floor and Mary took over my office on the fourth floor, we stayed in those two positions until December 1981. Robert "Bob" Kipp had succeeded John Taylor as city manager. Charles Wheeler had been elected to succeed Mayor Davis. Wheeler was interested in a strong mayoral form of government rather than the council–manager form. Although the charter didn't change, Wheeler continued to talk about change—but it never got traction with his colleagues on the council or with the powers that be throughout the city.

My Master's Thesis in Sociology, UMKC, 1973

My master's thesis in sociology was completed at the University of Missouri–Kansas City in 1973. Its title was "Social Organization, Social Tension, Social Change: The Role of Intermediary Groups." It turned out to be a perfect blueprint for what became the AdHoc Group Against Crime. Those who write theses with original research in their field of study present them to an examination committee for approval and acceptance to certify the student for the degree. Too often that's the end of it. My thesis was presented for the master's degree in sociology.

Although my thesis, like others, found its way to the shelves of my school's library, I seized the opportunity to test the theories of my thesis. I had a chance to put my academic study into practice to benefit the community by forming the AdHoc Group Against Crime. This group later brought national and international attention and accolades to Kansas City.

This crime-fighting group closed more Jamaican crack houses than the local police department, Jackson County prosecutors, and the Drug Enforcement Agency (DEA). Without guns, warrants, or SWAT—just a group of dedicated and committed Black men who became the vanguard of their community. Our women and youth also played an important role with prayer vigils, marches, and making posters denouncing drug and criminal activity in the community. The group formed an unprecedented relationship with the police, the Feds, the prosecutor's office, the courts, and most of all the community in which members lived.

More about the AdHoc Group Against Crime later.

City Manager Bob Kipp Wants Threatt to Return to Kansas City, 1977

One morning, City Manager Bob Kipp called me to his office and asked if I still was in close contact with Jim Threatt. From 1968 to 1972, Jim was the first director of Model Cities in Kansas City, a program designed to address problems of property, low-quality housing, and discrimination. I told Bob that I was, and, in fact, on my last trip to DC, Jim and I had dinner together. "I'd like to bring Jim back to Kansas City," Bob said. "You think he'd come back if the right offer was made?"

I told Bob I didn't know but I did know that Jim was proud of his accomplishments here in Kansas City—and a lot of folks in the city were, too. "Jim didn't leave mad at anyone," I said, "and I don't think there were too many people mad at him." We both laughed.

"That being the case, he just might consider coming back if the offer were right." Bob asked me if I wouldn't mind going to Washington to talk to him. I said I would.

About a week later, I found Jim out of his office. But one of his secretaries said she thought he was going home after his out-of-the-office meeting. She tried to reach Jim where he said he was going. He had been there but left when the meeting had ended. I called Jim's home. Doris, Jim's wife, answered and said that Jim called but was running late and wouldn't be home until 6:00 or 6:30. She told me, "Catch a cab and come out and have dinner with us. I hope Jim comes home before too long. Get a cab and come on out." I told her I would.

She gave me their address. When I arrived at the Threatts' home, Jim still hadn't arrived. I saw in the driveway that Bonneville Pontiac I had driven from Newark, New Jersey, to Kansas City. I kind of laughed to myself and rang the doorbell. One of the boys came to the door. They were surprised to see me. Doris hadn't told them I was coming for dinner.

Doris asked me why I was in DC. I didn't know what to say. I really wanted to talk to Jim first, but I didn't want to lie or avoid the question. I told her I wanted to see how they were doing and talk to Jim about some things that were going on in Kansas City that he might be interested in.

Doris asked, "Are they asking Jim to come back to Kansas City? Is Jim taking a job back there?" She said, "I'm not interested in going back to Kansas City. And Jim shouldn't be either."

I asked why not.

She began to tell me some of what I already knew that wasn't too pleasant. It was all about some of Jim's enemies. Most were no longer in the same positions or even in the city.

Jim came in. "Hey, Brooks, what the hell you doing in DC? They run your Black ass out of KC?"

I said, "Not yet, Jim."

Doris said, "No, the white folks sent him up here to bring you back to Kansas City. Something must be wrong, and they want you to straighten it out. Ain't that right, Brooks?"

And the arguing began. Doris almost cussed me out for coming up there disturbing their family. All with laughter.

Jim said, "I thought all you came up here for was to make me an offer Bob didn't think I could refuse."

I said, "Yes, something like that." Jim asked when I was going back. I told him the next day, afternoon.

The next morning about nine, Jim called and said he'd meet me in the hotel restaurant in about thirty minutes. That he did, except it was more like an hour. We ate and continued to talk about him and his family coming back to Kansas City, although Doris was not too happy about Kansas City or moving again. We went back up to my room and called

Bob Kipp. Joan would make reservations for Jim. Jim told her not to let what happened to him in November 1968 when he was discriminated against for trying to rent an apartment on Armour Boulevard, even though the city had made the reservation.

Threatt Returns to Kansas City, 1977

About a month later, Jim arrived back in Kansas City. Doris and the kids arrived later. Doris linked back up with her three main friends, my wife, Carol; Joyce Hill; and Hazel Martinez . . . and the gossip continued. Many times, Jesse, Joyce's husband; John, Hazel's husband; and Jim and I were topics of discussion. I can't repeat here some of the conversations. Doris got a job at Truman Medical Center and eventually retired from there. Jim retired as assistant city manager in 1994.

Jim and Doris Threatt, two of the best friends you could have, the best friends to Carol and me—both passed away and I spoke at each of their funeral services. I've pretty much kept up with the kids, especially Elliott "Ikie," who is a successful businessman here in Kansas City and a nationally renowned stand-up comic.

Chapter 6

ADHOC BEGINS AND FLOURISHES

Women of the Evening: A Serial Killer?

It was 1977, and homicides were on the rise. They were mostly Black on Black. I was an assistant city manager. That summer, a man named David Berkowitz, who became known as the "Son of Sam" serial killer, was arrested for committing multiple assaults and murders in New York City. At the same time, Kansas City was experiencing several murders of African American women. The Black community was enraged because it seemed like there was a crime pattern where the Black women's bodies were found and the causes of their deaths remained unknown.

The Son of Sam victims were all killed with a .44-caliber revolver. The women in Kansas City were murdered in different ways. None was a victim of gunshots. One had battery acid shot into her veins and was left down on the riverfront. Another was found in Brush Creek with multiple strips of wood driven into her vaginal area. All seemed to be done to make the police and the public believe that there was a serial killer loose in the Black community. Fear was rampant.

Career police Sgt. Al Lomax, my longtime friend, oversaw the murder squad assigned to investigate these murders. I called Al and inquired about the situation. Al told me no way were these homicides committed by a serial killer. He suggested we go over each of the cases. As I recall there were about nine at the time. After reviewing the cases with Sergeant Lomax, we determined that the murders had been committed by different persons—by different dope dealers, pimps, or johns.

I told Al I was going to convene a meeting with about sixty persons who represented a broad cross section of the Black community. I asked if he would be willing to come to that meeting and, without jeopardizing the investigation by disclosing too much information, share enough to allay the fear that there was a serial killer in the community. He said he would.

The first person I called was Miss Lucile Bluford, managing editor of the *Kansas City Call*, the weekly Black newspaper. After a long conversation, she agreed to hold the story until I had talked to the sixty folks from the Black community. There was "higher than high" anxiety about a serial killer. Some folks were spreading the rumor that it was a white police officer in the vice unit. Others believed it was a white man who hated Black prostitutes. One of the ten murdered women was white. Most of the women, if not all, had been victims of sexual or domestic abuse and were also drug users, alcoholics, or both.

One Sunday evening in November, Carol and I were sitting at our kitchen table watching the ten o'clock news. Our phone rang. I said, "Hello, Brooks residence."

"Brooksie?"

"Yes, ma'am," I said. "How are you, Miss Bluford?"

She said, "Not well. Did you see the news just now?"

I said, "Yes, ma'am, a tenth woman was found murdered."

"Brooksie, it's time to call that meeting you talked to me about. Have you talked to your sixty people yet?"

"Yes, ma'am, almost. But since I talked to you, I met with Sergeant Lomax, whose unit is investigating these murders. Miss Bluford, there are no similarities in these nine murders. All seemed to be committed by different individuals."

Miss Bluford said, "Well, now ain't that something? So, when you gonna call the meeting? Who are you inviting?"

I told her I had invited the two Black judges, an assistant prosecutor, other detectives working these cases, the Urban League and NAACP presidents, several Black businessmen, Black lawyers, ministers from different denominations, every neighborhood president who I could get a phone number for, several school principals, and the two Black members of the city council.

"Did all of them say that they would come?"

"Yes, ma'am, every one of them. A little more than sixty. Since we had the tenth murder tonight, I'm going to try and get a letter out tomorrow when I get to the office."

Miss Bluford said, "Well, don't wait until Friday to call the meeting. Remember we go to press Thursday."

I said, "Okay, Miss Bluford. I'll see if I can schedule the meeting for this Wednesday at 7:00 p.m. at the Linwood Multipurpose Center. You know, Miss Bluford, I'm not sending out a press release. If I do, we'll have hundreds of people show up, and we won't get anything done. Plus, you know how our people are when they get a chance to see themselves on television. The media is going to be mad at me, but so be it. I'm concerned about trying to alleviate the fear, and that can't be done with a bunch of screaming, hollering, fear-mongering folks showing up."

"Well, Brooksie, you're right. We will act a fool, and nothing will be heard, and nothing will come out of your meeting. Go ahead and do what you said. I'll see you

Wednesday evening if you can pull it off. This thing has gotten too serious. Ten women now killed in such a short period of time. I hope you can get the letter out tomorrow; otherwise, you'll have to call them. I'll talk to you later. Tell Carol I said hello."

"She's right here, and I'll tell her. Good night, Miss Bluford."

Carol and I sat there at our kitchen table while I sketched an organizational structure that should come out of this meeting. I thought there should at least be an "ad hoc group" formed to begin to work from inside the community to assist the police in solving these ten homicides. I said to Carol, "You know my master's thesis, although theoretical, is designed to do just what we're here talking about, create an intermediary group that's community based that can act between the community it represents and the established institutions—the police being a good example."

"Oh well," Carol said, "here we go again—you are getting involved in something that's not going to be short-lived."

I said, "Yeah. Yes, it'll be. That's what the 'ad hoc' means. Temporary. The organization is dissolved after it completes its mission. In this case, helping solve these ten murders."

The Formation of the AdHoc Group Against Crime, Wednesday, November 30, 1977, 7:00 p.m.

I personally contacted sixty people for the meeting, but the media picked up the story and several hundred people were there by the time it was called to order. Prayer was offered. The purpose of the meeting was announced: "To dispel some of the rumors in the community." Elbert Anderson was introduced as director of the Kansas City Council on Crime Prevention. Kansas City police homicide Sgt. Al Lomax was introduced. There was some applause, some boos. Al Lomax began his presentation.

He was never able to complete what he had set out to do. Even some of the so-called leaders, whom you would expect to at least want to hear Lomax's presentation out, were not interested because they had made up their minds that it was a serial killer. They were more interested in being on the news than hearing Lomax.

After the cameras were turned off, the crowd began to decrease. I thought I was skillful in controlling an unruly meeting. I had become the director of the city's Human Relations Department six weeks after the 1968 riot. By November 1977, I had nine years of experience—even, at times, speaking to racists, bigots, and crazies who wanted all Black folks to "go back to Africa." However, these were all Black folks who knew each other but didn't want to be troubled with the truth.

Well, the meeting did not go as long as Al and I anticipated. The meeting was adjourned. Those left were asked if they would like to meet again. We set another meeting for the second week in December.

The next meeting was held with only about seventy-five people, including most of the sixty-plus who had been personally contacted originally. Most of the loud, non-listening voices were not at the second meeting. We accomplished a lot. The group followed the agenda and was more respectful of each other. You could tell the attendees came for the purpose of becoming involved and cooperating with the police in order to get something done for the Black community.

It was suggested that a committee be formed to put together a list of goals that would be presented to a broad cross section of the community—goals that we would be willing and able to commit to and accomplish. The group also set out to develop a list of issues to present to the Board of Police Commissioners (BOPC). People volunteered to develop this list.

The group members felt they needed a name for the new group. I had given it some thought since our first meeting. I thought it needed a name that was representative of the discussion that had gone on at our first meeting and the discussion at the second meeting. I suggested: "The AdHoc Group of Community Leaders and Representatives Against Violent Crime in the Black Community." The group adopted the name. I included the words "Leaders and Representatives" in the name of the newly formed grassroots group to represent the Black community because I knew my Black community-village, especially the leadership, would be asked, if anyone came into the village without the proper identification, "Whom do you represent?"—so by adding "Leaders and Representatives" to the organization's name, few people could argue about who should be in attendance.

We also needed a vision and mission associated with the name for the group. A third committee was formed to hammer out the vision and mission. They agreed to meet once between Christmas and New Year's. At the next meeting, the three committees reported. One committee drew up twenty-one suggestions that the community would be asked to commit to work toward. Another committee drew up nine suggestions to present to the BOPC. The third committee offered the following suggestions for the vision and mission:

The vision was to work to improve the relationship between the police and the Black community.

The mission was to work within the community to prevent crime and assist the police in solving crimes in the Black community by implementing our twenty-one-point suggestions.

Two persons were selected to present both lists to the BOPC. Marvin L. Groves would present the nine suggestions to the BOPC and Haniff Khalil was selected to present the twenty-one suggestions for the community to carry out. I prepared the presentations. Another general meeting was held to reach a consensus on what was to be presented to the BOPC. There was unanimous agreement. I was asked to get us on the BOPC's agenda for the January meeting.

I met with Mayor Charles Wheeler, who was also a member of the BOPC by virtue of his office, and City Manager Bob Kipp about what had been accomplished since my discussion with them on November 30. They indicated that they were pleased that something was being done and that it had originated from the Black community. They offered their support if needed. I asked the mayor if he would place us on the agenda of the January BOPC meeting. I told him that two persons representing the group would like to make presentations to the board. Mayor Wheeler said, "Al, consider it done. Have your folks at the next meeting."

AdHoc's Presentation to the BOPC, 1978

A large group of Black ministers led by A. L. Johnson was also on the board's January agenda. They were presenting the same demands to the BOPC. They had all been at the November meeting but decided to make a trip to meet with Governor Joseph Teasdale in Jefferson City, the state capital.

(After they presented their "demands" regarding the police department to the governor, Police Commissioner Gwendolyn Wells reported to us that the governor told the ministers, "Gentlemen, I appreciate you coming to the state capitol to meet with me, but I'm not the one you should be bringing your demands to. You have the board of Police Commissioners and the mayor who is a member of the board, and the chief. Your demands should be presented to them. I'm sure they'll welcome you. I do appoint the four members to the board, but I don't have any control over what they do. I don't try to influence them at all. They hire the chief and make their decisions independent of me or my office. But it's good seeing you. Come down anytime.")

Clint Kanaga was president of the BOPC. James McNeill was vice president. Other members included Mayor Charles Wheeler, Frank Paxton, and Gwendolyn Wells. Manford "Manny" Maier was the board secretary and general counsel to the police department. It was embarrassing. The letter and demands the ministers presented had misspelled words and half sentences separated with a period or comma. I watched the expression on Gwen's face. Occasionally, she would look my way and shake her head.

When the ministers were finished, Kanaga asked if any board members had any questions. No one said anything. Kanaga thanked them for coming. They had not done their due diligence. From their meeting with the governor to their presentation of "We demand this, we demand that," etc., etc., not one question was asked. I could tell that Gwen was embarrassed. We certainly were. President Kanaga thanked them for coming and said they were welcome back anytime. I had already briefed Gwen on what we would be presenting to the board and had given her copies.

Mayor Wheeler said, "Al Brooks, the assistant city manager, has been working with the community to help improve its relationship with the police and to help solve some of these senseless murders. This group has brought the community together over some issues that I believe we need to hear about."

Kanaga said, "Thank you, Al, and thanks to all of you for coming down to meet with us and share your thoughts about how to improve the relationship between the Negro community and the police department and help reduce the violence."

I thanked the board for permitting members of the AdHoc Group of Community Leaders and representatives of the Black community to meet with them and make a presentation about some of the issues facing the police and the Black community. I thanked them for allowing us to offer suggestions to the police department and suggestions that we would be working to initiate with the Black community. I introduced the two representatives of the organization who would be making the presentations.

Attorney Sammie Edwards passed out copies of both Haniff Khalil's presentation and that of Marvin L. Groves. Haniff presented the twenty-one recommendations that the community was committed to begin working toward. All the ministers walked out. Haniff was asked several questions by Gwen, the mayor, and other board members. They offered congratulations and offered to assist any way they could.

Marvin then presented the nine recommendations that we were encouraging the board and chief to review, adopt, and implement. After Marvin finished, Kanaga turned to Chief VanKirk, board secretary/attorney Manny Maier, and Commissioner Gwen Wells and told them to review our recommendations and report back to the board at the next meeting. He also asked us to come back. I thanked the board and the chief for permitting us to present them with what representatives of the community had been diligently working on.

"No! No! No!" The Firing of Chief Marvin VanKirk, 1978

As Haniff was presenting our suggestions to the police department for consideration, one of the television stations caught a view over Chief VanKirk's shoulder of his copy of the nine recommendations on which he had written on the side of each, "NO." At the next meeting, the chief and Manny Maier presented what the department "could not do!"

This was seen as "insubordination" on the part of the chief. VanKirk was fired as chief by four members of the board. Commissioner Paxton was the only "nay" vote. The board reduced VanKirk in rank from chief to major, his permanent rank.

VanKirk asked for a formal hearing before the board. His request was granted. The board sustained its previous action. VanKirk appealed to the circuit court. The court upheld the board's decision. The board named Norman Caron as VanKirk's successor. Caron was Mayor Wheeler's candidate. Caron had been the liaison between the department and the county coroner's office. Wheeler had previously been the county coroner.

Caron and I had graduated from UMKC together in 1959. (Another officer who walked the beat in the downtown area had also graduated with us. We were the first full-time police officers to have completed college.)

An article appeared in the *Star* regarding the actions against VanKirk. The article gave the impression that AdHoc was the force that caused the action against VanKirk. I didn't necessarily want people to have that impression of AdHoc when we were just starting to work with the police in carrying out the suggestions for the community and those submitted to the BOPC for their implementation.

There was a lot of work ahead. Based on my position with the city as the liaison to the police department, I had to be cautious as to the role I played. I had to walk a tightrope. I didn't want anyone hollering "conflict of interest." Carol continued to remind me that she knew what I was doing with AdHoc: putting my theories in my master's thesis into practical action. She was right!

"Al B," I Want to Sit Down with the AdHoc Group, 1978

The third day after Norman Caron was sworn in as police chief, he called me at my office at city hall and asked, "Al B [for years, he had addressed me as Al B—ever since we were both patrolmen], "are you busy? If not, I'd like to come over and have a word with you about AdHoc."

I told him to come on over, I'd be waiting for him. Caron brought with him copies of the two presentations we had made before the BOPC. Caron and I sat at the conference table. He said, "Al B, I want to work with you and the AdHoc Group. VanKirk showed no consideration for what was presented to him and the board. I want to fully cooperate. I don't see any problem working with the group on all nine of the recommendations. And I'll do what I can, if needed, to work through what the group and the Black community want from the police. Please pass that on."

I told Caron, "I would like to set up a meeting with a small group of AdHoc members and you and have some dialogue to flesh out both sets of suggestions."

"Fine, Al B. You set it up and I'll be there."

"How about your office, Norm? Give them an opportunity to see how a big-city police chief lives." We both laughed.

"Set it up at my office." A couple of days later, Chief Caron sat with a half dozen AdHoc members who chaired task forces: Aasim Baheyadeen, Cliff Sargeon, Haniff Kahlil, Sammie Edwards, and Keith Hines. He went over all nine of the recommendations and assured the group's representatives "that as long as I'm chief, the AdHoc Group will have my full cooperation." One of the members asked if he was willing to make that commitment before the BOPC. He said, "Yes!"

AdHoc Reward Fund Established, 1978

The name of the group, "the AdHoc Group of Community Leaders and Representatives Against Violent Crimes in the Black Community," was shortened over time by the media and the community, and it became "the AdHoc Group Against Crime." Everyone said the original name was too much to remember and that just "AdHoc Group Against Crime" was easy to remember and say. So be it!

Members of the various "task forces," as they were called, rather than "committees," decided a community reward ought to be established for information that would lead to the arrest and filing of charges in all homicide cases—with emphasis placed on those homicides that caused AdHoc to come into being in November 1977. A five-member reward fund committee was established.

In May 1978, AdHoc teamed with radio stations KPRS-FM and KPRC-AM, the Black-owned radio stations—owned by Millie and Skip Carter. I visited with Millie shortly after our presentation to the BOPC about what AdHoc was attempting to do. I asked if she would join in a partnership with AdHoc to put on a "radiothon" to raise funds for a community reward fund. She called in their son, John Carter, to join this discussion. She told him to work with me to see that it got done.

John was somewhat resistant. He was not totally supportive even after Millie told him to get with me to see that it happened. John asked, "What's gonna happen to our ratings?"

Millie said, "Let me worry about that. I want us to cooperate in every way. Alvin's involved. Work with him and bring it back to me to see."

The reward fund committee met and set a goal of $10,000 to start the community reward fund. The radiothon was scheduled for the third week in May 1978. I suggested that we try a weekend from 6:00 a.m. Friday until 6:00 p.m. Sunday.

Millie approved the suggestion. Sixty hours of appeals for the AdHoc Reward Fund would be broadcast live from the second-floor conference room of the Multipurpose Center.

The on-air personalities involved would be at the center rather than at the radio station. Millie gave us one week of public service announcements leading up to marathon time. The on-air personalities announced the names of the ten murdered women and the purpose of the reward fund.

Elbert Anderson used money from his budget of the Kansas City Council on Crime Prevention to have some six phone lines and one dedicated line installed at the center for the live radio broadcast. He had the hotline for tips installed in his office at the Multipurpose Center. Volunteers were trained to answer the phones and record contributions, and schedules were set up. Elbert had set up a separate account for the fund. A news conference explained what the fund was for and identified and presented the reward fund committee. The chair was City Councilman Charles Hazley. Members were Miss Lucile Bluford of the *Kansas City Call* newspaper; the Reverend A. L. Johnson, pastor of Zion Grove Baptist Church; Elbert Anderson; and Aasim Baheyadeen.

The churches were asked to get involved by taking up a special Sunday collection and sending a representative afterward to join the on-air personalities who would announce the pastor's name, church, and amount donated to challenge other congregations. Volunteers answering the phones were asked to call relatives and friends to come by and bring donations. The Kansas City Chiefs organization called in and made a pledge of $10,000. At the end of the broadcast, Sunday at 6:00 p.m., volunteers counted actual cash and pledges. Collected funds and pledges totaled a little over $30,000.

Flyers that depicted the victims' photos and the dollar amount of the reward being offered were prepared. Several thousand flyers were given out to "secret witnesses" in collaboration with the members of the homicide unit. Photos of wanted persons were added to the flyers. And the calls began to come in. Rewards were paid for information called in on those crimes.

After the radiothon, I sat down with Millie Carter at the KPRS/KPRT studio. I told her of the relationship we at AdHoc had developed with the police department. I thought this was a moment we as a community needed to capitalize on. I asked her if she would allow me to do some commentaries on the air, both the AM side and the FM side. All would be within FCC guidelines. The broadcasts would be live from the police department and various parts of the community (when a violent act occurred). When a homicide occurred, I'd do a live broadcast from the crime scene on KPRS/KPRT. Because of the relationship we now had with the department, most of the time we would get the news of an incident before the other media. I also told her that I would like to host a weekly talk show on the AM side of the dial. For my guests, I'd have persons from the community or anyone who appeared to have a relevant message for the Black community. That relationship continues as I write this. In 1992, AdHoc began to broadcast "Voices from Midtown and

Beyond" live from our offices at 3336 Troost on Fridays from 4:00 to 5:00 p.m. At the present we broadcast live from the station at 11131 Colorado live on Tuesdays 12:30–1:00 p.m. on KPRS-AM.

Michael Carter, the grandson of Millie and Skip, is now the president of Carter Broadcasting Group.

From 1977 to 1988, AdHoc was strictly volunteer. Much of the operation was out of my office at city hall. All the task force planning and strategies took place in my office on the fourth floor in the Human Relations Department. Most of the Human Relations staff were involved with AdHoc. After Elbert Anderson changed jobs, the community hotline was transferred to my city hall office. When Caron became chief, he had a direct police line installed in my office. And when crack cocaine hit Kansas City in the early '80s, our hotline became the "24-hour community secret-witness hotline." We began to receive dozens of calls a day reporting crack houses and other crimes and suspects.

AdHoc Prepared to Become More than AdHoc, a Short-Lived Organization

The AdHoc Group had become highly active, but what really put it on the map nationally and internationally was its effort to close crack houses. More than 350 active crack houses had sprung up in the city. We had built quite a portfolio of active crack houses, and we shared it with the police and the Jackson County Prosecutor's Office (JCP) at one of our community meetings in 1991. The police and the JCP, in cooperation with the Feds, would determine what cases went to the state (via the JCP's office) and which went to the Feds. State prosecutions took longer to try, and the federal system was quicker. However, the federal judges gave a lot more time—sometimes, life without parole. Plus, it was difficult to make bond in federal cases, especially when Jamaicans were the defendants. The US Attorney's office indicated to the federal judges that the Jamaican defendants were flight risks, so they were held without bond. Both systems were too slow for AdHoc.

At one of our community meetings in 1987 (held on Wednesdays at 7:00 p.m. on the second floor of the Linwood Multipurpose Center), there was considerable discussion about the increased number of calls about crack houses, with neither the state nor the Feds acting fast enough. One of the group's fearless and active members, Aasim Baheyadeen (the husband of my secretary in the city manager's office, Mejeeda), suggested we should start a "crack house blitz" by mobilizing and marching on these crack houses and confronting the crack dealers. Baheyadeen's suggestion resonated with the members of AdHoc. Some, though, feared the crack dealers. They might harm us or pay someone to do so.

We decided to compile a list of suspected crack houses and have a team of AdHoc men check each residence identified over the phone and try to determine if it was, in fact, a "true" crack house. The group to carry out the blitz was called the "Anti-Drug-House Task Force." I convened the meetings. Since it was Baheyadeen's suggestion, I offhandedly, tongue in cheek, appointed him the chair of that task force. After a lot of laughter and offering motions with seconds from everyone, he agreed to chair the Anti-Drug-House Task Force. Joining him were Cliff Sargeon and Calvin Neal.

Cliff came up with a strategy to identify the crack house and the landlord. Cliff would telephone the owner and request a meeting. He would then bring a detective and a prosecutor along. They would tell the landlord that the state can seize a drug house. Sargeon would then offer the landlord a more palatable alternative: evict the tenant. Oftentimes, it worked when we were able to identify the landlord. In addition to Cliff's strategy, we moved forward with Baheyadeen's anti-drug-house blitz, because Cliff's strategy—and our marching on one house here and one house there—was not getting the job done fast enough. So when the number of active crack houses rose to more than 350, the Anti-Drug-House Task Force decided to step up its blitzes; rather than one or two houses here and there, the task force decided to blitz a group of more than a dozen, all in one afternoon. Someone suggested we ask the police chief to provide an escort for us so we could blitz the larger number.

It became my job to inform Police Chief Larry Joiner, who had succeeded Chief Caron, of our intent. We did not ask for "protection," but we wanted escorts through traffic from one crack house to the next. I called Chief Joiner and made our request. He was aware that we were gaining attention here and there identifying crack houses, but I told him that we were expanding our crack house blitz.

His first response was, "Al, you all can't do that. That's just too dangerous. These drug dealers are vicious and don't mind shooting someone, especially when you're interfering with their business. It's just not safe. Our joint task force has everything to defend ourselves because we know how dangerous they are. And in some cases, they out-gun us with more powerful weapons than we have."

I responded, "Larry, we've made up our minds that we're going to do this, respectfully, with or without your support."

"Oh, Al. Okay. When and where do you plan to start?" I told him we had done our own investigation on fourteen crack houses and planned to meet at Leon Jordan Park at Linwood Boulevard and Benton at 10:00 a.m. on Saturday.

That Saturday was a beautiful fall day. We had about fifteen cars loaded with AdHoc members—men, women, and kids—about forty in all. Only the task force members knew the addresses of the crack houses. And only task force men knocked on the doors and confronted the occupants. The kids made all kinds of drawings depicting the consequences of drugs to them and their families and their community. We began to haul a casket borrowed from Lawrence A. Jones Funeral Home on a truck bed. We'd roll it up in front of the crack house.

The kids' artwork surrounded the casket. Chief Joiner had one of the police officers drive either Baheyadeen or me with them in the lead car.

The first house we blitzed was my neighbor around the corner from my own house, on East 33rd Street. The crack dealer was Danny McCutchen, who, when I would drive past his house, would yell, "Hey, Brooks. Don't you want some of this?" He also put the word out, "Tell Brooks: until he can make a hundred thousand dollars a year tax-free, stay off my ass." When we were holding the blitz in front of McCutchen's house, he came to the door and opened it because he heard all the chants from Baheyadeen and Neal: "No more crack in our neighborhood!" More chants.

Channel 4 television caught McCutchen close-up with his door open. It appeared on the six o'clock news. McCutchen got sent up months after that. He was indicted, charged, pleaded guilty, and given twenty years without parole. So, who had the last laugh?

A little anecdote here. I think it was in 2014 when a school teacher asked me to speak to her class. The teacher was the daughter of Danny McCutchen. She introduced me by saying, "If it were not for this man, Mr. Brooks, I would probably be dead. My daddy was a drug dealer, but he got caught due to the work of Mr. Brooks and the AdHoc Group, and my daddy was sent to jail. Not only do I have my undergraduate degree, but in a few months, I'll have my master's." I was invited and did attend her commencement ceremony, and I gave her a bouquet of flowers.

From our impatient action to close crack houses, AdHoc drew national and international attention. Local, national, and international television, radio, and reporters followed us day and night. Reporters, some with camera people in tow, even came from the United Kingdom and Canada. Newspapers all over the metroplex carried AdHoc's stories as did national publications like *USA Today, Reader's Digest,* and the *Wall Street Journal.*

We made no arrests. We didn't go to court. We were just a group of determined citizens at the grassroots level who planned strategies and confronted the crack dealers face to face because we were tired of seeing what the scourge of crack was doing to our people, our families, and our community. A group of Black men—truly men, not just grown-up boys—came together and made a difference.

The Street Narcotics Unit (SNU) Was Formed

I don't remember exactly when the Street Narcotics Unit (SNU) was created, but it was created because of the success of that group of Black men closing crack houses. Police Captain Robert "Bob" Mathis, first commander of the Street Narcotics Unit, contacted AdHoc. He listened to our suggestions. Bob and Aasim worked together to identify and close crack houses. Aasim and I occasionally went undercover with Bob in different decoy vehicles.

At this time, crack cocaine was entering Kansas City from a Jamaican group. There were two, three, sometimes four crack houses on a single block.

Our collaborative efforts caused the number of Jamaican crack dealers to dwindle. As the Jamaicans were arrested, jailed, and eventually brought to trial and sentenced, many of them who had federal fugitive warrants fled the country and ended up back in Jamaica.

Black men began to fill the void, cooking, buying, and selling the drugs. Hundreds, particularly in the Black community, became crack addicts. Their customers were all ages, all professions, all races—even mothers with children. The problem had reached epidemic proportions.

Buys were made, and arrests followed. The US Attorney's office, the FBI, a KCPD officer, and AdHoc worked together. Rob Larsen, the assistant US Attorney for the Western District of Missouri, was assigned full-time to work these crack cases.

The rallying cry from all corners of the city was "Lock 'em up and throw away the key." No one was talking about prevention and treatment or saying that drug addiction was an illness.

With thirty to forty task force members and residents who sometimes joined our ranks, we marched on crack houses. In order to maintain surprise when we moved to the next house on our list, only a couple of task force members knew which were the active crack houses. Addresses were kept closely guarded because at times our ranks were infiltrated by dope dealers or those who sold for them. Because of the success of the group of Adhoc's Black men, the group took on the name of Black Men Together.

Mobilizing "Black Men Together," 1988

Black Men Together was formed to take on the work of the Anti-Drug-House Task Force as more and more local Black men (and some women) were making the crack house drug sales. And murders and assaults were increasing, making our work more dangerous.

I should mention that at one of our early meetings, we were searching for a name. It was my grandson, Damon Brooks, who suggested Black Men Together. Some thirty Black men would take the lead on marching on drug houses. We all had caps and jackets, gold on blue, that depicted us with our arms locked together. We were closing more drug houses than the police, the FBI, the county prosecutor, and the US Attorney all put together.

We discovered, however, that all we were doing by exposing them was pushing them toward another location in the inner city. So, we moved some; the criminal justice agencies arrested and convicted some; and some got long-term sentences. We all had an important role to play and the collaboration was enormous.

The AdHoc Group Against Crime really was ahead of the game. Cliff Sargeon was AdHoc's board chair. Black Men Together made the front page of *USA Today* for the success we were having with our "drug house blitzes," headed by Aasim Baheyadeen and Calvin "Big Timber" Neal. Both led the marches and the chants, some of which were "Down with dope—up with hope!" and "Dope dealer, hey, you—Black men are watching you!" and "No more drugs and no more crack—we just want our children back!"

Because of the success of Black Men Together, I was flown to Canada to appear as part of a television series, which again caused the national and international news media to pick up on what was being done in Kansas City to confront crack cocaine drug dealers and close crack houses.

Bill Dunn Sr. Promotes AdHoc, 1988

Early in 1988, Bill Dunn Sr., of the J. E. Dunn Construction Company, one of the largest construction companies in the world, and I were in a meeting. Bill, a well-respected businessman, civic leader, and philanthropist, asked me how AdHoc was doing. I told him that we were doing as much as we could but that with the crack cocaine epidemic, our city was really in trouble. Crime was increasing because so many people were getting hooked on crack and doing whatever they needed to get money to buy their drugs, and we already were seeing an increase in violence. Therefore, the demands for crack had become so great, the dealers had a great unwritten marketing campaign, and crack houses were springing up all over certain sections of the city, sometimes four crack houses in one block. Bill asked me what could be done. I told him the first thing would be to bring the various criminal justice folks together and let them give their assessment of the situation.

About ten days later, Bill convened a luncheon meeting at the Vista Hotel with about thirty persons: Jan Kreamer, of the Greater Kansas City Community Foundation, and others, including Jackson County Prosecutor Albert Reiderer; Rob Larsen from the US Attorney's Office; Kansas City Mayor Richard Berkley; KCPD Police Chief Larry Joiner; representatives from the Crime Commission; and representatives from several large businesses. Bill Dunn told the group about the conversation he had with me regarding the crack cocaine trade and violence. He asked Chief Joiner how he assessed the situation. Joiner told Bill Dunn it was probably worse than I had told him. He identified the kinds of resources and collaborations it would take to curb it. Reiderer gave his analysis of the situation and then Rob Larsen added to the discussion. Mayor Berkley suggested that those on the enforcement side should continue to meet, maybe weekly, and become more collaborative. Everyone agreed that was the thing to do. Mayor Berkley's suggestion came to pass and AdHoc was right in the middle of each meeting and had a voice at the collaboration table.

County Prosecutor Albert Reiderer Proposes Anti-Drug Tax, 1989

In the fall of 1989, Albert Reiderer, Jackson County prosecutor, held a Saturday breakfast meeting at the Vista Hotel with civic leaders to present his new brainchild—that the voters of Jackson County pass a quarter-cent sales tax to fund an anti-drug program to be executed by the prosecutor's office, the courts, and law enforcement.

AdHoc was the first organization to support the initiative and to campaign for it. AdHoc was the first to distribute yard signs in the high-crime area of the city. AdHoc encouraged residents to register to vote and to vote "yes."

At the meeting, some thirty men of AdHoc performed an anti-drug-house chant led by Aasim Baheyadeen and Calvin Neal. At the close of the meeting, I challenged those in attendance who wanted to get firsthand knowledge of drug houses in the community to "join Black Men Together on anti-drug-house marches at two o'clock this afternoon. We'll meet at the W. E. B. DuBois Center, 5501 Swope Parkway." There were no takers from the all-white crowd.

As people began to leave, Mr. Miller Nichols, businessman and civic leader, came up to me and asked, "Mr. Brooks, can I go on that march with you this afternoon?"

I said, "Yes, sir, you certainly can." I asked, "Do you know where the DuBois Learning Center is?"

Mr. Nichols said, "I do roughly, but I'm sure my security man does."

I asked, "Is your security man retired deputy police chief Jim Keiter? Oh yes, Jim knows where it is."

As we walked to the elevators, Jim Keiter caught up with us and asked, "Al, is it safe for the boss to be out there marching on drug houses?"

I said, "Sure, Jim, if we can do it, Mr. Nichols and the rest of you can, too!"

"Okay, Al," Mr. Nichols said, "we'll be there at two. Oh, can my wife, Jeanette, and my sister and brother-in-law come, too?"

I said, "Yes!"

At two, we had forty to fifty anti-drug-house marchers—men, a few women, and youth. Among them was Mr. Miller Nichols. The other four who were with him got out of the car driven by Keiter, but they were not marching. Jim asked if it was all right if they followed in their car. I told him they could. Aasim and Calvin began to warm the group up with our chants. Mr. Nichols caught on to the repetitiveness of the chants and joined in. Several police cars were lined up to give free passage to the dozen or so houses we had identified when our "advance team" visited them after dark to check for drug activity. In different cars, we would stop persons emerging from the house and ask what they were selling there. Normally, they would tell us. That's the way we confirmed what was reported to us on our hotline.

After we marched on about a dozen drug houses and returned to DuBois, Mr. Nichols asked if he could talk to me for a minute. I said yes. He said, "I like what you all do. I want to help. If there's anything I can do, give me a call."

I said, "I certainly will. Thank you for coming." Jim Keiter and the three others got out of the car to hear our brief "de-briefing."

Chapter 7

RECOGNIZED BY THE PRESIDENT

The US Drug Czar Visits AdHoc, 1989

In the early spring of 1989, AdHoc member Aasim Baheyadeen was on a bus tour with Missouri Senator Jack Danforth through Kansas City's inner city. During the bus tour, Aasim invited the senator to attend one of AdHoc's public meetings to hear how AdHoc was closing crack houses with the police, prosecutor, and courts involved.

When Danforth returned to Washington, he asked Drug Czar William Bennett to visit Kansas City to see what AdHoc was doing. Senator Danforth later attended an AdHoc public meeting and heard residents and the police tell how AdHoc's Black Men Together closed crack houses and, in some cases, helped police identify crack dealers who pleaded guilty to federal or state charges because of the overwhelming evidence after they were either indicted and arrested or arrested without indictments.

Senator Danforth was impressed and said he wanted to help. He was asked to impress upon the drug czar to come to Kansas City and witness what some forty to fifty Black Men Together were doing to help rid the community of crack dealers and crack houses. We explained that AdHoc had the full support of Police Chief Larry Joiner, the Jackson County prosecutor Albert Reiderer, Assistant US Attorney Rob Larsen, and other federal officers and agencies. Senator Danforth committed to the group that when he returned to Washington, he would suggest to Bennett that he make a trip to Kansas City and visit with AdHoc.

Shortly after Danforth returned to Washington, I received a call from Bennett indicating that he had been impressed with the conversation he had had with Senator Danforth and wondered if AdHoc could host his visit to Kansas City to meet with AdHoc, residents, and the police.

In early May, Bill Bennett came to Kansas City. The word had reached Washington about this unique, grassroots, community-based crime-fighting organization that had garnered national and international recognition in media including the British Broadcasting Corporation in Europe, a Canadian television station, NBC, the *Wall Street Journal*, the

New York Times, the *Christian Science Monitor, Reader's Digest, Jet, USA Today*, and even *Penthouse* magazine.

Bennett and his entourage brought so much attention to Kansas City and to AdHoc. AdHoc was a great host—if I say so myself. We took Bennett to a number of drug houses we had closed, including a couple of apartment buildings. We provided him with information about cases where we assisted with arrests and prosecution leading to prison time for offenders. Miss Lucile Bluford, owner and managing editor of the *Kansas City Call*, quickly developed a special relationship with Bennett. She and all other media, locally, nationally, and internationally, accompanied us every step of the way.

Three hundred crack houses were closed because of AdHoc drug house rallies, marches, and chants with women, children, and youth, led by members Aasim Baheyadeen and Calvin Neal. But it was AdHoc's Black Men Together, also led by Baheyadeen, Neal, Cliff Sargeon, and me, who knocked on doors, confronted the crack dealers, and told them they had to close and move on. Police were there in the streets, not to protect us but to give our caravan of cars safe passage through stop signs and traffic lights as we went from crack house to crack house. But certainly, the dealers didn't know the difference as they looked out and saw the street lined up with police cars. Sometimes we were threatened, but with our numbers and determination, although we were unarmed, we continued our efforts. It wasn't long before these crack houses were closed.

I Am Interviewed for the President's Drug Advisory Council

After Bennett left Kansas City, on Tuesday, August 8, 1989, I received a call from President George H. W. Bush's longtime friend William "Bill" Moss. Bill Moss said Bennett had reported to President Bush what he had seen in Kansas City after visiting with me and members of the AdHoc Group Against Crime and our group Black Men Together. He said Bennett was excited about what he had heard and seen and that the president was as excited as he was after receiving his report. Moss said the president had told Bennett to tell him to reach out to me to see if I might be interested in accepting an appointment on an advisory council President Bush was forming through an executive order later in the year. Moss said Bennett had given him my contact information.

So, Moss asked me if I might be interested in serving on the council, and if so, he would like to meet with me personally the following Monday morning, August 14, at 9:00 a.m. Our interview would take place over breakfast. A reservation would be made for me at the Watergate Hotel, where he would also be staying. Moss said someone from the White House staff would call to make travel arrangements. I said I was interested but wanted to run it past the group and that I would get back to him within the next twenty-four hours.

The active AdHoc membership gave me their blessings and thought it would be an honor not only for me but AdHoc as well. I called Bill Moss back and told him I would accept the president's appointment. Later I got a call from someone in the White House with my reservation information.

I arrived in DC Sunday afternoon. As I exited the plane into the terminal, a man in black uniform held a sign with my name. I identified myself and off we went to the Watergate Hotel. As I was being seated for dinner in the hotel dining room, an elderly white gentleman, who was already seated and sipping on a cocktail, walked over to me and said, "Good evening, Al Brooks. My name is Bill Moss." I stood and extended my hand; we shook hands, and I introduced myself. Moss said, "I guess you're wondering how I recognized you. Your face and members of Black Men Together were all over the media." He invited me to join him for dinner. During dinner we talked more about his relationship to the president, how he and others had urged Bush to run for president, and how he had supported him. He said that the president had asked him what he wanted in his administration. He said he knew the president's passion for addressing the scourge of illegal drugs was one of his top priorities. Moss said he told the president he would like to chair the drug council the president was going to appoint. The president promised him that appointment. We ate dinner and said good night.

The next morning, after a two-hour breakfast meeting, I told Bill Moss that I would be honored to serve on the president's drug council if appointed. Bill Moss said he had to interview some twenty other persons over the next couple of days to fill out the council, which would be ready to go following President Bush issuing his executive order. Moss said I was the first one to be interviewed. He said he would contact me for the appointment date, the swearing-in ceremony, and our first meeting.

By Executive Order 12696, issued November 13, 1989, President Bush established the President's Drug Advisory Council. The executive order states: "The council shall be composed of not more than thirty members appointed by the president from among citizens in private life." The function of the council was to "recommend to, and advise, the president and the director of National Drug Control Policy on developing methods and means to explain national drug control policies to the American people."

The administration was making an unprecedented commitment of government personnel and funds ($9.48 billion in fiscal year 1990 and $10.4 billion in fiscal year 1991), but the president recognized that the government's efforts have to be complemented by the whole-hearted involvement of the nation's non-governmental entities: the business community, schools, and religious, fraternal, and volunteer organizations.

President Bush directed the council to find:

better ways to encourage employers to ensure that their workplaces are drug-free;

better ways to enlist the aid of the many Americans who want to volunteer their time and energy to winning the war on drugs;

better ways to communicate to all Americans, especially our young, the importance of staying off drugs;

better ways to coordinate the many existing private sector and nonprofit anti-drug efforts; and

better ways to involve the private sector in the building of prisons and jails.

President Bush stated the twenty-seven members of the council were chosen carefully to address those concerns.

The members nominated by Bill Bennett, director, Office of National Drug Control Policy, and accepted by the president were present and witnessed the president's signing of the executive order in the Roosevelt Room of the White House. It was followed by a briefing from Bill Moss and Bill Bennett at the Old Executive Office Building. At the close of the briefing, we were told we would later receive the date set for our swearing-in ceremony and our first council meeting.

Following Bennett's meeting with AdHoc earlier in the year, I received a call from him in December 1989. Bennett said after telling President Bush of his visit to Kansas City with AdHoc Group Against Crime, he had witnessed how a grassroots group was challenging drug dealers and closing crack houses. Bennett said the president had talked to Senator Jack Danforth, who had praised the AdHoc program. He said the president told him that he would like to come to Kansas City and visit with this group. So, Bennett was asking if I thought AdHoc could host the president's visit.

I responded the same as I did when he called about his own visit. "Bill, I think the AdHoc governing body will welcome the opportunity to host President Bush coming to Kansas City, but give me a couple of days so I can call them together to share your request, as well as discuss this with Pastor Hartsfield, whom you met during your visit at Metropolitan Missionary Baptist Church." I told Bennett, "I believe this is such an honor and an exciting moment for AdHoc and Kansas City that our work will be strengthened by the president's visit."

I called a meeting of the governing body. Again, they responded with a roaring "Yes!" Then I met with Pastor Hartsfield at his church office and told him that I had the go-ahead from AdHoc, and if he was still okay with hosting President Bush at the church, that I would call Bennett back and give him the green light.

I called Bill Bennett the next day. He said, "Fine, Al. I'll pass that on to the president and you should be getting a call from the advance team coordinator who'll be scheduling with you."

A few days later I got that call. The coordinator said he and his team would be flying out to Kansas City and he gave me a date. I alerted the governing body and Pastor Hartsfield, so that as many members as possible could be at the briefing. I rushed to meet with Pastor Hartsfield because the church would become the center of activity, and I was sure that space would be checked from top to bottom and everywhere in between. Pastor Hartsfield felt honored that his church would be where the president's visit would take place.

The advance team arrived, about a dozen in number. We had most of the governing body present. I had also invited Jackson County Prosecutor Albert Reiderer, Police Chief Larry Joiner, Mayor Richard Berkley, US Attorney Rob Larsen, and, of course, Pastor Hartsfield.

The president was the leading Republican in the nation, and as Mayor Berkley was also a Republican, I thought it was the right thing to do. Also, the mayor was a friend of mine. There were several other politicians present who heard about the meeting. One of the Republicans told the lead advance team member that he wanted the president to attend another meeting with a certain group. I don't remember the person who made the request, or where he was inviting the president, but the lead advance team member replied, "I'm sorry, sir, but the president is coming to Kansas City to see Mr. Brooks and the AdHoc Group Against Crime. And most of that will take place right here in the space we are in right now. There will be another stop by the president, but that's already being planned as I speak."

The team asked a million questions, from the structural makeup of the church to the layout of the surrounding area. The lead advance team member asked Pastor Hartsfield if he had any objections to anything he had said. Pastor Hartsfield said, "No, none at all." We were finally told when the president planned to be at the church. The date was January 23, 1990, mid-morning Tuesday.

At about 3:00 a.m., I was awakened by a call from Alfred "Big Boy" Sims, a well-known crack dealer who lived on East 33rd Street, just around the corner from one of the designated stops for the president. "Hey, Brooks, the cops are over here and tearing up my place, saying I'm a drug dealer and that I need to find someplace until the president leaves town tomorrow afternoon. Brooks, you know me; I wouldn't sell an aspirin. What's wrong with cops? They're telling me I've got to get out of my own house until the president leaves. Brooks, they act like I would try to do something to the president. What for? He ain't done nothing to me. I wish you could talk to these cops. I wish you would come over here and see what they've done to my house—and then waiting here to escort me out of my own home. Ain't this against the law, Brooks?"

"Sims, you do know that the police did find a body in Swope Park and traced it back to your house on Montgall where the victim had been killed. And just two weeks ago, they found a dead body under a pile of wood under your back porch. The smell is what brought the police to your house. So, Sims, I suggest you talk to your attorney tomorrow."

"Okay, Brooks, thanks for listening, man. Just remember I reported it to you," were Sims's final words to me.

President Bush Arrives in Kansas City

When President Bush arrived in Kansas City, 11:00 a.m. Tuesday, January 23, 1990, his first stop was the Metropolitan Missionary Baptist Church's Fellowship Hall. The president was accompanied by national drug policy coordinator Bill Bennett, Attorney General Dick Thornburgh, members of the Missouri congressional delegation, Mayor Dick Berkley, Police Chief Joiner, and others.

I presented an overview of what AdHoc had done since 1977, how we had rallied the community to report crack houses, and what we were doing presently. I spoke about how crack was the drug overrunning urban communities across America. I said AdHoc was founded on mobilizing the community, especially the African American community, which was feeling the brunt of the crack cocaine addiction and violence. "Not only do we need interdictions, but we also need education, prevention, and treatment. As a small grassroots group, we're doing our part with a small staff and a host of volunteers. We've developed a unique relationship with the police, the prosecutor's office, the US Attorney, the FBI, and the courts."

President Bush said, "I applaud you, Al, and all that Bill Bennett told me about Black Men Together, the members of the AdHoc Group. This is truly a grassroots movement here in Kansas City." He said, "I have delivered an anti-crime package to Congress, and it awaits action." He opened the floor for discussion and questions. He thanked Pastor Hartsfield for "giving AdHoc space in your church. There's got to be a better and broader connection between the faith community and neighborhood groups and organizations."

Just before the president left the church, Pastor Hartsfield presented him with a Bible. Pastor Hartsfield mentioned that his wife, Matilda, was entering the hospital for an operation the next week. The president said thank you for the Bible, wished Mrs. Hartsfield well, and said he would keep her in his prayers. After a little more than an hour and a half, we moved on.

On the president's agenda we had placed a walk-through of one drug-infested block on Park Avenue, 33rd to Linwood Boulevard. We (Black Men Together) had closed crack houses and put out of business the street crack dealers who used the basketball court there as a decoy for crack sales. Dealers had sat in an old car seat, pretending to be innocent like the youths who played basketball during the crack dealing.

I had made arrangements for the president, Attorney General Thornburgh, Bill Bennett, Chief Joiner, and myself to meet Mr. James Kerr and his wife, Mrs. Mable Kerr, in their home on the 3200 block of Park Avenue, next door to the crack house we had closed. (And they had invited one of their neighbors over.) The Kerrs shared with the president what they had gone through for months until AdHoc came along. They said, "We were reluctant to call the police because of the threat of retaliation. But when AdHoc came along, they did what the police couldn't—they shut them down and ran them off. Thanks to AdHoc's presence and chanting and out-numbering them and taking over the basketball goal and getting that old car seat taken away, we are able to sleep better now."

The president thanked them for their hospitality. When he walked outside, a dozen or so members of Black Men Together, with jackets and caps to match, and with a couple of chants, greeted the president in the yard of the crack house we had closed next door to the Kerrs' home. The president praised them for their courageous stand for their community.

The next stop before the president left Kansas City was a meeting with law enforcement officers from across the metroplex at the Music Hall at the Municipal Auditorium in downtown Kansas City. Cliff Sargeon, AdHoc's board chair, rode with the president and Attorney General Thornburgh, and I rode with Bill Bennett, in bulletproof limousines. Bill Bennett said, "The president wants you to sit on stage with him. He wants to introduce you." I did, and he did introduce me.

Also on the stage with me were Missouri Governor John Ashcroft and Kansas Governor Mike Hayden, both Republicans; US Senator Kit Bond, a Missouri Republican; Democratic Congressman Ike Skelton and Republican Congressman Tom Coleman, both of Missouri; Kansas City Police Chief Larry Joiner; and the five members of the Kansas City Board of Police Commissioners. Bush was introduced by Kansas City Mayor Dick Berkley. After the president thanked Mayor Berkley for the introduction, the president praised me and the AdHoc Group Against Crime with a standing ovation.

After speaking for about forty-five minutes, as the president was leaving the stage under the direction of the Secret Service, he asked me to follow him. We exited the rear of the Music Hall. Then he asked if I wished to accompany him to Air Force One at the downtown airport. I did, along with several others, and had an opportunity to tour the presidential airplane.

AdHoc was really known nationally now. Our "stock" went up as though it were on the stock exchange. We began to get calls from everywhere across the nation.

I received my letter from Bill Moss stating that the President's Drug Advisory Council swearing-in ceremony was scheduled for Tuesday, May 22, 1990, at 4:00 p.m. in the Old Executive Office Building, and would be conducted by Director Bennett, with a reception to follow at the offices of the council at 708 Jackson Place and a dinner after that at the Madison Hotel. The president came by to greet everyone, specifically recognizing me and the AdHoc Group Against Crime. He also asked about Pastor Wallace Hartsfield and his wife, Matilda.

On Wednesday morning, May 23, at our first meeting of the council with Chairman Bill Moss presiding, Moss appointed a National Coalition Subcommittee to be chaired by council member Alvah Chapman. I was named to serve on the committee that was to meet the following day, May 24, in the library of the US Chamber of Commerce. The assignment for the subcommittee was to plan for a national conference. To begin the planning, five community organizations or coalitions had been invited to present their organizations' efforts at addressing the illicit drug problem in their communities to the planning committee. AdHoc was one of the organizations selected. The other four groups or coalitions were from Cincinnati, Ohio; Orange County, California; Denver, Colorado; and Washington, DC. The National Coalition Subcommittee was to carry out its mission statement and objectives and bring to the full President's Drug Advisory Council plans for a national conference to address the national drug crisis in the near future.

Each organization was given forty-five minutes to present their mission and vision statements and report their efforts at addressing the illicit drug problem.

Mary Weathers, the AdHoc executive director, did an extraordinary job making the presentation for AdHoc. After she outlined how AdHoc worked with the entities of the criminal justice system, confronted drug dealers, and closed crack houses, it was clear no one could match AdHoc's success. Bill Bennett's comments had already highlighted AdHoc: "I've been to Kansas City and have seen firsthand what they're doing."

The first President's Drug Advisory Council National Forum was held November 9–10, 1990, in Washington, DC. There were twelve presenters. I was one of the twelve.

President George H. W. Bush named me and AdHoc Board Chair Cliff Sargeon 398th and 399th Daily Points of Light on September 30, 1991, for community service. This announcement was made by the Office of National Services. We were flown to Disneyland along with other Point of Light recipients for a special ceremony. We each received a gold-colored medallion with the inscription, "AN AMERICAN POINT OF LIGHT." The medallions were presented by representatives of the Walt Disney Company on behalf of President George Herbert Walker Bush. Each recipient also received a limited edition Mickey Mouse watch.

Early May 1992, I got a call from a staff member for US Representative Charles Rangel, chair of the Select Committee on Narcotic Abuse. I was told Representative Rangel would like me to appear before his committee to testify at a hearing Thursday, May 14, 1992, on the topic of Community-Based Anti-Drug Initiatives. Congressman Alan Wheat, my Fifth District congressional representative, was to have introduced me but for some reason could not make it. My appearance lasted about forty minutes: twenty minutes of testimony and twenty minutes of Q&A.

A Mr. Hope also testified during the hour allotted. I don't remember the agency or organization he represented, but his part of the hour was brief, and he was asked only a couple of questions.

We both were thanked for answering the call to appear before the Select Committee. After the committee adjourned, several committee members and their staff persons continued the questioning and I responded. They asked for my contact information.

A Study to Determine the Direction of AdHoc, 1990

In the summer of 1990, at the suggestion and direction of Jan Kreamer, executive director of the Greater Kansas City Community Foundation, we were able to get a grant from the foundation to contract with a researcher to study AdHoc's effectiveness in the community, in improving the relationship between the Black community and the police, and ways to improve AdHoc's working relationship with other entities within the criminal justice system.

After meeting with a cross section of the community, the police, and the county prosecutor, the researcher had completed the evaluation of AdHoc and presented his findings with recommendations to the community foundation and the governing body of AdHoc. AdHoc received an outstanding evaluation with a set of recommendations. The consultant applauded our loosely put together bylaws and mission statement. The major recommendation was that the group should immediately form a board of directors and apply for 501(c)(3) status. It was suggested that we expand our services and recommended that we hire or contract with a grant writer to submit proposals to foundations and the private sector for funding to conduct additional programs that could help meet more of the Black community's needs. It was suggested we try to raise enough funding to secure or purchase our own offices in keeping with our expanded program. Further, it was proposed that the organization try to attract me from my position with the city to lead the AdHoc Group Against Crime, with me as executive director and Mary as director of programs with the same salary.

I told Carol what was being proposed. She, of course, asked the question, "Do you want to leave the city and take over AdHoc? That is your brainchild. You spent months researching and writing you master's thesis. That's what AdHoc is, your thesis."

"Well, it's something to think about," I said. "I can retire from the city. Let me think about it, and you and I can talk more later."

Carol asked, "What would Mary Weathers do?" I told her that the proposal was for Mary to become director of programs and for me to become the executive director. I would be hunting down additional funding and developing programs that would meet the needs of our community for the long haul.

"Will Mary accept the demotion?" Carol asked.

"I don't know," I replied. "She knew about it when the person who did the evaluation for the community foundation released his report. So, everybody is waiting for my decision."

The newly formed AdHoc board, which I chaired, was supportive of me becoming the executive director. Mary Weathers was not happy but stated she understood and could adjust to the change.

I submitted my resignation as assistant city manager/director of human relations to David Olson effective about April 17, 1991. On May 1, 1991, I became the executive director of the AdHoc Group Against Crime. My mission was to take AdHoc to another level. We had assembled a great staff under Mary Weathers's leadership. Several months after I took the position, Mary decided to go off on her own as a consultant. It was a loss, but because of her hard work, we were ready to move ahead.

In the fall of that year, I received a call from Mr. Willie Newby, branch manager of the Laurel American Bank at 3330 Troost. He asked if I could stop by and talk to him regarding an important matter. I told him I would. I went the next afternoon. Mr. Newby said the bank's president and board of directors wanted to close the Troost bank location and direct the Troost customers to the Armour and Main location. Almost all the customers of Laurel American Bank were from the neighborhood and businesses in the area. The bank president wanted to pick my brain to figure out the best way to close the bank so that the customers wouldn't feel it was being closed just because it was in a predominantly Black area.

The truth was there was no growth at that location. Area customers had died, and no new customers had appeared. Mr. Newby wanted to know if I would meet with the president at the Troost location at my convenience. A couple of days after that meeting, I returned and met with Mr. Newby and the president of the bank. He got right to the point. "Mr. Brooks, I need your expertise on what is the best way for me to close this facility while still making Black customers feel we value them. They will be directed to our headquarters at Armour and Main. I'm willing to pay you for your help. What would your consultant fee be?"

I thought for a minute and came back with an offer. "I'll take the challenge and you can give the bank building to AdHoc." I laughed—as did Mr. Newby.

But the bank's president didn't. He took me seriously. He said, "There's a possibility I can make that happen."

"Seriously?" I asked.

"Seriously," he replied.

"You've got yourself a consultant," I said. The bank president asked me to give him a couple of days to consult with his board of directors. I passed this news on to the AdHoc board of directors. (By then we had obtained our 501(c)(3) status and were using the "board of directors" language.) We were all optimistic.

About a week later, the bank president called, asking me to meet with him again at the Troost bank. "I still want your service in closing this bank," he said. "I can't deliver what I had hoped, but I can let AdHoc have this facility if you can pay off the balance due."

I asked how much, and he said, "In the neighborhood of $30,000." I asked if he could get me the exact balance on the facility. He said, "Why don't you let me set up a meeting with Charlie Price, chairman of the board? He has the final say on how we dispose of this space." The president made a phone call and asked me, "Have you got a minute? Charlie Price is in the office on Main right now, and he can see us, if you have the time."

Charlie Price was the son of the founder of the Price Candy Company. He was also a former US ambassador to the United Kingdom.

"I understand your group is in need of space and you like our bank on Troost," he said.

"Yes, that's right," I told him. "We're now at the Metropolitan Missionary Baptist Church at Linwood and Park. The pastor, Wallace Hartsfield, and the congregation provided space for us a little over a year ago, and we are grateful; but our staff needs more than the 600 or so square feet of space there. But I don't know what we would have done if Pastor Hartsfield hadn't offered us the space at no charge."

Charlie Price said, "The bank space on Troost is worth three to four times the outstanding debt. Can you raise the money to pay it off?"

"I'll certainly do everything I can," I told him.

"Okay, it's yours," he said. "You work the particulars out with the president. Alvin, thank you for your help. I hope things work out with the building."

I knew we had some money left over from the funds raised by Mr. Nichols and Mr. O'Neal for renovating the building at 3300 Troost. But for staffing, we'd need to go into another fundraising mode.

I told Jan Kreamer, executive director of the Greater Kansas City Community Foundation, that AdHoc had acquired the bank building at Troost for office space but needed money for a small staff. She asked, "How much, Alvin?"

I said, "I need a three-year commitment totaling $150,000." Jan said she would work with me to raise the money. I met with her, and we sat and drew up a list of possible donors.

The Founding of the Community Anti-Drug Coalitions of America (CADCA), 1992

After the election of 1992 and the change in administration, several members of the President's Drug Advisory Council, with the vision and leadership of Alvah Chapman (the retired publisher of the *Miami Herald* and chairman/CEO of Knight Ridder), became charter members of the newly formed Community Anti-Drug Coalitions of America (CADCA), a 501(c)(3) non-profit organization. The CADCA's mission was "to build and strengthen the capacity of community coalitions to create safe, healthy, and drug-free communities, and support member organizations with technical assistance and training, public policy, media strategies, conferences, and special events." The CADCA board was composed of some twenty members representing a broad cross section of leaders, from Fortune 500 businesses to community coalitions, so it was able to attract funds from the government and foundations.

As I recall, two executive directors served the organization before we selected retired Army General Arthur T. Dean to be chairman and CEO in 1998. (Jim Copple from Wichita, Kansas, was the first executive director. I had met Jim when he had asked me to speak in Wichita.) General Dean, a true visionary, took CADCA to a level none of us who were charter members could have envisioned. CADCA services more than 5,000 community coalitions across more than thirty countries from offices in Alexandria, Virginia.

I was a member of CADCA, and had served as one of the vice presidents, when we were searching for another CADCA leader. I urged the search committee to ensure that persons of color were among the candidates. I recall there were three finalists, two Black males among the three. General Dean rose to the top. I said to myself, "With all due respect, what does a retired army general know about coalition building, substance abuse, drug treatment, developing relationships across a broad spectrum of the nation, and motivating them to become committed to the cause? Strong administrator, yes, but?"

After the interview and a short time after he began the job, I saw we made the right decision. So after almost two decades, CADCA, under General Dean's leadership, became the premiere nationally and internationally recognized organization to demonstrate that all sectors of a community can come together to bring about significant healthy change such as reducing the use of illicit drugs, underage drinking, youth tobacco use, and the abuse of medicines. Thank you, General Dean, and your great board and highly professional staff for a job *well done—and still doing!*

I served on the CADCA board from October 1992 until retiring in February 2012. Both Carol and I were fighting cancer at the time. I was presented the Distinguished Service Award "in recognition of your long-standing commitment to CADCA's mission, and for providing outstanding leadership, energy, and expertise as a member of the board of directors." I truly hated to leave the board, General Dean, and his team because CADCA had accomplished so much and expanded its influence organizing coalitions beyond the continental boundaries of the United States.

Chapter 8

MY POLITICAL CAREER

I Made a Run for the City Council, 1997

Kay Barnes, a longtime friend and colleague, called me one day in March 1997 to discuss her run for mayor of Kansas City. During our breakfast at First Watch in Westport, Kay said she was positioning herself to run in 1999 and hoped I would consider running with her for the city council's Sixth District at-large seat and become her mayor pro tem. Kay shared with me her vision for the city, particularly her vision to revitalize Kansas City's downtown. She called it her "River Crown Plaza Redevelopment Plan," which was from the river to the Plaza.

I told Kay the furthest thing from my mind was running for public office. She said she was sure I could win, and our interests would complement each other. I asked Kay for a little time to think about her offer and talk to my wife, kids, and other close friends. We agreed to get together again in two or three months.

I did what I promised I would do. The main question everyone asked (first by my wife, Carol) was "Is this something you really want to do?" The kids had different opinions, from "That's cool, Dad," to echoing their mother: "Is this something you really want to do?"

The friends I discussed the question with gave somewhat similar responses:

"Brooks, do you have the fire in your belly to do this?"

"Great! We need additional Black folks on the city council."

"I don't know of anyone in the Black community who can win at-large from that district except you and Cleaver, and he's mayor and can't run again. And he's from the Fifth District anyway. The Sixth is much whiter than the Fifth, but you'd be running at large as Cleaver did for mayor. You can make it. Go for it."

"You've certainly done enough for people across this city. I don't know anyone who's done as much to bring folks together across this city."

"I think you can even carry the Northland."

In talking to family members and friends—Black, white, Hispanic, Christian, Muslim, and Jewish—the word had gotten around that I was considering running for the city council. Before Kay Barnes and I met about this, people began to call and see me at meetings and ask me if it was true, and if so, they committed themselves to help. Kay and I met in June at the same place, First Watch in Westport. I asked a lot of questions and I was satisfied with her answers. I told Kay that I would run with her. I told her I appreciated the confidence she had in me and thanked her for thinking of me as one of her running mates.

Both of us began to tell the Kay Barnes story and share her vision. She set up a meeting with Pat Gray, a well-known political strategist. He had a long history and record of handling candidates' campaigns, as well as initiatives, and had developed quite a record in the "win column" for himself. I had done some PSAs for initiatives under Pat's direction. Behind the scenes we started pulling together folks to support Kay and myself. I didn't use Pat as much as Kay did.

I hired Beverly "Bev" Livingston to direct my campaign. Bev had directed a congressional campaign for a candidate for the Fifth District congressional seat. I asked two-term Sixth District city councilman and retired business executive Arthur "Art" Asel to be my treasurer. Art was a conservative Republican, although Kansas City's mayoral and council races are nonpartisan.

Art and I had done some battling with each other on at least one occasion when he was on the city council and I was director of the Human Relations Department. One of Kansas City's leading businessmen and civic leaders had a complaint filed against him, charging him with discrimination. Art met with me and said that he personally knew this particular businessman and that he wouldn't treat anyone with discrimination and suggested that I dismiss the case. I told him I couldn't and wouldn't do that. The investigation had to run its course. Art went to the city manager and told him that he should tell me to dismiss the case and stop the investigation. The city manager supported my decision and told Art he couldn't do that. Well, I think Art had forgotten that disagreement, because he so readily said yes, he would be my treasurer.

Everyone I told wondered how I got Art Asel to say yes. My office was in the small strip mall at Red Bridge Road and Hickman Mills Drive. Art knew the owner, who gave it to me for free. I won the Sixth District at-large council seat without any opposition, and Kay won the mayoral race. Dr. Charles "Chuck" Eddy was my Sixth in-district colleague. Chuck and I worked very harmoniously. Kay, Chuck, and I ran for our second four-year terms in 2003, and all three of us won. Once again, I was unopposed, and once again Kay appointed me mayor pro tem.

Kay asked what committees I wanted. Since I had the role of mayor pro tem, I told Kay I didn't want to be chair of any of the committees. I was appointed vice chair of committees. Kay and I further developed our relationship. As mayor pro tem during Kay's absence, I presided over council meetings and business sessions and made numerous speeches representing the city, welcoming our visitors, both national and international. I sat in on the Board of Police Commissioners during Kay's absence. Kay continued to push her agenda, revitalizing downtown Kansas City, from the river to the Plaza.

As she neared the end of her first term, preparing for the second, a group of her detractors met with me with the intent of getting me to run against her. They agreed to finance my candidacy. They said that Kay had not done anything and was not worthy of their support for a second term. They felt that since I had won and won big in my first candidacy at-large, I would be a shoo-in for mayor in 2003.

Kay heard about what some of her detractors were trying to get me to do before she and I got a chance to talk about it. She came down to my office the same morning that I had met with the group at one of their homes and I told them, "Thanks, but no thanks." Kay and I were friends and you don't betray your friends. We were also political colleagues, and she depended on my support. We differed only a few times in the eight years we worked together.

There were two big incidents when I was called on to lead as mayor pro tem. One was the untimely death of Governor Mel Carnahan, who was running for the US Senate. Carnahan was killed in a small plane that crashed during a storm. At the time, Kay was out of the country on city business. The second time when I stepped in for Kay was after the terrorist attack on 9/11—in meetings, meetings, and more meetings, trying to bring different racial, ethnic, and religious groups together to address the rising issue of anti-Muslim sentiment.

Kay Barnes Selects First African American City Manager

As we began our second four-year term in 2003, we faced the task of selecting a new city manager. Kansas City has a council–manager form of government. The city manager is the person responsible for the day-to-day operation of the city. We contracted with a search firm to seek out candidates who would best serve our city. Mayor Barnes appointed three city council members, including me, to serve with her on the selection committee. The search firm screened dozens of résumés and settled on three, all males, to submit to the committee.

The first candidate we interviewed was the former city manager of Lawrence, Kansas, whom I had met while he was in that position. At the time of the interview he was a professor at one of the large universities in the Washington, DC, area. He was impressive but not my first choice. The second candidate was not quite as impressive as the professor, and the third candidate was my first choice.

After the third candidate was interviewed, the discussion began. The top two finalists were the professor and the third candidate. I predicted that the professor would call the search firm from the airport where we had met to withdraw from consideration. The search firm representative meeting with us got a call and excused himself. As I recall, two of our colleagues were moving for the professor. The mayor and I favored the third candidate. During our discussion, the search firm rep returned to the room and said the phone call he had just received was from the professor. "He wanted me to tell you, Mayor Barnes and councilmen, that he certainly appreciated meeting each of you and seeing you again, Councilman Brooks, but wished not to be considered any further for the city manager position." My colleagues asked why I thought he would back out. I reminded them as I had said earlier that just as a part-time professor he was making more money than we were offering him.

The mayor's and my choice was Wayne Cauthen, who happened to be Black, with twenty-five years of professional experience in both the private and public sectors. Wayne's current position was chief of staff for Wellington Webb, the mayor of Denver, Colorado. Out of twenty-five persons listed as the "most powerful people in Denver," Wayne was number eight. One colleague didn't think Wayne would be accepted by the "powers that be," by the "blue bloods" in the city, because of his "somewhat drawl."

After considerable discussion, the mayor and I persuaded two "holdouts" among us, and finally the one who raised the questions about Wayne's "drawl" conceded, so when Kay submitted Wayne Cauthen as first choice, she was able to report the committee's vote was unanimous. (I can't remember if the "advice and consent" rule had been passed by the city council at that time. The advice and consent rule is where the mayor submits his or her choice of a city manager to the full city council to be accepted or rejected. Since Cauthen, the council has never rejected a mayor's choice.)

Wayne accepted the offer and became the city's first Black city manager. He started work in April 2003. Wayne was the primary negotiator with the Cordish Company that proposed the Power and Light District, Kansas City's largest entertainment area, and the developer of the arena for which Sprint was awarded the "naming rights." Both the Power and Light District and the Sprint Arena draw from all over the Midwest. They were key to the remarkable revival of downtown and transformed it into an amazing place attracting both businesses and thousands of residents in older renovated lofts. One need only go to downtown Kansas City today to see Kay's and Wayne's footprints all over the place. Wayne also took Kay's River Crown Plaza Development Plan seriously and began working to bring her vision to reality. Beyond the naming of the Kay Barnes Grand Ballroom at the Kansas City Convention Center, I hope a suitable way to honor Kay for her remarkable achievements and vision can be found soon.

Mayor Barnes's vision was not shared by the mayor who succeeded her, Mark Funkhouser, who defeated me in the 2007 election by 950 votes. I was committed to seeing that Kay's vision proceed while also moving my agenda forward, including funding for our decaying infrastructure and a long-range plan for areas east of Troost, including affordable housing, attracting development with a special appeal to developers of color, bringing the police department back under city control, setting into motion a broad-based public effort to improve race relations and community-police relations, and moving the department into a true community policing mode. And several other initiatives that the broad community would support and achieve during eight years as mayor, following my eight years of experience as city council member and mayor pro tem.

Mayor Funkhouser lasted one turbulent four-year term. He was defeated overwhelmingly by the city's second Black mayor, Sylvester "Sly" James. (Emanuel Cleaver was the first, 1991–1999; he now serves as Fifth US District Congressman, beginning in 2005.)

Funkhouser unceremoniously dismissed Wayne Cauthen as city manager by ordering him to leave city hall immediately after the 2007 mayoral and city council election. Wayne's initiative and leadership gave Kansas City a running start toward the vision of the River Crown Plaza Development. He and Kay began the transformation of Kansas City.

The Precious Doe Murder Case, 2001–2008

A new nonprofit organization called Project Neighborhood, with financing from the Robert Wood Johnson Foundation, was formed to address the problems of substance abuse. AdHoc's mission was to reduce crime and violence within the same community. It was decided to combine the two organizations under a new name: Community Movement for Urban Progress (Move UP). Its first director was Jim Nunn, a retired deputy police chief.

On April 28, 2001, the nude, decapitated body of a three-year-old girl was found in the wooded area at 59th and Kensington. Two days later her head was found nearby in a plastic garbage bag. Move UP became the community meeting place where vigils were planned. Flyers were developed and search parties were organized. The media followed the case closely every day. Volunteers gave the baby the name "Precious Doe." Sketches, computer drawings, and busts of Precious Doe were distributed by hundreds of volunteers. All this activity went nationwide. Crime programs around the nation picked up on what we were doing. For some of us, Precious Doe became an obsession.

Who is this baby and who would dare do this to her? This case was assigned to KC police Sgt. David Bernard and his squad of detectives. Calls came in from around the nation. Sergeant Bernard's squad tried to run down every lead and even took the case international.

To illustrate how overwhelming the attention to the case was, here is an example. Late one night I received a call from a man who said he wanted to remain anonymous. He had some photos to share that might lead to the identification of Precious Doe. He said that his girlfriend was an employee at a Walgreens drugstore and had been told by the store's manager to dispose of a batch of old photographs left without anyone claiming them. His girlfriend was curious about the photographs and at random went through them. In one batch she saw a group of women with a beach background; in front of one of them was a small child. The caller and his girlfriend thought the child fit the description that had been circulated of Precious Doe. The caller, to avoid being identified, said he would leave the packet of photos in my home mailbox within the next twenty-four hours. I knew he already had my address because he called me on my landline phone.

I told him, "Fine, I look forward to receiving the photos and sharing them with the authorities." I looked in the mailbox the next morning, and there they were. After thumbing through them, I saw that several of the photos included a young girl. The group of women suggested that the occasion might have been a beach wedding. The photo envelope had a name, address, and phone number identifying the person who left them to be developed. I turned this over to Sergeant Bernard, who had two members of his squad call on the person whose name appeared on the envelope.

Officers went to the address, a Jamaican restaurant. It was not actually open, but a Black male came to the door and immediately ran out the back door. The officers did not give chase but went to the beauty salon next door and asked there about the person whose name was on the photo envelope. The beauty salon owner was the woman whose name appeared on the envelope. She owned the salon and the restaurant.

When asked about why the man they had just encountered ran from them, she told the detectives she didn't know who he was, just a clean-up person, and didn't know why he ran. She told the detectives she was from Jamaica and the child in the photos was a part of the wedding that occurred recently in Jamaica. She was sure that the child in the photo was very much alive. She gave the detectives names and contact information for the people in the photographs. The FBI was asked to check on this information as well. The local detectives passed it on to the national office to assign Jamaican authorities, who found that this young child was indeed alive and of course not Precious Doe.

Yes, Precious Doe became an obsession with Sergeant Bernard and so many others of us. Vigils, some for twenty-four hours, were held in Hibbs Park just across the street from where Precious Doe was found. The park also became a gathering place for people from all over the metro area. People of all races and faiths participated.

Precious Doe was first buried in December 2001 but was exhumed in 2003 as part of the police investigation. Precious Doe again remained in the Jackson County morgue. Numerous persons helped raise $14,000 for a reward fund. The account was set up with Move UP to administer. The media were constantly attentive and helpful. They were often—it felt like constantly—reporting from the park.

Four years later, on May 5, 2005, the baby's grandfather, Thurmon McIntosh, passed certain information on to a local community activist, Alonzo Washington. Washington passed the information on to the police, and Precious Doe was found to be named Erica Michelle Marie Green, born May l5, 1997, in McLoud, Oklahoma. Erica had come to Kansas City with her mother, Michelle, and her mother's boyfriend, Harrell Johnson.

On one occasion while passing out flyers throughout the community, a woman who was with us said to me, "Mr. Brooks, I hope we find out who this baby is." That woman was Erica's mother, Michelle! Michelle and Harrell returned to Muskogee, Oklahoma, and got married. Kansas City detectives went to Oklahoma and interrogated both suspects. Both Michelle and Harrell Johnson were arrested there. Michelle gave a full confession and statement. Both she and Harrell were extradited to Kansas City and arraigned on murder charges based on the information provided by McIntosh, Erica's grandfather, and her statement.

After Michelle and Johnson were charged, the police released Erica's body. The Precious Doe committee, organized under the umbrella of AdHoc, the police, and the Park Lawn Funeral Home, arranged funeral services in Memorial Park Cemetery on August 18, 2005. Thanks to Park Lawn Funeral Home for their contribution.

The media person for Move UP was Calvin Williford. He prepared all the news releases and did the on-camera appearances for the organization. Nunn was not one who liked media attention. Nunn passed in 2002 after two years as director of Move UP. He was succeeded by board chair J.T. Brown, who passed away in 2004.

In 2004, the board asked me to come back until a permanent executive was hired. I was Move UP's interim executive director when Michelle Green Johnson and Harrell Johnson were identified, arrested, and extradited back to Kansas City and charged shortly thereafter.

The Reward Fund Committee decided that Mr. McIntosh, who gave the information that solved the case, should receive the $14,000 reward money. I got a cashier's check in that amount. Kansas City Police Major Anthony Ell, who was commander of the violent crime's division, drove me to Muskogee. At a news conference there, both Major Ell and I made remarks praising and thanking Mr. McIntosh for the information he provided that led to identifying the slayers of Precious Doe. Then I presented Mr. McIntosh the reward check.

Michelle later took a plea bargain and testified against Harrell. She was sentenced to twenty-five years in prison. With Michelle's testimony, Harrell was convicted of first-degree murder and sentenced in October 2008 to life in prison without the possibility of parole. I sat through both trials. Michelle described what happened to her baby girl, Erica—how Harrell kicked her in the head, how neither of them checked on her or took her to the hospital, and how, after they realized she was dead, they took her lifeless body and placed it in a dumpster behind a church across from the wooded area. Johnson had second thoughts, though, removed her body from the dumpster, and sent Michelle back to the house to get hedge clippers. He then decapitated the child. He left her body in the wooded area just a few blocks from where they were staying and threw her head inside a trash bag in the same wooded area—several hundred feet away, east of where the body was.

There was not a dry eye in the courtroom, including mine. The case has a separate entry on Wikipedia.

The Gilder Family Reunion: Roots to Branches, 2004

The Gilder Family Reunion was held September 3–5, 2004, in Memphis, Tennessee, the first reunion after my mother's death in 1985. Memphis is the origin of the Gilders. Some still reside there. Carol and I decided to make the first reunion. Keith Williams, our daughter Estelle's husband, drove.

Despite his poor and frightening driving, we did reach Memphis in one piece. We checked into the motel and then went to the restaurant where the big social event was being held. Most of the family was there. At night we fanned out. Some of us went to a casino about thirty miles away in Tunica, Mississippi. The family picnic was scheduled for Saturday at a local park. The most important event, at least to me, was the brunch scheduled for Sunday.

At the brunch, I met my two oldest living female relatives, ninety-two-year-old Virgil Bynum and her ninety-one-year-old sister. Cousin Virgil was blind and unable to walk but sharp, articulate, and witty; she was the historian of the family. She was the niece of my grandfather, Thomas Gilder. Her mother was my grandfather's sister. Virgil was able to give the birthdates and ages of my mother and other family members. She had all the facts about our great-grandparents, George Washington Gilder and Caroline Young Gilder, and about my grandparents, Thomas and Susie Brooks Gilder. Grandma's maiden name was also coincidentally Brooks. My grandmother and adoptive father were not related.

When cousin Virgil was naming all my aunts and uncles and got to my mother, she gave a startling account of my mother and the Brookses. She stated that my mother, Thomascine, was adopted by the Brooks family. I had never heard that before, and I have not been able to substantiate it since. So, as of this writing, my mother remained a Gilder and went back to her home in Memphis as a Gilder. She was born in Memphis on August 6, 1917. Her parents were Suzie and Thomas Gilder. My mother was the fifth of seven children. I found later that she was affectionately called "Tommie" by relatives and friends.

Not knowing whether or not I would have the opportunity again to find out "who I am" and "how I got here," I decided to take advantage of every moment I had with my mother and other family members in Memphis. I found that I am the descendant of Caroline Young Gilder and George Washington Gilder. They were my great-grandparents who were born in slavery in South Carolina. As far as I know, their son was Thomas Gilder. He married Suzie Brooks. Quite a coincidence, to say the least! I don't know how she got the name Brooks. Maybe it was her maiden name. At least at this time, no one seems to know. Suzie married my grandfather Thomas Gilder and therefore, Suzie became Suzie Brooks Gilder. Their union produced seven children. The eldest was Uncle Roland, then Aunt Mozella, Uncle George, Aunt Ruth, Aunt Katherine, and then my mother Thomascine. Aunt Thelma was the youngest.

The children of my uncles and aunts are as follows: Uncle Roland's daughter was Katherine; Aunt Mozella's children were Dosey, Willa Bell, Marvin, Josephine, Julian, and Thomascine (named after my mother); and Uncle George's son was John Ivan. John Ivan was adopted like me. Aunt Ruth had triplets: Joan, Jean, and Joyce—then Bobbie, George, Katherine, and Margaret. Aunt Katherine's son was Melvin. Finally, Aunt Thelma's daughter was Orelia.

Listening to ninety-two-year-old cousin Virgil was the most important three-day event for me.

A Run for Mayor, 2007

As I approached the end of my second term as city councilman and mayor pro tem, there was considerable talk in many political camps as to who was going to run for mayor in 2007. By early spring 2005, names were being floated and candidates were already gearing up. The names of candidates eligible to run for mayor would appear on the March ballot in 2007 as soon as all signatures were in, counted, and certified.

Mayor Barnes and a host of friends and political organizations encouraged me to put my hat in the ring. But I had to get the green light, especially from my wife, Carol, then my five daughters and grands. The one who had the most questions was Carol. After a long "pro" and "con" discussion, she gave me her blessings and full support. Everyone else was excited. When I announced my candidacy in December 2005, Kay Barnes was one of the first to give me her support.

As I mentioned previously, I hired Pat Gray, probably the number one campaign strategist for candidates as well as civic causes. Pat and I sat down with several other politicos whom we both thought would be helpful in my campaign. Numerous items had to be taken care of before I could become a viable candidate. I had to determine when to announce my candidacy. I had to raise a lot of money, including money to pay Pat, who was handling several other candidates for city council seats as well. I needed to prepare a list of supporters, political action committees (PACs), and political organizations I would reach out to for support. Where would my headquarters be located? And I needed to develop a large cadre of volunteers to cover all of Kansas City.

But the most important thing I had to do was to prepare myself to tell, to convince folks, whether one-on-one or in a large crowd, how my platform would help the city; I also needed to demonstrate my willingness to listen to people, whether they were for me or for one of the other candidates. And I had to form a "Committee to Elect Al Brooks."

My treasurer this time was Lou Austin, a friend, local attorney, real estate salesman, and developer. I had appointed Lou as my representative on the Public Improvement Advisory Committee (PIAC).

His backup was Lee Moore, also an attorney, who worked closely with Pat Gray and was the treasurer for several candidates. Like Pat, he handled more than one candidate and cause at the same time. I felt, as did many others, that Pat and Lee were the best and most professional in their respective fields. As I mentioned, Pat had an exemplary record of wins. Other mayoral candidates tried to retain Pat, but he had already committed himself to my campaign.

I had a speech writer, Mary O'Halloran, who was great. But she had a problem with me not using the material she prepared for me, mostly because my wife, Carol, stopped me from using written speeches, both those prepared by myself and those others wrote for me. "Baby, you're too good. You don't need a prepared speech," Carol would say. "You sound better, look better, are more convincing, and capture your audience's attention better. It's like you're talking to them as individuals. You may not get everything in as you would if you were reading what you wrote or what someone wrote for you, but you seem more relaxed and you command your listeners' attention. Remember, I'm out there in the audience, and I watch people's reactions. Get away from writing your speeches. Your audience remembers more of what you say when you speak directly to them."

Mary always fussed at me, but I listened to Carol's free advice more than what I paid Mary to do. Mary was to be paid out of Pat's budget. The money began to come in steady. Mary also suggested what I should wear. I cannot say enough good things about Mary. She gave good advice and truly gave me her undivided attention. But it just so happened that I had to go home to Carol at the end of the day—and at the end of the campaign.

I kicked off my campaign at the former campaign headquarters of Kay Barnes at 51st Street and Main. I then opened just one official office at 75th and Holmes. I went to every labor union meeting, every PAC. The unions were divided among three, maybe four candidates. After the primary narrowed the candidates to Mark Funkhouser and me, Kay Barnes hosted a breakfast for me and raised about $50,000 in that one morning. After the primary, I believe I had all the unions except the firefighters. Local 42 of the

International Association of Fire Fighters supported Councilwoman Becky Nace in the primary election but went with Funkhouser in the general election.

First There Were Twelve, Then Just Two, 2007

After the primary, when it was just Funkhouser and me, came the debates, at least one of which was televised in its entirety over our PBS station, KCPT Channel 19, moderated by Nick Haines. I often accused Yael Abouhalkah, a columnist for the *Kansas City Star*, of being Funkhouser's campaign manager. Yael didn't like me calling him out during our debate sessions or presentations. I would say, "I'm happy to see Mr. Funkhouser's campaign manager is here with us." Both Yael and Funkhouser were irritated when I said that. But after I said it so often, people began to believe it. It was rumored that Yael was the one who encouraged Funkhouser to run and often met with him during the campaign.

During the campaign, I received a call from a member of the editorial board of the *Star* that the decision had already been made to endorse Funkhouser. I was interviewed by just two members of the board and Yael. The *Star* was not interested in my platform or my vision for Kansas City. If I had known what a patronizing gesture the interview would be, I would have declined and told the paper's editor why.

A few days after the primary, I got endorsements from four of those candidates who had entered on the journey with me but didn't make it through the primary—Albert Reiderer, Henry Klein, Dr. Charles "Chuck" Eddy, and John Fairfield.

When to Place Phone Books under Your Butt, 2007

In preparation for a debate to be held at the Liberty Memorial, the *Kansas City Star* wanted a photo of Mark and myself for the Sunday, March 25, 2007, edition. The *Star* photographer had us sit almost shoulder-to-shoulder to each other. I noticed that Mark was about nine inches taller than me. (Mark is 6'8". I am 5'11".) I said to myself, "No, no, I can't let this appear in the paper with Mark that much taller than me." I don't know why I felt as I did. So, I told the photographer, "Hold it just a minute!" I left the set fast and went into the office area and asked folks if I could please borrow their phone books. You see, I had remembered a Hollywood trick in the American TV historical drama mini-series *Freedom Road,* starring the greatest boxer, Muhammad Ali, and Kris Kristofferson. The trick camera made Kris Kristofferson taller than Muhammad Ali.

Whether my memory served me right or not, I decided I wasn't going to let that photo in Sunday's paper show Funkhouser nine inches taller than me. After collecting several phone books, I returned to the set and began to adjust the phone books under my butt until I had enough phone books to make Mark and me the same height. Those folks I borrowed phone books from—and others—had followed me back to the set, to see why I was borrowing the phone books. They knew we were there to have our photo taken. They all began to laugh when they saw me adjusting the phone books so I would be equal in height to Mark. I don't think Mark thought anything about what I had done until we appeared on the front page of the Sunday paper. When I got up early for church, I went out and got the paper. Standing on the porch in my house shoes, pajamas, and robe, I opened the paper, laughed out loud, and went back inside and hollered, "Carol, here it is!" I went upstairs and threw the paper on the bed.

She spread it out and said, "Man, you're crazy." After they got up, the kids all had a laugh. I bet Mark and his supporters said, "What the hell? How did Brooks grow nine inches or Mark shrink nine?"

My supporters said, "What the hell?" also. I know because I got several phone calls before church with folks laughing and asking the question at the same time. "Brooks, what the hell did you do?"

I even got a call from the director of my campaign, Pat Gray. "Alvin, how the hell did you pull that shit off where you're as tall as Funkhouser?"

I responded, "I grew!" We had a big laugh. When the family and I got to church, folks were asking about the photo. The photo became the "talk of the town" that Sunday and a couple days beyond. Folks were still asking, "What the hell?!"

Why I Lost My Bid for Mayor: An Analysis, 2007

I lost to Mark Funkhouser by 950 votes. I think the Black political organization Freedom, Inc. and many others in the Black community took for granted that I would win, that "no one knows 'the Funk,' but everybody knows Al Brooks." I did beat Mark by 10,000 votes south of the river. Mark made up the difference north of the river in Clay and Platte Counties.

My thirty-one years in Kansas City government had come to an end. As I reflect, I thank you, Kansas City, for twenty-three years in administration and eight years as a member of the city council. I have truly been blessed with so much love, respect, and friendship, but my journey of service is not over yet.

I Am Western Missouri Spokesperson for Obama: Change We Can Believe In, 2007

Shortly after my run for mayor in 2007, I began volunteering for Barack Obama's 2008 presidential campaign. In February 2007, Obama announced that he was going to run for president before a crowd of thousands in Springfield, Illinois. I felt so energized by Obama's speech that I knew somehow, some way, I had to become a part of this new movement. His first Kansas City office was set up at 39th and Main Street. Carol and I went by to pick up materials, placards, bumper stickers, and yard signs. We volunteered to answer the phones and make calls. Carol took her lists home to make calls. Sophie McCarthy was the Kansas City Obama campaign office manager. Steam was building up. The campaign slogan became: "Change we can believe in." Our chants were: "Yes We Can!" and "Fired Up, Ready to Go!"

Although I had been asked to start up AdHoc again, I put that on the back burner but kept it in mind. After being in the local Obama 2008 office for a while, I was asked to talk to volunteers and participated in their orientation and training. Later, I was asked to talk to the media. When Senator Claire McCaskill and other Democratic office holders held a news conference and rally, I was asked to make opening remarks and to introduce the speakers. I became the spokesperson for the Obama campaign for western Missouri.

Soon the organization needed more space and we moved the campaign headquarters to 31st Street and Gillham. We had volunteers from all over the metro area, including the Kansas side. We had volunteers of all ages, genders, religions, races, and ethnicities. The campaign office was open almost 'round the clock. I witnessed the multicultural energy of the Obama campaign and the growing enthusiasm. I saw how Obama was electrifying throngs of folks at rallies across the country. I shared with Carol my gut feeling: *This just might be the time that America elects an African American as president of the United States.* Yes, we did!

Missouri Delegate to the 2008 Democratic National Convention

The Missouri Democratic Convention in 2008 was held in Jefferson City on May 28 for the purpose of electing delegates to the national convention to be held August 25–28 at the Pepsi Center in Denver. I was one of three elected Obama delegates from Kansas City. Another three were Clinton delegates. I was able to get Carol a "special guest" convention pass. My young protégé Jermaine Reed, a bright, articulate, up-and-comer, somehow managed to be at several convention events without obtaining a pass. I knew he was destined for politics! At the convention, I attended both the African American Caucus and the LGBT Caucus. The finale was August 28 at Invesco Field at Mile High Stadium. The convention elected Barack Obama as the first African American to secure the presidential nomination of any major political party in the United States and chose Joe Biden as the vice presidential nominee. Obama was nominated on the first ballot, with enough superdelegate endorsements before the convention; Hillary Clinton conceded. Later, Hillary moved to "suspend the rules" and placed Obama's name in nomination. The Republicans nominated John McCain for president and Sarah Palin for vice president.

Chapter 9

ADHOC RENEWED

"You Really Need to Start AdHoc Again," 2008

After I lost the election to Mark Funkhouser on April 1, 2007, Carol and I thought I would rest awhile and give some serious thought to writing my autobiography. Well, that didn't happen. No rest. No writing of my autobiography then.

As I mentioned, that fall I began to hear from numerous persons in the community, including police officers, people in the prosecutor's office, and even a couple of judges. I listened to community people and neighborhood leaders. "What are you going to do in your spare time? Why don't you think about starting AdHoc again?" I really hadn't thought much about that.

Carol and I had a long conversation. She, of course, said, "Whatever you want to do. You know when you start doing something, you don't let go until you're so deep into it that you give it your all, and that means 24/7. Which means that I'm shortchanged again. But I'm used to it. What's new? Do what makes you happy. I'll be all right."

I began to talk to folks representing a broad cross section of the community. Everyone I talked to thought there was a void in the community without AdHoc, and they urged me to strongly consider starting it again. But Obama's run for the presidency came first for both Carol and me. After Obama won the election and was sworn in on January 20, 2009, I decided to listen to the voices urging me to start the AdHoc Group Against Crime again.

Move UP had become just another social service agency. Its doors closed in December 2007. The need was clear. There was so much grieving and anger in the community about the many unsolved homicides in the city, especially of African American men.

Right after the first of the year in 2008, I talked to Don Lee, executive director of City Development Corporation (CDC) of Kansas City, which owned the old Linwood shopping center. I told Don of my desire to start another AdHoc and my need for office space. I told him that I had no money to pay for rent or a lease and that I would appreciate it if he would consider letting me have some space in the shopping center. I would take the responsibility of painting, getting carpet laid, and getting furnishings. Don agreed to let me have the vacant office space that had been the headquarters for one of the previous city council candidates. I got with my longtime friend, attorney John Kurtz. I told John what my plans were for 2008, to give rebirth to the AdHoc Group Against Crime. I told him that I needed 501(c)(3) nonprofit status. John graciously completed the necessary federal forms after I asked two other persons to act as a temporary AdHoc board.

While we were waiting for our state and federal nonprofit status to be approved, I signed an agreement with Don Lee and the CDC of Kansas City and took over the vacant space at 3116 Prospect. I had the keys for approximately 1570 square feet of office space, but no carpet and no office furniture. It was winter by then—and cold in that office! The lights and water were on, but there was no gas or heat.

I got a call from a Boy Scout leader in Blue Springs. One of his scouts was working toward his Eagle Scout rank. The scout chose to gather up bicycles, repair them, and work with AdHoc to distribute them during Christmastime to inner-city youth who needed them. It would take him about six weeks to collect the bikes, refurbish them, and bring them to AdHoc.

Four days before Christmas, the scout, his parents, and several other adults and youth delivered the bikes. I had gone on the radio stations KPRS and KPRT and told my listeners to call in or come by the AdHoc office to sign up. Bikes, one per family, would be distributed by age and gender of the child. This information was placed on each bike based on our inventory. Then two days before Christmas, folks came with their kids to pick up their bikes. The first year, we had over seventy girls' and boys' bikes of all sizes. Many of the bikes were new. That scout and his helpers made so many of our kids happy.

In 2008, right after the first of the year, I began to handpick the new AdHoc board of directors and asked them to stay at least two years. I asked Peter Yelorda, vice president of Blue Cross/Blue Shield; Gayle Krigel, a great development person; David Ross, retired from Bank of America's trust department; Steve Israelite, retired executive of the Jewish Heritage Foundation; David Odegard of Odegard Outdoor Signs; the Reverend Kenneth Ray, my boyhood friend, now retired pastor of Highland Avenue Baptist Church; John Kurtz, a great lawyer; Deputy Police Chief Darryl Forté; Dr. Stacey Daniels-Young from the Black Health Care Coalition; and retired Catholic priest the Reverend John Wandless.

Peter Yelorda hosted the first of several meetings at his office at Blue Cross/Blue Shield. Peter committed $15,000 from Blue Cross/Blue Shield. Fr. John Wandless contributed $25,000. Others also gave. I called a longtime friend, reserve police officer Michael Sharp, who had been the owner of a carpet company, and told him I needed enough carpet to cover the concrete floor in what was going to become the new home of the AdHoc Group Against Crime. Mike called the person he sold his business to and got enough carpet to cover the floor. I got another friend to install it.

I told Peter that I also needed office furniture. He sent over enough from the Blue Cross/Blue Shield storage to furnish the office. A friend, LaTosha McCall at Western Blue Print, had a beautiful, colorful sign made. With the help of a maintenance man, I excitedly placed it on the front of the building. Unofficially, AdHoc was ready for business in March 2008, but it wasn't until October 2008 that AdHoc opened officially.

On staff were Beverly Livingston and Janae Reliford. And I cannot forget my number one volunteer, who gave so much of her own personal time and talent to the organization, Berdina "Nae-Na" Oliver, who later became a full-time employee. I received my first check from AdHoc in February 2009, and only after our funding was strong enough to include a salary for me.

I thought AdHoc needed a change of direction. My vision for the new AdHoc was to serve those families who had been victimized by homicide, especially families of color—to provide them with professional counseling from people who were certified and licensed and, most importantly, experienced and sensitive to grieving African Americans.

The "old" AdHoc worked with the police to solve violent crimes, particularly homicides. The "new" AdHoc continued that relationship. We had the hotline for persons to call in and report criminal behavior, regardless of where it was. We worked in collaboration with COMBAT to identify those in need of treatment and got them into treatment centers. Early on, I was able to write proposals (although that was one of my greatest weaknesses) and submit them to the Health Care Foundation and Jackson County COMBAT and was awarded significant funding.

The organization of old had an HIV/AIDS component. We hired staff to go out, teach prevention, and get people tested for the virus. We had a component that did outreach for drug abuse and treatment. With COMBAT, we were able to get people who wanted treatment into treatment.

The reborn AdHoc continued the hotline for people to report criminal behavior, regardless of the location, and raised money for a reward fund. We also continued the youth helpline for kids who had problems at home and school, were bothered by bullies, or were runaways.

Turning AdHoc over to the Younger Generation, 2011

In December 2011, I told my board that I believed it was time for us to look for a successor to take over the helm of AdHoc. Keep in mind, this was a group of great supporters who bought into my vision for the new AdHoc. We were, I felt, ready to transmit the organization to a new generation, which I had in mind as early as 2010.

In addition, Carol and I were facing health challenges. I had been diagnosed with prostate cancer in January 2011, and Carol had been diagnosed with a rare form of cancer that required surgery in February 2011. In 2011 and 2012, we both were going through cancer treatments at the same time. Shortly thereafter, Carol went through her first operation.

The board began to look for my successor in early March 2012. Two candidates were hired, but both candidates and the board did not feel it was a good fit.

The board then turned to the chair of the AdHoc board, Jermaine Reed, one of my protégés who came up in AdHoc from the age of nine. We asked him to keep the organization running until we found a permanent successor. He was a Kansas City, Missouri, city councilperson and a full-time student working toward his master's degree in public administration at UMKC. Jermaine served from February 2014 to February 2015. Those twelve months were not months of progress but maintained the current operation while the board was looking for the right person to take over leadership. In early February the board again advertised for my successor. Several persons applied and were interviewed by the AdHoc Personnel Committee. Damon Daniel was selected to be my successor and took over the helm on March 1, 2015.

As I write this, Damon has demonstrated that he possesses all those qualities that I mentioned earlier. His vision is to take AdHoc to another level by maintaining the programs we had dealing with prevention and intervention and broadening the original vision to include "healing and justice." I believe this is so important, considering the suffering within the African American community.

Many people, including some of my family members, kept telling me, "You'll never turn AdHoc loose." I responded with a quotation from the country and western singer Kenny Rogers: "You've got to know when to hold 'em, know when to fold 'em, know when to walk away, and know when to run." I've got enough good sense to do just as Kenny Rogers says. Let it go. Get out of the way. Let Damon do his thing, take the organization to another level. And he has. It becomes his brand now.

Chapter 10

CAROL'S TRANSITION

The Chapter I Don't Want to Write

The loss of my bride of sixty-three years remains painful, so you'll understand why I don't want to write this chapter. But it has to be done, so here goes. Carol had been diagnosed with numerous ailments as far back as 2007. We thought these were controlled with medication and frequent visits to doctors representing many disciplines. In February 2011, Carol complained of pain in her groin area. This had appeared rather suddenly. After a CT scan and a biopsy, a mass was removed. Malignancy was suspected. After all the tests, Carol was diagnosed with peritoneal cancer, which is quite rare. Among the options, surgery seemed best.

After Carol's operation on February 23, 2011, she went through several chemotherapy and radiation treatments. When I brought her home, she was exhausted. I would have to pull off her shoes and help her undress, but sometimes she was so wiped out she would just lie in bed. Sometimes she would ask, "Just lie here with me for a few minutes." I did, and it wasn't long before she was fast asleep, and I would slip away and work from home or go back to the AdHoc office. When she woke up hours later, she would call me and ask me, "Why did you leave without waking me up? I didn't intend to sleep that long."

At one point during her battle, she had to take injections in her stomach. She'd say, "My nerves won't let me do this. So you'll have to be the doctor." I would prepare the syringe, sterilize the area, and be playful. "Hold still, just a little stick here—a little stick there." I was just touching her with my finger. Finally, "Here goes." It was all over. "You see, that didn't hurt me at all," I said. I would get a good cursing.

I had to have another toilet, taller, installed because at times Carol was so weak, after she sat, she couldn't get up. My son-in-law, Rodney Lloyd, our daughter Diana's husband, installed it. She told Rodney, "Rodney, I'm so glad you'll able to do this kind of work; otherwise, I would have to stand up to do my business or wait for Alvin to come home and help me off the pot."

Rodney replied, "Anytime, Momma Carol." This was Rodney's pet name for Carol.

"Am I Your Girlfriend?"

With all the ailments Carol had even before she was first diagnosed with cancer, she was not feeling very good about herself as a result of the medication and then the radiation, the chemo, and all of the side effects: she was concerned about losing her hair, the swelling, and other things that would distort her looks. She was really concerned about what I would think of her and how she would look to me. We had a long discussion, and I assured her regardless of how she looked, even if was for the rest of our lives, I would love her just as much. Out of the clear blue, she began to ask, "Am I your girlfriend?"

I assured her she was. But only for a lifetime and a day! And then I'd counter with, "Am I your boyfriend for the same period of time?" We'd laugh.

It was during this time that Carol also reminded me of the song by Nat King Cole that became our love song, the love song of two teenagers who decided to get married without any coaching, "Too Young." That was Alvin and Carol's love song! The lyrics were by Sylvia Dee and the music by Sidney Lippman. I don't remember all of the words to the song, but I can never forget what the words meant to Carol and me. To us it meant everyone thought we were too young to know what true love is, but we showed them through sixty-three years and seventy-one descendants. We were not too young at all.

The Cancer Is Back

When Carol went back in late 2011 and 2012 for a series of tests, they found that the cancer was back, this time on both sides of the aorta—a dangerous place for surgery. It was suggested that we get a second opinion, which we did. The previous diagnosis was confirmed. So we had to decide whether to take a chance with this operation. This would be Carol's third operation. After a full family discussion, Carol decided she would go through with "whatever it takes to rid me of this cancer."

Now we had to select an oncologist and a hospital. We chose KU Medical Center and oncologist Dr. Gary Johnson. After Carol and the family had a long and thorough conversation with Dr. Johnson, her operation was set for Wednesday, April 10.

At church the Sunday before Carol's operation, our pastor at St. Monica Catholic Church, Father Terrell Finnell, announced that Carol was having surgery on Wednesday. The church prayed for her. Later, one of our church members, Kelly Artis, a social worker who also does hospice, said that when she visited with Carol, Carol told her, "I'm ready. I am tired."

Four days after Carol's operation, I was asleep in her room on the bed they provided for me, when Carol hollered, "Alvin, I'm going to vomit." I jumped up, turned on the light, hit the call button, grabbed a pan, and placed it under her chin. But nothing came up. She had aspirated and hollered out, "Alvin, help me!" She went limp. "Code blue" was called. Carol was not breathing. More than a dozen hospital personnel responded.

I asked, "Is Carol breathing?" No one responded right away.

Then someone said, "We're helping her now."

I asked, "She isn't gone, is she?"

Someone responded, "No!"

I was asked to step out of the room. I began to call the kids. Carol still was not breathing. A gurney was brought in and Carol was rushed to the operating room. Our kids and grands, some greats, came to meet me in the waiting room. It seemed like an hour, but it was a much shorter time when a doctor emerged and said, "Mrs. Brooks is okay. No brain damage. She'll be taken to the ICU shortly." In a few days, she was back in her room.

Sometime later Carol was released to rehab at Select Specialty Hospital, located in Research Medical Center. Things didn't go well there. All of the services were very poor. Carol finally ended up back at KU and the ICU via Dr. Johnson's office.

Carol was in the ICU a little more than a week. She was intubated, heavily sedated, and not responsive. We could tell she was worsening. Several of her organs were shutting down. But we could not give up on the possibility of a miracle. From our prayers individually, as family, and those of our religious friends—Jewish, Christian, Muslim, Buddhist—we realized that, like the beginning of life to this very moment, it was up to the Creator.

I asked the social worker to set up a meeting for the family, Dr. Johnson, and other members of the medical team. The family was given the latest prognosis. Carol was not getting better. She was getting worse. Several members of the medical staff gave their opinions.

I turned to Dr. Johnson, sitting next to me on an end table, and asked him what he thought we should do. He responded in a matter-of-fact way: "Just let her die." One of my granddaughters screamed. Others began to cry. Some members of the medical team walked out of the room. It wasn't that we didn't know that Carol was not progressing and her future was very bleak. It was the way Dr. Johnson responded. "Just let her die." Just like we were at the animal hospital with one of our pets. I jumped up. Looked at him. I didn't know if I wanted to strike him or curse him or both.

Instead I responded loudly, "No! We're not going to 'just let her die.'" I walked out of the room.

One of the female members of the medical team walked out with me and put her hand firmly on my shoulder and whispered, "I am so sorry." I got the feeling that she was apologizing and showing her displeasure for the manner in which Dr. Johnson had responded to me. Other members of the medical team apologized to family members. One of the nurses who was our neighbor said she was embarrassed and hurt. I let it be known that it was better for Johnson and me that we not come in contact with each other anymore.

We knew it was time to move Carol to hospice. The question was which one. I remembered when they were building the new facility out on Wornall Road: Kansas City Hospice and Palliative Care. As city councilman representing that area, I had participated in the groundbreaking ceremony. The social worker checked earlier in the day but there was no vacancy.

She approached me later in the day and said they had just had a vacancy and they would hold it for Carol if I still wanted it. I told her to tell them, "Yes, we want the room."

On Thursday, June 13, Carol and I took our last ride together. Coincidentally, the room now available to Carol was Room 33, which our longtime friend James "Jim" Wilson had just occupied. Jim's wife, Yvonne, and I grew up together.

Carol and all of our family and so many friends were treated like family by the staff.

On Sunday, July 21, 2013, at 11:40 p.m., My Queen Carol Made Her Transition

My "queen," Carol Lavern Rich Brooks, was born May 24, 1935. Dr. Henry B. Lysons delivered Carol at 2:00 a.m. at General Hospital #2 in Kansas City, Missouri. Her early years were spent in the Leeds-Dunbar all-Black community.

Family and friends described Carol as a "virtuous woman" (Proverbs 31:10–31). She lived a Christian life. Not only did she talk the talk, she walked the walk. She was truly her brothers' and sisters' keeper. Carol accepted all people as children of the same God, and so she loved them.

A Gospel Tribute and Celebration of Life Service for Carol

A Gospel Tribute and Celebration of Life Service was held for Carol on Friday, July 27, at 7:00 p.m. at the St. James United Methodist Church, with hundreds of family members and friends in attendance. Representatives from three religious communities spoke along with daughters, granddaughters, great-granddaughter, grandsons, and a son-in-law. I know Carol was proud.

In Fondest Memory: Carol Lavern Rich Brooks, May 24, 1935–July 21, 2013

Saturday morning, July 28, 2013, at 11:00 a.m. the Home Going Service was held for Carol, my queen. Just as at the previous evening, there was a capacity crowd, this time at our church, St. Monica Catholic Church. The Reverend Philip Egan, pastor, officiated. My dear friend, then–Kansas City Police Chief Darryl Forté, gave Carol the greatest send-off from

St. Monica's to Park Lawn Memorial Cemetery. Police cars and motorcycles, all with lights flashing, and a helicopter led the way. What a sight!

Carol, I know, was proud. The traffic was stopped from the church to all the way to 71 Highway and south to the cemetery. Persons stopped in traffic by the police thought the president was in town. The Reverend Terrell Finnell officiated at the grave site.

Without my girlfriend, without my wife, without my queen, my life was changed forever. Thank God for loving family and friends.

Chapter 11

A FAMILY ADVENTURE

Beginning a Six-Day Journey with My Five Queens

I thought I was done writing, but before you close this book, I must tell you about a trip I took with my daughters, the Five Krazy Women.

After six days with these daughters, aged forty to sixty-four, I was ready to go home—NOW!

Let me start at the beginning. On the night of August 23, 2017, my five daughters and I were on a conference call remembering the sixty-seventh anniversary of the wedding of their mother and me. Since Carol's transition, the six of us have made it a family tradition to come together by conference call at least once a month—Estelle, Diana, and I in Kansas City; Carrie in Phoenix; Rosalind in Augusta, Georgia; and Tameisha in Atlanta.

After some general discussion among us for about a half hour, I said, "I think the six of us ought to go on a trip together to DC, New York, Cambridge and Boston, Newark, Philadelphia, and back to DC." I suggested several venues: the Holocaust Museum, the National Museum of African American History and Culture, the Martin Luther King Jr. Memorial, and several other attractions in DC and Virginia. I suggested we board a train to New York City, rent a car, and drive to Cambridge and Boston and stop at Dedham, Massachusetts, to visit Endicott House, where I stayed while attending a six-week program for urban executives at the Massachusetts Institute of Technology in 1973.

I wanted to drive back to New York and take the train to Trenton, New Jersey, to visit my two sisters and brother and then take the train to Philadelphia to visit several historical sites before returning by train to DC. On the sixth day, we would leave for Atlanta and Augusta and then on to Kansas City.

The girls were excited! "I think it is going to cost us about $8,000." There was complete silence. I said that I thought we should divide it among the six of us, about $1,333 each. Again, complete silence. Except it seemed maybe five people breathing deeply. "Is everybody still on the call?"

Everyone said yes.

Then I said, "Carol and Alvin are paying for everything!"

Now the enthusiasm was off the chart! Now all the daughters had their own thoughts about the trip with Dad. I asked Carrie and Rosalind to pull everything together and report back in a week. They came back with the costs of airfare, renting a four-bedroom house in DC, train fare, theater costs—and the list just kept growing.

Roz and Carrie, who both travel for a living, felt that it would be impossible to do all that I suggested in one week. There just would not be enough time to do everything and get back by Monday, October 1. They suggested that we should eliminate Boston, Cambridge, or Dedham. I said we should begin with DC, go to New York, and on the way back to DC, stop in Trenton, New Jersey, to say hello to my two sisters and youngest brother, then DC again before heading back to our respective homes.

Carrie went online and came up with just the right house in DC, an old four-bedroom row house. Rosalind was able to get airfare for everyone on Southwest. Carrie flew to Kansas City on her own. The four of us—Carrie, Estelle, Diana, and I—flew from Kansas City to DC together. Rosalind drove up to Atlanta, and she and Tameisha flew to DC together. We landed at Reagan International Airport and met up with Tameisha and Roz. I suggested we take a Metro train that would let us off near the house at 215 T Street. Then the complaining started. . . . It was quite a walk over cobblestone streets and sidewalks.

It was suggested we get a taxi from where we got off the Metro train. I suggested we walk, and, to all the girls' dismay, we started walking—with all our luggage! They all had luggage with rollers, but my bag had a shoulder strap, or I could carry it by the handle. I should note that I had one small bag while all the girls had several huge bags. Those rollers did not roll too easy over the cobblestones.

We were about eight to ten long-ass blocks from the house. Every one of the girls complained *all the way*. Cars were honking and people kept laughing at all of us with those bags. One lady yelled, "Why are you dragging all of those bags?"

Carrie yelled back, "Our dad is making us do it!"

The girls were exhausted when we finally arrived and began to unpack. After unpacking, we all began to review the plans for the rest of our trip.

I suggested we have dinner at Florida Avenue Grill, a soul food eatery at 1100 Florida Avenue NW, directly across the street from Howard University. The distance from the house was a little farther than from the Metro to the house, and there were *more complaints*. "Why can't we get an Uber?" I kept walking and acted like I didn't hear the girls. Estelle and Diana set the pace.

Carrie contacted my sister, Tomette Herring, who lives in Maryland. She came over and joined us for dinner.

The girls all thought it would be a five-star restaurant. It was not. But the soul food was beyond a five-star restaurant. *More complaints.* Carrie thought we needed reservations! We were the only ones in the restaurant, so we had Martin Luther King's booth all to ourselves! After dinner we took photos outside the grill and started walking back.

They Continue to Complain

Tomette offered to take us back to the house, but she would have had to make three trips, maybe four, because she had a two-seat sports car. I said, "Let's walk." After stopping at a CVS Pharmacy for water and snacks, we were lost. An Uber was ordered. I don't remember who made the order, but I didn't have to pay for this one.

After breakfast Wednesday, we started our day with Uber taking us to the National Museum of African American History and Culture.

There is a year-long waiting list to get into the museum, but we were fortunate. Carrie called now Kansas City Councilman Jermaine Reed, who used to live in DC, as did Carrie. Both had deep roots there. He had a friend on the board of the museum, and we got reservations. But there was a little glitch. Carrie gave one of the staff members at the museum our reservations, but our names were not on the reservation list, not even my name. That person referred us to someone who seemed to be a supervisor. She had no knowledge of our reservation. So, I called the person Jermaine told me to call if we ran into any problems. I made contact and he asked to speak to the supervisor. We all got in!

My God, what a beautiful building! And the crowds inside and outside—multi racial, multi ethnic—by the busloads!

There was barely room to walk after we got beyond the information desk, where there were at least a half dozen or more staff members positioned around an oval-shaped station who gave a brief orientation about the history of the museum and described what there was to see on each floor. They also give us a map of the museum.

Inside was a beautiful cafeteria with a broad range of foods. Delicious but expensive! But that was okay. None of us complained, nor did we hear anyone else complaining. We did receive generous portions. We were a little early, but we were allowed to enter and sit until they were officially open. After we ate, we started the tour on our own.

There were many guides on every floor who could direct you if you hadn't listened to a representative at the orientation station or couldn't remember the information. There was a fascinating exhibit on the African slave trade, which began on the West Coast of Africa—Senegal, Mali, Gambia, and many from other African nations. More slaves were sent from Senegal than from any other West African nation.

It just so happens in April and May 1977, I was with a team of seventeen to study the water and food resources after the terrible drought. One Saturday, despite it being closed, four of us convinced a tour guide to take us by boat to the Island of Gorée (Slave Island), which lies off the coast of Senegal opposite Dakar. It was a chilling and unforgettable experience of "man's inhumanity to man."

Off to the Big Apple

On Friday morning, after a continental breakfast, we took Uber to the Northeast Regional Washington Station to board the 5:30 a.m. Amtrak to New York City. Rosalind had made reservations for us. It was almost as expensive as airfare.

I intended for us to spend all day in New York, then rent a car and drive to Dedham, Cambridge, and the Boston area. But because of the distance, we would have needed at least two more days unless we went by plane. So, by mid-morning we were in the "Big Apple," the town Frank Sinatra sang about in "New York, New York."

As soon as we got into Penn Station, we were bombarded by people of all races and colors offering us tour packages. I decided that we should walk first. That didn't go over too well. But without *too* many objections, the walk was on.

I did finally give in and bought six tickets on a double-decker tour bus where you can get on and off at places you'd like to visit.

It was quite cool on the upper deck where we chose to sit. The recordings by the tour guide gave an accurate description of what was coming up. I really wanted my daughters to visit Harlem, so we got off the bus in front of the historic Apollo Theater on 125th Street at Adam Clayton Powell Jr. Boulevard. The Apollo came to fame near the end of the Harlem Renaissance. We entered the Apollo just to say we had seen it and been there. And then the walk was on again.

When lunchtime came, we were seated outside at the Harlem Red Rooster Restaurant located on Lenox Avenue. The Red Rooster is owned by Marcus Samuelsson, who was born in Ethiopia. I should hasten to say that Carrie Lynn picked up the tab for the six of us, about $184, not including the tip for which I gave $40. After lunch, we walked.

I tried to give an overview of what the Harlem Renaissance was about and what effect it had on African American artists, on all kinds of performers, and how many of the stars we know today had been given their opportunities at the Apollo on talent nights.

The famous corner of 125th Street and Lenox doesn't look like it did when Carol and I visited in the 1980s. It was dirty then and there were boarded-up storefronts. Now it is dirtier, with even more boarded-up storefronts.

It appeared everyone on the streets of Harlem had a hustle. The streets were lined with vendors. The fast-food places, like McDonald's, Burger King, and KFC, all had a rule that you could use the restroom only if you could show that you had either purchased something or had placed your order and were waiting for it. On one occasion, Estelle and I really had to find a restroom. We went into McDonald's. The security guard announced, "No receipt, no use the restroom." We left in a hurry.

Our bladders were being stretched to their limits. Our next stop was Burger King just up the street. There was a line waiting because the men's restroom was "out of service." Both sexes were in line for the women's restroom. The next person in line was a woman. One of the girls asked her if I could be next. A comment was made about my age. The woman made some very affectionate remarks about me.

When a woman came out of the restroom, the next woman in line gave me the green light to go. No one in line argued with her or me. Somehow the woman who let me go ahead of her also permitted another woman to go next. I think Estelle followed her. Then the same kind woman also let another woman who was large go next. Again, no one who was waiting argued.

The large woman seemed as though she was not coming out. The woman who was directing restroom traffic knocked on the door real hard and yelled, "Come out of there! It's not taking you that long! Your ass is so big you have to stand up 'cause you're too big to sit on the stool!"

Now it was tense. Plus, for some strange reason, my daughter Carrie was laughing, egging the woman on. I thought it was past time for us to leave.

As we were leaving, the large woman did come out, but the other woman never let up on the heckling. The large woman didn't respond in kind. Carrie was laughing at both women while those of us who had good sense found our way to the sidewalk and distanced ourselves from Burger King. We began to make our way back to the Apollo where we would catch the next tour bus.

One of my daughters, I believe it was Estelle, said we had walked *14,000 steps*. Meaning, "It's time to do some more tour bus riding."

Our tour bus came and took us to the older part of Manhattan where there are several Jewish museums. The tour guide recording gave some great historical facts about the museums and the Jewish area of old. Even though they were on a bus, *the girls were complaining about the walking.*

Estelle, the oldest, said, "I think Dad is trying to break us down with all of this walking."

Diana, the second to the youngest, said, "Dad can't break me down!"

Carrie, the second daughter, said, "He's already broken me down! I can't take any more." She looked like she was going to cry at any moment.

Roz, the pray-er in the group, just kept praying softly and humming gospel songs. Tameisha, the baby who is almost twenty years younger than the rest, just laughed.

When the tour was over, we went to Times Square. The girls loved Times Square! Roz started dancing with one of the street performers who was dressed as a Transformer. Rozzie loves to do "the Robot." Then we made our way back to Penn Station, where we were to catch the train to Trenton.

From the Big Apple to Trenton, New Jersey

We arrived in Trenton and took Uber (to the girls' delight) to a town near Burlington, New Jersey, where my sister Ella had made reservations for us at a place just a half hour from her home. Rosalind and I were hungry, but the kitchen was closing. Only two women were left cleaning, but one was the cook. After hearing about my trip with my daughters and how we had come in from New York—*and all the walking*—both women felt sorry for us. They prepared what we ordered from the menu.

Early Saturday morning, after breakfast, Ella picked us up and we all piled into her SUV and headed to her home. We were joined by Robert, Ella's husband; Donald, Ella's son, and his son; my sister Julia; and my two nieces, Ella's daughters. We spent the day bringing everyone up to date on what was going on in our lives. Three of my siblings were not there—Lamar, Wilbur, and Tomette. The youngest, William Steven (everybody called him Steven), was to meet us with his wife and kids at the Chinese restaurant on our way back to Trenton. We were told that my brother Wilbur was still in Oakland, California, and Lamar was somewhere in Florida. As you'll recall, Tomette had dinner with us in DC.

At one point, I looked over and saw that two of my girls had fallen asleep: Diana and Carrie were passed out from exhaustion.

Steven and his family joined us at the restaurant as planned. None of my daughters had met them before. There were about fifteen to twenty of us eating from the buffet.

After dinner, we again piled into Ella's SUV and were off to Trenton to catch our DC train. Our train was late, but we ventured down to the track so we wouldn't miss it because it was the last one to DC. Shortly after we arrived, there was a train to Baltimore—I saw the destination sign on the train. The conductor hollered, "All aboard!"

Diana and Tameisha ran, trying to catch the Baltimore train. I ran to catch them and hollered, "Come back here! That's not our train!"

Their loving sister Rosalind hollered, "Let them go! Let them go!" Carrie and Estelle were bursting their sides laughing hysterically.

Diana was loaded down with bags in both hands, so she was shuffling rapidly behind Tameisha. Tameisha kept yelling, "All aboard, everyone!" Several passengers started running for the train as well. The conductor yelled even louder, "All aboard! All aboard!" I was finally able to catch them, but I had to full-on run, and I mean my knees were hitting my chest! If they had gotten on the train, they would have gotten kicked off, since I had everyone's tickets!

When they finally came back, we all laughed at Diana and Tameisha until our DC train came. At every stop, one of us (excluding Diana and Tameisha) hollered, "All aboard! All aboard!" for the two-hour-and-thirty-five-minute, 170-mile trip to DC. At least we were on the right train. Upon arrival, one of my daughters ordered an Uber, and we returned to where we were staying. It was late, and we were tired, but we began to pack because we had to be out of the place by 10:00 a.m. the next day.

"I Wanna Go Home—I'm Tired of These Five Women!"

It was Sunday morning and we had all gotten up early. All five of my daughters took part in preparing breakfast. Rosalind and Diana were doing most of the work. Just like their mother, they love to cook. When I came in the kitchen, the girls were all singing "Grateful" by Hezekiah Walker.

As the music played and the girls sang off-key, Diana said, "I love you, Roz." The two of them fought constantly as children and still do. But now Diana gave Roz a big sisterly hug. All the girls laughed!

Breakfast was almost ready. We sat down together, and I offered a prayer for the food we were about to receive. I thanked God for my daughters, for their mother, for the beauty of our trip together, for our family, and for generations yet unborn. I also prayed for a safe trip back to our respective homes. Amen!

After breakfast, everyone chipped in to clean. We had to leave the kitchen as we found it. It was a beautiful morning. We all hated to leave.

An Envelope to "Dad"

As we were cleaning up, I found an envelope on the table with "Dad" on it. I opened it. There was a card inside: "I Want to Say More Than THANK YOU" was on the face page. Inside were comments from my five daughters:

"Dad, I can never express how much I love and respect you. You will always be my *hero!* I'd go right over a cliff for you. Thanks for a great vacation. Love, Carrie."

"Daddy, I have always appreciated everything you do for me and my kids. This trip was a blessing. It allowed us to bond as sisters and as a family. You are a true example of a great man who has always taken care of his family. I thank you and love you for all that you do. Love you, from your Best/Favorite/Baby daughter, Tameisha."

"Dad, we know your steps are ordered by God for you to plan a trip like this. What man on Earth would plan a trip with *five* women with different personalities but a 'man of God!' How *amazing!* Memories that you shared will be forever in our hearts. Our bodies will never be the same from all the walking! The pace was slow like a turtle and timely so that you never missed a beat. God, forever we stand on the foundation you have set. Everlasting love! Rozzie."

"Daddy, the *best* is left for last. Words cannot express how important this trip meant. We were raised on the importance of family and we are grateful for that. We were not able to pick parents, but we hit the jackpot!! I am so glad to be a Brooks Girl!! Love you so, so much, Estelle."

"To: Daddy, Thank you for taking the time and spending all your money on your girls. It has been a wonderful, fun-filled family trip! Nothing but *love* **** Kisses for you, Daddy. Love you! Diana, Second Baby Girl."

I placed the card back in the envelope and thanked them and went back downstairs. I didn't want them to see me cry. Plus, I was afraid if I did cry in their presence, all of us might have ending up crying. Sometimes when people love each other, and that love is so obvious, crying can become contagious. I thanked God again for my five girls and the fun we'd had together as a family for the past six days. I prayed, wishing Carol could have been with us, but I thanked God because she was there in each of our daughters and certainly in my heart.

We all got home safe. *Thank God for it all!*

Chapter 12

RECENT ACTIVITIES

My Last Hurrah!—On the Board of Police Commissioners, 2010–2017

I was appointed to the Kansas City, Missouri, Board of Police Commissioners by Governor Jay Nixon on February 4, 2010. I had come quite a distance since I was a police cadet in 1954, quite a distance since that 1978 presentation by AdHoc to the BOPC.

I succeeded my long-time friend James ("Jim") Wilson and filled out his final year. Jim was married to my "homegirl" (that is, a childhood friend from the same Leeds neighborhood) and a retired state senator. I continued to serve until I resigned in 2017. I served two years as president of the five-member board. Four members are appointed by the governor to four-year terms. There are no term limits; tenure depends on how one is favored by the sitting governor. The fifth member of the board is the mayor by virtue of the office.

You may recall that Carol was given the very same hospice room at Kansas City Hospice and Palliative Care that had been the room of Jim Wilson, who died the day Carol entered hospice.

I had promised Carol, my daughters, and myself that this was my last public hurrah, the last public office I would hold, appointed or elected. The 2016 election resulted in a new governor, Eric Greitens, a Trump Republican. The Democratic candidate, Chris Koster, who had been Missouri attorney general, would have re-appointed me since my term as commissioner had expired. I knew that I would not be re-appointed by Greitens, so I decided to resign in March 2017. I enjoyed serving seven years and some months as a police commissioner.

As I mentioned earlier, as one of the few Black cops on the department in the '50s and '60s, I had risen as far as possible, from a rookie uniform cop to a corporal and then detective . . . and finally to president of the Board of Police Commissioners, the policy-makers for the department. I developed a great relationship with rank-and-file police officers, the command staff, and the deputy chiefs.

I was the first strong advocate for Darryl Forté to become the first Black police chief. Some of my colleagues on the board wanted to look outside the department for the new chief.

Lisa Pelofsky, a close friend and fellow commissioner, joined me in advocating for Forté. After interviewing several candidates, the list was narrowed down to three finalists, including Forté. Then, with unanimous support of the board, he was appointed chief of police in October 2011.

My Long and Continuing Radio Career

As I noted, I began a presence on the radio stations KPRS 103.3 FM (the contemporary station) and KPRT 1590 AM (the religious station), both part of the Carter Broadcast Group, in 1978, shortly after the seventy-two-hour AdHoc radiothon. The immediate need has long passed, but I have continued all these years without any interruption because a voice was needed for the Black community and beyond. I both do commentary and host a live call-in show each Tuesday (12:30–1:00 p.m.) on KPRT, "Voices from Midtown and Beyond." Sometimes people come into the studio and I add them to the mix.

Everything and everybody gets discussed, including present issues and some historical perspective that mostly impact the Black community. For example, I've had Congressman Emanuel Cleaver call in from Washington several times to bring us up-to-date on congressional matters. Dr. Yolanda Cargile, superintendent of Hickman Mills School District, talked about the challenges caused by a system with declining enrollment not fully accredited. The police department, civil rights activists, and neighborhood groups always have important contributions. In recent years, I have been sharing these Tuesdays in rotation with Melissa Robinson, another one of my young protégés, recently elected to the city council, and Jermaine Reed, her predecessor, and with Damon Daniel, my successor at AdHoc. As a public service to the community, Michael Carter, president and CEO of Carter Broadcasting, has embraced this way of helping the community be informed about issues that affect it. After so many years in public service, this is certainly a way my voice can continue to be heard.

On the Hickman Mills School Board

I live in the Hickman Mills C-1 School District. For some time, its board had been in turmoil and the district became unaccredited. Its test scores had fallen below the state's standard in several academic areas.

The district had a little more than 6000 students with a steadily declining student enrollment over the previous ten years. The student population is about 90 percent African American. About 90 percent of the students in the district were eligible for free lunch. There's a mortality rate of 61 percent. Because of the sudden resignation of two board members after the April 2017 board election, there were two vacancies on the seven-member board.

I received calls from several board members, from the superintendent, and from numerous parents to become a candidate for appointment by the board to the board. Yolanda Cargile had been named superintendent in June 2017 but officially began July 1, following Dr. Dennis Carpenter, who had been appointed to the neighboring Lee's Summit School District.

Since Carol had passed, I couldn't discuss with her what I had been asked to do, taking on the challenge of helping turn around the Hickman Mills School District. But I did run the idea by my five daughters, who revealed some interesting opinions, in favor and against. On Carol's birthdate, May 24 (she would have been eighty-three), I officially resigned from the Kansas City, Missouri, Board of Police Commissioners.

But despite the many calls from so many different people, I had to have a better reason than those calls to even think about becoming a candidate for the school board. Most of my adult life I've had real concern for young African American males, and I've tried to help them as much as I can. You see, I know the difficulties little Black boys in this society face to become men. From so many being raised by single mothers, with little interaction and support from the father (if he's even known), to having problems in school, often beginning in kindergarten. Even by the time they are just five or six, the die has been cast. Too often you can predict their dismal future—dropping out at an early age, the streets raising them, being vulnerable to gangs, guns, and drugs, becoming teenage fathers—and eventually entering the juvenile justice system and then graduating to the "big" prison.

With all of the above in mind, with my early career in police work and urban education, and with my long civic experience, I decided to see if I could get on the Hickman Mills School Board and help some of our Black boys from a different vantage point. Education is one of the key factors that help boys (and girls, too!) rise out of poverty, which, in turn, reduces all those negative forces that offer bleak alternatives.

Certainly I couldn't do this alone, but with six colleagues on the board and a new young superintendent, I thought (maybe naively) I just might be able to help keep a number of young Black males out of family court and out of those orange-colored jumpsuits in adult prison. (By the way, I do possess a lifetime teaching certificate from the State of Missouri.)

So, I entered my name to be considered for one of the vacancies on the Hickman Mills School Board. The five remaining members of the board would make the selection. There were four candidates for two positions. I was elected unanimously, along with my neighbor, Luther Chandler, who had already served several years on the board. Luther had even served as president for a period. We both were sworn in on the evening of May 24, 2017.

For these seven months as a board member, I have found it to be a real challenge, for both the board and for Superintendent Cargile. But there are more positives than negatives. I hope the board will coalesce as policy-makers and leave the day-to-day operations to

Superintendent Cargile. And I hope the superintendent will be able to surround herself with committed and dedicated administrators and teachers and attract and recruit Black men and women, as many as possible, to join the district in various positions, mainly as teachers and good role models. The board and the superintendent together make every effort to engage our parents and youth, with education challenges that can bring the district back from provisional to full accreditation.

I was elected by the citizens of the district for a three-year term on the Hickman Mills C-1 School Board on April 3, 2018, and was sworn in on April 12. As an optimist, I believe I can help my fellow board members, along with the superintendent, over the next three years, following our Five-Year Plan to regain full accreditation and to better lead the Black boys and all students into a more fulfilling future. Then my becoming a member of the Hickman Mills C-1 School District really will become my Last Hurrah, rather than the police department.

Don't you agree, Carol? And my switching the position of my Last Hurrah will not have been in vain.

My Queens and Me in Vegas; Plans for 2020

You've read about my taking my daughters to Washington, DC, and New York in 2017, so here is an update. In April 2019, I took my five daughters (my queens) to Las Vegas for a week of fun, frolic, and constant sibling rivalry—twenty-four hours every day. "Let's go here!" one would say. Another would say, "No, let's do that." They couldn't agree, so they would end up saying, "What do you want to do, or where do you want to go, Dad?" With years of experience, and without Carol being present, I was able to make these executive decisions. But no one ever told a true story of how much money was lost at the casinos, not even me. But I will testify that I paid all expenses.

Plans are being made by my five queens to bring all of Carol's and my descendants to Kansas City for Father's Day weekend, June 18–22, 2020—some sixty-one children, grandchildren, great-grandchildren, and great-great-grandchildren from at least eight cities around the country. That's as I write this, but please remember, there are several months intervening; and I frequently hear the number of Carol's and my descendants has grown again.

I've commissioned my five queens to put their rivalries aside to plan the festivities. But as in the past, I am footing the bill, so please buy an extra copy or two of this book for your friends!

Chapter 13

A FINAL PRAYER

The Little Black Boy from North Little Rock, Pulaski County, Arkansas, 2020

On August 23, 2014, I built a memorial in our backyard to my son, Ronall, and to Carol. This would have been Carol's and my sixty-fourth wedding anniversary. The unveiling was a big event with family members and friends present. The memorial has three fountains and I go there often to talk to Carol and Ronall and to meditate and pray.

After talking to Carol, meditating, and praying, I've finally reached the conclusion that this, the last chapter of my autobiography, should be "upbeat," as Craig Salvay had suggested to me. (He is a cousin of Bruce Krigel, and Bruce and Gayle have been dear friends of Carol's and mine for a long time.) Let me share an interesting event with you.

I was sitting on the bench at the memorial, eyes closed. I really can't say what I was thinking. Just sitting, eyes closed. I opened my eyes and there, about thirty feet from me, stood a beautiful young doe. We stared at each other. Neither of us moved for two or three minutes. I eased my hand down to my side and grabbed my cell phone. I tried to get the camera in position to take a photo of "Bambi," and I did. In fact, I got a couple. She and I were still staring at each other. I wondered what she was thinking. I figured it must have been, "That's one of those humans. But he's not moving. I've got my eye on him. If he makes any false move, I'm gone faster than he can do anything crazy to hurt me."

The doe was standing just beneath what we used to call a "horse apple" tree, a tree whose branches have thorns and that produces a large, light-green, round fruit with a milk-like substance inside that is very sticky. When I was a kid, we called these things hedge balls or horse apples. This tree was right next to a beautiful northern pine tree. Bambi stretched her neck up and grabbed a mouthful of the leaves off the horse apple tree, took a couple of deliberate steps, jumped the stream, and disappeared into the wooded area behind my house. I could not hear her moving through the woods at all. When I returned to my computer, my head was clear as to how I was going to get into this final chapter.

How do you thank all the people who have entered your life and taken you down a journey of eighty-eight years? Eighty-eight years of not too much interruption. Some setbacks here and there along the way, but all in all, what a journey! What a life is all about! "God has looked over you, Al Brooks," I often tell myself. "And most people have given you so much love and respect. You've been honored far beyond your imagination, by block clubs and neighborhood organizations; by fraternities and sororities; by various religious groups, social, and civic clubs; by mayors, governors, and other state and local officials; by national organizations; and even by the president of the United States."

If I'm in any way worthy of any of these awards and recognitions, it's because of that lovely queen, Carol Rich Brooks, and the six kids. All of them loaned me to the community for so many years and gave me their abiding love either as a husband or as a father. In return, I have given them my abiding love. But I often feel that I shortchanged them by being out in what Carol often called "your community."

Through prayer, I've often asked God, Carol, and Ronall for forgiveness and acceptance of my apology for my shortcomings and human frailties. I didn't ask for any of these awards and recognitions. I didn't seize the opportunity to get in front of local and national television cameras or chase down reporters or editorial writers. It just happened. I feel so loved, so highly thought of by so many people across this city. The people of this whole metropolitan area have been so good to me. And I thank them. As I've often said before, I try to live with the scripture in mind that we are made in the "image" and "likeness" of God, our Creator (Genesis 1:26–27). As I lie in bed every night, I thank God for my four parents—my mother, Thomascine Gilder; my father, Wilbur Lamar Herring; my adoptive mother, Estelle Brooks; and my adoptive father, Cluster Brooks—for the roles they have played in my life.

All men and women, girls and boys, are brothers and sisters; all 7.7 billion of us on planet Earth are children of the same God. People who have never met me, but who saw me on television, heard me over the radio, read my remarks in one of the local newspapers, heard me speak at a grade school promotion, or give a high school, college, or university commencement address. People I met when I conducted a workshop or seminar on race relations or interpersonal relationships or when I spoke at a church, synagogue, mosque, or Buddhist center. We are all children of the same God.

For some reason, sometimes some people who know me, and even people who don't, have asked me for advice in all kinds of situations, sometimes just encouragement, sometimes changing direction, sometimes a little financial help, sometimes social or political advice, sometimes something intimately personal. Well, I've been around now going on nine decades. Maybe my experiences—you've read about quite a variety—have helped me understand some things, and my faith and the love from two mothers have pulled me to see a little of how things can fit together and be better for all. In both public and private ways, I am grateful for the opportunities I've had to serve others.

Like all human beings, I have an ego. But whatever I've done or said, it was my intent to do it for the common good and not to bolster my ego. But I must admit, it felt good deep inside when someone would call me, send a note, or see me somewhere and tell me how much they appreciated what I said, or had done, or was doing. That was a good feeling. And when I was introduced to an audience as "one of Kansas City's jewels" or as a "Kansas City icon" or "Wherever you go across this metro area and mention Al Brooks, people say, 'Amen,' or 'Praise the Lord.'" Even young people will say, "I know you. I heard you over the radio. Can you give me a shout-out?"

I've also been introduced as the drug czar and the first African American police officer in Kansas City. I'm more like an anti-drug czar, and I have to set the record straight: the first African American joined the Kansas City police force in 1854.

I admit, most of what I've done has been for the good and advancement of my people, particularly African American males. I don't apologize for that. I've also worked for other minorities—Jews, Muslims, Native Americans, religious groups, and LGBT people, to help the wider culture see them as God's people. But I don't like the word "minorities" because to me it means "less than."

Life is full of surprises, even as I complete this autobiography. Here is a very unexpected example. As I was reviewing what I had written, I realized I have no proof that I was ever legally adopted by the man and woman who raised me, even as I have dedicated this book to my two mothers, the one who raised me and the one who gave birth to me. As I shared a nearly final draft of these pages with my daughters, my queens, here is what Queen Carrie wrote, which she titled "Tales My Mama Told Me":

I watched in delight as my dad completed his memoirs! His excitement and pure glee were contagious! I watched Dad struggle to write, determined to leave a written legacy for the family he and Mom created (six children, seventeen grandchildren, thirty-one great-grandchildren, and thirteen great-great-grandchildren, a total of sixty-seven descendants)—and we continue to populate as I write! Dad always said we are like rabbits: we breed every thirty-one to thirty-five days!

As he finished the last chapter, my mind was flooded with memories of previous conversations. I remember how concerned I was at one time about Dad's birth. After graduating from high school, I moved to San Francisco, where Thomascine Davis lived. I got to know Grandma very well. She told me she hired a private eye who worked for years to locate Dad. I was confused since we all knew and loved our Grandfather Cluster (Grandma Estelle had passed).

I went home for a visit and asked my mom what happened, and she told me about Dad's birth. I can see her in my head leaning against the kitchen counter and nodding her head a tad bit to the right as she spoke. Mom always spoke with such confidence and strength. Mom said Dad was born to Thomascine Gilder in 1932. His mom was only thirteen or fourteen. In 1932 it was unacceptable to have a child out of wedlock. To be pregnant at such a young age was a terrifying experience and unacceptable. His mom's family had neighbors, the Brookses, who were childless. They volunteered to let Thomascine live with them until the baby was born.

After the baby was born, the Brookses cared for the baby and Thomascine. It was not an unusual situation in Black families. Babies born out of wedlock were often given to other family members or close friends who could afford to raise the child. Every Black family has cousins who are extremely close, but you just cannot determine how exactly they are related. You see, in those days everyone in the community looked after the children. It could be the owner of the neighborhood store, your next-door neighbor, or Mrs. Johnson from around the corner. They all cared for the children. It was not unusual for any adult to whip a child straight out for doing wrong. And you got another whipping after your mom found out!

The Brookses decided to move to another city but promised to keep in touch with Thomascine, but soon after they left, Thomascine stopped receiving letters. She had lost her child!

My mom said the year I was born, 1954, Dad received a letter from his mom. Mom said Dad was confused but said he would meet with her anyway. Mom said she and Dad were pretty sure it was a mistake. Later that year Dad's mom came for a visit. It was clear she was his mom—he looked just like her (a "spitting image").

The Brookses clearly loved Dad. I know this because of the man my dad became. I asked Mom, "Did they steal Dad? Who are we really?"

I distinctly remember her placing her hands on her hips and looking at me straight in my eyes. She said, "We are Brookses because that's who your dad is." She said, "Do not ever forget who your parents are: Alvin and Carol Brooks!" She said that Dad is "a self-made man, a man who loves his children, a working man, a good husband and father, a provider, a man of God!" Mom said always be proud of who you are and where you came from and to always represent my dad in a positive way. "We build our own legacy," she said. "The footprints that we leave for others to follow are what matters." She asked me, "So what footprint will you leave?"

I was reluctant to share this memory with my dad, but strongly felt the Brooks generations to come should know their true beginning. So, I did share this story with Dad. Although he had never heard the story in his entire life, he listened calmly without interrupting. When I finished, he looked up at me over his glasses with tears in his eyes and said, "Daughter, we must always face the truth in life." Dad will always be my Hero!

What Carrie has recalled helps me so much to make the point I'm trying to make, the footprints we leave, about my sense of divine direction through all the surprises of my life, in my upbringing, in my family, in my work.

The bottom line to all of this is that early on I knew the role God played in my life and that of my family. I believe I'm blessed. No! I *know* I'm blessed. God and I talk every night and every day. Black American guitarist Albert King sang, "If it wasn't for bad luck, I wouldn't have no luck at all," but I feel so lucky. If it weren't for the good fortune I've had, I wouldn't have had any fortune at all! From a sickly child about to die, saved by goat's milk, to now, at eighty-eight, knowing I've helped so many other people, the good fortune has always outweighed what I call the "other" fortune. The majority of the things I've participated in have been successful not because of me but because of the people I was able to develop relationships with.

Despite the transition of my son, Ronall, on January 18, 2003, at the age of fifty-two, and the transition of Carol on July 13, 2013, at the age of seventy-eight, the Brooks family can celebrate a great journey together. We'll leave a great legacy for generations to come and perhaps bless many others.

At least once a month, my five daughters and I have a Sunday night conference call. We pray and laugh, and they bring up old events that they say Carol and I didn't know about, or that they lied to us about who committed the act. Sometimes, the wrong person was punished. And so on and so on. We reminisce and even cry sometimes.

One time recently there were twenty-seven of us on the phone: all the girls and their children, three of Ronall's five, and several of my other grandchildren. There were several greats on. Not everyone wanted to talk, but they all identified themselves when I called the roll. They stayed on the call and heard the conversation of their parents, grandparents, and their great-grandpa.

Because of the pushing, urging, and support from Carol, and my kids seconding the motion, I was able to do unbelievable things and go to unimaginable places that I had never dreamed. I've learned about so many people, from so many places, in so many circumstances, and I've gained from all of this.

Let the record show that I never did any of what I've mentioned herein for fame and fortune. I've known some trouble myself. My urge has been to help someone along the way. If I've done any good, then as Mahalia Jackson sang in her song, "If I Can Help Somebody," my life has not been in vain.

Momma, I remember you picking up your Bible and sitting in that old lime-green rocking chair with the wooden back and calling me to kneel down and place the side of my head in your lap. You prayed, "Lord, please help my baby become the kind of man you want him to be."

Momma, I pray that I turned out to be the kind of man you prayed to God for me to be.

Photo Credits

Every effort was made to secure permissions at the time of printing. Any permission corrections will be amended in subsequent printings.

All photos reproduced courtesy of the Brooks family except where noted.
Page 10 reprinted with permission of the DeGraffenreid family.
Page 13 reprinted with permission of the Buie and Bumpus families.
Page 14 reprinted with permission of the Boudreaux family.
Page 17 reprinted with permission from the local *New People Paper*, April 9, 1968.
Page 19 (top) reprinted with permission from AdHoc, photographer Mary Watson.
Page 20 reprinted with permission from *The Call*, 1985.
Page 21 reprinted from *USA Today*, May 23, 1989.
Pages 22, 23 (top), 25, 28 (top) courtesy of The White House.
Page 26 reprinted with permission from the *Kansas City Star*, December 1, 2005.
Page 27 reprinted with permission from the *Kansas City Star*, 2007.
Page 28 (bottom) photographer Percy Meyers.
Page 30 reprinted courtesy of the mayor's office of Independence, Missouri.

ALVIN BROOKS was elected to serve as the Sixth District at-large councilman in 1999 and re-elected in February 2003. After his first election, Brooks was appointed as mayor pro tem by Mayor Kay Barnes. In addition to serving as mayor pro tem, Brooks chaired the Public Safety Committee, the Police Capital Improvements Oversight Committee, and the Police Site Selection Committee; and served as vice chair of the Aviation Committee and the Finance and Audit Committee.

In 1991, Brooks was selected as president of the AdHoc Group Against Crime, a broad-based grassroots community organization he founded in Kansas City, Missouri, in November 1977.

EDUCATION
- Lincoln Junior College: September 1952 to May 1954, AA degree
- University of Missouri—Kansas City: September 1956 to May 1959, Bachelor of Arts Degree, History and Government
- University of Missouri—Kansas City: May 1973, Masters of Arts Degree, Sociology

Brooks holds a State of Missouri Lifetime Teacher's Certificate. He has been a reserve teacher and a visiting instructor at University of Missouri—Kansas City, Penn Valley Community College, and Pioneer Community College.

EMPLOYMENT
- Police officer and detective (Kansas City, Missouri)
- Home school coordinator, Kansas City School District
- Director of neighborhood youth corp (NYC) Kansas City—St. Joseph Diocese
- Director of school, parents, community relations, Kansas City School District
- Director of human relations department (Kansas City, Missouri)
- Assistant city manager (Kansas City, Missouri)
- Founder, AdHoc Group Against Crime
- Move UP (a merger of the AdHoc Group Against Crime and Project Neighborhood)

Brooks has been a consultant to many business executives in the area of diversity minority and women matters. He has also been a motivational speaker and lecturer for governmental agencies and the private sector. He has conducted hundreds of lectures, seminars, and workshops on the subjects of cultural/racial diversity, religious tolerance, civil rights, crime and violence prevention, community involvement and police community relations, and understanding the criminal justice system. He has also been a motivational speaker at numerous colleges, universities, and high school commencements.

Brooks has served on numerous boards and committees, some of which include:
- Board of Governors, Avila University
- Board of Directors, Midwest Center for Holocaust Education, Inc.
- Charter Board Member, Community Anti-Drug Coalitions of America (CADCA)
- Board of Visitors, Park University
- Advisory Committee, Supreme Court of Missouri
- Board of Regents, Central Missouri State University
- National Conference of Christians and Jews
- Board member, National Youth Information Network
- Board member, National Conference for Community and Justice
- Board member, Prime Health Foundation
- Mid-America Regional Council
- Board of Missouri Commission on Human Rights
- Board of Midwest Center for Holocaust Education
- Board of Directors Hickman Mills C1 School District

AWARDS AND HONORS
- Honorary Doctor of Law, Rockhurst University
- Honorary Doctor of Law, Park University

Alvin Brooks

- Honorary Doctor of Humane Letters, University of Central Missouri
- Honorary Doctor of Humanities, Western Baptist Theological Seminary
- Honorary Doctor of Philosophy, University of Missouri—Kansas City
- Annual Peach Award, Crescent Peace Society
- Bodhisattva Award, Rime Buddhist Center and Monastery
- William Booth Award for spiritual dedication and service to others, the Salvation Army
- Kansas City Globe's 100 Most Influential Black Kansas Citians
- National Conference of Christians and Jews Outstanding Citizens Award
- The William F. Yates Medallion for Distinguished Service, William Jewell College
- Peace Man Award, the African American Student Union,
    University of Missouri—Kansas City
- Cincinnatus Award, the University Club
- Kansas Citian of the Year, Kansas City Press Club
- Centurion Leadership Award
- Spirit Award
- Alumni of the Year Award, University of Missouri—Kansas City
- Distinguished Alumnus Award, Kansas City Tomorrow
- Alumni Achievement Award, University of Missouri—Kansas City
- Distinguished Alumnus, Missouri Community Colleges
- Whitney Young, Jr. Service Award, Boy Scouts of America
- Diversity Exemplary Practices Award, American Public Works Association
- Alumni Hall of Fame Metropolitan Community Colleges,
    Penn Valley Community College
- Humanitarian Award, Heartland Muslin Council
- Award of Excellence, Nigeria Women Association of Greater KC
- Honorary Member, Organization of Kenyans of Greater KC
- Humanitarian Award, American Red Cross
- Mid-American Education Hall of Fame
- Distinguished Alumni Award, Metropolitan Community Colleges Foundation
- Midwest Innocent Project lifetime Achievement
- ACLU 50 Years Liberty Award
- Community Anti-Drug Coalition of America (CADCA) 20 Years Dedicated Service
- 2016 Harry S. Truman Public Service Award*
- 2019 Kansas Citian of the Year, Greater Kansas City Chamber of Congress
- CRES Award, Center for Religious Experience and Study
- The Crescent Peace Society Annual Peace Award for Outstanding Community Service
- Honorable Recipient of the James B. Nutter Community Enhancement Award

Brooks was honored by President George Bush in November 1989 for his work with AdHoc Group Against Crime. His efforts brought President Bush to Kansas City, Missouri, in January 1990. Brooks was named by President Bush as one of America's Thousand Points of Light. He was also appointed by President Bush to a three-year term (1989–1992) on the President's National Drug Advisory Council. Former drug czar William Bennett recognized Brooks as being one of the nation's "front-line soldiers in our war against drugs."

*The Harry S. Truman Award for Public Service is the highest honor bestowed by the City of Independence. The award is presented annually to an outstanding American citizen who best exemplifies and possesses the qualities of dedication, industry, ability, honesty, and integrity that distinguished President Harry S. Truman. Brooks is the forty-second recipient of this national honor and joins an elite list of honorees including former presidents Jimmy Carter, Gerald Ford, and Bill Clinton. Throughout his life, Brooks has served as a volunteer, leader, and consultant to numerous community groups, organizations, and causes.

Andrews McMeel Publishing
a division of Andrews McMeel Universal
1130 Walnut Street, Kansas City, Missouri 64106
www.andrewsmcmeel.com

21 22 23 24 25 RR2 10 9 8 7 6 5 4 3 2 1

ISBN: 978-1-5248-6776-8
Library of Congress Control Number: 2020950410

Editor: Jean Z. Lucas
Art Directors: Julie Barnes, Diane Marsh, and Holly Swayne
Production Manager: Carol Coe
Production Editor: Dave Shaw

ATTENTION: SCHOOLS AND BUSINESSES
Andrews McMeel books are available at quantity discounts with
bulk purchase for educational, business, or sales promotional use.
For information, please e-mail the Andrews McMeel Publishing
Special Sales Department: specialsales@amuniversal.com.